Thinking of Necessity

A Kantian Account of Modal Thought and Modal Metaphysics

JESSICA LEECH

Great Clarendon Street, Oxford, OX2 6DP,
United Kingdom

Oxford University Press is a department of the University of Oxford.
It furthers the University's objective of excellence in research, scholarship,
and education by publishing worldwide. Oxford is a registered trade mark of
Oxford University Press in the UK and in certain other countries

© Jessica Leech 2023

The moral rights of the author have been asserted

All rights reserved. No part of this publication may be reproduced, stored in
a retrieval system, or transmitted, in any form or by any means, without the
prior permission in writing of Oxford University Press, or as expressly permitted
by law, by licence or under terms agreed with the appropriate reprographics
rights organization. Enquiries concerning reproduction outside the scope of the
above should be sent to the Rights Department, Oxford University Press, at the
address above

You must not circulate this work in any other form
and you must impose this same condition on any acquirer

Published in the United States of America by Oxford University Press
198 Madison Avenue, New York, NY 10016, United States of America

British Library Cataloguing in Publication Data
Data available

Library of Congress Control Number: 2023938849

ISBN 978–0–19–887396–9

DOI: 10.1093/oso/9780198873969.001.0001

Printed and bound in the UK by
Clays Ltd, Elcograf S.p.A.

Links to third party websites are provided by Oxford in good faith and
for information only. Oxford disclaims any responsibility for the materials
contained in any third party website referenced in this work.

Contents

Acknowledgements	ix
1. A Methodology for Modality	1
1.1 Why Kant? Why Modality?	1
1.2 A starting point for modal metaphysics	4
1.3 Some questions	11
1.4 Chapter plan	12
2. Kant on Modality	16
2.1 Thought and cognition	16
2.2 The modalities of judgment	19
2.3 The postulates of empirical thinking	25
2.4 Relative necessity	34
2.5 The function of real modal judgment	41
2.5.1 The Principle of Possibility	41
2.5.2 The necessity of necessity	44
2.5.3 Modality and objectivity	46
2.6 A Kantian's guide to modality (or a modal metaphysician's guide to Kant)	49
3. The Function of Logical Necessity	50
3.1 Introducing logical necessity	50
3.2 Belief in logical necessity	54
3.3 Suppositions and reasoning	56
3.4 Reasoning and thinking	58
4. The Source of Logical Necessity	75
4.1 An answer and a question	75
4.2 Logical necessity and the laws of thought	76
4.2.1 Constitutive and normative laws	76
4.2.2 Immunity to rational doubt	78
4.2.3 Explaining immunity	82
4.3 Competing features of logical necessity	84
4.3.1 TRUTH and THOUGHT	84
4.3.2 Essentialist logical necessity	85
4.3.2.1 Logical functions	86
4.3.2.2 Logical concepts	88
4.3.3 Conventionalism	91
4.3.4 Constitutive norms	95

vi CONTENTS

5. Objectivity and Modality 98
   5.1 A series of bold claims 98
   5.2 The Problem of Reality 99
   5.3 Objective, subjective, neither 107
   5.4 Objectivity and modality 112
   5.5 Objective thinking 120

6. What Is Metaphysical Necessity? 132
   6.1 Metaphysical necessity as a target notion 132
   6.2 Extensional neutrality 134
   6.3 The space between 137
   6.4 The strictest real necessity 140
   6.5 Objective necessity is the strictest real necessity 147
   6.6 Metaphysical necessity is objective necessity 150

7. Relative and Absolute Necessity 156
   7.1 Relative and absolute necessity 156
   7.2 Metaphysical necessity is relative necessity 158
   7.3 Relative necessity: arguments from linguistics and similarity 162
      7.3.1 The argument from linguistics 162
      7.3.2 The argument from similarity 165
      7.3.3 Modal differences 168

8. What Is Metaphysically Necessary? Metaphysical Necessity and
   De Re Necessity 171
   8.1 Conditions on objectivity are general 172
   8.2 *De re* modality and metaphysical modality 173
   8.3 *De re* modality and relative necessity 177
   8.4 Relative necessity and Quine's challenge 181
      8.4.1 Quine's challenge again 181
      8.4.2 Quantification into sentence position 184
      8.4.3 Quantification into name position 186

9. Essence, Existence, and Modal Knowledge 191
   9.1 Necessary and contingent existence 191
      9.1.1 Necessary existence 191
      9.1.2 Contingent existence 193
   9.2 Essentialism 199
      9.2.1 Essential preliminaries 199
      9.2.2 Essentiality of kind and a general problem for essentialism 201
      9.2.3 Essence and identity 207
   9.3 The necessary *a posteriori* 214
   9.4 Two kinds of conceivability 219

10. Metaphysical Necessity in a Formal System 223
   10.1 The conjunction property 224
   10.2 Metaphysical possibility, absolute necessity, and duality 225

10.3	Modal principles and iteration	228
10.4	Possible worlds semantics	232

Concluding Remarks	235

Bibliography	237
Index	245

Acknowledgements

First of all, thank you to Fabrice Correia and Bob Hale for being superlative doctoral supervisors, and for overseeing the early development of many of the ideas in this book. Their intellectual influence is also evident from my engagement with their work throughout the book. Thank you to Bob Stern for his support and encouragement, and for sparking my interest in Kant on the function of modal judgment. Thank you to the participants of seminars and colloquia in Cambridge, King's College London, Leipzig, Nottingham, Stirling, and Zürich, and especially to Arjun Devanesan, Alex Franklin, Lucy Mason, Penelope Mackie, Roope-Kristian Ryymin, Thierry Schütz, and Cansu Yuksel for helpful discussion of various parts of the book. Thank you to Bill Brewer, Sam Kimpton-Nye, Nils Kürbis, Carlo Nicolai, David Papineau, Andrew Stephenson, and Tobias Wilsch for feedback and discussion on work in progress and draft chapters. Particular thanks to John Divers, who kindly spent an afternoon helping me to plan out the shape of the book. Thank you to the team at Oxford University Press, and to three readers for the press whose comments led to significant improvements. One reader in particular was extraordinarily helpful and constructive in their comments. Last but by no means least, thank you to Mark Textor for providing all possible forms of support, both philosophical and personal.

1
A Methodology for Modality

I make bold to say that there cannot be a single metaphysical problem that has not been solved here, or at least to the solution of which the key has not been provided.

(Kant, *Critique of Pure Reason*, Axiii)

1.1 Why Kant? Why Modality?

Modality abounds. Both in everyday usage of words like 'can', 'must', and 'could', and throughout philosophical practice. There is a curious sense of the 'oomph' of necessity and the ethereality of the merely possible, which is ripe for philosophical explanation, even more so if modality permeates our world so widely. And indeed, philosophical theories of modality are not thin on the ground. But there is still much dissatisfaction. The aim of this book is to present a new option, or rather to reinvent an old one.

What kind of account of modality should we aim to give? We shouldn't assume that our aim is to *reduce* modality to something else, i.e. to give an account of modality in terms of something wholly non-modal. One might think that possibility and necessity, impossibility and contingency, are such fundamental or core notions that it would be fruitless to seek a reduction of these into other terms. It just doesn't seem clear that what *is* could ever provide an adequate account of *what could be, what must be, what couldn't be,* and *what could have been otherwise*. However, giving up the expectation of a reductive account of modality is not to give up hope of an illuminating account of modality at all. It is still open to us to provide an elucidation of key modal notions, even if this is given in other modal terms. We can still learn more about how modality behaves, where we should locate its source, and what the most basic modalities are, without needing to do this in non-modal terms. For example, realists and anti-realists may disagree over whether the source of necessity is in the mind-independent modal properties of things (such as essences or potentialities),[1] or in the rules governing our use of language (where rules are understood in terms of deontic modality, what one may and may not

[1] See, e.g., Hale (2013); Vetter (2015).

Thinking of Necessity: A Kantian Account of Modal Thought and Modal Metaphysics. Jessica Leech,
Oxford University Press. © Jessica Leech 2023. DOI: 10.1093/oso/9780198873969.003.0001

2 THINKING OF NECESSITY

do).[2] In both cases, a non-reductive account is given, in modal terms, but there is still a genuine and interesting disagreement to be resolved.

Why do we need a new account of modality? I will not rule out all of the alternatives on offer: my aim in this book is to focus on the motivation, development, and defence of my preferred option, rather than showing that it outplays all competitors. But it is worth offering some brief remarks here on why one might harbour doubts about some of the better known alternatives.

First, possible worlds accounts, fuelled by the enormous influence of David Lewis's philosophical work,[3] give an account of modality in terms of quantification over possible worlds: necessity is truth at *all* worlds, possibility truth at *some,* impossibility truth at *none.* There is no doubting the utility of talking about modality in terms of possible worlds, especially when it comes to employing a possible worlds semantics for modal logics. But I think we can do better when it comes to a *metaphysical* account of the nature of possibility and necessity.[4]

There are myriad accounts of the nature of possible worlds, given in modal or non-modal terms, providing non-reductive and reductive accounts of modality accordingly. According to a reductive account, modal facts reduce to facts about what worlds there are, and what is true, or false, or what exists at those worlds. Worlds are not defined in modal terms, e.g., as what there *could be.* For example, Lewis defines worlds as spatiotemporally closed sums of individuals: alternative worlds are spatiotemporally unconnected to ours.[5] In my view, reductive worlds-based accounts fail to capture something important about modality. Necessity is something more than universality, i.e. being *everywhere* true: we want to capture the idea that things *really couldn't have been otherwise,* not just that they *are not anywhere otherwise.* In general, we shouldn't seek to reduce modality to the non-modal: the modal is too fundamental and important to be done away with. Non-reductive accounts of possible worlds avoid this error by characterizing worlds in modal terms, for example, as sets of propositions that *could be* true, or properties that the world *could* instantiate. However, they seem to me to still avoid answering the really interesting question. Yes, we can explain the possibility of, for example, talking donkeys in terms of possible worlds, but what about the possibility of worlds? We have just postponed the interesting question about the nature of possibility and necessity to a specific case, namely, that of the possibility of worlds.

Possible worlds accounts are usually taken to be realist accounts of modality. There exist some mind-independent entities—*worlds,* whatever they may be—that

---

[2] See, e.g., Thomasson (2013, 2020). In fact, Thomasson would class what I call "realism" here as "heavyweight realism", and frame her own view as a kind of "simple realism". There are many ways to draw the line between realism and anti-realism. My emphasis here is simply the range of views over which we may disagree without going reductionist.

[3] Particularly Lewis (1973, 1986).

[4] In Chapter 10 I discuss how to reconcile a worlds semantics with a non-worlds metaphysics.

[5] See Lewis (1986, 2) for a nice outline of the view, and Divers (2002, 45–6) for a precise account of the nature of Lewisian worlds.

determine facts about possibility and necessity. But they are not the only realist options. Realism about modality has, in recent years, tended towards accounts based on special modal features of things, such as the essential natures of things,[6] or the potentialities (disposition-like properties) of things.[7] There is also a large family of anti-realist views, whereon modality is understood in terms of something subjective or mind-dependent such as attitudes, linguistic conventions, habits, or social practices.[8]

In the midst of all these options, what can Kant offer the metaphysican of modality? The realist will typically situate key notions as part of mind-independent reality, which one might find too strong. Do ordinary objects really contain the "oomphs" and ethereals of genuine metaphysical necessity and possibility? The anti-realist may render key notions as subjective attitudes projected onto the world with no reality to speak of at all, which one might find too weak. Surely those oomphs are something stronger, that isn't down to mere human convention or attitude? The Kantian view promises to be just right.

A Kantian framework includes the idea of transcendental conditions—features of experience which are a necessary condition of the very possibility of having experience of the world at all. Although Kant describes these features as being *a priori* and having their source "in us", they nevertheless form part of the reality that we experience and of which we can have knowledge. Thereby a Kantian view treads the thin line between a realism which is too strong and an anti-realism which is too weak. We can explain key notions as having their source "in us" where we find it implausible that they are primitive features of a completely mind-independent reality, without giving up the idea that they nevertheless do shape reality in important respects that go beyond mere conventions and attitudes. As Thomas Baldwin puts the point:

> Of the alternatives to full-blooded realism, the Kantian position appears, to me at least, prima facie the most attractive. For it offers the prospect of an account which does not treat modality as a primitive feature of reality, in the way that an appeal to Aristotelian essences appears to, while equally avoiding the subjectivism of Humean projectivism.   (Baldwin, 2002, 9)

This is all so much intuitive motivation. But in the course of the book I will present more robust reasons in favour of a Kantian account and further detail on what makes the view I propose "Kantian".

Crucially, one of the most useful insights of Kant's work is that he doesn't primarily offer us a metaphysics of modality, but rather, modality appears in

---

[6] Fine (1994, 1995, 2005); Hale (1996, 2013).
[7] Kimpton-Nye (2018); Vetter (2015).
[8] See, e.g., Cameron (2009, 2010); Sidelle (1989, 2009); Thomasson (2020).

4 THINKING OF NECESSITY

the context of a kind of feature that all judgments must have (the modality of a judgment), and a suite of modal concepts (modal categories) the possession of which is a necessary condition of possible experience. Kant is not so much concerned with what modality *is*, but with the *role* that various different modal notions play in our capacity for thought and experience. This then shapes what we can say about the nature of modality—it must at least be compatible with, and may well be determined by, the role of modal judgments and modal concepts. It is this crucial methodological aspect that will make Kant so helpful for the present book. In the next section, I introduce a methodology that takes the function of modal judgment to be a guide for a metaphysics of modality.

1.2 A starting point for modal metaphysics

What is logical necessity? What is logical possibility? What is metaphysical necessity? What is metaphysical possibility? And what are the relations between them? I aim to answer these questions in the following pages. But where should I start? It would be customary to take for granted that there are necessary and possible truths of these kinds, and/or facts about what is necessary and possible, and jump straight into an account of the truth conditions for those truths, or the nature of those modal facts. However, there is an alternative way to approach these questions which, one might hope, will set us on a more promising path. According to this alternative, we should first investigate what, if any, important purpose is served by our ability to make judgments with modal content—logical or metaphysical— and, relatedly, the possession and ability to apply logical and metaphysical modal concepts.[9] It is only once we have a clear view of what these kinds of modal judgment and concepts are for that we will know what kind of wider account of modality is appropriate.

In this context, I am taking a judgment to involve the thinking of a thought, what some might call the entertaining of a proposition. By contrast, judgment understood as something like the mental correlate of the speech act of assertion is often taken to also include a *commitment to the truth* of the thought or proposition. So the act of judgment is a mental act of thinking or grasping some thought *with commitment*, and a judgment understood as the product of that act is an occurrent mental state, a thought, with a particular content and force. When I move on to discuss Kant's views, the complication will arise that, for him, a judgment need not involve commitment—an assertoric judgment, as we shall see, is just one mode of judgment. This is why I favour the weaker understanding of judgment, which does not require commitment to truth. Nevertheless, both conceptions of judgment—contemporary and Kantian—agree that a necessary condition of (making) a judgment is (thinking) a thought.

---

[9] See McFetridge (1990); Blackburn (1993); Divers (2010); Divers and Elstein (2012); Divers and González-Varela (2013); Thomasson (2013, 2020).

A METHODOLOGY FOR MODALITY 5

Why start with a question about the function of modal judgment? What benefits could this bring, and what mistakes might it help us to avoid?

Firstly, we need to verify whether there is any legitimate and ineliminable function to be played by these modal judgments and concepts. If there is not—if we can make all of the judgments we need to make, and can think about all of the things we need to think about, without modal judgments or concepts—then it would seem that we don't need to bother with much of an account of modality at all (other than to debunk it). For example, one might think that all modal judgments are simply epistemic judgments in disguise: we mistake judgments about what we already know for judgments of necessity, and judgments about what we don't know for judgments of possibility. If this were the case, then we should be able to get by just with epistemic judgments and epistemic concepts. As such, there would be no need for an account of genuinely modal truths and/or facts; we would rather only need to do some epistemology, to give an account of known and unknown truths and/or facts. Therefore, it seems a good idea to ascertain whether we need to give an account of modality at all, before charging ahead with one.

Compare: someone who believes in or practises homeopathy will make a host of homeopathic judgments and apply homeopathic concepts. Do we need to include facts about homeopathy in our account of the world? No, because there is no legitimate and ineliminable function to be played by serious homeopathic judgments. For example, perhaps homeopathy has the potential for a useful placebo effect, or other incidentally positive effects on well-being: someone might feel happier from the experience of feeling that they are being treated for an illness by an understanding practitioner. However, one doesn't need homeopathy in particular to produce these effects. So even if the function of making people feel better or happier is legitimate, homeopathy is not an ineliminable path to fulfilling that function. Moreover, homeopathy makes false claims about, for example, the behaviour of water. Including false claims does not in and of itself render a kind of judgment illegitimate—for example, we presumably want to allow that normal scientific practice is legitimate even though sometimes scientists get things wrong[10]—but there is an important question whether a practice that is mostly involved in making false claims is fit for purpose. If the function of *curing disease* is a worthy pursuit, then one might reasonably suppose that such a function will be better served by a body of judgment that is mostly true, and that is at the very least sensitive to empirical evidence. Whether or not people *do* make homeopathic judgments, then, they don't need to, and we don't need to take account of purported homeopathic facts in our metaphysical picture of the world. Our question, in a way, is whether modality is like homeopathy.

One might retort: we need modal concepts to be able to think about *modality*. But this would be to put the cart before the horse. We are looking for a good

---

[10] Or perhaps, even, we should assume that most current science is still progressing towards the truth, and so strictly speaking false. More radically, the aim of science might not even be truth at all (van Fraassen, 1980).

6   THINKING OF NECESSITY

reason to suppose that there is any such thing as modality that we need to think about. Of course, if it turns out that we can't make full sense of the world without having modal concepts because the world itself contains real modal properties and facts, then we can conclude that we need modal concepts to be able to think about modality, i.e., about the modal features of the world. But this methodology urges us to consider that this is not a foregone conclusion, and so we must think more carefully about the function of modal judgments and concepts first.

Second, even if there *is* some ineliminable function for modal judgment and concepts, we might not need *the full range* of modal judgments and concepts. This would mean that we would be required to account only for a smaller range of modal judgments and applications of modal concepts, and would thereby potentially reduce our modal commitments. For example, in various places John Divers makes the point that, within a possible worlds framework, different families of modal judgment carry different ontological commitments. This means that whether or not we need to introduce non-actual possible worlds into our ontology will depend upon which kinds of modal judgment we need to make, and for what purpose. According to a possible worlds analysis of modality, necessity is truth in all worlds, and possibility is truth in some world. A necessity claim is analysed as a universally quantified statement, which can be true without being existentially committed to worlds. It is only the possibility claims, analysed as existentially quantified statements, that commit us to the existence of worlds. However, if the ineliminable role of modal judgment is only to make judgments of *necessity*, then our practices, thus far, of modal judgment do not require us to commit to an ontology of alternative possible worlds. We are only required to make those judgments which, as universally quantified statements about worlds, do not require the existence of alternative worlds for their truth. And hence we are only required to include the actual world in a metaphysics of modality; we may remain agnostic about the existence of *possibilia*.[11]

Both of these points are aspects of what Divers calls 'the functional constraint' on giving an account of modality.

> One ought to accept no more substantial a theory than is required in order to account for the body of (functionally) de jure modal assertion. The body of de jure modal assertion comprises the kinds of modal assertion that we (in some sense) *need* to make in order to serve whatever are the legitimate and identifiable purposes of our modalizing.   (Divers, 2010, 205)

---

[11] See Divers (2010). My sketch here is a vastly simplified version of the modal agnostic view proposed in Divers (2004). But the general principle is the same: one's ontological commitments—the picture of modal space you need metaphysically to introduce—depend upon one's purposes in modalizing. One need not take for granted that the whole pluriverse of worlds is required.

He argues that since there is the potential for the de facto cases of modal assertion to outrun the de jure cases of modal assertion, this opens up the potential for the body of de facto modal assertion to incur theoretical commitments that go beyond the theoretical commitments accumulated by the body of de jure modal assertion. But then:

> The advocate of the functional constraint...finds this prospect intellectually unacceptable and takes the view that commitments so acquired are unjustified.
>
> (Divers, 2010, 205)

Theoretical commitments are unjustified, then, if they arise from illegitimate or eliminable modalizing. Because there is the potential for the function of modal judgment to make a difference to the justification of our theoretical commitments, we must ask the question of the function of modal judgment to ensure that any commitments we incur are, in the end, properly justified.

To restate, the first issue was that there may be no legitimate or identifiable purposes of our modalizing, or those purposes may be served entirely by non-modal assertion, such that there is no body of modal assertion that we need. In such cases, according to the functional constraint, we need *no* theory to account for the body of functionally de jure modal assertion, for there is none. The second issue was that there may be fewer legitimate or identifiable purposes of our modalizing, or that some of those purposes may be served by non-modal assertion, such that there is a smaller body of modal assertion that we need. In such cases, according to the functional constraint, our theory is likely to be more modest. Note further that both points can be applied to different kinds of modality; we will need to ask what the function of judgments and concepts of *logical* necessity and possibility is, as well as the function of judgments and concepts of *metaphysical* necessity and possibility, and so on for other modalities of interest. Finding a genuine role for judgments and concepts of one kind of modality will not necessarily guarantee a genuine role for judgments and concepts of another kind.

Divers's primary application of the functional constraint concerns the theoretical commitments that a philosophical theory of modality may incur. He takes those commitments to include semantic or conceptual commitments (e.g., to the intelligibility or analysis of a body of modal assertion); epistemological commitments (e.g., the body of modal claims that one believes); and ontological commitments (e.g., the existential commitments arising from the body of modal beliefs).[12] However, I plan to exploit an additional aspect of this approach which takes the function of modal judgment seriously, namely, that the kind of function we discover for modal judgment may tell us something about the kind of modal

---

[12] See also Thomasson (2020, 18), who draws a connection between the function and the meaning of metaphysical modal terms.

8 THINKING OF NECESSITY

metaphysics we require. For example, if the function of modal judgment turns out to be closely tied to our understanding of causal relations in the world, we may well expect that to be reflected in our metaphysics, e.g., in a realist metaphysics that closely allies modal facts to causal powers.

One might object that we don't usually need to give an account of the function of some body of judgments before providing an account of whatever kinds of facts those judgments concern. Moreover, one might think that we *couldn't* do so without having a better understanding of the body of judgments, via a better understanding of what they are about. As Daniel Nolan puts it,

> It might be counterproductive to insist on a story about what a set of judgments are good for before we have a good story about what they amount to. If you don't understand a topic, you are unlikely to be able to perfectly understand what the information is good for, as anyone who has filled out a grant application aimed at non-specialists can probably tell you.   (Nolan, 2010, 222)

Nolan expresses further concern. In essence, it seems greatly unreasonable to say that a science—astronomy, or geology, say—has gone wrong because its theorizing and discoveries go beyond what is strictly required by the function of that science at a given time. For example (simplifying greatly): at one time the primary functions of judgments of astronomy were to tell the time and to navigate. Around that time Newton developed an astronomical theory that was able to explain much more than just what was needed for telling the time and navigation. But it seems wrong to criticize Newton for this reason.

> If your account of astronomical method condemns Newton's *Principia* as poor astronomical theory construction—in this case, because it took on too many commitments that took us beyond the pre-established "function" of astronomical judgment—then that is a *reductio* of the functional constraint, not a problem for Newton's astronomical theory. The fact that Newton's theory went well beyond what we need to tell the time or find out which way is north does not tempt anyone I've ever met, at least, to think we should be instrumentalist about it.
>
> (Nolan, 2010, 223)

One might think that science benefits from, perhaps even depends upon, pioneers who think beyond present-day concerns and purposes. Is this kind of thinking ruled out by the functional constraint?

I don't believe so. It is important to recognize that these kinds of examples are uncontroversially cases of judgments about various matters of fact—astronomical or geological. The present approach to theories of modality can grant that it might be a perfectly uncontroversial and legitimate function of some kinds of concept and judgment to represent certain kinds of facts. For example, it may well be the primary function of astronomical concepts and jugdments simply to represent astronomical facts, even if we also use those facts to navigate and tell the time, etc. The cosmos is out there for us to discover, and we will need appropriate conceptual resources to do so. The case of modality is different. We are not assuming from the outset that there is a body of modal fact to be represented.

What, after all, might a modal judgment be attempting to represent in the world? Suppose one makes a judgment of mere possibility, say, that the sky could have been green instead of blue. Well, the sky *isn't* green rather than blue, so what can the judgment be getting at? Similarly, suppose one makes a judgment of necessity, say, that $2+2$ must be equal to 4. Well, $2+2$ *is* equal to 4. What is added by the additional force of judging this to be necessarily so? We can make similar points concerning other kinds of modal judgment, such as counterfactual judgments.[13] For example, suppose one judges that if it hadn't rained today, the road wouldn't have flooded. But it *did* rain, and the road *did* flood. Such judgments may serve a purpose, e.g., in planning how to prevent flooding in the future, but it is still not a given that we are simply reporting modal facts. More consideration is required. In such cases, it is reasonable to proceed cautiously, by first considering what modal concepts and judgments are required for in our cognitive lives, and then asking to what kind of modal theory this guides us. It may turn out that there is a body of modal facts that we need to (or are at least able to) represent. But since this is not obvious from the outset, as in the case of astronomy and geology, we would do well to avoid assuming so.

Moreover, the functional constraint need not be understood as recommending that work on the function of modal judgment take place and conclude *temporally before* further work on modal metaphysics. Nolan is probably right that we do need some understanding of modal judgment in order to inquire about its function, even if this understanding may be revised in due course. When one calls for an answer to questions about the function of modal judgment prior to pursuing modal metaphysics, the "prior" should be read as *justificatory*, not strictly temporal, in nature. It is an important underpinning of modal metaphysics that we consider the function of modal judgment, for if there is no legitimate, ineliminable function for modal judgment in mere descriptive reporting of modal facts, then any modal metaphysics that assumes so will lack motivation and justification.

Beginning with the assumption that there are modal truths and facts out there to be explained ushers in a range of potentially intractable philosophical problems. For instance, there are *epistemic problems*, concerning how we could know about these modal features of reality, and *metaphysical problems*, concerning the nature

---

[13] Williamson (2007), for example, takes the function of modal judgment primarily to lie in the importance of counterfactual judgments. Ultimately, I take a different route, since I will argue that concepts of logical and metaphysical possibility and necessity are implicated in our capacity for thought and for objective thought, aside from any further role that counterfactual judgments might play.

10 THINKING OF NECESSITY

of the modal features of reality, and how they relate to the non-modal. Thus, Amie Thomasson (2013, 144) complains that 'while virtually everyone is familiar with these epistemic and metaphysical problems of modality, hardly anyone has any idea how to solve them'.

The hope, then, is that in beginning with a preliminary examination of *what modal judgments and modal concepts are for,* we will be able to develop an account that is in a better position to address these problems. Partly, if we develop an account for just as much modality as we need to account for the body of de jure modal assertion, then there is at least more chance of a more modest account, for which the epistemic and metaphysical problems are accordingly less serious. More generally, in relation to epistemic problems, one would hope that the ineliminable requirements of our cognitive activities would not draw us into making judgments about facts that are at the same time hopelessly epistemically inaccessible to us. Perhaps more ambitiously, as noted earlier, I plan to use the function of modal judgment not just to determine the extent of a metaphysics of modality, but also the *kind* of metaphysics required. Hence, starting with the function of modal judgment promises to also feed into answers to the metaphysical problems. In brief: the function of modalizing will be connected to our ability to *think* and to our ability to have *objective representations,* i.e., to think about the world. As such, the modal theories offered will draw a close link between modality and conditions of thinking, as opposed to a link between modality and mind-independent features of the world.

In the course of the next few chapters I will present an account of the function of the concepts and judgments of logical and metaphysical necessity and possibility— an account of why (if at all) we must possess and be able to apply these concepts and/or to make these judgments. I will assume that the ability to apply concepts of a certain kind goes hand in glove with the ability to make judgments involving those concepts, and so I will take the questions of the function of concepts and judgments to be answered by the same arguments.

I am restricting my discussion in this book to logical and metaphysical modality. This is not to say that there aren't similarly interesting and important questions about other kinds of modality, such as natural modality or the family of doxastic and epistemic modalities. There are a variety of philosophical and practical reasons for my choice of focus here. It is logical and metaphysical modality that promise to have some connection to our capacity for thinking in the Kantian context, hence there is a distinctive philosophical interest in developing these ideas. There is also a question about what kind of necessity is *absolute necessity,* where a kind of necessity is absolute just when if anything is necessarily true in that sense, then there is no sense of possibility according to which it is possibly false. The usual suspects for absolute necessity are logical and metaphysical necessity, hence a focus on these lends itself to an examination as well of absolute and relative necessity.

To conclude this introductory chapter, I will say a little more to clarify the different questions we might ask about the function of modal judgments and concepts, before presenting a summary of the rest of the book.

1.3 Some questions

Recall, Divers recommends to us that 'we ought to accept no more substantial a theory than is required in order to account for the body of (functionally) de jure modal assertion' (Divers, 2010, 205). If we take this recommendation seriously, then our task is to investigate 'the body of (functionally) de jure modal assertion', which 'comprises the kinds of modal assertion that we (in some sense) *need* to make in order to serve whatever are the legitimate and identifiable purposes of our modalizing' (Divers, 2010, 205).

Divers introduces the functional constraint in terms of assertion; a kind of speech act. I will reframe matters in terms of judgment and thought: mental acts rather than speech acts. My concerns here are primarily conceptual rather than linguistic, and the general methodological point is not harmed by this shift: it is not likely that the core legitimate and identifiable purposes of the speech act of modal assertion are not correlated with an accompanying mental act of modal judgment.[14] We can ask why, if at all, we need a modal conceptual repertoire just as much as we can ask why, if at all, we need modal terms to express that repertoire.

The functional constraint invites a family of different questions, depending on the sense in which we 'need' to make modal judgments, and on the kind of modal judgment under consideration. When we ask about the *function or purpose* of making modal judgments, or applying modal concepts—why we *need* to do so— we might have one of at least two different questions in mind.[15]

The practical question: What is the practical use of modal judgment? How would a thinker be practically worse off if they didn't or couldn't make modal judgments, or if they didn't have modal concepts?

---

[14] One might contrast the case with the speech acts of actors on a theatre stage. Arguably, such speech acts are not accompanied by a mental act of judgment, understood as a commitment to truth. So this is a case where it makes a difference whether we focus on linguistic or mental acts. Although, recall, I have in mind a weaker notion of judgment; in the theatre case, presumably the actors still entertain the relevant propositions, and so a parallel between the linguistic and the mental re-enters.

[15] See Leech (2021f). Divers (2010) discusses potential *instrumental*, rather than practical, functions. Although he cautions against assuming that a function for modal assertion would be instrumental (p.196), he also seems suspicious of other options. Of particular interest to me is his brief criticism of the view that modality is in some way essential to thought (pp.199–201). I will not respond to those arguments directly, but rather indirectly in the course of the following chapters which argue at more length for the role of modal concepts in our capacity for thinking.

The transcendental question: What is the transcendental role of modal judgment? Would there be a thinker at all if they didn't or couldn't make modal judgments or if they didn't have modal concepts?

My primary focus here will be with the transcendental question. This is partly due to my Kantian inspiration: it turns out that Kant offers some interesting proposals for why thinkers need to be able to make certain kinds of modal judgment in order to be a thinker at all. As we shall see in due course, there are then reasons to take these functions to feed into the metaphysical account of modality. This is not to say that the practical question is not of interest. But if there is a role for modal judgment to play in our very capacity to think *at all*, then this will subsume, at least to a great extent, any other function for modal judgment. i.e., if modal judgment is needed for *any* thinking, then it will *a fortiori* be needed for practical thinking.

There are many different kinds of modality. We often distinguish between logical necessity, metaphysical necessity, nomic necessity, natural necessity, normative or deontic necessity, epistemic necessity, and so on, to name just a few. Insofar as we can identify different families of modal concepts, we need to ask the questions outlined above separately for each kind of modality in which we are interested. In this book I will be concerned with logical modality and metaphysical modality. So the following questions are at issue.

The logical modality question: What is the transcendental role of judgments and concepts of logical modality? Would there be a thinker at all if they didn't or couldn't make judgments of logical modality or didn't have logical modal concepts?

The metaphysical modality question: What is the transcendental role of judgments and concepts of metaphysical modality? Would there be a thinker at all if they didn't or couldn't make judgments of metaphysical modality or didn't have metaphysical modal concepts?

Ultimately, logical modality will be connected, via the laws of logic, to our ability to think and reason at all. Similarly, I will argue that the possession of metaphysical modal concepts, and an ability to apply and make judgments using them, is constitutive of our ability to have *objective* thoughts, thoughts that succeed in being about the world. So whilst something of a thinker might remain without these metaphysical modal concepts, it would not be much of a thinker that couldn't think *about* the world we live in.

1.4 Chapter plan

Having set out my methodology here, the rest of the book will proceed as follows. In Chapter 2, I gather together the relevant elements of Kant's philosophy, to present the historical background inspiring many of the ideas and arguments that follow. (Readers who are less interested in origin stories may skip straight to Chapter 3.) Through the course of the chapter, I draw out in particular the following key ideas. (1) Kant draws a distinction between mere thought and cognition. Mere thought is subject to merely logical constraints, whilst cognition is subject to additional constraints that constitute the *objectivity* of a thought. (2) Kant's distinction between mere thought and cognition has ramifications for the distinction between objective and subjective representations. Objective representations (cognitions) are to be distinguished both from subjective representations and from representations which are neither objective nor subjective (mere thoughts). (3) Kant also distinguishes between logical modality and real modality. Logical modality concerns the possibility and necessity of thoughts and concepts and is to be understood in terms of the laws of thought. Real modality concerns the possibility and necessity of things (objects, broadly conceived) and is to be understood in terms of the laws of cognition (in other words, conditions of possible experience). So again, the distinction between thought and cognition is important. (4) One can understand Kant as bearing some commitment to taking at least some kinds of necessity and possibility to be *relative modalities*. In line with this, and drawing on the previous points, I propose to understand *real modality* as *relative* to conditions of possible experience. (5) Kant provides accounts of the function of various kinds of modal judgments and concepts. Logical modal concepts have a role to play in the unity of consciousness, and real modal concepts have a role to play in the possibility of objective representation.

In Chapter 3, I begin my task in earnest, by presenting an account of the function of logical modal judgment. I present and defend the following general line of argument: (1) Reasoning from suppositions depends upon a belief in logical necessity (and hence the possession of concepts of logical modality and the capacity to apply them in judgment). (2) Any logical reasoning at all depends upon an ability to reason from suppositions. And (3) any thinking at all depends upon logical reasoning. Hence, any thinking at all depends upon the possession of concepts of logical modality and the capacity to apply them in judgment. We have our answer to the logical modality question.

Chapter 4 builds on the results of Chapter 3, presenting an account of the source of logical necessity. I introduce and defend an account according to which logical laws, and hence logical modality, have their source in thought, more particularly, in *constitutive norms for thought*. These are norms evaluability in light of which is constitutive of thought. I then introduce a test that I take it all accounts of logical modality should pass. In short, any account of logical necessity must account for two important features: logical necessity is factive (if it is logically necessary that *p*, then *p*); and some logical necessities are immune to rational doubt. I argue that my favoured account passes the test, and that some rival accounts fail.

Chapter 5 returns to the metaphysical modality question. I argue that there is a kind of modality that is relative to conditions on objective thought, and that having a conception of that kind of modality is itself a condition on having

14 THINKING OF NECESSITY

objective thoughts. In order to do so, I introduce the Problem of Reality and introduce conditions on objective thought as a solution to that problem. I then argue that the objective/subjective distinction is not a true dichotomy, and that there is a third option of being neither objective nor subjective (nonjective). In order to grasp this three-way distinction, I contend, one needs modal concepts and, in particular, concepts of a kind of modality relative to conditions on objective thought. Next, I argue that we need a conception of objectivity in order to have objective thoughts. From which it follows that we need the selfsame conception of modality in order to have objective thoughts.

In Chapter 6, I argue that the conception of modality isolated and motivated in Chapter 5 should be understood as *metaphysical modality*. I proceed by clarifying what the target notion of metaphysical necessity is, namely, *the strictest real necessity*, and argue that the kind of necessity introduced in Chapter 5 fits the bill for providing an account of the strictest real necessity.

Chapters 7–10 further develop this account of metaphysical necessity. In Chapter 7, I explore the claim that metaphysical necessity is a kind of relative necessity. I clarify what is meant by 'absolute necessity' and 'relative necessity'. I address the issue of where to draw the line for absolute modalities, and why absolute modality should not stop short with metaphysical modality. I then consider some arguments in favour of treating metaphysical modality and other alethic modalities as relative, drawing on linguistic considerations as well as more general considerations of similarity and difference between different kinds of modality.

Having proposed an account of what metaphysical necessity is, Chapters 8 and 9 aim to answer the further questions: What is metaphysically necessary, and how can we know that? Chapter 8 explores the extent to which the proposed account can accommodate *de re* metaphysical necessity. I argue that the conditions on objectivity, to which metaphysical modality is relative, are general, and that therefore they primarily give rise to *de dicto* metaphysical necessities, however, I introduce a notion of *conditional metaphysical necessity* which can be *de re*. Considerations of *de re* modality raise the spectre of Quine. Quine challenges the intelligibility of a combination of ordinary objectual quantification and logical modality operators. This combination is a feature of my proposed view. I therefore take the opportunity to present a response to Quine: we can make sense of conditions that apply to objects, independent of how we refer to those objects, due to the logical features of the conditions and without appeal to the idea of inherent modal properties of the objects. We can thus defend the intelligibility of *de re* modal predication without being drawn into the metaphysical jungle of Aristotelian essentialism.

Chapter 9 considers more particular purported cases of metaphysical necessity. First, I argue that it is likely that, on the proposed view, nothing exists metaphysically necessarily, and so everything exists contingently. This requires a comment on the Barcan Formulas, which can be used to argue for necessitism; the view that everything that could exist exists necessarily. I argue that we should reject the Barcan Formulas for logical, and hence for metaphysical, modality, by rejecting an existence assumption in classical logic. This is in line with the conclusions of Chapter 4: if logical necessity has its source in the laws of logic, understood as constitutive norms for thought; and if the laws of thought are not, on their own, laws of objective thought; then we should not expect logic and logical modality alone to bear consequences for the existence of real things. I then consider the extent to which essentialist necessity claims, such as the essentiality of kind, can be accommodated by the account of metaphysical necessity. I raise a general problem for any such claims, stemming from the generality of the conditions of objectivity. However, I then propose an alternative way to accommodate essentialist claims as claims of generalized identity.

Towards the end of Chapter 9, I also address some epistemological issues. Metaphysical necessity is often associated with the necessary *a posteriori*. I explain where *a posteriori* knowledge might figure in our knowledge of conditional metaphysical necessities, using the template of deduction models of modal knowledge. Finally, I briefly address the issue that lies at the heart of an epistemology for metaphysical necessity: how can we come to know conditions of objectivity and thereby come to know metaphysical necessities? I suggest that the distinction between thinking and objective thinking can help to shed light on the notion of conceivability as a guide to possibility. We may distinguish between conceivability understood in terms of what is *thinkable,* and conceivability understood in terms of what is *objectively thinkable.* Logic helps us to explore the first kind; transcendental philosophy helps us to explore the second.

In the final chapter, I give attention to some of the more formal aspects of the proposed account and formulation of metaphysical necessity and possibility. I present definitions of metaphysical necessity and metaphysical possibility that could be added to a formal modal logical system for metaphysical modality. I consider how, in such a system, we might accommodate the conjunction property: that if it is metaphysically necessary that A, and metaphysically necessary that B, then it is metaphysically necessary that A and B. I defend the result that, strictly speaking, metaphysical necessity and possibility are not duals in the system, and show how this interacts with our understanding of absolute necessity. I consider whether we should endorse the validity of familiar modal schemas such as T, 4, and 5, and discuss in general what to make of iterated metaphysical modalities. I also explain the extent to which it is justified to continue using a possible worlds semantics for this modal logical system in spite of also endorsing a non-worlds modal metaphysics.

2
Kant on Modality

The aim of this book is to present an account of modality—in particular logical modality, metaphysical modality, and the relations between them—that builds on some of the key ideas that we can find in Kant's views on modality. A first step is to lay out those views that Kant held about modality upon which I will be basing my account. In this chapter I outline the main ideas and claims that feature in, and crucially support, Kant's claims about modality. But before I begin, a few caveats. First, I will not be able to properly defend my interpretation of Kant here. To do so would take us too far afield from the primary aim to apply these ideas in a theory of modality. For those readers who are interested in matters of Kant interpretation, I include pointers towards other texts where I and others discuss Kant's writings in more depth. Second, I will not include discussion of everything that might be thought of as a claim that Kant makes about modality. I have chosen what I take to be central and important ideas that can be fruitfully developed into an interesting and defensible theory of modality. Finally, I do not attempt to defend Kant's claims in this chapter. In the course of developing my theory of modality, I will have more to say about the defensibility and plausibility of the key Kantian ideas, but first I simply want to say what they are.

2.1 Thought and cognition

Kant makes a distinction throughout his work between thinking (*denken*) and cognizing (*erkennen*).[1] Cognitions are objective thoughts—thoughts that conform to the conditions under which it is possible for them to represent objects in the world. Mere thoughts are not objective. This distinction has important applications in both Kant's theoretical and practical philosophy. In his theoretical philosophy, especially in the *Critique of Pure Reason*, Kant develops an account of the conditions under which it is possible for creatures with minds like ours to represent the world. There are certain conditions that a mental representation must satisfy if it is to count as objective. To say that a representation is objective is not to say that it is true, or correct, but that it is about the world. So, for example, my judgment that *the sky is pink*, when the sky is in fact blue, is still objective if it says something

---

[1] See Leech (2021g) for a more detailed account of the ideas in this section.

Thinking of Necessity: A Kantian Account of Modal Thought and Modal Metaphysics. Jessica Leech,
Oxford University Press. © Jessica Leech 2023. DOI: 10.1093/oso/9780198873969.003.0002

about the sky, even though it is wrong. Indeed, one might say that it makes sense to think of it as being wrong only because it does succeed in saying something about the sky, in being objective. So, a cognition, an objective thought, must conform to these conditions of objectivity.

However, many of Kant's most important claims and discussions concern matters beyond the limits of our capacity for objective thought, that is, they violate the conditions of objectivity. For example, Kant distinguishes between appearances and things in themselves. Appearances are objects as they are presented to us in experience; they conform to the forms of our capacity to be presented with objects (the "forms of intuition", space and time) and can be brought under the conceptual framework required by our capacity to think about objects ("the categories"). By contrast, things in themselves are 'things as they are independently of the forms of intuition (space and time) and of thought (categories qua functions for unifying sensible contents); things not as they appear but as they really are' (Hogan, 2021, 454). Such a distinction is at the heart of Kant's philosophy: we can cognize and experience appearances, but not things in themselves. Kant also discusses and criticizes the claims of rationalist philosophy concerning the world, the soul, and God. These, along with things in themselves, are all things that, according to Kant's own philosophy, we cannot cognize. Therefore, it is of the utmost importance that Kant has a way to make room for the meaningfulness of claims concerning such things.

> [E]ven if we cannot **cognize** these same objects [of experience] as things in themselves, we at least must be able to to **think** them as things in themselves.
>
> (Bxxvi)[2]

Hence, he makes the distinction between cognizing and thinking. We can certainly *think* all of these important ideas, but we should not make the mistake of assuming that we are thereby able to *think about* objects corresponding to those ideas.

The importance of leaving room for thought where there cannot be cognition is heightened by the role that these ideas play in Kant's moral philosophy. Transcendental freedom, the immortality of the soul, and the existence of God are all what Kant calls 'practical postulates'; they are ideas that we need to believe in, in order to make moral action rational for us. Again, these are not things that we can cognize.[3] But we can think them. If we could not even think these things, it would be hard to make sense of our believing in them nevertheless. But if we couldn't believe in them, then Kant's moral philosophy would be undermined. So we can

---

[2] All references to Kant's *Critique of Pure Reason* will use A/B page numbering. See Kant (1998) for bibliographic details. All other Kant references will use *Akademie* edition numbering along with edition and page number.

[3] To be more precise, Kant thinks that we cannot have *theoretical* cognition of these ideas, but that we can, in some sense, have *practical* cognition of freedom. See Kant (5:105; 1997a, 88).

18 THINKING OF NECESSITY

understand the notion of a mere thought, in distinction to a cognition, as a crucial underpinning of Kant's whole philosophy, practical and theoretical.

Why is this distinction important for understanding Kant on modality? Because Kant explicitly links it to another distinction he makes between real and logical modality.

> To **cognize** an object, it is required that I be able to prove its possibility. ... But I can **think** whatever I like, as long as I do not contradict myself, i.e., as long as my concept is a possible thought, even if I cannot give any assurance whether or not there is a corresponding object somewhere within the sum total of all possibilities. But in order to ascribe objective validity to such a concept (real possibility, for the first sort of possibility was merely logical) something more is required.
>
> (Bxxvi, footnote)

Simply put, logical modality concerns the consistency of thoughts and concepts, whilst real modality concerns things in the world. It is logically possible that p if and only if p does not entail a contradiction, and logically necessary that p if and only if $\neg p$ entails a contradiction. But, for Kant, these logical notions are not enough to tell us about the modalities of real things. The concept of a unicorn, for example, as well as the proposition *that there are unicorns*, may well be perfectly consistent, but that is not enough to tell us whether there really could be unicorns. Real possibility requires more than mere logical consistency. Broadly speaking, something is really possible just when the concept of it is non-contradictory *and* consistent with conditions of objectivity. Hence, we can see why Kant links real possibility with objective validity (i.e., applicability to objects) in the passage above.[4]

Another way to put things is that for logical possibility the concept or proposition need only be non-contradictory, but for real possibility it must also fulfil certain conditions such that it could be instantiated in experience.

> *Logical* possibility, actuality, and necessity are cognized according to the principle of contradiction. ... Real possibility is the agreement with the conditions of a possible experience.   (28:557; Kant, 1997b, 322–3)

---

[4] The attentive reader will notice that in the passage Kant does not straightforwardly draw a link between real possibility, objective validity, and cognition, but rather between the latter and *being able to prove* the real possibility of something. What is most important for present purposes is simply that there is a link between thought and logical modality on the one hand, and objective thought and real modality on the other. But it is worth noting that the passage is not clear cut. Kant writes that if we want to *ascribe* objective validity to a concept, we need to prove its real possibility. And indeed, if objective validity and real possibility are co-extensive, then this would seem to be a plausible way to discover objective validity. See Gomes and Stephenson (2016); Stang (2016); Leech (2021g) for discussion.

Conditions of possible experience determine what kinds of things could be encountered in the world, what concepts could be instantiated, what thoughts could be true of the world. As such, those conditions of possible experience will determine what *things* are possible, and hence ground real possibilities. Real modality is thus to be understood in terms of conditions of objectivity, i.e., those conditions to which a thought must conform if it is to count as a cognition. Kant takes logic to concern the rules of thinking, and so we can understand logical possibility and necessity also in terms of rules of thinking.

To summarize: It is logically necessary that p if and only if $\neg p$ entails a contradiction, and logically possible that p if and only if p does not entail a contradiction. The principle of contradiction is a condition of thought, hence, logical modality is to be understood in terms of conditions on thought. Furthermore: it is really necessary that p if and only if it follows from the conditions of cognition that p, and really possible that p if and only if it is compatible with the conditions of cognition that p. Hence, real modality is to be understood in terms of conditions on cognition.

These brief statements leave much to be determined. The next sections will add more detail.

2.2 The modalities of judgment

The two main places where Kant treats modality explicitly in the *Critique of Pure Reason* are his discussions of the modalities of judgment—the different modal forms that a judgment might take—and his discussion of the modal categories— the different modal concepts that we might apply in cognition. In this section, I present my preferred interpretation of the modalities of judgment.

Kant claims that there are three modalities of judgments—*problematic, assertoric*, and *apodictic*. He says that they express logical modality. But he is also clear that the modality of a judgment does not contribute to its content and does not concern the matter that is judged. So we cannot understand the modality of a judgment simply as whether the content of the judgment is (logically) possible or necessary. One way to make sense of Kant's view here is that, for Kant, the modality of a judgment concerns the location of that token act of judgment in a course of reasoning.[5] In short, all of our acts of judgment are connected to others by inferential relations, and hence all of our judgments have a modality, in the sense that they have a position in a course of inference. These relations in turn contribute to the unity of consciousness.[6]

It is important to be clear that Kant's account of the modalities of judgment is not an account of *modal judgments*, i.e., judgments that contain explicit modal

---

[5] See Longuenesse (1998) and Leech (2012).   [6] See Leech (2017a).

20 THINKING OF NECESSITY

locutions, such as *Necessarily 2 + 2 = 4*, or *There could have been blue swans*. Kant's claim is that *any* judgment has a modality, including judgments that are not explicitly modal, such as *There are two apples on the table*, or *The swan is white*. The challenge is to understand what modality has to do with judgment in general, not to give an account of only those judgments with explicit modal content.

According to Kant, a judgment can lack assertoric force. Making a judgment is more like entertaining a proposition than making a (mental) assertion. For Kant, any judgment has four determinables to be determined: each judgment must have some quantity, quality, relation, and modality. Each of these four determinables has three determinates.[7] The first three determinables involve the logical form of the content of the judgment, for example, *quantity* requires that every judgment be either *universal* (*All As are Bs*), *singular* (*The A is B*), or *particular* (*Some As are Bs*). Kant lays out what he claims to be an exhaustive list of the ways the constituents of a judgment can be unified, these determinates and determinables, in the Table of Judgments.

The final determinable—*modality*—differs from the first three. Kant writes,

> The modality of judgments is a quite special function of them, which is distinctive in that it contributes nothing to the content of the judgment (for besides quantity, quality, and relation there is nothing more that constitutes the content of a judgment).   (A74/B99–100)

> This determination of merely possible or actual or necessary truth concerns only *the judgment itself*, then, not in any way *the thing* about which we judge.
> (9:109; Kant, 1992, 605)

The modality of a judgment is distinctive in that it does not give form to the content of a judgment like the other functions of judgment. Nevertheless, there are three determinates for modality—*problematic, assertoric,* and *apodictic*—so any judgment must be either a problematic judgment, an assertoric judgment or an apodictic judgment. If these modal elements do not contribute to the content of the judgment, then what do they do?

Kant illustrates the modalities of judgment in terms of the different elements of a syllogism.

> The problematic proposition is therefore that which only expresses logical possibility (which is not objective), i.e. a free choice to allow such a proposition to count as valid, a merely arbitrary assumption of it in the understanding. The assertoric proposition speaks of logical actuality or truth, as say in a hypothetical syllogism the antecedent in the major premise is problematic, but that in the

---

[7] See Allison (2004, 138) for a nice way to explain the completeness and exhaustiveness of the Table of Judgments.

KANT ON MODALITY   21

minor premise assertoric, and indicates that the proposition is already bound to the understanding according to its laws; the apodictic proposition thinks of the assertoric one as determined through these laws of the understanding itself, and as thus asserting *a priori*, and in this way expresses logical necessity.

(A75–6/B101)

Consider Kant's example, the hypothetical syllogism.

If p then q

p

Therefore, q.

In the context of this course of reasoning, the modality of p in the first premise, *if p then q*, is problematic, as nothing is claimed or determined regarding the truth-value of p (the same goes for q). Insofar as one judges *if p then q*, one must also be judging p and judging q, in the sense that p and q are both at least entertained, albeit not asserted. Nothing determinate is thought regarding the truth or falsity of the antecedent and consequent of the conditional, so p and q are problematically judged. The conditional as a whole is taken to be true, as a premise, and is thus assertorically judged.

> In the above example ["If there is perfect justice, then obstinate evil will be punished"] the proposition "There is a perfect justice" is not said assertorically, but is only thought of as an arbitrary judgment that it is possible that someone might assume, and only the implication is assertoric. Thus such judgments can be obviously false and yet, if taken problematically, conditions of the condition of truth.   (A75/B100)

If a conditional is asserted, neither antecedent nor consequent are asserted, but these two constituent judgments are still made, in the sense that the propositions are entertained. Likewise in a disjunction, the whole may be asserted, without either disjunct being asserted. Hence, these constituent judgments of compound judgments can be understood as cases of problematic judgment. In the second premise, the modality of p is assertoric; here we take p to be true. In the conclusion, q is taken to be necessary, insofar as it is determined by the premises via the laws of thought; it follows logically. Given the premises and certain rules of inference (the laws of thought), the conclusion *must* be true.

The modalities of judgment can thus be understood in terms of the role a judgment is intended to play in reasoning. This is why the modality of a judgment does not contribute to the content of the judgment: whether a certain content is employed as a premise or as a conclusion, say, does not change that content.

22 THINKING OF NECESSITY

And this is why the modality of a judgment does not concern 'the thing about which we judge'. It is not a function of the content: *it is not a question of whether, considered on its own, that content is true or false, possible, impossible, or necessary.* Of course, the content of judgments is relevant to whether one is able to make a valid inference from some judgments already made to a further judgment, but there is nothing in any particular content to require that it be, for example, always a premise rather than a conclusion. Indeed, Kant notes that a judgment can be 'obviously false' and yet judged in such a manner as to leave its truth-value undetermined, i.e., judged problematically. In the very example offered by Kant, of the hypothetical syllogism, the same content, *p*, is judged first problematically then assertorically. But if the modality of a judgment were a function of its content alone, one would expect the same content, *p*, to yield a single modality. If we think about the form of a syllogism, it is clear that we can substitute pretty much anything in.

In short, the modality of a (token) judgment is a matter of where it appears in the course of reasoning of the judger. The judgment that is the conclusion of an inference is apodictic. We might think of this as capturing the idea that the conclusion is *necessitated* by its premises. Certain parts of the premises, such as the disjuncts of a disjunction or the antecedent and consequent of a conditional, are problematic. Although these judgments occur, they do not have assertoric force. The premises themselves are assertoric: we take them to be true, and see what follows. Finally, we can understand why one might call the modality of the modalities of judgment 'logical'. An apodictic judgment expresses logical necessity insofar as it is judged to follow logically necessarily from other judgments: it does not need to have a content that is logically necessarily true. The modalities of judgment concern logical modal connections between judgments, but not the logical modal status of the contents of those judgments independently of these connections.

It is these inferential connections between judgments that can also help us to understand why Kant posits modalities of judgment of this kind at all. If the modality of a judgment is its position in a course of reasoning, and if every judgment has a modality, then it follows that every judgment has a position in a course of reasoning. But why should this be so? In short, because judgment requires the judger to combine judgment constituents; combination requires a certain kind of unity of self-consciousness, namely, necessary connections between our mental states; and it is judging on the basis of other judgments—reasoning and inferring, rather than making judgments in isolation of one another—that constitutes those necessary connections, hence that unity of self-consciousness, and hence makes judgment possible at all.[8]

---

[8] See Leech (2017a).

Judgments, for Kant, are acts of unification: when we judge we combine representations together. This combination of representations is not something given to us, but must be contributed by the activity of thinking. Kant calls our capacity for thinking 'the understanding'. He writes,

[A]ll *combination*, whether we are conscious of it or not, whether it is a combination of the manifold or intuition *or of several concepts . . . is an action of the understanding.* . . . (B129–30, my emphasis).

For Kant, we combine representations by *representing them as combined*: combination is 'the representation of the synthetic unity of the manifold' (B130–1). Moreover, the combination must be *necessary*: it is a kind of necessary unity that distinguishes a judgment, which is objective, from merely subjective mental association.[9] What grounds this representation of necessary unity? What makes it possible? The unity of self-consciousness (apperception). This can be understood to involve the ability to prefix all of one's representations with 'I think': it only makes sense to say that, for example, *p* is one of *my* representations, if it is possible for me to also think 'I think that *p*'.

This ability is not, however, to be understood in terms of some individual thing, *a self*, acting as a locus for combination. Rather, there is nothing more to the requisite unity of self-consciousness than this ability to combine, which is manifested as a unity of self-consciousness.

Combination does not lie in the objects . . . but is rather *only an operation of the understanding, which is itself nothing further than the faculty of combining a priori* and bringing the manifold of given representations under unity of apperception. . . . (B134–5, my emphasis)

If this unity of self-consciousness were understood to be grounded by a self-object to which all of one's mental states belonged, then we would not be able to account for objective knowledge and representation in the right way. According to Kant, knowledge, cognition, and experience require a combination of several representations into one. For example, cognition of an object will involve a combination of what Kant calls 'intuition' (the object must be presented to us via our senses)

---

[9] See, e.g., A108–25, B142, B168. For Kant, there are two kinds of unity of consciousness: the transcendental unity of self-consciousness, through which representations are combined into cognitions, and a subjective or 'empirical' unity of consciousness, which concerns the contingent subjective stream of inner sense (B139). Merely empirical, contingent relations are insufficient for objective unity. Objective unity involves *necessary* connections (A108). Kant argues that it is through application of the logical functions of judgment that representations are brought to the transcendental unity of consciousness and combined with objective unity (B142). The result is then an objective judgment (B142).

24   THINKING OF NECESSITY

and concepts (the intuition of the object is brought under suitable concepts).[10]
That combination is made possible in turn by the unity of self-consciousness:
I can prefix all of my representations with 'I think', they are all mine, and so they
are all apt to be combined by one thinker. But how can I have knowledge of my
mental states—how is it that I have this prefixing ability? We might answer that I
have a privileged inner sense, a special faculty of introspection. We are presented
with a manifold of inner intuitions (of our mental states, etc.) which give rise to
knowledge of our inner states. However, this would be to explain my knowledge of
myself and my states on the model of knowledge of objects: this is just the special
case where the object of my knowledge is 'inner'. We still need to combine or
'synthesize' the manifold of intuitions—inner or outer—and so we still face the
question of how such combination is possible.

The answer is again the unity of self-consciousness, a certain kind of self-
knowledge. So we come up against the same question: how is this kind of knowledge or representation of self possible? Changing the object from outer to inner
does not change the structure of the problem. Combination of (inner) representations is still required, and still to be accounted for. Hence, if we are to break out of
this circle, there must be a fundamentally different capacity for self-knowledge at
work here. The unity of self-consciousness constitutes a kind of self-knowledge—
knowledge of the unity of one's mental states—not through detecting facts about
inner objects, but by the fact that its own activity constitutes that very unity.
As Patricia Kitcher puts it,

> Rational cognizers do not, and could not, recognize relations of necessary con-
> nection across their thoughts through an 'inner sense'. They recognise them,
> not through a special observational power, but through having produced those
> relations in judging whatever they are judging.   (Kitcher, 2017, 10)

The proposal is for a radically different model of knowledge. Knowledge of these
necessary connections is not to be understood on the usual model, with the
necessary connections being an object of knowledge that we must somehow gain
access to. Rather, knowledge of these necessary connections *just is* constituted
by our judging on the basis of reasons and thereby forming those connections.
Knowledge of the self and its unity as an object, via inner intuition, is not thereby
ruled out, but any knowledge of objects—including self-knowledge via inner
intuition—is only possible if there is also this distinct kind of knowledge of the
self through its own activity.[11]

---

[10] See Gomes and Stephenson (2016) for more on the role of intuition in cognition.
[11] The view that there are two kinds of self-knowledge, one as object, one connected to the activity
of the self, is explored elsewhere. See Moran (2001) and Boyle (2009).

At heart, the ability to judge is an ability to combine certain representations, using the logical functions of judgment (as set out in the Table of Judgments). But it is only possible for me to combine *my* representations. My ability to combine them goes hand-in-hand with my ability to represent them *as mine*. So combination in a judgment requires not only a unity of self-consciousness, but also some kind of cognitive access to that unity of self-consciousness. Kant's idea is that it is through making judgments that we both produce and become aware of the unity. *By actually relating judgments to each other through judging one on the basis of another we are able to produce the unity of self-consciousness, which is a condition of combination in judgment, and also thereby to become acquainted with it.*[12] In short, the unity of self-consciousness is constituted by necessary connections between our mental states, and those necessary connections and our awareness of them are built through our judging for reasons. Something is a judgment only if it relates to the unity of self-consciousness in the right way, and this is ensured if the judgment is part of a connected course of reasoning.[13]

In making a judgment, then, we not only apply the first three kinds of logical function of judgment (*quality, quantity, relation*) to combine the constituent representations, but we also judge on the basis of prior judgments. This means that every token judgment we make is located in a course of reasoning. This is precisely what an application of the fourth function of judgment—*modality*—looks like. Depending on the location of the token judgment in that course of reasoning, it is either problematic, assertoric, or apodictic.[14]

2.3 The postulates of empirical thinking

What kinds of things could there be in the world? What must the world be like? How could it have been different? These are the kinds of modal questions that we can address by considering Kant's account of real modality. Real modal concepts, as opposed to the modal forms of judgment we have just encountered, are primarily introduced in the *Critique of Pure Reason* in the Table of Categories and a section entitled the *Postulates of Empirical Thinking in General*. Whereas the modalities of judgment did not contribute to the content of a judgment, but rather the location of a judgment in a course of reasoning, the modal categories are concepts that can be employed in the content of a judgment.

---

[12] In this reading of Kant, I am indebted to Kitcher (2017).

[13] See also Marshall (2010). Marshall develops an 'effect-relative view' of the self according to which 'for any particular unified experience, whatever thing or things are immediately causally responsible for the unity of that experience compose a self' (p.16). So mental states form a self when they co-cause a unified experience, although it is left open what (further) relation may hold between those states that thereby form a self. The actual-inferential view I propose may fill this gap.

[14] See Leech (2012, 2017a) for more detail and defence of the ideas in this section. See also my entries on 'apodictic', 'assertoric', and 'problematic' in *The Cambridge Kant Lexicon* (Leech, 2021a,b,e).

26 THINKING OF NECESSITY

Logical modality concerns *thinking*; real modality concerns *things*. Cognitions are mental representations which are objective or 'objectively valid': they are about objects in the world. Experience is empirical cognition: cognition that involves input from empirical intuition given through the senses.[15] Cognition—objective representation—is possible only through a combination of concepts and intuition: the object must be both *thought* by the understanding (concepts are applied to it) and *given* by sensibility (an object is intuited, i.e., presented to us). So the move from conditions of *thinking* to conditions of *experience* means that not only logical criteria for thoughts, but now also additional criteria concerning the possibility of intuition and the interaction of intuitions and the understanding are brought in.

The categories concern groups of concepts—of *quality*, *quantity*, *relation*, and *modality*—one of each of which must be applied in any representation or experience of an object (A80/B106). One can understand them, again, as determinables and determinates. Every object must have a size, shape, causal profile, and so on.[16] One can think of the categories as together constituting our concept of an object in general. The categories act to synthesize intuitions according to this general framework of physical objects standing in causal relations. Intuition may present objects to cognition, but we need a general conceptual framework for how to think about objects if we are to be able, not only to have objects thus given to us, but also to apply concepts to them and thereby to cognize them—to have experience of them.[17] Particular features of objects of experience such as *being 1m tall*, *being yellow*, or *being squashed by a falling boulder*, are then supplied by input from sensibility, i.e., from sensation and empirical intuition, and conceptualized using empirical concepts, concepts derived from experience.

The modal categories, as they appear in the Table of Categories, are:

Possibility—Impossibility

Existence—Non-existence

Necessity—Contingency.

Kant does not say much more about these immediately following their introduction. Rather, it is in the *Postulates of Empirical Thinking in General*

---

[15] See B147; B161; B165–6; B218.

[16] Roughly speaking, *quality* corresponds to having or lacking properties to various degrees; *quantity* corresponds to size, shape, constitution from parts; and *relation* to there being substances in which properties inhere and which stand in causal relations.

[17] "Conceptualists" and "non-conceptualists" disagree over whether the activity of the understanding and its concepts are already involved in our capacity for intuition. The way I have put things here suggests a non-conceptualist reading, but this can be weakened for the conceptualist by claiming that this general conceptual framework is also involved in how intuition is able to present us with objects. See McLear (2021) for an overview of the debate.

(A218–35/B265–87) that Kant fleshes out the content of the modal categories when applied in experience.

The *Postulates* appears in the course of a larger part of the *Critique,* the *Analytic of Principles.* The general aim of this part is to provide instructions for how to apply the categories to appearances, i.e., to the undetermined objects of empirical intuition.[18] The categories are pure concepts, in the sense that they are concepts that are not derived from experience, but are part of our capacity for thinking about objects at all. So far, in the course of the *Critique,* we have learnt only minimally which concepts are categories, e.g., we have learnt that *causality* is a category, but we don't know much more about the things that fall under it. We have also learnt that these pure concepts are applicable to the empirical world (Kant's "transcendental deduction"), but again, we don't know in which particular circumstances which pure concept will apply. One thing we do know *a priori* about appearances is that they are in space and time. Kant has already argued in an earlier part of the book, the *Transcendental Aesthetic,* that the forms of space and time are necessary conditions of the possibility of our having sensible intuition at all, hence space and time are the pure forms of intuition. Time is the primary form, given that it applies to *all* empirical intuitions, whereas space only applies to the intuitions of outer sense.[19] Hence, much of Kant's strategy in the *Analytic of Principles* concerns what an application of the categories must look like if the intuitions to which they are applied are in time.

There are two ways for a category to contribute to cognition. First, consider: *The cat is on the mat.* This contains no explicit use of categories such as *substance* or *causation*, but nevertheless such a cognition relies on a background conceptual framework supporting the idea of two objects, each with a size, shape, density, causally interacting with each other. The categories contribute a unifying framework of objects and relations to any empirical experience. Second, consider: *The cat caused the mouse to run away.* In this case we have an explicit use of the concept *cause.* In both cases we want to know what the concept *cause* means: in the first case, to know what has been contributed to the framework of our experience; in the second case, to know what it means to make an explicit causal judgment.

The *Principles* aim to flesh out the categories. Here Kant presents in more detail the kind of content that each category contributes to the framework underlying judgment and experience, and thereby also the content of judgments explicitly involving these concepts, such as causal or modal judgments. In doing so, Kant

---

[18] See A20/B34.

[19] 'Time is the *a priori* formal condition of all appearances in general. Space, as the pure form of all outer intuitions, is limited as an *a priori* condition merely to outer intuitions. But since, on the contrary, all representations, whether or not they have outer things as their object, nevertheless as determinations of the mind themselves belong to the inner state, while this inner state belongs under the formal condition of inner intuition, and thus of time, so time is an *a priori* condition of all appearance in general, and indeed the immediate condition of the inner intuition (of our souls), and thereby also the mediate condition of outer appearances' (A34/B50–1).

28 THINKING OF NECESSITY

also provides specific arguments for why a concept with that kind of content is a necessary condition of the possibility of experience. One of the more well-known examples of this is Kant's *Second Analogy*, where he argues that a principle of causality—roughly, that every event must have a cause—is a necessary condition of the possibility of our experience of objective temporal succession (A189–211/ B232–56).[20]

In the *Postulates*, Kant presents three modal principles.

1. Whatever agrees with the formal conditions of experience (in accordance with intuitions and concepts) is **possible**.
2. That which is connected with the material conditions of experience (of sensation) is **actual**.
3. That whose connection with the actual is determined in accordance with general conditions of experience is (exists) **necessarily**. (A218/B265–6)

Kant then offers an elucidation.

The categories of modality have this peculiarity: as a determination of the object they do not augment the concept to which they are ascribed in the least, but rather express only the relation to the faculty of cognition. If the concept of a thing is already entirely complete, I can still ask about this object whether it is merely possible, or also actual, or, if it is the latter, whether it is also necessary? No further determinations in the object itself are hereby thought; rather, it is only asked: how is the object itself (together with all its determinations) related to the understanding and its empirical use, to the empirical power of judgment, and to reason (in its application to experience)?   (A219/B266)

There is much contained in this short passage. First, a negative point: that modal concepts do not further determine an object. Second, a positive point: that modal concepts express something about the relation between an object and our cognitive capacities.

First, then, Kant claims that the modal concepts do not add to the concept of a thing. Although we can use modal predicates, as in, for example, 'A talking donkey is possible', we do not thereby say anything about what the object is like. For example, to say 'That donkey is grey' tells us something about what the donkey is like, i.e., that it is grey. But to say that it is possible doesn't tell us what it is like, it tells us something else (roughly, that something like that could exist). In applying a modal concept to something, Kant says that 'no further determinations in the

---

[20] See Watkins (2010) for an introduction to the *Principles*, and Leech and Textor (forthcoming) for more on substance and causation.

object itself are hereby thought'. Stang (2016, 39) offers a more precise account of what Kant means by 'determination'.

> A concept P *determines* a concept C if and only if it is possible that there is an object that instantiates C and P and it is possible that there is an object that instantiates C but not P.
>
> A predicate P is a *determination* if and only if P determines at least one concept.

For example, the concept of being unmarried does not determine the concept of being a bachelor, because it is not possible that there is a bachelor that is not unmarried. But the concept of being tall does determine the concept *bachelor*, because there can be tall bachelors and short bachelors.

Given this framework, we might understand Kant's claim about the modal concepts as follows. Consider some concept, C_1.[21] Is it possible that there is an object that instantiates both C_1 and the concept of mere possibility as well as possible that there is an object that instantiates C_1 but not the concept of mere possibility? Only if there are merely possible (non-actual) objects and impossible objects. Is it possible that there is an object that instantiates both C_1 and the concept of actuality as well as possible that there is an object that instantiates C_1 but not the concept of actuality? Again, only if there are non-actual objects as well as actual objects. But there are no non-actual objects; to be is just to be actual. So the concepts of mere possibility and actuality do not determine C_1. The choice of C_1 was arbitrary, so we can conclude that these modal concepts are not determinations. Is it possible that there is an object that instantiates both C_1 and the concept of necessity as well as possible that there is an object that instantiates C_1 but not the concept of necessity? Kant has already argued that everything has a necessitating cause. He will argue in the *Postulates* that everything is hypothetically or conditionally necessary (subject to necessary, *a priori* laws of nature). Hence, everything is necessary (in this sense). Hence, it is not possible that there is an object that instantiates C_1 but not *necessity*. So the concept of necessity does not determine C_1. The choice of C_1 was arbitrary, so we can conclude that this modal concept is not a determination.

In his discussion of the modal postulates, Kant makes claims about the role of a modal predicate when it is ascribed to *a concept*, i.e., the concept of whatever thing may be possible, actual, or necessary. But according to Kant, we can only properly represent individuals by means of an *intuition*, not a concept, although sometimes

---

[21] C_1 may be more or less detailed. It might approach the detail of an individual concept, e.g., a detailed concept applying to Socrates. Or it might be much simpler, e.g., the concept of a bachelor. The question is whether the concept of mere possibility can serve to further determine C_1, e.g., whether being merely possible adds more to our concept of Socrates, to make the concept of a *merely possible Socrates*; whether being merely possible adds more to the concept *bachelor*, to make the concept of a *merely possible bachelor*.

30 THINKING OF NECESSITY

it may happen that a concept can be used to pick out an individual. Concepts, by nature, do not individuate things.[22] So we should be wary of understanding the emerging account of modal concepts in terms of *individual objects*, e.g., as including the claim that the modal predicate 'is possible' doesn't further determine the concept of the individual object, but rather tells us that there could be such an individual. Rather, given Kant's view of singular thought, it makes better sense to think of the view in terms of the concept of a *kind* of object. For example, the judgment that *a talking donkey is possible* represents that a kind of thing, a talking donkey, is possible. It does not represent of any particular *individual* talking donkey that *it* is possible. Of course, we can apply concepts to intuitions: that's an important part of Kant's theory of experience. But particularly in the case of claims of possibility, where there is no actual intuition but we want to claim that there *could be* (such a thing could appear in experience), the available candidate for the ascription of possibility—however that ascription functions—is a kind of thing, represented by a concept, not an individual, represented by an intuition.

This is what we should understand Kant's view to be, given his account of concepts and the crucial role that intuitions play in singular thought. With advances in logic available to us, we can now give examples of concepts that, if satisfied, could only have one thing falling under them, for example, *the tallest tree*. Even so, the majority of cases would still seem to fit in with the framework suggested, i.e., non-individual concepts for which we may ask if there could be such a kind of thing. Moreover, the examples suggested are still descriptive. They don't give us the resources to ask whether there could be a particular individual, e.g., whether there could be tree *a* rather than tree *b*, but only whether there could be such a kind of thing as a tallest tree. Hence, even these apparently individual concepts usher in the possibility only of a *kind* of individual. It is also worth noting that there is certainly no contemporary consensus on what to make of individual possibilities, i.e., whether there can be genuine *de re* possibilities concerning merely possible individuals, or whether they must ultimately be descriptive (and maybe also related to actual individuals, e.g., the seventh son of Kripke).[23]

Thus far, I have discussed general considerations for the modal postulates. What does each postulate in particular state? Each concerns conditions of experience: *formal, material,* and *general.* The forms of sensibility and the categories together

---

[22] For example, even a completely determinate conceptual description of a drop of water might pick out more than one individual thing. Intuitions are required for individuation. See (A263–4/B319–20). Concepts are *by nature* general representations that are able to pick out more than one thing. However, they may still often be *used* to pick out individuals, for example, if as a matter of fact there is a unique individual, we would be able to pick it out using a concept which was sufficiently determinate to exploit its unique qualities. See especially Kant (9:91; 1992, 589): 'It is a mere tautology to speak of general [*allgemeinen*] or common concepts—a mistake that is grounded in an incorrect division of concepts into general [*allgemeine*], *particular* and *singular*. Concepts themselves cannot be so divided, but only *their use*' (translation amended). See also Leech (2017b).

[23] See, for example, Stalnaker (2012).

comprise the *formal conditions* of experience: they provide experience with a framework of spatiotemporal physical objects, bearing properties, standing in relations, and so on. These *a priori* conditions of experience give *form* to the matter of experience.[24] The *material conditions* of experience are the particular input given from sensibility, i.e., sensation. For there to be an experience there has to be both form and matter. Kant has argued that there are formal conditions which are a necessary prerequisite of any experience whatsoever, but there also needs to be some input from sensation to which those formal conditions apply: 'Thoughts without content are empty, intuitions without concepts are blind' (A51/B75). Finally, neither the formal nor the material conditions of experience, thus described, concern any particular things. They require that everything conform to the formal and material conditions of experience, not that any particular thing should be of any particular form, nor that any particular thing should be given to us. Hence, the *general conditions* of experience can be understood to be a combination of the formal and material conditions.

The principles of modality provide a definition of each modal category in terms of one of these types of condition. Something is possible only if it agrees with the formal conditions of experience. This should come as no surprise. Within Kant's system, in order for anything to be an object of possible experience, it must conform to the forms of sensibility—or else it could not be presented to us—and to the categories—or else we could not cognize it.[25]

Something is actual only if it is connected to material conditions of experience. So, for some thing to be actual is for it to be connected to what is given through sensation. What does it mean for something to be "connected to what is given through sensation"? Simply that it is presented to us in sensation? That would mean that everything actual is presented in sensation, and hence that everything actual is sensed, leading us into a strong form of idealism according to which the only things that actually exist are things that are experienced. This seems unpalatable: if there is a tree in the heart of the forest, that as a matter of happenstance no sentient creature ever directly senses, surely we still want to claim that the tree *actually* exists? However, Kant stresses that we do not need *direct* perception of an object for it to be actual or existent, so long as we have some perception of something which is related by the categories of relation to the object.

---

[24] There are differences between the contribution made by the forms of intuition and the categories, but both have an impact on the form of our experience, whether by determining the form of the objects that can be given to us, or by determining the conceptual framework in which we can cognize and experience those objects. As such, I will be exploiting this important commonality. See Allais (2015, 292–7) for an account of the differences between *a priori* intuitions and *a priori* concepts.

[25] This states a necessary condition for real possibility. Later, I explain why this is not, on its own, also a sufficient condition.

32 THINKING OF NECESSITY

> The postulate for cognizing the **actuality** of things requires **perception,** thus sensation of which one is conscious—not immediate perception of the object itself the existence of which is to be cognized, but still its connection with some actual perception in accordance with the analogies of experience, which exhibit all real connection in an experience in general.   (A225/B272)

As long as an object is connected in this way to an actual perception, even at some remove, then the object counts as actual. Those connections are detailed by the *Analogies of Experience*, principles which purport to establish causal connections between all existing things.[26] According to the *Analogies*, any actual existent must be related to any other, in particular, to objects of direct, actual perception. Kant gives an example of something that cannot be seen by the naked eye (magnetic force) whose existence can be inferred from other perceptual experiences (the attraction of iron filings).

> Thus we cognize the existence of a magnetic matter penetrating all bodies from the perception of attracted iron filings, although an immediate perception of this matter is impossible for us given the constitution of our organs.   (A226/B273)

Hence there is no pernicious phenomenalism here. The actual world is the world of all and only objects standing in causal relations to the objects of direct experience. The actual world is, in fact, understood as closed under causal and spatiotemporal relations, which is now a rather familiar idea to contemporary metaphysicians.[27]

Necessity is defined as that which is determined in connection with the actual according to general conditions of experience. One might have expected that, just as possibility is defined as what is in agreement with formal conditions of experience, necessity would simply be what is *required* by those conditions. However, Kant defines necessity in connection with the actual. Why? He explains:

> Finally, as far as the third postulate is concerned, it pertains to material necessity in existence, not the merely formal and logical necessity in the connection of concepts. Now, since no existence of objects of the senses can be cognized fully *a priori*, but always only comparatively *a priori* relative to another already given existence, but since nevertheless even then we can only arrive at an existence

---

[26] See, e.g., A189/B232; A211/B256; Allison (2004) Part II; Watkins (2010).

[27] I have in mind David Lewis's notion of a possible world as of a maximal spatiotemporal causal sum, i.e., a sum composed of all and only parts spatiotemporally or causally related to any of its parts (Lewis, 1986). There will be other examples.

that must be contained somewhere in the nexus of experience of which the given perception is a part, the necessity of existence can thus never be cognized from concepts but rather always only *from the connection with that which is perceived*, in accordance with general laws of experience.   (A226–7/B279, my emphasis)

It is not possible, according to Kant, to have knowledge of existence *a priori*. All *a priori* knowledge has its source in subjective conditions of experience, but for something to exist it needs to be given in the matter of experience. So we could not know about the existence of something purely on the basis of subjective conditions of experience; we would also require the contribution of the matter of experience. Moreover, those subjective conditions of experience are all general, as explained above, and do not concern particular things. So it is hard to see how one could acquire *a priori* knowledge of some *particular* thing. Nevertheless, Kant grants that we could have *comparative a priori* knowledge of existence, i.e., if I have knowledge of some cause (the stove is hot), and of some empirical law (heat melts ice), then I can *a priori* infer the existence of an effect (a puddle—from a block of ice).

Kant is often understood to hold that *a priority* and *necessity* are co-extensive.[28] If this is correct, then, for Kant, nothing (no object of experience) exists necessarily, in an unqualified sense of 'necessity'.[29] However, objects of experience do bear necessary connections to one another. So, for example, a certain effect is necessary conditional upon its cause. This means that, whilst a concept of unqualified necessary existence may have no use for Kant, a concept of conditional necessity does. And indeed, this coheres with the idea that we can have comparative *a priori* knowledge of existence, *conditional on* another existent. Hence, the postulate of necessity concerns necessity conditional upon what is already actual: given some actual state, and given the laws of nature, some consequential state is conditionally necessary.[30]

We can now see that Kant effectively defines two different kinds of modality in the *Postulates*: one in terms of formal conditions of experience, and one in terms of general conditions of experience plus how things actually are. I will call the former 'formal modality' (following Stang),[31] and the latter 'material modality' (following Kant's use of 'material necessity').

---

[28] But see Stang (2011).

[29] For present purposes, it suffices to make this assumption. However, the precise relationship between *a priority* and necessity is rather more complicated. See, for example, the very illuminating discussion in Stephenson (forthcoming). At least: if necessity is a 'secure indication of an *a priori* cognition' (B4), then it would seem that necessary existence should entail some kind of *a priori* cognition of existence. But if that latter is ruled out, then the former is also ruled out.

[30] See Leech (2021d).   [31] Stang (2011, 2016).

2.4 Relative necessity

One key aspect of Kant's views on modality that I want to bring out and exploit is that they can be understood in terms of a framework of relative necessity. Notions of relative necessity and possibility are profuse and familiar. In everyday life, as well as in philosophical practice, we often make use of a variety of different notions of possibility and necessity that are qualified in relation to something or other. For example, we might say that something is necessary, given biological laws (e.g., it's necessary that this frog was once a tadpole), or that something is possible, given one's practical abilities (e.g., it's possible for me to build a wall). In philosophy of language and linguistics there is significant support for the claim that modal locutions vary wildly, relative to the slightest changes in context.[32] And most philosophers are familiar with distinguishing between notions such as logical necessity, metaphysical necessity, natural necessity and epistemic necessity. One plausible way to make sense of these different modalities and how they relate to each other, is to treat them as *relative modalities*. For example, something is physically necessary if it is necessary *relative to* the laws of physics, or something is morally necessary if it is necessary *relative to* a certain moral code, or something is epistemically necessity if it is necessary *relative to* a state of knowledge. Relative necessity is contrasted with *absolute* necessity. Roughly speaking, something is absolutely necessary if it is not merely relatively necessary—not necessary conditional upon something else—but necessary without qualification.

Kant has his own understanding of absolute necessity as that the non-existence of which would cancel all possibility. So, for example, the existence of a being that served to ground all of possibility would be absolutely necessary in this sense, for if it ceased to exist, the grounds of possibility would also cease, and hence there would no longer be such possibilities. This allows for different kinds of absolute necessity for different kinds of possibility, e.g., the non-existence of an absolutely *real* necessary being would cancel all *real* possibility.[33] I will not follow Kant's understanding of absolute necessity here: my interest in this book is in a notion of absolute necessity understood as necessity without qualification, which contrasts with relative necessities. There are clearly two interesting notions here that share a name, and I follow more recent usage of the name 'absolute necessity' rather than Kant's use. As I am about to explain, we can understand aspects of Kant's account of modality in terms of relative modalities. Since that notion comes along with the sibling notion of absolute necessity (necessity without qualification), it is not unreasonable to discuss Kant's work in these terms, even if he might have used the labels differently.

---

[32] See, for example, Kratzer (1977, 2008) and Lewis (1979). Lycan (1994) paints a particularly striking picture of the relativity of modal terms.

[33] See Stang (2016) for more extensive discussion.

There are various virtues of adopting a unifying framework of relative and absolute necessity as far as possible that I discuss later in this book.[34] But for the time being, I want to note that it is quite natural to think of Kant's view as having this structure. Something is formally possible *relative to* formal conditions of experience, and something is materially necessary *relative to* general conditions of experience plus how things actually are. Insofar as the relative necessity framework is attractive in general, then, the fact that Kant's view so easily lends itself to this makes it easier to draw on the benefits of Kant's view as well.

Beyond the *Postulates*, there are suggestions that Kant himself thought of modality as sometimes being relative. For example, in a lecture on metaphysics (from around 1782/3, between the two editions of the *Critique*), he stated that,

> Physical possibility is that which does not conflict with the laws of experience; this one can easily comprehend, e.g., that a large palace could be built in four weeks is physically impossible. Morally possible is that which is possible according to the rules of morals, and does not conflict with the general law of freedom.
>
> (29:812; Kant, 1997b, 166)

Here Kant can be read as applying a relative modality view to different kinds of modality. He also gives further examples of things which are possible or impossible relative to different conditions or 'hypotheses'.

> E.g. it is possible that a human being should arrive at vast riches, but due to laziness, unsuitability, and a lack of wealthy relatives it is impossible. Something can be possible in itself, while hypothetically, under either its logical or real hypothesis, it is impossible.   (29:813; Kant, 1997b, 167)

The same thing can be possible relative to some condition and at the same time impossible relative to another condition.

In more precise terms, one can define relative necessity schematically in the following way.

Relative$\Box$ It is Φ-necessary that p iff $\exists \phi (\Phi \phi \wedge \Box (\phi \rightarrow p))$[35]

This states that it is Φ-necessary that p if and only if there are some suitable Φ-propositions which strictly imply p, i.e., which imply p as a matter of logical necessity. So, for example, it is physically necessary that p if and only if there are

---

[34] See Chapter 7.

[35] Or alternatively: It is Φ-necessary that p iff $\exists \phi_1 \ldots \phi_n (\Phi \phi_1 \wedge \ldots \wedge \Phi \phi_n \wedge \Box ((\phi_1 \wedge \ldots \wedge \phi_n) \rightarrow p))$. For present purposes the simpler version should suffice, but see Hale and Leech (2017) on the more complex formulation. On the formulation of relative necessity see also Humberstone (1981, 2004); Hale (2013); Leech (2016). See Chapter 10 for further discussion.

36 THINKING OF NECESSITY

some basic truths of physics which strictly imply p (here 'Φ' is replaced by 'it is a basic truth of physics that'), or it is biologically necessary that p if and only if there are some basic biological facts which strictly imply p (here 'Φ' is replaced by 'it is a basic biological fact that').

Relative possibility might accordingly be understood as *not being ruled out* by certain propositions.

***Relative*◇** It is Φ-possible that p iff $\neg\exists\phi(\Phi\phi \wedge \Box(\phi \rightarrow \neg p))$

For example, it is physically possible that p if and only if there are no basic truths of physics that rule out p, and it is biologically possible that p if and only if there are no basic biological facts that rule out p. The crucial idea at issue is that important kinds of necessity and possibility can be defined as relative, in terms of logical necessity and a certain class of propositions.

It is tempting to straightforwardly plug Kant's principles of possibility and necessity into this framework. The postulate of possibility introduces a kind of possibility that is relative to formal conditions on experience. So we could formalize this as follows.

***Formal*◇** It is F-possible that p iff $\neg\exists\phi(F\phi \wedge \Box(\phi \rightarrow \neg p))$

where '$F\phi$' means 'ϕ is the conjunction of the formal conditions of experience'. We could then also define a cognate notion of necessity.

***Formal*□** It is F-necessary that p iff $\exists\phi(F\phi \wedge \Box(\phi \rightarrow p))$

One might similarly formalize the kind of necessity defined in the third postulate, and a cognate notion of possibility.

***Material*□** It is M-necessary that p at t iff $\exists\phi(G\phi \wedge \Box((\phi \wedge A_t) \rightarrow p))$
***Material*◇** It is M-possible that p at t iff $\neg\exists\phi(G\phi \wedge \Box(\phi \wedge A_t) \rightarrow \neg p))$

where '$G\phi$' means 'ϕ is the conjunction of the general conditions of experience', and 'A_t' stands for a statement of how things actually are at (up until) time t.

However, there are two problems with this first attempt at subsuming Kant's modal principles under this framework. The first problem is that it doesn't quite capture the sense in which conditions of experience are involved in possibility. For something to be formally possible, according to Kant, it must agree with formal conditions of experience. This implies that *there are* such conditions. So it doesn't seem right to formalize this as in *Formal*◇, where it is formally possible that p just when there are no formal conditions that are incompatible with p. For that could be the case when and because there are no formal conditions of experience at all. A more faithful formalization, which captures the important idea that formal conditions are the backdrop against which formal modality is defined, would thus be:

Formal◇*   It is F-possible that p iff $\exists\phi F\phi \wedge \forall\psi(F\psi \rightarrow \neg\Box(\psi \rightarrow \neg p))$

It is formally possible that p just when *there are* formal conditions of experience and p is not ruled out by any of those conditions. Likewise, the following is preferable.

Material◇*   It is M-possible that p at t iff
$$\exists\phi G\phi \wedge \forall\psi(G\psi \rightarrow \neg(\Box(\psi \wedge A_t) \rightarrow \neg p))$$

It is materially possible that p at t just when *there are* general conditions of experience, and it is not the case that any of these taken together with how things actually are at and up to t rule out p.

Formal◇* and *Material◇** have a noteworthy consequence: formal possibility and necessity and material possibility and necessity are no longer straightforwardly interdefinable, i.e., $\Diamond p \equiv \neg\Box\neg p$ and $\Box p \equiv \neg\Diamond\neg p$ fail for these modalities. I address this issue later in the book, when I develop a Kantian account of metaphysical necessity.[36]

The second problem is how to understand the necessity—the '□'—in terms of which these relative modalities are defined. The natural choice is logical necessity, as I have been assuming thus far. This would give us a view according to which logical modality is the fundamental kind of modality common to all relative modality, and relative modalities are simply qualified logical modalities. However, this stands in conflict with another aspect of Kant's view.

Included in formal and general conditions of experience are mathematical principles, for example, certain geometrical axioms. According to Kant, mathematics is *synthetic,* not analytic, and central kinds of mathematical reasoning, particularly geometrical reasoning, are also synthetic. Kant seems to want to leave room for a kind of non-logical implication in mathematics. This is in tension with taking all real necessities to follow logically from formal conditions of experience (and with taking possibilities to be logically compatible with those conditions). As Stang puts the point,

> It should be clear that formal necessity and possibility cannot be defined in terms of logical grounding (entailment)....If we analyzed formal possibility and necessity in terms of logical grounding, it would follow that geometrical

---

[36] See Chapter 10.

38 THINKING OF NECESSITY

axioms logically entail geometrical theorems, i.e., that all formally impossible propositions are logically incompatible with the axioms. But Kant holds that geometric reasoning is irreducibly synthetic because it relies on construction in pure intuition. Consequently the relation between forms of experience and what is formally necessary cannot be assimilated to the relation of logical entailment; the formal necessities do not follow *logically* from the forms of experience.

(Stang, 2016, 207)

Accordingly, Stang defines these modalities in terms of *real grounding*, a non-logical relation of explanation between things.

Must we therefore read '□' as a kind of necessity connected to a non-logical notion of grounding, such that A grounds B just when $\Box(A \rightarrow B)$? There are some passages from Kant which seem to support this interpretation. For example, in the lecture on metaphysics from which I quoted earlier, Kant seems to explain relative modalities in terms of grounds.

> Something is possible internally or in and for itself, and relatively in reference and connection with other things.... Much is possible internally *<interne>*, that in connection is not possible externally *<externe>*, i.e., conditionally possible as well; the condition is here as much as a ground, e.g., it is possible in itself that a human being can become rich, but also conditionally, for his parents are rich, so there is yet another ground for that.   (29:813; Kant, 1997b, 167)

Nevertheless, I find it strange that, if real grounding is so important to Kant's understanding of modality, he does not discuss it more explicitly in the *Postulates*. In fact, in this section of the *Critique* the word only appears twice, where Kant argues that the possibility of invented concepts such as *telepathy* is 'groundless', because they cannot be 'grounded in experience and its known laws' (A223/B270). It is not clear cut how to read this passage, but at least, if there is a claim to a real grounding relation, it is not to formal conditions of experience, as would be expected for possibility, but to 'experience and its known laws'. The problem Kant is discussing here is that certain concepts are defective insofar as they are neither necessary conditions for the possibility of experience, nor acquired from experience, but made up without taking heed of how things actually are and how properties are actually combined in the world. Such concepts may not be appropriately grounded and so cannot be assessed for agreement or disagreement with formal conditions of experience. But that does not tell us whether to understand 'agreement' in terms of real ground or logical entailment.

Still, the problem is an important one. To properly address whether Kant can be read as allowing for real necessity to be a relativization of logical necessity would take us too far into Kant exegesis and interpretation for present purposes. Later in the book I argue for the virtues of a relative necessity framework in which all non-epistemic alethic modalities are to be understood as relativizations of logical necessity. I also argue that metaphysical necessity is ill-understood, and that an account of metaphysical necessity that fits into such a framework is illuminating.[37] My aim is to develop the idea of real modality as relative to conditions of experience into an account of metaphysical necessity. This is obviously inspired by Kant's view, as I understand it, but does not follow Kant to the letter.

We have seen that Kant defines two different kinds of modality in the *Postulates*: *formal modality* and *material modality*. Above, I introduced the crucial distinction between real modality and logical modality, and introduced the *Postulates* as defining real modality. How do formal and material modality relate to real modality?

There are different ways to organize this cluster of modal notions. According to Stang (2016), formal and material modality are instances of a more general species of real modality.[38] Stang's view is well-motivated (I will not discuss the details here), but it does preserve an oddity of the postulate of possibility that I want to explain in a different way.[39]

The core idea of real modality seems to be a matter of *what there can be* in the most general sense. The most general sense, for Kant, concerns what can be an object of experience or cognition. There are non-logical conditions on being an object of experience. Hence, real modality is distinct from logical modality. Just because the idea of something is logically consistent, does not mean that there could be such an object. I explained earlier how it is an important part of Kant's view that there are both formal and material conditions of experience. Objects of possible experience must be compatible with the formal conditions of experience, *but they must also be given to us*. For something to be really possible, it must be possible for it to be given to us. What are the conditions of the possibility of something being given to us as an object of experience? The formal conditions of experience, yes. But Kant also argues—later in the *Critique*—that there is a material condition of possibility.

> [B]ecause that which constitutes the thing itself (in appearance), namely the real, has to be given, without which it could not be thought at all, but that in which the real in all appearances is given is the one all-encompassing experience, the material for the possibility of all objects of sense has to be presupposed as given in one sum total; and all possibility of empirical objects, their difference from one another and their thoroughgoing determination, can rest only on the limitation of this sum total. (A581–2/B609–10)

---

[37] See Chapters 6 and 7.

[38] Stang calls material modality 'empirical-causal' modality. According to Stang's interpretation, a kind of possibility is real just when it is non-logical, has real grounds in actuality, and does not depend upon how our minds are constituted. See Stang (2016, 198–9).

[39] See also Leech (2017c).

40 THINKING OF NECESSITY

Put simply, real possibility depends not only on formal conditions of experience, but also on the quite general requirement that we be given some matter of experience as well to which those forms may then apply. Kant also claims that this matter is given in a single sum total: the forms in which we can be given objects of sense are space and time, which are unities, hence the material condition of real possibility is that there is some matter of experience given to us in a single spatio-temporal unity. The particular spatiotemporal location of an individual object, which distinguishes it from other individuals, can then be understood in terms of a limitation of this sum total.[40]

The peculiarity of the postulate of possibility is that it does not make mention of this arguably crucial material condition of real possibility. One consequence of this is that the principle does not, therefore, give a completely general definition of real possibility. It states a *necessary condition* for real possibility—that the concept of something agrees with formal conditions of experience—but is not a *sufficient condition*, since it does not include reference to the material condition of real possibility. Hence, I don't think we should take formal possibility, as defined in this first postulate, to be a species of real possibility.

Why would Kant offer us a principle of possibility that falls short of real possibility in the very place where he is supposed to tell us about the possibility and necessity of things? This is because of the function of the postulate of possibility. I explain this more in the next section, but in brief, the principle of possibility is applied by Kant, in the *Postulates* discussion, only to pure representations, which are not derived from sense experience and hence need justification for their applicability to experience for their real possibility. Given the function of the principle of possibility, it only need concern formal conditions of experience, because it is in terms of their relation to those formal conditions that we can justify the applicability of pure representations. Empirical representations, by contrast, are applicable to experience because they were derived from experience. Hence, the real possibility of these representations is more closely tied to the material conditions of real possibility.

Real modality, as I understand it, is relative to conditions on cognition, conditions on there being objects of experience. So whatever is compatible with these conditions is really possible, and whatever is required by these conditions is really necessary. In the *Postulates*, Kant is particularly concerned with *a priori* principles that have some role to play in the possibility of experience. As such, although the principles there relate to real modality, they are not definitive of it. The principle of possibility, as I explain soon, has a role to play in ensuring the objective validity of pure representations, hence it only concerns formal conditions of experience. The principle of necessity has a role to play in ensuring necessary connections

---

[40] See Leech (2017b).

between things in experience, hence it concerns material necessity, not purely real necessity. It takes into account, not only what is required by purely general conditions of experience, but also what is actually given to us in experience.

2.5 The function of real modal judgment

It is significant that Kant includes modal concepts amongst the categories. The applicability of the categories to experience, and the principles to which they give rise, are necessary conditions of the possibility of experience. But why? Why does Kant think that we need modal concepts, as defined in the *Postulates*, as a condition of possible experience? In this section, I first briefly review the arguments that I think can be found for this in the *Postulates*. Then I introduce another important argument from Kant's *Critique of the Power of Judgment*.

2.5.1 The Principle of Possibility

> Whatever agrees with the formal conditions of experience (in accordance with intuitions and concepts) is **possible**.
>
> (A218/B265)

As I noted earlier, the *Analytic of Principles* not only tells us more about the content of the categories, it also provides specific arguments for why principles arising from these categories are necessary conditions of the possibility of experience.[41] If the *Postulates* are to follow the pattern of the rest of the *Principles*, then we should expect to find similar arguments concerning the modal principles. Indeed, I believe we can.

Kant presents the following argument for the principle of possibility.

> [T]he principles of modality are also nothing further than definitions of the concepts of possibility, actuality, and necessity in their empirical use, and thus at the same time restrictions of all categories to merely empirical use, without any permission and allowance for their transcendental use. For if they are not to have a merely logical significance and analytically express the form of thinking, but are to refer to things and their possibility, actuality, and necessity, then they must pertain to possible experience and its synthetic unity, in which alone objects of cognition are given. (A219/B266–7, translation amended)

---

[41] See Leech (2022a) for a fuller account of the interpretation presented in this section.

42   THINKING OF NECESSITY

From this, we can extract the following argument.

1. The categories are restricted to an empirical use: to application to objects of experience. (Otherwise they would have a merely logical significance.)
2. If the categories are to be restricted to an empirical use, then they must pertain only to possible experience and its synthetic unity (in which alone objects of cognition are given).
3. If the categories are to pertain only to possible experience and its synthetic unity, then the application of the categories must agree with the formal conditions of experience. (If a category did not agree with the formal conditions of experience, then there could not be an object of experience falling under that concept, and the category would therefore not be applicable to objects of experience.)
4. Therefore, if the categories are to be restricted to an empirical use, then the application of the categories must agree with the formal conditions of experience.
5. That a concept agrees with the formal conditions of experience just is an instance of the principle of possibility.
6. Therefore, the principle of possibility is a transcendental condition of the restriction of the categories to an empirical use.

This appears to be a transcendental argument for the principle of possibility.[42] Premise 1 states an assumed truth about the meaning or significance of the categories. Premises 2–4 present a chain of transcendental conditions (necessary conditions of the possibility) of 1. Premise 5 notes that the ultimate transcendental condition is equivalent to the principle of possibility. Hence in 6 we can conclude that the principle of possibility is a transcendental condition of the assumed truth in premise 1, that the categories have a restricted use.

The role of the principle of possibility in possible experience is thus to ensure that the categories are restricted to an empirical use. Having given this argument, Kant proceeds to apply the principle to a fairly exhaustive list of pure representations: 'We shall now make obvious the extensive utility and influence of this postulate of possibility' (A221/B268). First, he applies it to the three categories of relation: *substance* (A221/B268), *causation* (A221/B268–9), and *community* (A221/B269). Next, to concepts of magnitude, the categories of quantity and quality (A224/B271–2). This covers the non-modal categories. Finally, Kant also applies the principle to the concept of a triangle. This is not a category, but it is a pure representation, insofar as we can construct a representation of a triangle

---

[42] A transcendental argument is, in brief, an argument that begins with some assumed truth and charts back the necessary conditions of the possibility of that truth. For more on transcendental arguments see Stern (1999).

in the pure intuition of space (A223–4/B271). Hence, he covers an example of a mathematical concept as well. In each case, it is argued that the pure representation alone is not sufficient to guarantee its objective validity. Rather, it must agree with the formal conditions of experience. It must be shown that the representation has an empirical application.[43]

One can understand the requirement for a principle of possibility to play such a role as arising from Kant's theory of the formation and acquisition of concepts. According to Kant, concepts have a form and a matter. Their characteristic *form* is *generality*. They relate to an object 'by means of a feature which several things may have in common' (A320/B337). The generality of a concept is 'made', not given (9:93; Kant, 1992, 591). In other words, it is due to our cognitive capacities that we have general representations of this kind—concepts are not given to us, we form general representations of things when we notice and abstract out similarities in the world. We can think of the generality of a concept in terms of the concept having a sphere or extension, that is, a domain of things to which it applies (Newton, 2015, 473). An explanation of how the generality of a concept is made, then, will be an explanation of how a concept comes to have a sphere or extension at all. Proposals for this explanation vary.[44] Our present concern, however, is not with the generality of concepts *as such*, i.e., not with how concepts get to have an extension *at all*, but with how that extension comes to be appropriately *limited* (to empirical use only).

The form of a concept, generality, is made. But the *matter* of a concept might be made or given. Concepts that have a 'made' matter are constructed concepts, typically mathematical concepts. Concepts with a given matter divide into those with a matter given in experience (empirical concepts, such as the concept of a tree) and those with a matter given independently of experience (pure concepts, such as the concept of causation). The matter of an empirical concept is derived from empirical experience of the relevant kind, e.g., experience of various trees for acquiring the concept *tree*. The matter of the concept serves to limit the extension of the concept, e.g., to applicability to trees. But what is to serve as the matter of a category? The logical functions of judgment provide the basis for the content of the categories, but these alone are not sufficient to limit the extensions of the categories to the empirical world: they 'extend further than sensible intuition' (A254/B309), as they are forms of thinking, and do not take into account conditions of intuition. An additional element is therefore required

---

[43] For example, Kant says of his principle of substance that, 'If I represent to myself a thing that persists, so that everything that changes merely belongs to its states, I can never cognize from such a concept alone that such a thing is possible' (A221/B268). Rather, we can only cognize the applicability to objects of experience of such a concept in relation to 'the form of an experience in general and the synthetic unity in which alone objects can be empirically cognized' (A222/B269), namely, it must agree with the formal conditions of possible experience.

[44] See, e.g., Longuenesse (1998); Newton (2015).

44 THINKING OF NECESSITY

to ensure that the extensions of these concepts are restricted to possible objects of experience. Kant offers us the principle of possibility. When a concept is formed, it must be formed in agreement with the formal conditions of experience. In the case of an empirical concept this condition is satisfied by the fact that any concept acquired from *actual* experience is *a fortiori* in agreement with *possible* experience. In the case of a pure concept, not derived from experience, agreement with these conditions requires an additional principle: the principle of possibility. Given the fundamental role that such a principle plays, it must be *a priori*. We can now also see why the principle of possibility concerns only formal, and not material, conditions of experience. Its primary role is in application to pure representations, the content of which is not derived from the matter of experience, and so the real possibility of which is not to be found in their relation to the matter of experience, but in their relation to the formal structure of experience.

I have presented what, in my view, is Kant's argument for the principle of possibility. In the place where we would expect to find the next argument— one for the role of a concept of actuality—we find one of Kant's most famous transcendental arguments: the *Refutation of Idealism*. The *Refutation* purports to show that a necessary condition of the possibility of immediate awareness of my inner states is immediate awareness of actual objects outside of me. The exact aims, structure, presuppositions, and success of the Refutation argument are much discussed, and I have nothing in particular to add here. My focus in this book is on Kant's account of possibility and necessity, hence I will leave this issue to one side.

2.5.2 The necessity of necessity

> That whose connection with the actual is determined in accordance with general conditions of experience is (exists) **necessarily**.
>
> (A218/B266)

In the *Postulates*, Kant argues that we need a concept of material necessity in order to make necessity as it features in the world of experience *understandable* (cognizable).[45] This, in turn, is a condition on conditions of experience.

In section 2.3 we saw that, for Kant, we cannot cognize necessary existence. However, we can cognize a kind of conditional necessity: what is necessary given the actual state of things and the laws of nature. In his discussion of the principle of necessity, Kant presents us with four *a priori* laws of nature.

---

[45] See Leech (2021d) for a fuller account of the interpretation presented in this section.

KANT ON MODALITY   45

1. 'Everything that happens is hypothetically necessary; that is a principle that subjects alteration in the world to a law, i.e., a rule of necessary existence, without which not even nature itself would obtain. Hence the proposition "Nothing happens through a mere accident" (*in mundo non datur casus*) is an *a priori* law of nature; . . .' (A228/B280)
2. '. . . likewise the proposition "No necessity in nature is blind, but is rather conditioned, consequently understandable [*verständliche*] necessity" (*non datur fatum*).' (A228/B280, translation amended)
3. 'The principle of continuity forbade any leap in the series of appearances (alterations) (*in mundo non datur saltus*). . . .' (A228/B281)
4. '. . . but also any gap or cleft between two appearances in the sum of all empirical intuitions in space (*non datur hiatus*).' (A229/B281)

These laws are implicated in the possibility of the unity of experience (A229–30/B282). Moreover, they arguably correspond to the principles as presented in the *Analytic of Principles*.[46] In particular, the second law, *non datur fatum,* is singled out as a principle of modality. This law requires that *necessity in nature is conditioned and therefore understandable*.[47]

Kant contrasts *conditioned* (therefore understandable) necessity with '*blind*' necessity. By 'blind' Kant does not mean that blind necessity cannot itself see, but rather that it is something through which one cannot see, just as we might say that you can't see round a blind bend, or over a blind summit, or down a blind alley.[48]

> Blind means when one oneself cannot see; but also that through which one cannot see. Blind necessity is thus that by means of which we can see nothing with the understanding. (28:199 Kant, 1997b, 23)

A concept of unconditioned necessity is unsuitable for use by the understanding in cognition; the understanding can 'see' no objects using such a concept. Hence, a concept of unconditioned necessity is 'blind'. A concept of *conditioned* necessity, however, as defined in the *Postulates*, is 'understandable'. It is a concept of necessity that can be used in cognition.

Why do we need such a concept? In the Transcendental Deduction, Kant argues that a certain kind of necessary unity, introduced by the application of the categories by the unity of self-consciousness, is a necessary condition of experience

---

[46] 'The principle of no leap is related to quality, no gap to quantity, no chance to relation, and no fate to modality' (Watkins, 2001, 75).

[47] '. . . bedingte, mithin verständliche Notwendigkeit' (A228/B280). Guyer and Wood translate 'verständliche' as 'comprehensible', Kemp Smith as 'intelligible'. I prefer the more literal 'understandable'. This captures in English the obvious link between 'verständliche' and 'Verstand' that is present in German.

[48] See Thielke (2006).

46   THINKING OF NECESSITY

(see B164–5). The principles (in the *Analytic of Principles*), as we have seen, can be viewed as—or as importantly connected to—necessary *a priori* laws of nature. Such laws of nature concern the necessary combination of appearances. But this is precisely the concept of necessity captured by the postulate.

> That whose connection with the actual is determined in accordance with general conditions of experience is (exists) **necessarily**.   (A218/B266)

In order to be able to cognize the necessity implicated in the unity of experience, then, we need the concept of material necessity that is defined in the postulate.

Why do we need to be able to cognize this necessity? Although the *source* of the necessary unity of experience is a kind of pure necessity grounded in the unity of self-consciousness, this is transformed, in application to appearances given in space and time, into the material necessity of laws of nature. Material necessity is not given in experience; for Kant, experience can only teach us what is thus and so, and not whether it could have been otherwise (B3). But material necessity is nevertheless present in experience, insofar as the categories bring necessary unity to experience. So material necessity must be a contribution of the mind (i.e., the understanding). Hence, we must be in possession of such an *a priori* concept, i.e., the concept of material necessity. We need a concept of necessity that can capture necessity in the world of experience, that is suitable for application in cognition ('understandable'), and which, given that the relevant necessity is a condition of the possibility of experience, is pure.

Finally, note how this explanation of the role of the postulate of necessity relates to the role of the modal functions of judgment. The latter had a crucial role to play in the unity of self-consciousness, via contributing to the necessary connections between mental states required for this unity. This function is mirrored in the postulate of necessity and its role in contributing to the necessary connections between states of objects required for the unity of a world of experience. This is just as we would expect, if the same functions of unity are at work both in the forms of judgment and in the categories (A79/B104–5).[49]

2.5.3 Modality and objectivity

In the *Critique of Pure Reason*, the concepts of (formal) possibility and (material) necessity have a role to play in the possibility of objective representation. Kant presents a different line of argument for a similar conclusion in section 76 of

---

[49] 'The same function that gives unity to the different representations **in a judgment** also gives unity to the mere synthesis of different representations **in an intuition** . . .' (A79/B104–5).

the *Critique of the Power of Judgment*: we need modal concepts because we have distinct capacities for intuition and thought.[50]

Kant believes that creatures with minds like ours have distinct capacities for being presented with objects (sensibility) and for conceptual thinking (understanding). Due to this, so his argument goes, there is the potential for a mismatch between these two capacities: we might have presentations of objects (intuitions) for which we have no concepts, or we might have thoughts without also being presented with corresponding intuitions. This latter case is the more important, because it introduces the possibility for a certain kind of error: we can have thoughts that are not confirmed by intuitions, and which may therefore be false.

> It is absolutely necessary for the human understanding to distinguish between the possibility and the actuality of things. The reason for this lies in the subject and the nature of its cognitive faculties. For if two entirely heterogeneous elements were not required for the exercise of these faculties, understanding for concepts and sensible intuition for objects corresponding to them, then there would be no such distinction (between the possible and the actual).... Thus the distinction of possible from actual things is one that is merely subjectively valid for the human understanding, since we can always have something in our thoughts although it does not exist.... (5:401–2; Kant, 2000, 272)

In order to recognize this potential for error, we need to possess concepts of possibility and actuality, to allow us to capture the distinction between a thought about an object that is actually given in intuition, and a thought that does not have a corresponding intuition and is therefore about a merely possible object.

The problem with this argument is that it appears that a non-modal distinction between the actual and the non-actual would do the job equally well. Such a distinction would allow us to grasp that we can have 'something in our thoughts although it does not exist'; it doesn't appear that we also need to grasp that such a thing *could* exist. Moreover, there is a question concerning why we need to be able to grasp such a potential for error in the first place.

The answer to the latter question is that thinkers require possession of a conception of objectivity as a necessary condition of being able to think objectively. Is this a claim that Kant endorses? I won't attempt to answer that question here, although I at least think he *ought* to endorse the claim if his argument is to succeed.

The key to the former issue is to recognize that Kant's distinction between the objective and the subjective is not exclusive, but that there is an important

---

[50] See Leech (2014, 2021f) for a fuller account of the interpretation presented in this section.

48 THINKING OF NECESSITY

third option: *neither objective nor subjective,* 'nonjective' for short.[51] Cognitions—objective thoughts—succeed in being about objects of experience, even if they turn out to be false. But there are *two* quite different ways for a thought to fail to be objective. A thought or judgment might be *subjective.* This is when the connection between representations is merely contingent, and based on subjective associations and feelings.

> That the room is warm, the sugar sweet, the wormwood repugnant, are merely subjectively valid judgments.... [T]hey express only a relation of two sensations to the same subject, namely myself, and this only in my present state of perception, and are therefore not expected to be valid for the object.
>
> (4:299; Kant, 2004, 51)[52]

But a thought might also fail to be objective because it is *nonjective.* It fails to meet the standard of objective thought, not because it concerns merely subjective associations, but because it purports to represent beyond the bounds of possible experience. This brings us back to the distinction between mere thought and cognition that I introduced in section 2.1. Mere thoughts are nonjective. Cognitions are objective. And there are merely subjective representations besides.

Possession of a non-modal distinction between the actual and the non-actual may be sufficient to grasp a distinction between the objective and the subjective: objective representations can be wrong (may be of non-actual objects), whilst subjective representations cannot fail to be wrong (see, e.g., Peacocke, 2009). If all there is to the subjective thought that *the wormwood is repugnant* is a relation of a sensation of wormwood and a sensation of repugnance in a single subject at a time, then they can't be *wrong* about the wormwood seeming repugnant to them then. But an objective thought that *the body is heavy* (B142) can be wrong, because a claim is made that these two features—being a body and being heavy—are united in the object, not just in subjective experience of the object. The body might be light. However, the objective is to be distinguished not only from the subjective, but also the nonjective. So the non-modal distinction between the actual and the non-actual is insufficient for grasp of a conception of objectivity. *This* is why, on Kant's view, we need an additional distinction, between the possible and the impossible. Objective thoughts are of really possible things, nonjective thoughts are not, just as we saw earlier in section 2.1.

In sum, the function of (real) modal concepts for Kant is tied up with our capacity for objective thought (cognition). They are tied up with the formation and possession of suitable *a priori* concepts; with the necessary unity of experience; and with our grasp of the concept of objectivity.

---

[51] See Routley and Routley (1980, 155): 'Call the resulting account, which is neither objective nor...subjective, *nonjective* (short for, neither objective nor subjective: the term is ugly but memorable).'

[52] See also (B142).

2.6 A Kantian's guide to modality (or a modal metaphysician's guide to Kant)

This concludes my summary of some of the main ideas that we can take from Kant's thinking about modality. These ideas are the starting point for my Kant-inspired theory of modality.

Thought/Cognition   There is a distinction between mere thought and cognition. Mere thought is subject to merely logical constraints; cognition is subject to additional constraints that constitute the objectivity of a thought.

Logical/Real   Logical modality concerns the possibility and necessity of thoughts and concepts. It is to be understood in terms of the laws of thought. Real modality concerns the possibility and necessity of things/objects. It is to be understood in terms of the laws of cognition.

Relative Modality   Real modality is relative to general conditions on possible experience. Formal modality is relative to formal conditions of experience. Material modality is relative to general conditions of experience plus what is actually the case.

Objective/Subjective/Neither   Objective representations are to be distinguished both from subjective representations and from representations which are neither objective nor subjective.

Function (Unity)   Modal concepts have a role to play in the unity of consciousness.

Function (Objectivity)   Modal concepts have a role to play in objective representation.

These ideas form the basis of many of the claims and arguments that will be developed and defended in the rest of the book. The distinction between thinking and objective thinking (thought/cognition) will underwrite the different functions of logical and metaphysical modal judgments, and the consequent accounts of these kinds of modality. The logical/real distinction will therefore align similarly with the distinction between logical and metaphysical modality. The idea of relative modality will feature importantly in the account of metaphysical modality and its relation to logical modality. The rejection of an exhaustive distinction between the objective and the subjective, as well as the role of modal concepts in objective representation, is the inspiration for Chapter 5 and the account of the function of metaphysical modal judgment. The role of modal concepts in the unity of consciousness provides a template for the argument of Chapter 3 on the function of logical modal judgment.

3

The Function of Logical Necessity

3.1 Introducing logical necessity

What is the function of judgments or concepts of logical modality? We can't answer that question before first specifying what we mean by 'logical necessity'. I shall adopt a fairly standard characterization, also shared by Kant, that it is logically necessary that A if, and only if, it is logically contradictory that not-A (i.e., not-A entails a contradiction). Whilst this tells us what our target notion is, it does not yet tell us very much about it. For example, it tells us nothing of the source of logical necessities—what it is in virtue of which there are such statements the negations of which are contradictory. I will address the source question in the next chapter.

For now, let us extend this characterization to *that kind of necessity that is implicated in deductive validity*. As Ian Rumfitt explains,

If we assume a classical logic...we immediately have the following meta-theorem: whenever B follows logically from $A_1, \ldots, A_n$, the statement ⌜It is logically necessary that if A_1 and ... and A_n then B⌝ is true (where the conditional is understood to be material).[1] So logical necessity is implicated in logical consequence.

[1] For suppose B follows logically from $A_1, \ldots, A_n$. Then the statement ⌜It is logically contradictory that A_1 and ... and A_n and not B⌝ is true. So, if 'if...then' is read as a material conditional, the statement ⌜It is logically contradictory that not (if A_1 and ... and A_n then B)⌝ is true. So, on the recommended conception of logical necessity, the statement ⌜It is logically necessary that if A_1 and ... and A_n then B⌝ is true. (Rumfitt, 2010, 35)[1]

---

[1] Rumfitt specifies a classical logic, but there is nothing in this line of argument to prevent the conclusion also applying to the negative free logic that I adopt later in the book.
    Rumfitt further argues that this should not be taken to be the primary sense of logical necessity. For, given certain assumptions about the rule of necessitation, it would fail to distinguish logical necessity from some other kinds of necessity: 'An analogue of the meta-theorem will hold for any species of necessity which validates the 'rule of necessitation', a rule which is widely assumed to be valid for physical and metaphysical necessity, among other modalities. Our characterisation of logical necessity is far more exacting: it is physically impossible that a particle should have travelled from the Sun to the Earth in less than a minute, but it is not logically contradictory that it should have done so' (Rumfitt, 2010, 35).

Thinking of Necessity: A Kantian Account of Modal Thought and Modal Metaphysics. Jessica Leech,
Oxford University Press. © Jessica Leech 2023. DOI: 10.1093/oso/9780198873969.003.0003

It seems right to recognize the intimate relationship between logical necessity and logical consequence or deductive validity. Indeed, Ian McFetridge takes logical necessity, if anything, to be that kind of necessity attaching to deductive validity.

> Deductive validity is the central topic of logic. So, if, as Aristotle and others have taught, to think of an argument as deductively valid requires us to deploy *a* notion of necessity, then that notion, if any, will deserve the label 'logical' necessity. There will be a legitimate notion of 'logical' necessity only if there is a notion of necessity which attaches to the claim, concerning a deductively valid argument, that if the premisses are true then so is the conclusion.   (McFetridge, 1990, 136)

Both Rumfitt and McFetridge quote Aristotle with approval.

> A deduction is a discourse in which, certain things being stated, something other than what is stated follows of necessity from their being so.
> (Analytica Priora, 24b18–19)[2]

One may, of course, deny that deductive validity, logical consequence, logical truth, and by association logical contradiction, have any modality attaching to them. The rest of the argument of this chapter will, at some length, argue that a commitment to there being logical necessities is a necessary condition of our engaging in logical reasoning, and so can be considered a response to this worry. But there are other, well-known defences of the idea that we must think of logical consequence as involving modality.

John Etchemendy (1990), for example, attacks the (amodal) Tarskian account of logical consequence. It is standard to understand logical consequence and logical truth in terms of models: some conclusion p is a logical consequence of some premises Γ just when there is no model according to which Γ are true and p false; and p is a logical truth just when it is true according to all models. The Tarskian understands models in terms of different interpretations of the non-logical vocabulary of the language in question. As such, logical consequence is a matter of 'truth preservation on the basis of the meanings of the logical vocabulary' (Beall and Restall, 2016, 11). On an alternative understanding of models, they can be understood as representing different possible worlds or possible circumstances. On this different interpretation, logical consequence is a matter of *necessary* truth-preservation (and logical truth a matter of necessary truth), truth-preservation (truth) in all possible worlds.[3]

---

[2] McFetridge (1990, 136); Rumfitt (2010, 38). Note, this conception of consequence is stronger than our familiar notion, for we do not require the conclusion of a valid argument to be *something other than what is stated* in the premises. e.g., we usually allow that $\phi \vDash \phi$.

[3] One can also combine the two ideas: logical consequence is a matter of necessary truth preservation, no matter the meanings of the non-logical vocabulary. I won't discriminate this view here, though, as the crucial point is that it includes necessity.

52   THINKING OF NECESSITY

Etchemendy attacks the former approach and endorses the latter. I will briefly sketch one of his arguments.[4] First, notions such as *necessity* are important features of our understanding of logical consequence, and play an important role in how we use logical reasoning. They must therefore be accounted for in any conception of the latter.

> Surrounding the intuitive concepts of logical consequence and logical truth are a host of vague and philosophically difficult notions—notions like necessity, certitude, *a prioricity*, and so forth. Among the characteristics claimed for logically valid arguments are the following: If an argument is logically valid, then the truth of its conclusion follows necessarily from the truth of its premises. From our knowledge of the premises we can establish, without further investigation, that the conclusion is true as well. ... These may be vague and ill-understood features of valid inference, but they are the characteristics that give logic its *raison d'être*. They are why logicians have studied the consequence relation for over two thousand years.   (Etchemendy, 2008, 265–6)

In particular, an important feature of a valid argument is that it is supposed to give us a guarantee that, if the premises are true, then the conclusion must be too. That's one of the reasons why valid arguments are so useful. If I know some propositions to be true, and I also know a valid argument form with those propositions as premises, then I can find out that the consequence of this argument is also true—without needing to find out the truth of that conclusion independently.

However, Etchemendy argues that on the Tarskian view this feature of valid arguments is lost, because the question of the validity of an argument becomes confused with the question of the truth of the conclusion. Recall, the Tarskian understands logical validity in terms of truth-preservation in all models, understood as truth-preservation across all interpretations of the non-logical vocabulary. In effect, an argument is logically valid just when it is a member of a class of arguments all of which are truth-preserving and all of which share a certain form. Truth-preservation requires that either a premise is false or the conclusion true. However, consider a case where we know a set of premises Γ to be true, but we do not know whether the purported conclusion p is true. Etchemendy's complaint is that in such cases, 'any uncertainty about the conclusion of an argument whose premises we know to be true would translate directly into uncertainty about whether the argument is valid' (Etchemendy, 2008, 267). Since validity here is just membership in a particular class of arguments, the question of whether p is true is at the same time a question of whether the argument from Γ to p is valid: 'for if its conclusion turned out to be false, the associated class would have a

---

[4] As presented in his reprise article Etchemendy (2008).

non-truth-preserving instance, and so the argument would not be logically valid' (Etchemendy, 2008, 267). So it then seems circular to appeal to the argument to learn that p is true: 'Logical validity cannot guarantee the truth of a conclusion if validity itself depends on that self-same truth' (Etchemendy, 2008, 267). But this was one of the primary uses of logically valid argument; to establish a conclusion on the basis of known premises and valid argument.

The notion of a valid argument is only of any worth, then, if it gives us an independent guarantee of some kind.

> [We need] an independent guarantee—independent, that is, of the actual truth values of premises and conclusions—that all the instances of the argument form preserve truth. This independent guarantee, and only this independent guarantee, is what enables us to infer that a conclusion is true on the basis of the truth of the premises. (Etchemendy, 2008, 268)

Etchemendy concludes that the Tarskian view thus renders logical consequence 'a completely flaccid relation', such that 'it would be impossible to use valid arguments to extend our knowledge, to justify the truth of a conclusion, or to prove that a given theorem follows from accepted axioms' (Etchemendy, 2008, 270).

One may well disagree with Etchemendy's arguments here. I don't take them to be the end of the discussion, but rather to lend motivation and support to the idea that logical consequence should be thought of as modal. But there is more argument to come.

Let us return to our question of the function of a concept or judgments of logical necessity. As clarified earlier (in Chapter 1), I will focus on the transcendental question, and in this chapter on that question for logical modality.

The logical modality question: What is the transcendental role of judgments and concepts of logical modality? Would there be a thinker at all if they didn't or couldn't make judgments of logical modality or didn't have logical modal concepts?

From here on, I take *thoughts* to be constituted by concepts unified into something like a propositional form, and *thinking* most minimally to be the entertaining of a thought (although one could take a stronger attitude in thinking and *believe* the thought, etc.). So, for example, there can be the thought that *the moon has risen,* but not the thought that *moon shine night.* I am thus taking thought to be a relatively advanced cognitive achievement, and my claims here should be understood in relation to the capacity to think in this sense. There is also a broader sense of 'thinking' that includes processes and transitions from thought to thought, e.g., engaging in a course of reasoning, mulling something over,

54   THINKING OF NECESSITY

and so on. My principal focus in this chapter is on individual thoughts, insofar as the crucial feature to be accounted for is the unity of those thoughts. To the extent that the broader activity of thought chains and processes involves individual thoughts as well, the following argument also concerns 'thinking' in the broader sense.

My argument begins by drawing on McFetridge (1990), who argues that we must believe that there are logically necessarily truth-preserving rules of inference, as a necessary condition of our being able to reason from suppositions. But this argument alone will not suffice to give us a robust answer to the transcendental question. The ability to reason from suppositions is an ability to reason from premises that we do not necessarily assert or take to be true—we might only assume premises for the sake of argument. An argument that belief in logical necessity is a necessary requirement for this ability will only have force if our ability to reason from suppositions is important in the first place. I will thus supplement the argument with two additional steps:

1. Reasoning from suppositions depends upon a belief in logical necessity. (McFetridge's argument).
2. Any logical reasoning at all depends upon an ability to reason from suppositions.
3. Any thought at all depends upon logical reasoning.

Ultimately, the function of concepts and judgments of logical necessity will have a fundamental, transcendental role: they are implicated in the very possibility of thought. I proceed as follows: first McFetridge's argument, then step 2, then step 3. I will treat steps 1 and 2 fairly briefly. My focus will be on what I take to be the much tougher argument for step 3.

3.2 Belief in logical necessity

McFetridge takes the manifestation of (evidence for) someone having a belief that a rule of inference is logically necessarily truth-preserving to be their being prepared to employ that rule of inference in reasoning from any supposition whatsoever.

> I ... wish to suggest that we treat as the manifestation of the belief that a mode of inference is logically necessarily truth-preserving, the preparedness to employ that mode of inference in reasoning from any set of suppositions whatsoever. Such a preparedness evinces the belief that, no matter what else was the case, the inferences would preserve truth. And the suggestion is that it is just this preparedness which is built into the idea that the validity of an argument is quite independent of questions about the truth of its premisses. A central point of

THE FUNCTION OF LOGICAL NECESSITY   55

interest in having such beliefs about logical necessity is to allow us to deploy principles of inference across the whole range of suppositions we might make.

(McFetridge, 1990, 153)

I will have more to say about this later. But for the meantime, let us grant this view of belief in logical necessity.

McFetridge then argues that there are, indeed, rules of inference that we are prepared to employ in reasoning from any supposition whatsoever. Hence, our practice of reasoning from suppositions commits us to a belief in logical necessity, specifically, logically necessarily truth-preserving rules of inference.

In more detail: Suppose we abandon a belief in logical necessity, i.e., we believe that for *every* rule of inference R there is some supposition s such that, if it were the case that s, R would not preserve truth. In this case, either we know, for a given rule R, under which suppositions R would fail to preserve truth, or we don't. If we do know, then we could in principle construct a new rule, R/s, specifying the suppositions under which R alone would not preserve truth. This new rule would then preserve truth in reasoning from any supposition whatsoever.[5] If we don't know under which suppositions R would fail to preserve truth, then this undermines our whole practice of reasoning from suppositions. If we never know whether or not rules of inference such as R are going to be truth-preserving when reasoning from suppositions, because we don't know whether or not a given supposition s is precisely the supposition under which R fails, then we can never rely on R at all. This would be disastrous. And plainly we do carry on reasoning from suppositions quite happily.[6] Hence, as long as we want to preserve our practice of reasoning from suppositions, we should reject the initial idea that for every rule of inference R there is some supposition s such that, if it were the case that s, R would not preserve truth. Hence, we should believe that there are some logically necessarily truth-preserving rules of inference, *rules that we can assume to be sound when reasoning from any supposition whatsoever.*

I conclude then, that on the present view of what it is to regard a rule of inference as logically necessarily truth-preserving, we are constrained to believe that there are such rules. For if we abandoned that belief, we would be unable to reason from suppositions at all.   (McFetridge, 1990, 154)[7]

---

[5] For example, take a rule of inference that allows one to infer an existential claim from a universal claim: $\forall x \phi x \vdash \exists x \phi x$. Such a rule would seem to fail to preserve truth under the supposition that nothing exists. But we can then build this in to construct a rule that preserves truth under this supposition as well, for example: $\forall x \phi x, \exists x (x = x) \vdash \exists x \phi x$.

[6] Admittedly, we carry on doing lots of things regardless of disastrous consequences. However, in this case, I am optimistic enough to think that we do have a fairly successful practice of reasoning from suppositions.

[7] See Hale (1999) for discussion of objections to McFetridge's argument and some responses. I also discuss this in Leech (2015).

56 THINKING OF NECESSITY

3.3 Suppositions and reasoning

McFetridge also draws our attention to some basic lessons about logical inference. First, whether or not an inference is valid—whether the conclusion follows logically from the premises—is a distinct matter from whether or not the premises are true.

> When we begin logic, we are all told to distinguish assessing an argument as *valid*, and assessing its premises as *true*. These, we are told, are independent activities. In particular, then, the acceptability in an argument of some mode of inference, is supposed to be quite independent of whether or not the overall premises of the argument represent beliefs we have or mere suppositions we are making, as we put it, for the 'sake of argument'. Deductive inferences, then, are supposed to remain regardless of what suppositions they are applied to, or are made in the course of the argument.   (McFetridge, 1990, 151)

This is similar to Etchemendy's observation that the validity of an argument is supposed to give us an independent guarantee that the conclusion follows from the premises, independent of the actual truth-values of the premises and conclusion. At least, then, our familiar conception of inference *allows for* us to reason from suppositions as much as from premises that we believe or know to be true (or false). But this does not yet show us that we *need to* sometimes reason from suppositions.

Rumfitt argues the case. Rumfitt is arguing against Bertrand Russell's non-modal conception of logical consequence, but in so doing he provides us with an argument to show the importance of reasoning from suppositions. Russell writes:

> In order that it be *valid* to infer q from p, it is only necessary that p should be true and that the proposition 'not-p or q' should be true. Whenever this is the case, it is clear that q must be true. But inference will only in fact take place when the proposition 'not-p or q' is *known* otherwise than through knowledge of not-p or knowledge of q. Whenever p is false, 'not-p or q' is true, but is useless for inference, which requires that p should be true. Whenever q is already known to be true, 'not-p or q' is of course also known to be true, but is again useless for inference, since q is already known, and therefore does not need to be inferred. In fact, inference only arises when 'not-p or q' can be known without our knowing already which of the two alternatives it is that makes the disjunction true. Now, the circumstances under which this occurs are those in which certain relations of form exist between p and q. ... But this formal relation is only required in order that we may be able to *know* that either the premiss is false or the conclusion is true. It is the truth of 'not-p or q' that is required for the *validity* of the inference; what is required further is only required for the practical feasibility of the inference.   (Russell, 1919, 153)[8]

---

[8] As quoted in Rumfitt (2010, 38).

There are two key ideas in this passage. First, it is claimed that inference takes place on the basis of known, true premises—so not on the basis of mere supposition. Second, the validity of an inference from p to q is taken to depend solely on the truth of 'not-p or q', and so the passage presents a non-modal conception of validity.

However, Rumfitt argues that this account of inference harbours a hidden commitment to reasoning from supposition. According to Russell, we are only ever in a position to infer q from p if we know that p but not that q, for if we already knew q we would not require an inference from p to learn it. If q follows from p, according to Russell, this means that not-p or q. In the case of inference, we are supposed to be trading off our knowledge that p, and our knowledge that q follows from p, i.e., that not-p or q. We can't know that latter via knowledge that not-p, for we know that p. Nor can we know it via knowledge that q, for that is precisely what we stand to gain from the inference. *How else can we know the disjunction?* Rumfitt argues, by deductive reasoning on the basis of suppositions or hypotheses.

> Russell tells us that we can infer Q from P when we know that either not P or Q otherwise than through knowing that not P or knowing that Q. But *how* might a thinker know that either not P or Q without knowing that not P or knowing that Q? In many cases, I claim, there is no convincing explanation that does not at some point advert to our ability to apply our deductive capacities to suppositions—to things we suppose to be true or take as hypotheses—as well as to things that we know.   (Rumfitt, 2010, 40)

> So, for example, let us grant for the sake of argument that the thinker knows that either not P or P. How is that to yield knowledge that either not P or Q? In general, the answer must be: because the thinker is able to deduce Q from the supposition that P.   (Rumfitt, 2010, 40)

There are two lessons here. First, there is the straightforward argument against '*material* or *Philonian* consequence—the relation that obtains when either the conclusion is (actually) true or some premiss is (actually) untrue' (Rumfitt, 2010, 39), namely, that the most plausible explanation of how we might come to know that *not-p or q*, not via knowing that not-p or via knowing that q, is that we deduce q from the supposition that p. Second, there is the consequence of this for an account of inference that appears to rule out reasoning from suppositions, such as Russell's view that inference takes place on the basis of known premises. For, insofar as such an account of inference still relies on our knowing that *not-p or q*, not via knowing that not-p or via knowing that q, it still relies on our capacity to reason from the supposition that p. In general, any restriction of the proper application of logical reasoning to reasoning from known or believed premises (premises to which an attitude of more than supposition is taken) will face a similar consequence: such reasoning will only be worthwhile if we have independent knowledge of the validity of the argument—independent, that is, of knowledge (or belief, etc.) of the premises or conclusion. The most plausible explanation of

58 THINKING OF NECESSITY

this independent knowledge, as offered by Rumfitt, is that the thinker is able to deduce the conclusion from the supposition of the premises.

3.4 Reasoning and thinking

Let us grant, following McFetridge, that *if* we want to be able to reason from suppositions, we must be committed to a belief in logical necessity. So *if*, as we have seen, reasoning from suppositions is inseparable from logical reasoning at all, then if we want to be able to reason at all, we must be committed to a belief in logical necessity. However, one might now ask: why should we bother to engage in logical reasoning? One might think that—in answer to the practical question[9]—it would be inconvenient if we could not thus reason, but not that—in answer to the transcendental question[10]—we could not think at all if we gave up the practice of logical reasoning and thereby also reasoning from suppositions. At this point we can appeal to a key idea of Kant's: that logical reasoning has an ineliminable role to play in our ability to think and judge at all.

Recall, Kant claims that every judgment has a modality, in the sense that every judgment occurs in a course of reasoning. I claimed that Kant should think this for the following reasons.[11] He holds that judgment requires the judger to combine judgment constituents. That act of combination in turn requires a certain kind of unity of consciousness, namely, necessary connections between our mental states. And it is judging on the basis of other judgments—reasoning and inferring—rather than making judgments in isolation from one another, that constitutes those necessary connections. Hence, it is reasoning and inferring that gives rise to the unity of consciousness required, and hence makes judgment possible at all. If our very ability to have thoughts and make judgments—which are unities of constituent representations—depends upon a unity of consciousness, and if that unity of consciousness in turn depends on our ability to reason on the basis of suppositions, then we will have an answer to the transcendental question: a belief in logical necessity—a commitment to logically necessarily truth-preserving rules of inference—is a necessary condition of an ability to reason from suppositions, and that ability in turn is a necessary condition of being able to have any thoughts at all.

I shall outline the steps of argument, before proceeding to defend them.

1. Thoughts are unities of thought constituents.

---

[9] What is the practical use of modal judgment? How would a thinker be practically worse off if they didn't or couldn't make modal judgments, or if they didn't have modal concepts? See p.11.

[10] Would there be a thinker at all if they didn't or couldn't make judgments of logical modality or didn't have logical modal concepts? See p.12.

[11] See Chapter 2, section 2.2 and Leech (2017a).

2. Either the activity of the thinker combines thought constituents into a unity, or thoughts are prior unities.
3. Either way, the unity of a thought depends upon a single thinking subject. Either a necessary condition of being able to combine constituents into a unified thought is that all of the constituents "belong" to the same thinking subject. Or a necessary condition of discerning structure in thoughts is that thoughts be compared by the same thinking subject.
4. Such a thinking subject is not something we can experience or introspect; rather, we can make sense of the notion of a particular thinking subject via a unity of thoughts—actual inferential connections between (at least some of) their mental states.
5. Actual inferential connections between mental states are formed by judging on the basis of other judgments, i.e., reasoning.
6. Therefore, a necessary condition of thoughts is a thinking subject that engages in reasoning.

As noted earlier, I am taking a thought to be a well-formed combination of thought constituents (such as concepts and other thoughts) of propositional form. The most minimal kind of thinking is akin to 'entertaining a proposition'. But there will also be cases where we take a stronger attitude towards the content, such as judging that p (in the contemporary, not Kantian, sense), and (occurrently) believing that p, where a judgment is a mental act of something like 'making up one's mind that p', and a belief is the resultant state. If believing that p is a dispositional state, then we don't need to say that if S believes that p, then S thinks that p. That would be implausible at times when S isn't consciously reflecting on or drawing on their belief that p. But when S brings to mind, for whatever reason, their belief that p, and so are occurrently believing that p, they will also be thinking that p.[12]

I am deliberately taking these mental states to be combinations of thought constituents understood as mental representations, and not to be mental states that have combinations of concepts and suchlike, more abstractly understood, as their *contents*. Whatever relationship these (mental) thoughts and concepts have to abstract or shared contents is not something I wish to pursue here. The reader can, I hope, supplement my view with whatever account they prefer. The argument here is supposed to concern mental states, which are unities composed of constituent mental representations.

---

[12] I am setting aside details here of how thoughts might interact with time. See, for example, Geach (1958, 1969); Mouton (1969). In brief, it seems to me reasonable to suppose that there are 'achievements and/or commencements' (Mouton, 1969, 75), such as concluding a line of reasoning or a thought occurring to one, that could mark the end or beginning of activities and processes such as inferring, considering, entertaining, and so on. In particular, it seems plausible that one can think of an inference both as a process over time (considering the premises, working through the stages of a proof, etc.) and as the conclusion of such a process (achieving the conclusion). Thank you to Benoit Gaultier for discussion of this issue.

60 THINKING OF NECESSITY

1. Thoughts are unities of thought constituents. The claim that thoughts are unities of thought constituents (concepts, other thoughts, etc.) may be viewed as a fairly uncontroversial extension of familiar principles of compositionality. Compositionality is usually introduced to explain how it is that competent speakers of a language are able to understand and produce any of an infinity of novel utterances. The explanation is that language is compositional: given a finite number of atoms (vocabulary) and rules for composition (grammar), we can build and parse any number of combinations. It seems plausible that the same considerations apply to our capacity for mental, as to linguistic, representation. Competent thinkers are able to think any of an infinity of novel thoughts. Again, it seems reasonable to explain this in terms of the compositionality of thought; given a finite number of atoms (thought constituents) and rules for composition (the well-formedness of thoughts), we can entertain any number of combinations. (Note, this is not to say whether the thought constitutents exist prior to a combination into a thought, or whether thoughts are fundamental unities in which we can discern constituents. The guiding thought here is compositionality, which requires a certain kind of structure to our thoughts.)

I won't say any more to defend this starting point, other than to address one question that might arise. One might worry that this has implications for views according to which concepts can only have a meaning in the context of a judgment or thought. This would be something like a mental counterpart of Frege's context principle, that a word only has a meaning in the context of a complex expression, or perhaps even the whole language.[13] According to such a view, one might suggest, concepts only have a meaning in the context of a complete thought or system of thoughts, hence, one could not account for the meaning of the whole thought in terms of a combination of concepts that had a meaning prior to their combination in thought. I do not want to comment on the plausibility of such a context principle here; it is enough to note that such a principle can be compatible with a compositionality principle.[14] One may allow that the meaning of a whole thought is determined by the meanings of its constituents and their mode of combination, whilst also holding that no thought constituent can have a meaning outside of such a combination.

2. Either the activity of the thinker combines thought constituents into a unity, or thoughts are prior unities. One might take thoughts to be unities that are grasped as a whole, but in which structure can be discerned, or take thoughts to

---

[13] 'Only in a proposition have the words really a meaning. . . . It is enough if the proposition taken as a whole has a sense; it is this that confers on its parts also their content' (Frege, [1884]1950, section 60).

[14] 'Even if words are meaningful only because they occur as constituents within sentences, there could still be a function (perhaps even a single function across all possible human languages) that maps the structure of a sentence and the meanings of its constituent words to the meaning of that sentence' (Szabó, 2013).

THE FUNCTION OF LOGICAL NECESSITY   61

be made up of constitutents that are put together in thought. The first kind of view is broadly Fregean, the second broadly Kantian. At this point, my line of argument splits into two strands, which will again reunite at step 4.

Let us take the view that a thought is composed from prior thought constituents. Then, new thoughts do not appear ready-made, ready-unified for us to think. For the very conception of a thought as a combination of constituents implies that these constituents must be somehow put together. And how else could that combination be achieved than by the activity of the thinker? To be sure, the generation of certain thoughts may well be caused or otherwise inspired by something else—for example, I hear someone utter 'It is raining in town' and so I think that it is raining in town (if not also come to believe it)—but it would seem odd to thereby conclude that the combination of those thought constituents is effected by that something else alone. It is not as if, in making that utterance, someone else thereby combines mental representations that are not their own.

One might take an alternative view: that in fact thoughts come to us as unities, and that in understanding them and comparing them to other thoughts, we thereby discern structure and constituents of the thoughts. There are different approaches one might take to accounting for this discerning of structure, but we need to account for it if we are to make room for compositionality. We might, for example, base an account on comparison of thoughts and recognition of similarities. Suppose that I think that *grass is green*, and that *limes are green*. I could then compare these (and perhaps other) thoughts and recognize that they have something in common, namely, they both predicate *greenness* of something.

3. Either way, the unity of a thought depends upon a single thinking subject. Either a necessary condition of being able to combine constituents into a unified thought is that all of the constituents "belong" to the same thinking subject. Or a necessary condition of discerning structure in thoughts is that thoughts be compared by the same thinking subject. Again, our argument runs in two strands.

Let us take the first case: a thinker combines the constituents into the thought. The question is now upon what this kind of unity of thought, effected by the thinker, depends. First, it seems quite straightforward that all of the thought constituents that are (to be) combined into the thought are available to one and the same thinker. Compare: suppose I want to build a table. I go to my workshop. I have various pieces of wood at my disposal—some would do as legs, there's a nice big flat piece that will do as a top, and so on. I can only build a table from the pieces I have available to me. It doesn't help me at all if, *somewhere else*, Bert has a nice set of table legs in his workshop. There will only be a table if someone, say me, builds it; and I can only build a table from my pieces of wood,

62 THINKING OF NECESSITY

not from those belonging to anyone else, located in workshops other than mine. (Of course a team of carpenters could build a table. But the same kind of point holds: if Bert and I combine forces and materials to build a table, we still can't use the timber that Bertha has in *her* workshop, if Bertha and her workshop are unavailable to us.)

Likewise, I have already claimed that there can only be a thought if a thinker produces it; and that thinker can only produce thoughts by combining those thought constituents that are *theirs*, in a sense yet to be determined. Now of course, the analogy is not perfect. When it comes to wood, workshops, and builders, we can move wood from workshop to workshop, and work together as builders. The important disanalogy is that as thinkers, we cannot access each other's thought constituents in order to make thoughts from them, or team up to think thoughts. (We can engage in communal projects such as working through a logic proof together, but we don't literally think each other's thoughts, or co-think thoughts, in so doing. We merely closely causally influence each other's thought processes so that they are, perhaps, very similar.) The point is that, given this obvious restriction, a thinker can therefore only produce thoughts by combining *their own* constituents, just as if Bert and I cannot get into each other's workshops, we can only build out of the components we each already have.[15]

Take the second case. The suggestion was that a thinker could discern structure, or shared constituents, or structure or constituents understood as shared properties, by comparing different thoughts to each other. Suppose a thought is not composed of antecedent constituents, but is rather what we might call a prior unity, in which some parts might consequently be discerned. How might a thinker discern such parts, or such structure? If the thought itself is fundamentally a whole it won't, speaking metaphorically, have any joins to betray any internal structure. A better way to discern structure would be, rather than considering each thought alone, to compare thoughts and look for similarities. As suggested earlier, even if one doesn't take the concept *green* to be a part out of which the thought *that grass is green* has been composed, one could still recognize that this thought and the thought *that kale is green* have something in common. Enough of these shared properties and resemblances would seem to provide an analogue of parts and structure more literally understood. But importantly, this process of comparison only makes sense if there is one and the same thinker thinking each of the thoughts. It won't help if *I* think that grass is green, and *Alice* thinks that kale is green, but neither of us thinks both thoughts, and so neither has both in mind for comparison. Of course, Alice might say to me, 'Kale is green', thereby inviting me to think the thought and allowing me to make the comparison, but us each

---

[15] Compare Kant: representations that are 'divided among different beings (e.g., the individual words of a verse) never constitute a whole thought (a verse)' (A352).

THE FUNCTION OF LOGICAL NECESSITY   63

thinking one of these thoughts alone is not sufficient. Therefore, the requirement of a single thinking subject to which all the thoughts belong remains.[16]

What does it mean to say that a thought (or thought constituent) "belongs" to a subject? The metaphor of ownership is well-known, but not illuminating on its own. An option which takes it most literally would be the existence of a Cartesian ego—some independently existing soul-like entity—that is related in some important way to all of its thoughts (and thought constituents). I wish to set aside this option, because I don't think we have good reason to think there is such a thing. I agree with David Hume that such an entity is not something we can encounter in experience.

> When I enter most intimately into what I call *myself*, I always stumble on some particular perception or other, of heat or cold, light or dark, love or hatred, pain or pleasure. I never can catch *myself* at any time without a perception, and never can observe any thing but the perception.   (Hume, 1739, 1740, I.IV.vi, 252)

So if we are to believe in an ego or soul, we must have some theoretical reason. But, I shall argue, there is another way for us to make sense of the ownership of thoughts and of our grasp of the first person that does not rely on the introduction of a Cartesian ego.

An alternative way to make sense of ownership is in terms of the ability to self-ascribe thoughts (and their constituents). A thought T "belongs to" some subject S, just when S has the ability to think 'I think T'. Again, this is a Kantian idea—drawing on his characterization of the unity of self-consciousness and the 'I think'. The proposal seems a reasonable one. Rather than positing the existence of some mysterious soul *substance* of which we have no experience, substitute in the idea of an *ability* to think certain thoughts, namely, thoughts that self-ascribe thoughts. Primarily, we might understand this in terms of thoughts, rather than constituents, as it is most natural to take 'I think' to be completed with a thought. But we can extend this to thought constituents by modifying what has the form of a sentential operator to take other kinds of terms: 'I think of . . .', e.g., 'I think of green', 'I think of grass', 'I think of Bert's lawn', and so on.[17]

---

[16] I have sketched two broad options here. There are further options, but they will fall under the same general line of argument. To give two brief examples. (1) Suppose one takes thought constituents to be put together into thoughts at a sub-personal level which are then grasped as a whole at the level of conscious thought. One will either try to account for compositionality at the sub-personal or at the conscious level. If the former, the first line of argument will apply: the components to be unified all belong to a single subject; if the latter, the second line of argument will apply: the thoughts to be compared all belong to a single subject. (2) One might tell an inferentialist story about how thought constituents are to be individuated, i.e., in terms of their inferential role. But to recognize an inferential role, one must be able to recognize an inference, which involves a relation between thoughts of one and the same subject. So again, we have the idea of a subject to which various thoughts all belong. Thank you to seminar participants in Zürich for raising some of these issues.

[17] Note: in the Fregean case, the thought is taken to be an abstract entity that can be thought by many, rather than a mental entity belonging to one thinker. The discussion here can be transposed,

64 THINKING OF NECESSITY

We can appeal, then, to an ability of a thinker to append 'I think (of)' to her thoughts and thought constituents. However, how can we be assured that any two tokens of 'I think that T' would "belong" to the same thinker? After all, Alice can think 'I think that grass is green', and Bert can think 'I think that kale is green', but the two component thoughts do not thereby belong to the same thinker. What more is required is an account of how it is that some and not other first-personal thoughts belong together in this sense, that does not appeal to the existence of distinct Cartesian egos.

4. Such a thinking subject is not something we can experience or introspect; we can rather make sense of the notion of a particular thinking subject via a unity of thoughts—actual inferential connections between (at least some of) their mental states. We are seeking a minimal grasp of a single thinker of several thoughts, where that thinker is not something we can experience in introspection, and we cannot assume it is a substantial entity. Kant's notion of the transcendental unity of self-consciousness is this kind of idea; the idea of some locus to which all of "a subject's" mental states belong, and nothing more. The idea of such a locus doesn't provide us with an entity, nor with a relation between that entity and its mental states, but it is the idea of something that makes possible the combination of mental states by "having" them. One way to get at this locus of the thinker, then, is not to focus on the purported entity, the thinking thing—for there is nothing really to get hold of there—but on the relations that stand between a unified class of mental states that belong to it. As there is no entity that is the thinking thing, we cannot understand this relation in terms of all of those states being related to *it*; we need a relation that holds amongst the states themselves.

To clarify, there is no assumption here that this locus of thought is to be identified with a person, or the thing you (as a whole) are. That is, this should not be taken to intervene in debates about personal identity or about what kind of thing we are (persons, animals, minds, etc.). The locus of thought made reference to in 'I think' might bear different relations to *you*, or to a person, depending on your wider views. For example, perhaps the locus of thought is a person, or not a person but a part of one, or the thinking part of a human animal, and so on. The present aim is to make sense of the conditions of a capacity for thought, where there are different ways to think about the nature of the things that have such a capacity, and how they relate to the locus of thought that we are in the process of isolating as a part of that capacity. There is, admittedly, a background working assumption in operation, that there is likely to be one locus

---

however, to consider individual acts of thought undertaken by individuals such that an abstract thought becomes the content of that act. In order to discern structure, an individual thinker still needs to grasp the relevant thoughts in order to be able to compare them, i.e., they must perform acts of thinking with the relevant thoughts as their content.

THE FUNCTION OF LOGICAL NECESSITY   65

of thought per person—I use examples involving, for example, *my* thoughts vs. *Alice's* thoughts vs. *Bert's* thoughts. However, this should not be taken to be a serious claim about personal identity, but rather about making sense of different loci of thought. And indeed, it is an assumption that may well be undermined, for example, depending on what we want to say about various mental disorders.

The proposal to be worked out in the next pages is, in sum, as follows. We can make sense of the identity of one thinker rather than another by recognizing relations holding between some mental states, relations that are sufficient for those states to count as belonging to the same thinker (locus of thought). I think it is unlikely that we will find such a relation that is also *necessary* for states to belong to the same thinker, such that we could understand a single thinker in terms of a relation holding between *all* of their states. As such, the proposal requires a kind of bootstrapping. Some mental states are related in a way that is sufficient for them to belong to the same thinker, we can then identify a thinker as *the locus of those states,* and then appeal to other relations between that thinker and other states which are sufficient for them to belong to that thinker, but which would not be suitable to provide the right kind of unity of states at the first stage.

Is causation a suitable relation to play this role? Perhaps the mental states of a single thinker are causally related: every state in the relevant class is caused by another. However, there are several problems with this. First, this would allow what we would intuitively classify as the mental states of someone else to be counted in, hence a causal relation between mental states would be insufficient for their belonging to the same thinker. For example, Alice's thought that it is raining in town could cause Bert's thought that it is raining in town, via a causal chain involving Alice making some utterance, e.g., 'It is raining in town', and Bert hearing and understanding it. One might think that this could be rectified by requiring that the causal relation between mental states in a single thinker be *direct*, i.e., unmediated by any intermediate causes and effects. States of distinct thinkers can be causally linked, but only when mediated by other events (such as utterances and the hearing of them, inscriptions and the reading of them, facial expressions and the interpretation of them, and so on). However, that invites several difficult questions about mental causation. What are mental states? Are they the right kinds of entities to be causally related? Or should we think of them as merely realized in brain states that are the proper relata of causal relations? Even if we grant that they can stand in causal relations, the account assumes that the causal relations between mental states belonging to the same thinker are unmediated by anything that is not a mental state. But why should this be so? Without a detailed account of how mental states can be causally efficiacious, it is not clear. For example, one might think that one mental state can cause another in virtue of causing some intermediary chain of brain states, culminating in the effect of the latter mental state. Such a view wouldn't appear to invite us to include mental states that do not belong to our purported individual thinker, as was the worry above, so it is

66   THINKING OF NECESSITY

not clear why such a view should be ruled out, from the off, by our account of the unifying relations of the thinker.

An alternative is to draw on *conceptual or inferential* connections between the contents of thoughts. The thought that *it is raining in town*, and the thought that *if it is raining in town, then the streets will be wet*, are related in this way, insofar as the first has the same content as the antecedent of the latter. And moreover, these two thoughts would be related to a third, that *the streets will be wet*, by virtue of logically entailing it. A thought that *Alice is a wife* will be related to the thought that *Alice is married*, insofar as the latter is a conceptual or broadly logical consequence of the former. The problem with this kind of relation between thoughts, though, is that again it allows thoughts from different thinkers to be thus related, and is thus insufficient for mental states to belong to the same thinker. The content of *my* thought that *Alice is married* is no less a consequence of the content of *Bert's* thought that *Alice is a wife*, but in spite of this connection, we do not want the result that my and Bert's thoughts belong to the same thinker, and hence that I and Bert are the same thinker.

A suggestion made by John Campbell may help here. In Campbell (1994) he presents a series of arguments against the reductionist view of the self. Campbell's arguments here are put in terms of a *person*. As already noted, I am discussing something much more minimal; just a locus of mental states. But we can make use of Campbell's line of thought.

> The reductionist view of the self demands a noncircular definition of the identities of persons in terms of more fundamental relations holding between more basic entities than persons. In particular, the reductionist appeals to bodies, experiences causally dependent upon them, and causal relations between those experiences. The reductionist is explaining what a person is in these more fundamental terms.   (Campbell, 1994, 157)

He makes a similar point to mine above, that 'there seems in fact to be no causal relation, or set of causal relations, that characteristically holds among the psychological states of a single person' (Campbell, 1994, 175). His alternative proposal is to appeal to inferential connections between first-personal thoughts.

> Consider the 'I' thoughts of a single thinker. They are inferentially integrated, in the following sense: from any two premises, both stated using the first person, the thinker is entitled to draw inferences which trade on the identity of the thing referred to in the two premises. For example, from 'I am F' and 'I am G', the thinker is entitled to move directly to the conclusion 'I am both F and G'.
>
> (Campbell, 1994, 175–6)

Campbell's proposal only makes sense if we take these to be *token states*. For two different thinkers can each engage in the same (type of) line of first-personal reasoning. The crucial point is that, for example, if Alice thinks *I am F* and *I am G*, it is only Alice who is entitled to conclude on this basis that *I am both F and G*; Bert can't conclude *I am both F and G* on the basis of Alice's premise thoughts (even if, for example, Bert is also thinking *I am F* and *I am G*).

The suggestion we can take from this is that the relation we are seeking is an inferential relation between token first-personal thoughts.[18] This would provide us with a core class of mental states related in a way that is sufficient for them to count as belonging to the same locus of thought. However, there are two problems with this. In responding to those problems, we will arrive at our final proposal.

First, the first-personal inference relation is not sufficiently reductive. Campbell himself emphasizes that we cannot *reduce* the notion of a single thinker to these first-personal inferences.

> In describing why these norms of inference hold between first-person thoughts, we have no choice but to appeal to the notion of being the same person.
>
> (Campbell, 1994, 184)

Campbell's worry here is that the kinds of inferences to which he is appealing precisely trade on the notion of a single person. Transposing the concern to our present purposes, we could not use these kinds of inferences to introduce or identify a single locus of thought.

Second, the proposal relies on our actually having some first-personal thoughts. Our task was to make sense of an *ability* to have certain first-personal thoughts, namely, those beginning 'I think...'. But there was no requirement that one ever actually exercise that ability. Should one do so (more than once), then inferential relations of the kind Campbell discussed may well hold between them, but that wouldn't help us to identify a locus of those thoughts, given the previous objection. The initial suggestion was that we could bootstrap our way up from a nexus of token mental states that are related to each other in some way. The current proposal requires that at least some of those mental states are first-personal thoughts.[19]

---

[18] I am taking for granted here that there are token mental states, such as token thoughts that it is raining. One might disagree, as does, for example, Marcus (2009). I will not defend my assumption here, other than to say that it seems clear to me that we can distinguish between, for example, Alices's thinking that *p* and Bert's thinking that *p*, as *different* thoughts in one important sense, whilst at the same time taking them to be the *same* thought in another sense.

[19] At least some, but not necessarily all, for non-first-personal thoughts may feature in a relevant inference. For example: I am a woman; all women are mortal; therefore I am mortal.

68 THINKING OF NECESSITY

But should one, as a matter of fact, never exercise the ability to prefix one's thoughts with 'I think', and should one, moreover, never happen to have any other first-personal thoughts, there would be no thoughts of the requisite type available to stand in the crucial relation.

My proposal is thus as follows: to take on board the suggestion of some kind of inferential relation between token mental states, but not to require them to be first-personal. The function of the first-personal element was to ensure that the inferential relation would be sufficient for sameness of thinker—to rule out, for example, inferential connections between Alice's thoughts and Bert's thoughts. If we remove that restriction, it must be replaced with something that will similarly guard against this. My suggestion is to take the inferential relations to be *token inferential relations* between thoughts, that is, that one token thought is, on this occasion, inferred from another (or others), rather than *types of inferential relation* that hold between the contents of thought, that is, the kind of relation that holds between Alice's thought that Clive is a bachelor, and Bert's thought that Clive is a man. Indeed, this move to tokens rather than types was already needed in the case of first-personal thoughts.

One way to think of familiar inferential and conceptual connections between thoughts is in terms of what *can be* inferred from a thought or thoughts. If one thinks that *it is raining in town,* and that *if it is raining in town the streets will be wet,* one *can* infer from those thoughts that *the streets will be wet,* but one might not actually do so for any number of reasons. Just because one *can* have a certain thought or thoughts, it does not follow that one *does.* Let us then consider the connections that are forged by the inferences that a thinker *actually* performs. We often make judgments or think thoughts on the basis of other judgments or thoughts. I judge that it is raining in town, I already know that if it is raining in town, the streets will be wet, and so on the basis of these I judge that the streets will be wet (and determine not to wear my brand new suede shoes, and so on). Or, I entertain the thought that Alice is a wife, and on the basis of that think that Alice would also have to be married, if that were so. These thoughts are thereby clearly connected inferentially—the one follows from the other or others—but it is important that we only take into account those inferential connections that are *actually* forged in the actual thinking of thoughts or making of judgments, rather than those that *could be* forged, given the relations that hold between the contents of these thoughts.

This relation—which I call an *actual inferential relation*—does not hold between the thoughts of distinct thinkers. It is the relation that holds between a thought and some (other) thought or thoughts when the former is inferred from the latter. There are no non-inferential mediating steps between the relata of this relation. As such, it may be the case that Bert utters 'Alice is a wife', and then I finish our joint inference by first thinking and then uttering 'Alice is married'. But that would not be a case of me inferring my thought directly from Bert's thought, for there is

THE FUNCTION OF LOGICAL NECESSITY 69

obvious mediation between those two thoughts, in the form of expression of an utterance and the hearing and interpretation of the utterance. This captures the idea that I can't, as it were, reach into Bert's mind (i.e., locus of thought) and infer conclusions directly from his thoughts—we need some kind of mediation to make our thoughts apparent to one another.

This provides us with a core locus of thought, understood as *the thinker of those thoughts,* where *those thoughts* are actually inferentially connected. Recall, my claim is not that this relation is *necessary* for mental states to belong to the same thinker, only that it is *sufficient.*

We also want to make sense of *thought constituents* belonging to the same thinker. Having introduced a locus of thought via actual inferential connections between thoughts, we can now trade on the identification of this locus and also ascribe thought constituents as belonging to *it.* Those constituents may belong to it by virtue of being constituents of the thoughts that are actually inferentially related, or via the bootstrapping move proposed. They belong to the thinker insofar as that thinker—identified via the nexus of actually inferentally related thoughts—can prefix them with 'I think of . . .'.

In a similar way, we can accommodate thoughts that are not actually inferentially related, but which we may want to count as belonging to the same thinker. There are two cases I have in mind. First, mental states that are not actually inferentially connected to any others; be they apt for such connection— thoughts or judgments prompted by something other than, and not leading onto, inference—or not. Second, it is plausible that discrete clumps of thoughts might be actually inferentially related, such that the thoughts in each clump form a unity, but such that the clumps themselves do not come together to form a unified thinker where we might expect to find one.

What to make of extraneous thoughts that are not actually inferred from others, either because a thought has a different instigation, or terminates without inference, or because the mental state is not apt to be inferentially connected? For example, I may wake up and immediately think that I feel refreshed, where my thought is caused by a good night's sleep and is not part of a course of reasoning. Or my thought that it is raining in town may arise because I heard Alice say so even though I hadn't been thinking (or reasoning) about town or rain at all just beforehand. The answer is that all of these thoughts belong to the same thinker, meaning that the same thinker has the ability, in each case, to prefix the thought with 'I think' (or otherwise prefix the mental state with a first-personal locution). Before, this account was inadequate because we had no account of how to distinguish between the token first-personal attributions of different thinkers. We now have an account of how to identify a single thinker in terms of thoughts that are related together by actual inferential relations; they are the thing that has or thinks these thoughts. This is sufficient to identify our thinker, as no other thinker could be actually inferentially related to these thoughts.

70 THINKING OF NECESSITY

The same solution can be applied to the case where there are discrete clumps of thoughts closed under actual inferential relations. For example, one might think that Alice could begin a discrete chain of reasoning at 3pm on a Tuesday and complete it at 11pm that same night, and commence a distinct chain of reasoning at 2pm the next day and complete it at 4pm.[20] Does that mean that there are (at least) two distinct thinkers, where we thought there was just one (Alice)?[21] Not necessarily. Again, as soon as we have one such clump of thoughts, this will allow us to fix on the idea of the individual thinker of those thoughts. Once we have the idea of this individual thinker, we can use it as a locus to which belongs many other mental states, including other thoughts and the clumps to which they are actually inferentially related. One might worry that two different thought clumps in what we want to think of as the same thinker would compete to play the role of the clump that identifies the thinker. For example, is it the thoughts that Alice had on Tuesday, or those she had on Wednesday, that can do the work of identifying to her the locus of her thoughts? However, such a worry is a red herring. We need not think of any such clump of thoughts as privileged in this way. As explained, the clump is there so that we can identify the thinker of the clump of thoughts, but then we can take the idea of this thinker for granted and allow that she has access to all her other thoughts and mental states. Any such clump can do this work, and as long as distinct clumps in "the same thinker" would eventually be related via their belonging to the same thinker, if not by actual inferential connections, the end result is the same; they all belong to one and the same thinker.

I have made a suggestion here for how to treat distinct actually inferentially related clumps of thoughts that we may intuitively think of as belonging to the same thinker. But note, there is also an option to bite the bullet. The task was to make sense of a locus of thought underlying the 'I think (of)', in order to account for the unity of thought. This task is discharged when we have more than one nexus of actually inferentially related thoughts. So one may choose to stop here, and ignore the temptation to go further in accommodating our intuitions about how many loci of thought there are. Especially so if we distinguish this from a distinct set of

[20] This kind of description can accommodate various views about how thinking interacts with time, *pace* Geach (1958, 1969). It is commonplace and plausible to say that a course of reasoning took place over time, even if one disagrees over what to say about the temporal location of constituent thoughts and inferences. What is crucial for my argument here is that there appear to be two clusters of *actually inferentially related* thoughts, not the precise timings of those thoughts.

[21] This kind of case might seem to usher in fission-type problem cases. For example, Alice starts the chain of reasoning, and as she carries it out she steps into a teletransporter and is beamed to another location, reasoning all the while. But the transporter malfunctions and leaves original Alice intact. Arguably, Alice1 and Alice2 are the subjects of a chain of reasoning that connects together the thoughts of just one thinker at an earlier time, Alice1, and two thinkers at a later time, Alice1 and Alice2. However, this case does not raise the same kinds of problems as it does for someone dealing with personal identity. Our challenge here is to identify a locus of thought that can explain the unity of individual token thoughts. In this case, any token thought has some locus to which we can refer it. What to say about the persistence conditions of such loci, and how they relate to persons, is beyond the scope of this chapter. Thank you to Roope-Kristian Ryymin for raising this case.

THE FUNCTION OF LOGICAL NECESSITY   71

questions concerning personal identity. Nevertheless, it is worthwhile noting that one can take two or more such clumps to belong to the same thinker. Such a nexus allows us to make sense of a locus of thought, but we can then say more about the relation between this and other thoughts and other loci, where that relation may turn out to be identity.

5. Actual inferential connections between mental states are formed by judging on the basis of other judgments, i.e., logical reasoning.   We can now grasp the idea of an individual locus of thought, understood as *the thinker of those thoughts,* where *those thoughts* are a collection of thoughts that are actually inferentially connected. These relations between these mental states are sufficient for us to make sense of them belonging to the same thinker. The next step is to claim that these actual inferential connections are forged by logical inference. That is perhaps the obvious move, but there are some important points to be considered.

First, there are kinds of non-logical inference. So, perhaps actual inferential relations could be forged by, for example, inductive reasoning. If this is sufficient to establish our loci of thought, then my overall argument fails. It's not *logical* reasoning that is needed to underwrite the unity of thought. But it is logical reasoning that ushers in a belief in logical necessity.

In response to this concern, we can draw again on McFetridge's argument, that any reasoning on the basis of suppositions requires a commitment to logically necessarily truth-preserving rules of inference. Suppose, for example, that one is reasoning using a rule R^* that does not preserve truth, but according to which the premises have a weaker relation to the conclusion. For the sake of argument, let us suppose that R^* says to infer the conclusion from the premises just when the premises make the conclusion *more probable* (i.e., when the probability of the conclusion given the premises is higher than the probability of the conclusion alone). R^* is not necessarily truth-preserving, because there can be cases where the premises are true and the conclusion false: such cases are unlikely but possible. However, given such a rule, it is not that it is *inapplicable* in those cases where the premises are true and the conclusion false: after all, it is still true that the conclusion is more probable given the premises. From this, we can construct an argument analogous to McFetridge's. Suppose that for every such rule of inference R^* there is some supposition s such that, if it were the case that s, R^* would not apply (e.g., under the supposition that s, the rule no longer licenses inferring the conclusion on the basis of the premises). In this case, either we know, for a given rule R^*, under which suppositions R^* would fail to apply, or we don't. If we do know, then we could in principle construct a new rule, R^*/s, specifying the suppositions under which R^* alone would not apply. This new rule would then apply in reasoning from any supposition whatsoever. If we don't know under which suppositions R^* would fail to apply, then this undermines our whole practice of reasoning from suppositions. If we never know whether or

72 THINKING OF NECESSITY

not rules of inference such as R^* are going to function properly when reasoning from suppositions, because we don't know whether or not a given supposition s is precisely the supposition under which R^* fails, then we can never rely on R^* at all.

Some care is needed here. First, this argument does not commit us to some rules being *truth-preserving* under any supposition: it *does* appear to commit us, though, to some rule working—however the rule may function—in reasoning from any supposition whatsoever, so, to the necessary validity (albeit not deductive validity) of the rule. The thought here is that the argument commits us to there being rules of inference, even if non-deductive, that apply when reasoning under any supposition whatsover. This is not to say, for example, that if a rule says to infer the conclusion from the premises just when the premises make the conclusion *more probable,* and if that rule applies under any supposition, then any suppositions whatsoever will increase the probability of any conclusion. Rather, the thought is that when such a rule applies under any supposition, that means that whatever one supposes, one may always infer to a conclusion *if* it is made more probable by the supposed premises.

Second, McFetridge took *preparedness to employ a mode of inference in reasoning from any set of suppositions* to be the manifestation of a belief in *logically necessarily valid* rules of inference. In light of the adapted argument just presented, this must be read with care. McFetridge takes this preparedness to 'evince the belief that, no matter what else was the case, the inferences would preserve truth' (McFetridge, 1990, 153). But we can now see that there are two elements to this, one of which can be exploited in the present context. First, there is the belief that *no matter what else was the case,* the inferences do whatever they are supposed to do. Second, there is the kind of inference in question: one that preserves truth. What we need for reasoning from suppositions is the commitment to rules that apply under any supposition whatsoever, which captures the logically necessary applicability of the rule. There is then space to recognize different kinds of rule: those that preserve truth under all of those suppositions, and those that do something else (e.g., preserve a probabilitistic relation).

In short, a condition of reasoning—deductively or otherwise—from suppositions commits us to a belief in logically necessarily valid rules of inference, whether validity be understood deductively (in terms of necessary truth-preservation), or otherwise. Nevertheless, there are wider reasons to think that logical reasoning— i.e., employing logically necessarily truth-preserving rules of inference—should still have a central role to play. In the next chapter, I argue that logical necessity has its source in laws of logic understood as constitutive norms for thought, that is, norms evaluability in light of which is constitutive of thought. This both supports and is supported by the proposal here that a necessary condition of a capacity for thought is engaging in logical reasoning. Perhaps one should see these two chapters, then, as mutually supporting. As a whole package, I think there is an interesting view which has a central role for logical reasoning, rather than other types of reasoning. Henceforth, I shall assume that the actual inferential relations implicated here are logical inferential relations.

The second issue is whether the logical reasoning that thinkers engage in, which we are taking to underwrite the unity of a thinker, must always be *successful*. To answer this question, let us review the line of argument. When we reason logically, and thereby when we reason logically from suppositions, we are committed to a belief in logically necessarily truth-preserving rules of inference. To link a capacity for thought to a belief in logical necessity, then, we need to link a practice with this commitment to the condition on the unity of thought. Now, there is nothing in McFetridge's argument that requires that we are always *successful* in our reasoning from suppositions: it is just that to make sense of that practice we are committed to belief in logically necessarily truth-preserving rules of inference. We might make mistakes about what the rules are, or in applying them, but we believe in them. Similarly, imperfect attempts at logical reasoning will forge connections between mental states, but still—given the point just made—usher in a commitment to logical necessity. Again, the considerations of the following chapter may go some way to reinforcing this point. As the laws of logic are taken to be to some extent *normative*, even mistaken reasoning can count as inference, so long as it is evaluable as mistaken in light of the laws of logic. Such imperfect reasoning then, can count as logical reasoning, and it can usher in the commitment to logical necessity.

6. Therefore, a necessary condition of thoughts is a thinking subject that engages in logical reasoning.   Where does all this leave us? We need some kind of unity to get the unity of a whole thinker up and running, but as soon as we have any unity of this kind—as soon as some actual inference occurs—we have something to start with. Then we can appeal to an account in terms of the ability to prefix one's thoughts (and other mental states) with 'I think' (or similar). Crucially, then, in this account of the idea of our thoughts belonging to a thinker, *some inference must actually take place*. Without some actual inference taking place no thoughts would be actually inferentially related, so there would not be the kind of unity that could introduce the idea of the locus of those thoughts, the thinker; and without the idea of this thinker we couldn't make sense of thoughts and thought constituents belonging to the same thinker; and without this, I have argued, combination of thought constituents into thoughts (or discernment of shared structure) could not take place, so there would be no thoughts at all. Therefore, a necessary condition of the thinking subject, and of them having thoughts, is that they engage in logical reasoning.

Earlier, I drew together some arguments to show that a belief in logical necessity is a necessary condition for reasoning from suppositions, and that reasoning from suppositions is a requirement of our engaging in logical reasoning at all. We can now add a further conclusion: a necessary condition of the thinking subject, and of them having thoughts, is that they engage in logical reasoning. Putting this all together, we find that a belief in logical necessity is a necessary condition for a subject to have thoughts at all. This, then, is the (or at least *a*) function of a concept of, and an ability to make judgments of, logical necessity.

4

The Source of Logical Necessity

4.1 An answer and a question

In the previous chapter, I introduced logical necessity as that kind of necessity that is implicated in contradiction and deductive validity. More particularly: it is logically necessary that *A* if, and only if, not-*A* entails a contradiction. I then argued for an answer to the transcendental question for logical modality.

The logical modality question: What is the transcendental role of judgments and concepts of logical modality? Would there be a thinker at all if they didn't or couldn't make judgments of logical modality or have logical modal concepts?

My answer: A belief in logically necessarily truth-preserving rules of inference—and hence the concept of logical necessity required for such a belief—is a necessary condition of an ability to reason from suppositions. An ability to reason from suppositions is a necessary condition of an ability to engage in any logical reasoning at all. Engaging in logical reasoning is a necessary condition of thinking. Therefore, the role of judgments and concepts of logical modality is to ensure the possibility of thinking. There would be no thinker at all if they didn't have the ability to make judgments of logical modality, or have logical modal concepts.

We thus have a characterization of logical necessity and an account of its role in the possibility of thought. But what is the source or nature of this logical necessity?[1] A range of different answers are compatible with these results. We might agree, for example, that it is logically necessary that *if grass is green, then grass is green*, logically possible that *if grass is green, then the sky is green,* and logically impossible that *grass is green and it is not the case that grass is green.* And we might agree that we must possess the kinds of modal concepts that would allow us to think about these cases, as a condition of being able to think at all. But what is the source of these apparent modal facts? Ostensibly, the laws of logic. It is the laws of logic that prohibit contradiction and that determine what follows logically from what. But now our question becomes: what is the source of these laws of logic? Do they arise from mind-independent features of the world, or do they depend on something to do with thinkers like us?

---

[1] See Chapter 6, section 6.4 for more on the notion of *source.*

Thinking of Necessity: A Kantian Account of Modal Thought and Modal Metaphysics. Jessica Leech, Oxford University Press. © Jessica Leech 2023. DOI: 10.1093/oso/9780198873969.003.0004

76 THINKING OF NECESSITY

Given the intimate link between thought and the role of logical modal judgment and concepts, one might suspect that the latter is more likely. Thus far, however, that is a mere suspicion. In the course of the argument of this chapter, it should emerge that there is a particularly intimate link between the laws of logic and our capacity for thought. This will vindicate our answer to the logical modality question. And we shall also see how that answer to the question provides additional support to the account of the source of logical necessity proposed here.

In the present chapter, I introduce and defend an account according to which logical laws, and hence logical modality, have their source in *constitutive norms for thought*. I then introduce a test that I contend all accounts of logical modality should pass. I will argue that my favoured account passes the test and that some rival accounts fail.

4.2 Logical necessity and the laws of thought

4.2.1 Constitutive and normative laws

The proposal is that the laws of logic are laws of thought.[2] And so logical modality ultimately has its source in the laws of thought.

There are different ways that one might take laws to govern some state or phenomenon. Laws might be normative, constitutive, or constitutive norms.

Laws for *F*s are *normative* if they determine what counts as a good *F* or a bad *F*. For example, the laws of a nation (i.e., laws for actions in a particular jurisdiction) determine what actions are legally permissible, legally obligatory, and legally impermissible. But they do not thereby determine what counts as an action: even an illegal action is an action.

Laws for *F*s are *constitutive* for *F*s if they determine what counts as an *F* and what doesn't count as an *F*. For example, one might think that the rules for the form of a sonnet determine what counts as a sonnet and rule everything else out. If a poem closely follows the right rhyme scheme, but is only twelve lines long, then it isn't a bad sonnet—it doesn't count as a sonnet at all.

Laws for *F*s are *constitutive norms* for *F*s if evaluability in light of the laws determines what counts as an *F* and what doesn't count as an *F*. For example, if I am on a large field with goals at opposite ends, surrounded by other players, etc., I only count as playing football (soccer) if certain actions are evaluable as wrong or right according to the laws of football. For example, all other things being equal, if passing the ball using my hand counts as wrong, but kicking it forward counts as permissible, I am playing football. If those actions have no normative status at

---

[2] My argument here closely follows that presented in Leech (2015) and parts of Leech (2017d).

all, or a different status, then I'm not playing football. If I punch the ball towards goal using my hand, I can still count as playing football, so the laws are not purely constitutive. I am playing football as long as my actions are held to the standards (norms) of football. In this case, I am playing football as long as punching the ball towards the goal (when I am not the goalkeeper) counts as an illegal move.

If the laws of logic are normative laws for thought, then thoughts that violate the laws are still thoughts, but are bad thoughts. For example, suppose that the law of non-contradiction is a normative law for thought: on this view, one can still think contradictory thoughts of the form *p and not-p,* but they are bad, and ought to be corrected. If the laws of thought are constitutive laws for thought, then so-called "thoughts" that violate the laws are not thoughts at all, but something else. For example, if the law of non-contradiction is a constitutive law of thought, then one literally could not think thoughts of the form *p and not-p.* If the laws of logic are constitutive norms for thought, then thoughts that violate the laws are thoughts so long as they are evaluated as bad in light of those laws. For example, if we understand the law of non-contradiction in this way, then according to this view one can think contradictory thoughts of the form *p and not-p,* so long as doing so counts as bad in light of the laws.

I will argue that the laws of logic are *constitutive norms of thought.* In brief:

1. Some logical principles are immune to rational doubt.
2. The best explanation of (1) is that the laws of logic are constitutive norms of thought.
3. Therefore, the laws of logic are constitutive norms of thought.

Before I sketch a defence of the three premises, some remarks are in order.

First, this is not a logically valid argument, it is an argument to the best explanation. Hence, it does not purport to show definitively that the laws of logic are laws of thought, but it at least gives us good reason to favour the view. Second, it is not quite right to call it an argument to the *best* explanation. I don't consider or rule out all possible competing explanations. My focus is primarily on showing how my proposed view provides a good explanation. Hence, we might call this an argument to *a good* explanation.

Third, let me briefly clarify the kind of normativity at play. There are different ways we might think of a norm. Sellars (1969) distinguishes between 'oughts-to-do' (rules of action) and 'oughts-to-be' (rules of criticism). A rule of action is of the form: if one is in circumstance C, one ought to do action A. In such cases, Sellars argues, to conform to the norm an agent needs to possess concepts of C and A (Sellars, 1969, 507–8). A rule of criticism is of the form: Xs ought to be in state φ, whenever such and such is the case (Sellars, 1969, 508). In this case, Sellars drops the conceptual requirement. This distinction is important when we consider what kind of norms—including those imputed in constitutive

78 THINKING OF NECESSITY

norms—may apply in the case of laws of logic. If we take laws of logic to be oughts-to-do that are constitutive of thinking, then it would also be constitutive of thinking to possess certain concepts, namely, explicit grasp of the laws of logic (A) and of the circumstances in which those laws apply (C). I did argue in the previous chapter that all thinkers must possess a concept of logical necessity, but it's not clear how far those conceptual resources stretch, and whether they should be taken to stretch this far. As such, it is more plausible, and still enlightening, to understand the norms as rules of criticism, standards against which our mental activity must be evaluable in order for that activity to count as thinking, where we needn't be explicitly cognisant of the laws. Nevertheless, thinkers need at least some implicit awareness of the laws, such that, for example, they would be prepared to correct themselves when shown a logical error. Hence, the truth lies somewhere between the two extremes. Let us not require thinkers to have full logical recognitional capacities in order to count as thinkers (they shouldn't need to be accomplished logicians). But they should be sensitive to logical correction and tuition. If the laws of logic are norms that are genuinely constitutive of thought, it is not surprising that, given enough prompting, we should be sensitive to them, but it doesn't follow that we should be able to start out as thinkers with a clear and explicit grasp of them.

Finally, as before, thinking can be as minimal as entertaining a proposition, and more broadly includes transitions from one thought to another. If we think something, then we have meaningful thought constituents put together in a meaningful way, into something like propositional form. There will thus be some constitutive rules for thoughts, namely, those that ensure their meaningfulness. Thoughts must be 'grammatical', or 'well-formed'; put together in the right way. These are the kinds of rules that would normally appear in the definition of a formula in a formal logical system (e.g., 'if ϕ is a formula and ψ is a formula then $\phi \wedge \psi$ is a formula'). The rules that I am taking to be *constitutive norms* are those that govern already well-formed formulas, for example, that contradictions are not true, or that the consequent of a conditional follows from the conditional taken together with its antecedent.

4.2.2 Immunity to rational doubt

In this section I sketch an argument to show that there is indeed a phenomenon to be explained in our argument to a good explanation, i.e., I defend premise 1: *some logical principles are immune to rational doubt.*

The first step of the argument is a simplified version of the argument at the heart of Hale (2002a). We have already seen, in Chapter 3, an argument that we are committed to belief in logical necessity as a condition of our ability to reason from suppositions (and ultimately, I have argued, our ability to think at all).

Hale (2002a) links this commitment to a belief in logical necessity to the idea that there are certain principles that are immune to rational doubt. He argues that there is a 'minimal toolkit' of logical principles that are involved in the very practices of doubting and reasoning about the soundness of logical principles. Hence, we cannot rationally doubt the soundness of these principles. The argument runs as follows.

Suppose we want to rationally doubt the soundness or validity of some rule of inference. What will be involved in this? If the doubting is rational, it will involve some reasoning.[3] So, in any case of rational doubt of a rule of inference R, we must be relying on some rule of inference R', to carry out our reasoning. R' cannot be the same rule as R, on pain of vicious circularity. Hence, for any case of reasoning about a rule of inference R, there will be some other rule of inference R' which is assumed to be sound for the purposes of reasoning about R. Hale suggests that we should extend the conclusion to the claim that there is (are) some rule(s) of inference R' that we assume to be sound in any context of reasoning whatsoever. Hence such a rule is itself immune from rational doubt, as it is part of our very practice of rational doubt that the rule be assumed sound in all such contexts.

> If what I've said is right, *any* vindication of a doubt about the conservativeness (or, more generally, the soundness) of *any* rules of inference must involve reasoning which doesn't use those rules, but uses *some* other rules instead—rules whose reliability is assumed in that reasoning. It does not, of course, follow from this that there must be *some* rules whose reliability must, and may properly, be assumed in *any* demonstration we can give of the conservativeness or non-conservativeness (more generally, soundness or unsoundness) of *any* (other) rules. It does not *follow*, but it is—or so I believe—*true*.   (Hale, 2002a, 297)

Hale points out towards the end of this passage that the final step of this argument does not follow: we may have shown that in any case of rational doubt there is some rule of inference assumed sound, but it does not follow from this that there is some rule of inference assumed sound in any case of rational doubt. Hale works to bolster his conclusion by presenting plausible examples of rules of inference that we would expect to be assumed sound in all contexts. I return to these examples soon. First, though, note that we can draw on McFetridge's argument to help plug the gap.[4]

McFetridge has argued that in any case of reasoning, which we can presume to include cases of reasoning in the aid of rational doubt, we are committed to the belief that there is some rule of inference assumed sound under any supposition

---

[3] We are not interested in irrational foot-stamping here: of course we can refuse to believe things for all sorts of irrational motives.

[4] See Chapter 3, section 3.2.

80 THINKING OF NECESSITY

whatsoever. That is, such a rule of inference is assumed to be sound in reasoning under *any* supposition, and therefore in any case where one is engaging in rational doubt.[5] Hence, we can add this to Hale's argument to conclude that each of us must be committed to a belief in or assumption of the soundness of some rules of inference in all contexts of reasoning, including in cases of rational doubt.

I conclude, then, that for each of us there are some principles immune to rational doubt. Is there any reason, though, to conclude that they are *the same* for each of us? The argument does not straightforwardly show this, but there are some reasons for thinking that, nonetheless, there are some shared rationally indubitable principles.

First, we might simply appeal to the fact that we can often easily engage in shared inferences.[6] This is not to say that we can literally think each other's thoughts in a group inference (against which I argued in the previous chapter), but we can work through an argument together—mediated by utterances of premises and inscriptions on the whiteboard, etc.—which, it seems, is underwritten by a shared standard for reasoning. And we can engage with others' inferences and arguments. This at least strongly suggests that we all hold fixed some shared core of rules of inference.

Second, Hale outlines several plausible examples of the kinds of rules that we would expect to be part of this 'minimal toolkit'.

> Any rule(s) of inference whose soundness we may wish to consider will—or so I think we may assume—be both *general* and *conditional*—general, in the sense that their explicit formulation tells us that a conclusion of some specified general form may be drawn from premises of some specified general form, and conditional, in the sense that they tell us that *given* premises of the specified form, a conclusion of the specified form may be drawn. Any reasoning *about* what inferences they permit—as distinct from reasoning that simply uses those rules—will, at least if fully articulated, involve reasoning from explicit formulations of the rules.... If this is right, then there is what might be called a *minimal kit* of inference rules—including at least rules for the conditional and universal quantifier—required for any reasoning about the soundness of any rules of inference.   (Hale, 2002a, 299)

This suggests that it is not simply that we need to be able to hold some rules fixed in order to reason from suppositions in general, and about the soundness of rules of inference in general, where those rules may vary from thinker to thinker. Rather, the very shape of reasoning about rules of inference requires particular

---

[5] The argument thus far doesn't assume that we know which rule (or rules) this is: the point is that we are committed to a belief of something like the form '$\exists r \forall s Srs$', i.e., there is a rule (or rules) such that under any supposition that rule is sound. I discuss potential examples of such rules later in this section.

[6] See, e.g., Williamson (1997, 650).

THE SOURCE OF LOGICAL NECESSITY   81

kinds of rules—at least rules for the conditional and universal quantification—to be assumed universally valid by anyone engaging in that kind of reasoning.

A different but complementary line of argument from Suki Finn supports this. She argues that the logical rules of Modus Ponens (MP) and Universal Instantiation (UI) have a special status: 'they govern all logical rules of inference, including themselves' (2021, 4908) because all logical rules of inference are conditional and universal, and hence presuppose MP and UI.[7]

> Logical rules of inference are, very generally speaking, universal and conditional in their structure. To be of a universal structure is to apply in *all* cases of a certain kind. To be conditional in structure is to say what to do *if* one is in a case of a certain kind. Logical rules of inference take us from premises to a conclusion via a conditional, and are universal meaning that they apply in all cases when the antecedent of that conditional is satisfied.   (Finn, 2021, 4913)

Since all rules of inference are conditional and universal, they are governed by rules for the conditional and the universal quantifier. Finn's application of this point is to argue that such rules are distinctively self-governing, and that they cannot be adopted, i.e., cannot be taken on by a thinker who was not previously using these rules, because to do so they would already need to be able to think conditionally and universally. For our purposes, Finn draws out that rules for the conditional and the universal must be part of a minimal logical toolkit.

> Logical rules seem to presuppose that we can make sense of instructions of the form 'if . . . then', and recognise instances as instances of general forms. Therefore a grasp of UI and MP is central to the notion of a logical rule of inference, and that is what makes them basic, unadoptable, and required at the meta-level for any adequate logical system. Without UI and MP, there is no way to make sense of, or apply, any other logical rules, since all of the logical rules depend on UI and MP to govern them.   (Finn, 2021, 4920)

Moreover, if any logical reasoning—including that employed in rational doubt—must therefore presuppose rules governing the conditional and the universal quantifier, we have again the conclusion that such rules are immune to rational doubt.

Note: Finn focuses on MP and UI, but there are other relevant rules, such as Conditional Introduction.[8] Finn's line of argument would seem to apply here too:

---

[7] MP: $A \supset B, A \vdash B$

UI: $\forall x A \vdash A(x/a)$, where $A(x/a)$ is the result of substituting a for every free occurrence of x in A, and (in classical logic) where either a has already been introduced in the proof, or no constants have been introduced so far.

[8] CI: Assume A, derive B, then $\vdash A \supset B$.

82 THINKING OF NECESSITY

if we need rules governing the conditional and the universal quantifier in order to be able to engage in logical reasoning, surely we need introduction as much as elimination rules. Moreover, thus far, we need make no assumption about the precise formulation of those rules. For example, the form that quantifier rules take will depend upon whether or not we are working with a free or a classical logic.[9] But the point stands that we need some quantifier rules, whichever logic we ultimately favour.[10]

4.2.3 Explaining immunity

So, some logical principles are immune to rational doubt. Why? One might suggest: because their negations are unthinkable. The logical principles express laws of logic that are constitutive laws of thought, and so it is not possible to think the opposite of them. However, I take such a view to be seriously mistaken: we should not understand the laws of logic as constitutive laws for thought. If the laws of logic were constitutive laws for thought, then any mental activity—any purported thought—that failed to conform to the laws of logic would not count as thought. For example, suppose one (purportedly) thought that *p and q* but also that $\neg p$, and that one made this connection in thought, i.e., $(p \wedge q) \wedge \neg p$. Such a thought is in violation of the law of Conjunction Elimination.[11] Since this entails $p \wedge \neg p$, the (purported) thought is contradictory. However, since this is in violation of at least one law of logic, this "thought" would be no thought at all. But we *can* think contradictory thoughts like this, so the laws of logic are not constitutive of thought. We can recognize logical mistakes, including logical contradictions, and correct ourselves. Indeed, contradictions feature in purportedly valid rules of inference, such as *reductio ad absurdum* and *ex falso quodlibet*. When we encounter a logical mistake, it is not that thought *ceases*, and so we are alerted to some problem that must be corrected before we can continue on with a train of thought. If that were so, surely any interruption to thought could potentially be counted as logically relevant, for example, a momentary blackout, or a string of nonsense. But that is not the case. Coming across a logical mistake calls for a rational response: we recognize the mistake for what it is, and accommodate it into our reasoning accordingly. For example, if we encounter a contradiction, we might recognize it for what it is, and then conclude that whatever led us into contradiction, such as accidental violation of a law, must be wrong.[12]

---

[9] Thank you to an anonymous reader for raising these two points.

[10] See Chapter 9, section 9.1.2 for more discussion of free logic.

[11] $A \wedge B \vdash A, A \wedge B \vdash B.$

[12] I have argued at more length for the thinkability of contradictions elsewhere. See Leech (2015, 2017d).

THE SOURCE OF LOGICAL NECESSITY   83

The laws of logic are not straightforwardly constitutive. Nevertheless, a good explanation of their rational indubitability would be that they are constitutive of thought in some sense. That would explain why we can't rationally doubt them; they form part of the framework for rational thought—including doubt—in the first place. The compromise is thus to take them to be constitutive-*normative* laws. We can explain the intimate connection between thought and the laws of logic by taking thought to be constitutively evaluable in light of the laws of logic; to think is to be subject to the laws of logic, even if it is possible to violate those laws and thereby to err in thinking.

Suppose for some law of logic L that it is indeed a constitutive norm of thought. One counts as thinking insofar as one's activity counts as right or wrong as evaluated against L (and other laws). Now, suppose one tries to cast rational doubt on L. One finds that it is not possible to coherently do so. Why? Because any course of reasoning, such as is involved in the attempt to rationally doubt L, only counts as reasoning because it is correct or incorrect in light of, amongst other things, the standard laid down by L. Such a thinker just does not have the mental resources to rationally doubt L, because rational doubt itself presupposes the authority and correctness of L. Hence, it makes good sense to think of the laws of logic as constitutive norms of thought.

To conclude, the laws of logic are normative laws, evaluability in light of which is constitutive of thought. That's just what thought *is*: a mental activity which is subject to these kinds of rules. If logical necessity is the necessity distinctive of valid inference and its laws, then logical necessity thereby has its source in the laws (constitutive norms) of thought.

This conclusion also vindicates the conclusion of the previous chapter, that the function of judgments and concepts of logical necessity is, ultimately, as a necessary condition of thought. We have, effectively, reached the same conclusion here. If the laws of logic are constitutive of thought in any sense—even our normative sense—then if there were no such laws, there would be no such thing as thought. And if those logical laws carry with them logical necessity, then again, without logical necessity there would be no thought.

Moreover, the result that the function of logical modal judgment is that it is a condition on our very capacity for thought is not merely vindicated by the argument that the laws of logic are laws of thought. We can also take the former conclusion to add independent support to our conclusion here about the source of logical necessity. For consider: if a capacity to make judgments of logical necessity is a condition of our capacity for thought, what, as a consequence, should we expect (the source of) logical necessity to be like?

Compare a view according to which logical necessity has its source in the mind-independent natures of abstract logical objects (such as logical functions of conjunction and negation), and a view according to which logical necessity has its

84 THINKING OF NECESSITY

source in the nature of our capacity for thought.[13] In the former case, insofar as our capacity to think depends upon logical necessity (i.e., on logically necessarily truth-preserving rules of inference), and insofar as logical necessity depends upon (has its source in) the nature of abstract logical objects, it follows that our capacity to think depends upon the nature of, and so presumably also the existence of, abstract logical objects. Now, that view isn't immediately or obviously false, but it is at least strange. Why should a certain kind of mental capacity—*thinking*— have anything to do with what mind-independent objects exist, and what they are like? You may perhaps be of the view that any thought at all depends upon there being something to think about, e.g., as Kant writes, 'all cognition begins with experience; for how else should the cognitive faculty be awakened into exercise if not through objects that stimulate our senses . . . ?' (B1). But even then, it is hard to see why some objects rather than others should exist for these purposes. This view at least raises a set of challenging questions to be addressed.

By contrast, a view according to which logical necessity has its source in the nature of thought leaves no such gap to be explained. It is constitutive of thought to be evaluable in light of logical laws, which shows up in the immunity to rational doubt of those laws, and which is explained by the role that logical laws play in the very possibility of thought, namely, they contribute to the unity of a locus of thought that is presupposed by the unity of thoughts. We have a self-contained package that requires no reference to or dependence on seemingly unrelated parts of reality, and hence which avoids the additional challenges faced by the alternative.

4.3 Competing features of logical necessity

4.3.1 TRUTH and THOUGHT

Logical necessity has two notable features. First, I have just argued that some logical principles are immune to rational doubt. At least some logical necessities are thus immune to rational doubt: they are intimately connected to what we are able to think and doubt. Second, logical necessity is factive: if it is logically necessary that p, then p is true. I call these two features THOUGHT and TRUTH respectively. I have just argued for THOUGHT; TRUTH is a relatively uncontroversial platitude about logical necessity (although I will briefly discuss some non-cognitivist scruples). Taken together, they create a tension. Why should something be true, and indeed necessarily so, just because we're not able to subject it to rational doubt?

---

[13] One might take a view according to which our capacity for thought is a capacity to grasp abstract objects, namely, Fregean thoughts (Frege, 1956). But this is distinct from the view I have in mind as a contrast, where the abstract objects in question are logical entities such as functions, as in Hale (2013). I maintain that there remains a mystery how such things of the latter kind should be so intimately related to our capacity for thought.

And conversely, just because something is true, albeit necessarily so, why should that affect what we're able to doubt? I take an important desideratum on an account of the nature and source of logical necessary to be that it can provide a resolution of this tension, i.e., that it can account for both THOUGHT and TRUTH. In what follows, I consider whether and how some central accounts of the nature of logical necessity can meet this challenge. Unsurprisingly, I will conclude that my proposed account—that the source of logical necessity lies in constitutive norms for thought—is more successful on this front.

4.3.2 Essentialist logical necessity

Essentialist theories of modality take metaphysical modality to have its source in the natures of things, and logical necessity to be a special case of this, with its source in the natures of a sub-class of things, logical things.

The nature or essence of some thing is often understood in terms of the Aristotelian notion of real definition, 'what it is to be' something. So, for example, Fine (1994) writes,

> The metaphysically necessary truths can then be identified with the propositions which are true in virtue of the nature of all objects whatever. Other familiar concepts of necessity (though not all of them) can be understood in a similar manner. The conceptual necessities can be taken to be the propositions which are true in virtue of the nature of all concepts; the logical necessities can be taken to be the propositions which are true in virtue of the nature of all logical concepts. . . .
> (Fine, 1994, 9)

And Hale (2013) writes,

> By the nature or identity of a thing, I mean what it is to be that thing—what makes it the thing it is, and distinguishes it from every other thing. We may think of the nature or identity of a thing as what is given by its definition—that is, the definition of the *thing,* and not that of some word for the thing or concept of the thing.   (Hale, 2013, 132)

Where p is a logical truth, we can explain why it is necessary that p by citing some facts about the nature of the logical functions involved. Using Fine's handy sub-scripted box notation, our explanation can be represented schematically as:

$\Box p$ because $\Box_{X_1,\ldots,X_n} p$

where $X_1, \ldots, X_n$ is a list of the relevant logical entities. We can read this as saying: 'It is necessary that p because it is true in virtue of the natures of $X_1, \ldots, X_n$ that p'.
(Hale, 2013, 145)

86 THINKING OF NECESSITY

There are a number of questions one might raise for the essentialist view, not least why one should think that things have their natures or essences necessarily. Hale's view explicitly relies upon and argues in defence of the claim that things have these natures absolutely necessarily.[14] It is for this reason that they can provide a basis for what seem to be absolute necessities, such as logical and metaphysical necessities. I think there are reasons to doubt the claim that these natures or essences are indeed guaranteed to be necessary, but I will set this concern to one side here.[15] My focus is on resolving the tension between THOUGHT and TRUTH.

As is evident from Fine and Hale's remarks, there are two main ways to flesh out the idea that logical necessity has its source in the essence of logical things: those things might be logical concepts, e.g., the concept of conjunction, or something non-conceptual, logical functions understood as abstract entities, e.g., the truth-function *conjunction*. I will argue that neither view is able to adequately accommodate both TRUTH and THOUGHT.[16]

4.3.2.1 Logical functions
Consider the version of the view in terms of logical functions.

ELF   It is logically necessary that *p* because it is true in virtue of the nature of the logical functions that *p*.

For example,

It is logically necessary that a conjunction *A and B* is true if and only if *A* is true and *B* is true because it is true in virtue of the nature of *conjunction* that a conjunction is true if and only if both its conjuncts are true.[17]

If it's *true* in virtue of the nature of the logical functions that *p*, then it is *true* that *p*. So the factivity of logical necessity, and hence TRUTH, is easily and straightforwardly accommodated.

But what about THOUGHT? The question arises: why is it that the essences of *logical* entities in particular are so intimately related to what we are able

---

[14] See Hale (2013) section 5.5.2, especially the top of p.133.

[15] See Leech (2018, 2021c); Mackie (2020).

[16] There is another branch of essentialist accounts which deny that essentialist statements need to be committed to the existence of objects, but rather can be understood in terms of statements of generalized identity, e.g., 'what it is, in part, to be conjoined is to be such that the conjuncts are true if and only if the conjunction is true'. Such a statement does not obviously bear commitment to the function or concept of conjunction. However, I can't see how this could make any advance on explaining THOUGHT, for there is no reason in general to suppose that identity statements are immune to rational doubt, or lead to immunity to rational doubt. (Consider, for example, 'what it is to be water is to be H_2O'.) Hence, I will not discuss this option here. See Correia and Skiles (2019); Leech (2021c). See also Chapter 9, section 9.2.3.

[17] See Hale (2013, 134–5).

THE SOURCE OF LOGICAL NECESSITY   87

to rationally think or doubt? In general, one would not expect the essence of something to constrain what one is able to think or doubt. On the contrary, many essentialist necessities are taken to be *a posteriori*. So, for example, even if it is essential to water to be H_2O, this is not *a priori*, and so it makes sense to think that water might be something other than H_2O. Even once one grasps the nature of something, e.g., that water is essentially H_2O, there may still be circumstances in which it would be rational to doubt that water is H_2O, for example, if one was presented with compelling evidence of historic and pervasive mistakes in the natural sciences.

So what, if anything, makes the (essences of) logical functions different? Why is it that, for example, the essence of the function *conjunction* constrains our capacity for rational doubt, but the essences of other things such as water, or Socrates, do not? The obvious answer is: there is no reason to think that mind-independent abstract entities such as truth functions have any bearing on our capacity for rational thinking. Why should they? For a start, there is almost by definition no causal connection between us and them. Note, the problem is not simply one of the epistemology of abstract objects. Just because we can account for our *knowledge* of a class of entities, does not yet say anything about whether or why these entities have a particularly intimate relation to our ability to think.

It may be that the details of an epistemology for abstract objects, however, would have that consequence. After all, if some class of entities constrain one's ability to think, one might take this to provide a route to knowledge of them; take the principles that cannot be rationally doubted as a guide to the nature of these entities. To review all the promising epistemologies for abstract objects would be a significant project in its own right, far beyond the scope of this book, but let me explain why I think it would nevertheless be unlikely to yield a satisfactory explanation of THOUGHT.

I would assume that the more promising epistemologies for abstract objects would be fairly uniform. It would be strange if one class of abstract objects received one treatment, the rest another. Insofar as they are similar enough to all be classified as abstract, and insofar as, being thus classified, they all share the same general epistemological problem, it is reasonable to expect the same kind of epistemological solution to be available to most or all of them. Suppose, then, that one's epistemology of abstract objects does yield an explanation of THOUGHT. In this case, given the uniformity we might expect of such an epistemology, this would also yield the result that *all* abstract objects have essences that give rise to principles that are immune to rational doubt. But this seems highly implausible. Compare, for example, two functions—where a function is a many-one relation, that is, a relation that maps one or more arguments to a unique value. The truth function *conjunction* maps pairs of true propositions (say, A and B) to a single true proposition ($A \land B$), and other pairs of propositions to a single false proposition. The essentialist story has it that this behaviour is essential to the function, and thus

88 THINKING OF NECESSITY

grounds the logical necessity of a conjunction of two propositions, *A and B*, being true if and only if *A* is true and *B* is true. Such a principle is also supposed to be immune to rational doubt. Compare: there is a function that maps (parts of) the names of a couple (Kim, Kanye; Brad, Angelina) to form a single name for that couple (Kimye; Brangelina). We might even allow that it is of the essence of that function to do so. However, it would be absurd to suggest that there is a principle here immune to rational doubt. Not all of the essences of abstract objects (in this case, functions) give rise to truths that are immune to rational doubt, hence, we cannot use a blanket epistemology, covering all abstract objects, to accommodate THOUGHT.

There are two obvious responses to this. First, what if the only abstract objects were logical entities? I take it this is implausible. It would be *ad hoc* to accept only a few functions, and thereby only a very few relations, into one's ontology. Any rationale for accepting the logical functions is likely to be general enough to cover other abstract entities as well. Second, one might argue that there is an important dissimiliarity in the examples above, namely, that only one of them involves a *logical* function. And only the *logical* functions will have this compelling effect on our thought. However, this is just to reintroduce our problem, and to accept that a general epistemlogy for abstract objects is not going to help us.

In short, even if we can give an account of how our minds gain access to these entities, this does not yet tell us why those entities should in turn impose constraints upon our minds (other than determining whether our thoughts about them are true or false). On this version of essentialism about logical necessity, then, there is no clear route to accommodating THOUGHT. Hence, the tension between THOUGHT and TRUTH does not receive a satisfactory resolution.

However, there is a third, more serious, response: that there *is* a special kind of abstract object that we *do* have good reason to treat differently to others, namely, *thoughts* understood as the senses of declarative sentences which belong to the third realm (Frege, 1956). If thinking just is the apprehension of these abstract entities, then the existence of these abstract entities may well constrain our capacity for thought and, furthermore, we might expect functions that govern important features of these entities (such as truth functions) also to thereby constrain our thinking. It looks like such a view could then accommodate THOUGHT and also account for TRUTH in terms of the essences of these logical entities—thoughts included. This view is now quite similar to a version of the next view to be considered: that logical necessity has its source in the nature of logical concepts, and logical concepts are to be understood as Fregean third-realm entities. In which case, I postpone my reservations until the next section.

4.3.2.2 Logical concepts

Does the concepts version of the view fair any better? The view states that:

ELC   It is logically necessary that p because it is true in virtue of the nature of the logical concepts that p.

For example,

> It is logically necessary that a conjunction A *and* B is true only if A is true and B is true because it is true in virtue of the nature of the concept of conjunction that a conjunction is true if and only if both its conjuncts are true.

The consequences of this view obviously depend upon what you take concepts to be. Let us consider three broad options: (1) concepts are worldly entities, properties or functions; (2) concepts are mental entities, the constituents of our thoughts; (3) concepts are abstract modes of presentation, neither (1) nor (2), but of a 'third realm'.[18] I shall argue that none of these options allows one adequately to accommodate both TRUTH and THOUGHT. Note: my arguments concern how these views of the nature of concepts interact with essentialism; they are not arguments for or against these views of concepts *per se*.

(1) is Frege's use of 'concept'. For Frege, our words express modes of presentation, senses or thoughts, which in turn determine a reference. The things to which we refer are further divided into two kinds, objects and concepts. On this understanding, concepts are roughly equivalent to the kinds of entities I discussed in the previous section: properties and/or functions, such as the function *conjunction*. As such, on this view of concepts, ELC collapses back into ELF, and the same conclusions can be drawn as above: only TRUTH, but not THOUGHT, can be accommodated.

If (2), concepts are understood as mental entities, then it is easier to explain THOUGHT. It is more plausible that mental entities could have a significant impact on our capacity for thought. After all, we use these concepts to think. However we conceive of these concepts—as mental processes, or mental pictures, or mental words—it seems plausible that a view could be developed according to which, as the mind works by using these concepts, they thereby constrain what the mind is able to do and hence our capacity for rational doubt. That said, however, it is harder to understand how such a view could accommodate the importantly *normative* character of the laws of logic. If we are to attribute their source to something like the mental mechanisms of thought, then it would seem that they would have to be constitutive laws of thought, which I have argued is wrong. Moreover, such a view threatens to introduce an unpalatable psychologism. Where option (1) was unable to account for the constraint placed upon thought by the laws of logic at all, option (2) goes too far.

---

[18] Frege (1956, 302).

90 THINKING OF NECESSITY

Finally, then, what of option (3), that concepts are abstract modes of presentation? We might say, in Fregean terms, that they are senses that inhabit a third realm that is neither mental nor physical. As Hale (2013, 142) points out, whereas mental entities (option (2)) are contingent and thus seem inadequate as a source or ground for logical *necessity*, according to the option that takes concepts to be abstract modes of presentation the existence of concepts is plausibly no longer tethered to the contingent existence of minded creatures or mental entities. Hence, this immediately looks like a better prospect. Moreover, these senses are connected in important ways to their referents. In simple terms, we might say that sense determines reference.

Hale discusses Peacocke's more precise notion of a *determination theory* for each concept: 'a theory of how the semantic value of the concept is determined from its possession conditions (together with the world)'.[19] But the core idea is the same: there is a systematic connection between concepts *qua* abstract senses and the reference or semantic value of those concepts. One might hope, therefore, that this systematic connection between concepts and the world makes the view favourable to TRUTH, whilst at the same time being able to explain THOUGHT in terms of these concepts with which we think.

Hale argues that, at least on Peacocke's theory of concepts, this connection between concepts and their semantic values results in the natures of the semantic values, i.e., the truth functions that are the semantic values of our logical concepts, wearing the metaphysical trousers when it comes to the grounding of logical necessities.

> While we might, speaking somewhat loosely, present [Peacocke's] theory as tracing the necessity of the principle of conjunction elimination back to the concept of conjunction, it is really the semantic value of the concept (i.e., the truth-function itself) which plays the key role in explaining necessity: the concept of conjunction ... determines ... a certain truth-function, and because that truth-function takes the value truth only if both its arguments do, it is impossible for a conjunctive propositional content to be true without both of its conjuncts being true. (Hale, 2013, 143)

Setting aside the details of a particular version of the view, such as Peacocke's, I think we can see in quite general terms why this third version of ELC provides no advance on the first two options.[20] On a view according to which concepts are abstract senses, those senses determine referents or semantic values in a systematic way, such that the truth value of propositions or thoughts composed of those

---

[19] Peacocke (1992, 17), cited in Hale (2013, 142).
[20] For more detail on Peacocke's view and Hale's discussion of it, see Peacocke (1992); Hale (2013, 141–3).

senses is systematically related to the behaviour of those referents. Hence, when it comes to the necessary truth or otherwise of a proposition or thought, the ultimate ground or explanation will lie in the natures of the referents, rather than the nature of the senses, i.e., in the natures of the logical functions, say, rather than in the nature of the logical concepts. As such, ELC collapses back into ELF and faces the same challenges.

One might respond that, in fact, ELC makes progress on ELF, because these logical functions now bear systematic relations to our thoughts, i.e., they are determined by the concepts of which our thoughts are composed. However, this raises some difficult questions. The appeal to concepts was supposed to provide an explanation of THOUGHT: because we use concepts to think, our capacity for thought is constrained by the nature of those concepts. Conceptual and logical necessity, if they have their sources in the natures of concepts, and particularly logical concepts, should be expected to be intimately connected to what we are able to think using concepts. However, it now turns out that in order to properly accommodate TRUTH we need to make appeal to the fact that these concepts determine their semantic value and, in turn, that it is the nature of that semantic value that in fact is the source of necessity, not the concept. Hence, on this view it would seem that we accommodate both TRUTH and THOUGHT, and thereby resolve the tension between them, only by equivocating. i.e., TRUTH is accommodated by a view according to which logical necessities are true in virtue of the nature of the logical functions, which are the semantic values of our logical concepts, and THOUGHT is accommodated by a view according to which logical necessities are true in virtue of the nature of our logical concepts, which we use in thought. Hence, TRUTH and THOUGHT are in fact not shown to both be accommodated by one and the same account of the source of logical necessity.[21]

4.3.3 Conventionalism

Conventionalism, broadly speaking, holds that the source of logical necessity is in linguistic or semantic conventions that govern the meanings of our words and sentences. To give a well-worn example, it is a mere linguistic convention that the word 'bachelor' means the same as the expression 'unmarried male'. But, given the associated conventional semantic rules for these expressions, it is necessary that if something is a bachelor, then it is an unmarried male. Again, it is a mere convention that the word 'and', when conjoining two sentences, produces a true sentence if and only if the two sentences conjoined are both true; we may well have chosen the word 'or' or 'if' to have such a meaning. So, one might think

---

[21] Some essentialists might be happy to build an hybrid view out of this conclusion, but more trouble lies ahead. See Keefe and Leech (2018); Leech (2022b).

92 THINKING OF NECESSITY

that a conventionalist account of logical necessity could adequately accommodate both TRUTH and THOUGHT. TRUTH, because it is due to these conventions that necessary *truths* arise, for example, 'All bachelors are unmarried'. THOUGHT, because we can only express ourselves using language, so the expression of our thoughts is bound by these (conventional) linguistic rules, and to suppose that there are thoughts inexpressible by language is implausible, or at least requires significant defence.

One might think that conventionalist approaches to necessity were debunked long ago by Quine (1936/1976; 1963/1976). Nevertheless, there remain some defenders, such as Alan Sidelle. Setting aside the wider debate over the merits of and problems for the conventionalist view, I focus here on the potential of conventionalism to meet the present challenge. First, I discuss a potential objection to conventionalism being able to account for THOUGHT, the answer to which will provide help elsewhere. Second, I present the decisive blow; it is not convention that accounts for either the truth or the necessity of necessary truths, and so convention is nothing more than a red herring—our explanation of TRUTH must lie elsewhere.

The first worry is based on the contingency of convention.

> According to Conventionalism, what is necessary, or essential, is so because of our conventions, our ways of conceiving and/or talking about the world. But our conventions, whatever they are, might have been different. If so, the Conventionalist must admit that what is necessary or essential might not have been so. But, then, it is not really necessary or essential then! So conventionalism is false. (Sidelle, 2009, 224)

If correct, this is clearly a significant problem for the conventionalist. At best, they will either have to find a response to the objection, or find a way to justify denying the S4 axiom (that whatever is necessary is necessarily necessary). Setting aside these wider concerns, though, one might worry what this means for THOUGHT. The challenge was to explain why it is not possible for thinkers like us to rationally doubt logical necessities. Suppose these necessities are to be understood as linguistic conventions and the consequences of these conventions. Suppose these conventions are also contingent. Presumably, part of the reason we take them to be contingent is because we can clearly and easily conceive of them being otherwise: we can perfectly well conceive that things had gone differently, such that 'bachelor' meant the same as 'costermonger', and that had that been the case, it could often have been false, of some bachelor, that he was unmarried, being a married costermonger. Moreover, perhaps we don't even need to use our imaginations. There are cases where words change their meanings over time. 'Nice' is a particularly nice example, having variously meant over the course of history

THE SOURCE OF LOGICAL NECESSITY   93

'timid, faint-hearted' as well as 'precise, careful', which are hardly synonyms.[22] But now it seems hard to fathom how such apparent necessities could be taken to be immune to rational doubt. They are quite straightforward to doubt.

This way of posing the objection risks overstating the problem. Indeed, a beginner to English may very reasonably and rationally doubt whether 'bachelor' and 'unmarried male' mean the same; they don't yet have any knowledge about these expressions and their relations to any other expressions of English. The point is rather that a competent speaker of English may perfectly well know the rules associated with these two expressions and yet be perfectly rational in accepting that they might have been otherwise, and hence that it might not have been true that all bachelors are unmarried males.

Sidelle (2009) offers what seems to me to be a convincing response to the contingency worry. He asks us to consider a possible situation where, indeed, the convention for 'bachelor' is different, such that it applies to anyone—woman or man—who has never been married. In that situation, according to that convention, 'All bachelors are male' would be false, as would 'Necessarily, all bachelors are male'. However, Sidelle crucially asks *how* we should describe this possible situation, given our actual situation and actual linguistic conventions.

> How should *we* describe this situation? Is [unmarried] Linda a female bachelor? Of course not—someone counts as a bachelor only if they are male. Our rules for applying 'bachelor' tell us that one must be (give or take) 'a never-been-married, but eligible male'—so *ipso facto*, the rules tell us that what rules the speakers *in* that world use is quite irrelevant to whether or not someone is a bachelor. They are no more relevant than the rules of Spanish if we are, in English, describing a situation in Mexico.   (Sidelle, 2009, 229)

---

[22] **nice (adj.)**

late 13c., 'foolish, ignorant, frivolous, senseless,' from Old French *nice* (12c.) 'careless, clumsy; weak; poor, needy; simple, stupid, silly, foolish,' from Latin *nescius* 'ignorant, unaware,' literally 'not-knowing,' from *ne-* 'not' (from PIE root *ne- 'not') + stem of *scire* 'to know' (see **science**). 'The sense development has been extraordinary, even for an adj.' [Weekley] – from 'timid, faint-hearted' (pre-1300); to 'fussy, fastidious' (late 14c.); to 'dainty, delicate' (c. 1400); to 'precise, careful' (1500s, preserved in such terms as *a nice distinction and nice and early*); to 'agreeable, delightful' (1769); to 'kind, thoughtful' (1830).

> In many examples from the 16th and 17th centuries it is difficult to say in what particular sense the writer intended it to be taken.   [OED]

By 1926, it was pronounced 'too great a favorite with the ladies, who have charmed out of it all its individuality and converted it into a mere diffuser of vague and mild agreeableness.' [Fowler]

> 'I am sure,' cried Catherine, 'I did not mean to say anything wrong; but it *is* a nice book, and why should I not call it so?' 'Very true,' said Henry, 'and this is a very nice day, and we are taking a very nice walk; and you are two very nice young ladies. Oh! It is a very nice word indeed! It does for everything.'   [Jane Austen, 'Northanger Abbey,' 1803]

https://www.etymonline.com/search?q=nice.

94 THINKING OF NECESSITY

We can only describe counterfactual scenarios using our own language. When we do so, the rules of our own language apply. It doesn't matter if the counterfactual scenario we are describing involves language users adhering to different linguistic rules; we can still only describe that in our own terms. As such, from our perspective, in any scenario, all bachelors are male, even if the locals happen to use the word 'bachelor' differently.

The contingency of conventions, then, is somewhat of a red herring. And, indeed, this kind of response can be employed in combatting a similar challenge to a Kantian approach. If one takes logical and metaphysical necessity to have their sources in the laws of thought and of objective thought respectively, as I shall propose, then one might reasonably ask, couldn't *those* laws have been different? Couldn't there have been radically different thinking beings, with radically different constraints on their thought? Whether or not we can make sense of such a proposal,[23] we may now stand ready with an answer: what matters is how *we* can think of alternative situations and scenarios, and in all of those scenarios our necessities hold steadfast, given that they have their source in the very conditions under which we are able to think about anything at all.

There is, nevertheless, a more serious objection to conventionalism: conventions do not determine what is true, nor what is necessary, they merely determine what it is that a sentence says (what proposition it expresses), and it is what it says (the proposition) that is true (or not) and necessary (or not). At a first step, conventions allow us to transform one truth into another, but they do not account for that truth. For example,

> [A] convention to the effect that, say, 'bachelor' means, or is to mean, the same as 'unmarried man' enables us to transform 'No bachelor is married' into 'No unmarried man is married'. But it is simply a confusion to suppose that the convention is what makes the former statement true. If that statement is, or expresses, a necessary truth, that is because it is a definitional contraction of another necessary truth—the logical truth that no unmarried man is married— the necessity of which is not to be accounted for by reference to that convention.
>
> (Hale, 2013, 117–18)

The next step, then, is to consider the status of the more basic necessary truths into which we may transform others via conventional definitions, and whether we can account for *them* in terms of convention. There are familiar problems with how to account for a potential infinity of necessary truths in terms of convention, which I will not repeat here.[24] I wish to focus on what to make of the basic necessary truths, setting aside whether they can proliferate in a suitable manner.

---

[23] See, for example, Davidson (1974); Conant (1992).
[24] See Quine (1936/1976, 1963/1976).

The issue is whether we can simply stipulate or otherwise engender a convention for some sentence S to be true (or to express a truth), where it is *the convention* that explains the truth of S. What does the convention do? It sets the meaning of S. Perhaps some semantic rules for the constituents of S are specified. In any case, in setting the meaning of S, the conditions under which S will be true are determined (even if that turns out to be, in all circumstances). But, importantly, it is not now the *convention* that determines that S is necessarily true, it is the truth condition with which it is conventionally associated. Hale makes the point better than I can.

> The objection rests upon two claims: first, that only what has a (more or less) determinate content—in the sense, minimally, that it is associated with some (more or less) definite condition for its truth—can be true or false; and, second, that once a declarative sentence is thus associated with a truth-condition, it is— already, as it were—an objective and independent matter whether that condition is or is not fulfilled, so that there is simply no room for a stipulation to settle its truth-value. (Hale, 2013, 120–1)

I demanded above that an adequate account of logical necessary should be able to resolve the tension between THOUGHT and TRUTH. It turns out that the conventionalist may appear to do so only because they are explained by very different things. THOUGHT is accounted for in terms of conventions, as described above, but TRUTH is not; the explanation of the latter is provided, if at all, by the nature of the truth conditions with which our sentences are (conventionally) associated, and not at all by the conventions themselves.

4.3.4 Constitutive norms

I have argued that neither the essentialist nor the conventionalist accounts of logical necessity just considered can meet the challenge to relieve the tension between THOUGHT and TRUTH. Can the view developed earlier in this chapter— that logical necessity has its source in constitutive norms of thought—fair better?

If the laws of logic are constitutive norms of thought, and we understand logical necessity in terms of logical laws, then there is a straightforward explanation of why THOUGHT holds. If the laws of logic are constitutive norms of thought, then one counts as thinking only insofar as one's activity counts as right or wrong as evaluated against these laws. One will therefore be unable to rationally doubt these laws, because any course of reasoning, such as is involved in any case of rational doubt, only counts as reasoning because it is correct or incorrect in light of, amongst other things, the standards laid down by these laws. We just don't have the mental resources to rationally doubt logical necessities, because rational

96 THINKING OF NECESSITY

doubt itself presupposes the authority and correctness of the laws from which they arise.

What about TRUTH? Why should facts about our capacity for thinking have any consequences for how things must be? Ostensibly there is no such reason why—that is precisely the tension at issue. There are several complementary lines of thought, though, that allow us to accommodate TRUTH.

First, recall what kind of commitment was required by the function of logical modal judgment, namely, a commitment to there being rules of inference that would be *truth-preserving* under any supposition whatsoever. In other words, no matter what, these rules of inference preserve truth. No matter what the premises, if they are true, then whatever conclusion can be reached via the rule of inference, it will also be true. For any rule of inference there is an associated material conditional that is logically necessary just when the rule of inference is necessarily truth-preserving. For example, the rule of Conjunction Elimination— $A \wedge B \vdash A, B$—has an accompanying material conditional of the form 'If A and B, then A'—$(A \wedge B) \supset A$. If the rule is truth-preserving in all circumstances, then the material conditional must be true in all circumstances as well. For suppose that it were false in some circumstance. Then it would be the case that the antecedent of the conditional was true but the consequence false. But the antecedent corresponds to the premise of an argument and the consequent to its conclusion. Hence, this circumstance would also be one in which the premises would be true and the conclusion false, and hence a circumstance in which the rule of inference did not preserve truth. Hence, all logical necessities that derive from necessarily truth-preserving rules of inference are themselves true. At least for any logical necessities of this kind, then, TRUTH holds.

Second, recall that it is logically necessary that p just when $\neg p$ entails a contradiction. Suppose, *contra* TRUTH, that it is logically necessary that p but not true that p. Then it is true that $\neg p$. But since $\neg p$ entails a contradiction, it follows that some contradiction is true. But no contradiction is true. Therefore, we must reject our supposition that it is logically necessary that p but not true that p. TRUTH holds.[25]

Third, there is an argument that piggybacks on the factivity of metaphysical necessity. My Kant-inspired account of metaphysical necessity will be developed in more detail later in the book, but for present purposes, suffice it to note the following. One, everything that is logically necessary is also metaphysically necessary, as is standardly assumed. And two, metaphysical necessity is connected to the conditions of objective thought—thought that succeeds in being about the world—and an explanation of the factivity of metaphysical necessities will be based upon this.[26] With these points in hand, the argument runs as follows:

---

[25] Thank you to an anonymous reader for suggesting this argument.
[26] See Chapter 6, especially section 6.5.

1. If it is logically necessary that p, then it is metaphysically necessary that p.
2. If it is metaphysically necessary that p, then p.
3. Therefore, if it is logically necessary that p, then p.

Therefore, TRUTH holds.[27]

Finally, there is a feature of a Kantian approach that makes it uniquely suited to accommodate both THOUGHT and TRUTH, namely, that it takes seriously the view that conditions of thought might genuinely shape facts about the external world. As just noted, later I will present an account of the factivity of metaphysical necessity that draws on the connection between metaphysical necessity and the conditions of objective thought. The conditions under which we can think about objects, it will be argued, should be taken to have implications for the possibilities and necessities for objects, i.e., for metaphysical modality. Now, the laws of thought in general are not in themselves sufficient conditions of objective thought. Nevertheless, objective thoughts are a species of thought, and hence the laws of thought are amongst the laws of objective thought. Insofar as the laws of thought are included in the laws of objective thought, then, this explanation can be extended to show why not only must all objects conform to laws of objective thought, but also to the laws of logic. If the laws of objective thought are true, as will be argued, then so must be the laws of logic. Hence, we can not only accommodate TRUTH, but also show how its source is closely related to that of THOUGHT. The tension is not merely relieved; THOUGHT and TRUTH share a deep connection.

---

[27] Such an argument could be exploited by any account of modality that takes logical necessity to imply metaphysical necessity, and metaphysical necessity to imply truth.

5

Objectivity and Modality

5.1 A series of bold claims

In this chapter, I shall make a number of bold claims about objectivity and objective thought. I shall argue that thoughts must conform to a set of principles to be objective; that one needs a certain conception of modality in order to grasp a conception of objectivity; and that one needs to grasp a conception of objectivity in order to have objective thoughts, thus introducing an additional constraint on objective thought along with the set of principles. These claims may seem hard to swallow, but they are motivated by taking seriously a deceptively simple philosophical question, indeed, a question that arguably drove much of Kant's theoretical philosophy. How is it possible, how on earth can we make sense of the fact, that mental states—goings on of the mind—get to be genuinely *about* other things out there in the world? As Kant phrased the question:

> What is the ground of the relation of that in us which we call 'representation' to the object?   (Letter to Herz, 21 February 1772)

One might attempt many different approaches to answering this question, but the question itself is philosophically compelling. As Sebastian Gardner puts it:

> Whatever allows reality to be an object for us cannot be merely postulated or taken for granted as a primitive fact—it stands in need of philosophical explanation, if anything does.   (Gardner, 1999, 34)

The intended upshot of this chapter is to argue that there is a kind of modality relative to conditions on objective thought, and that having a conception of that kind of modality is itself a condition on having objective thoughts. In the following chapter, I argue that this modality is best understood as *metaphysical modality*. I then proceed to develop this theory of metaphysical modality and chart out some of its consequences. The argument as a whole, then, promises to show that a concept of metaphysical modality has a fundamental role in our capacity for objective thought, and thereby to assure metaphysical modality a central role in our thinking, rather than being a mere philosophical conceit.

I shall proceed as follows. First, I introduce the Problem of Reality and introduce conditions on objective thought as an answer. I then argue that the

Thinking of Necessity: A Kantian Account of Modal Thought and Modal Metaphysics. Jessica Leech, Oxford University Press. © Jessica Leech 2023. DOI: 10.1093/oso/9780198873969.003.0005

OBJECTIVITY AND MODALITY   99

objective/subjective distinction is not a true dichotomy, and that in fact there is a third option of being neither objective nor subjective (nonjective). I argue that in order to grasp this three-way distinction, one needs modal concepts, and in particular, concepts of a kind of modality relative to conditions on objective thought. Next, I argue that we need a conception of objectivity in order to have objective thoughts. From which it follows that we need the selfsame conception of modality in order to have objective thoughts. One could probably write a whole book on each of these steps alone. My aim here is draw together these threads to weave an account of a deep-set function for modal concepts and judgments.

5.2 The Problem of Reality

In 1772, Kant famously wrote a letter to Markus Herz. In that letter, he posed a question which is often taken to mark the beginning of Kant's critical turn: 'What is the ground of the relation of that in us which we call "representation" to the object?' Kant is puzzling over how representations—in particular, mental representations "in us"—are able genuinely to represent—to bear a suitable relation to—objects out there in the world.[1] In his commentary on the *Critique of Pure Reason*, Gardner takes Kant to be introducing 'The Problem of Reality'.

> There is, we naturally suppose, a real world. The proposition that there is such a thing as reality is one that can scarcely allow itself to be doubted. We suppose, furthermore, that reality is known or in principle knowable to us, if only in part. Reality is then naturally conceived as that which fundamentally explains how objects of experience and thought are possible for us.
>
> Now in order for reality or any part of it to become known to us, some sort of condition must obtain whereby it becomes an *object* for us. As it may also be put, something must bring it about that the objects composing reality *appear* to us. But the question is: what makes reality into an object for us?
>
> (Gardner, 1999, 33–4)

Although such a question informs Kant's thinking, it is not confined to Kantian philosophy and Kant commentary. In contemporary philosophy of mind, for example, Naomi Eilan asks 'how is objective knowledge possible from within the perspective of consciousness?' (Eilan, 1997, 236). And Michelle Montague asks 'how do we achieve access to the things with which we stand in mental intentional

---

[1] What about representations of *ourselves*? Kant allows for a kind of self-knowledge and self-representation which treats the self as an object of experience, roughly, a unity of the various mental states we can observe in ourselves. These goings on are not "out there in the world". But I use this informal way of speaking to try to keep a complex discussion more tractable. I thus set aside self-knowledge and self-representation for the time being. Thank you to Koshka Duff for raising this point.

100 THINKING OF NECESSITY

relations?... What mechanism determines what a thought or perception is of?' (Montague, 2013, 27) (she labels this 'The Access Problem'). Eilan and Montague tend to answer the question for perceptions rather than thoughts, but they both formulate the problem as general. Further back, William James recognizes the existence of the problem, although he thinks that his Radical Empiricism can dissolve, rather than solve, it.

> The first great pitfall from which such a radical standing by experience will save us is an artificial conception of the *relations between knower and known*. Throughout the history of philosophy the subject and its object have been treated as absolutely discontinuous entities; and thereupon the presence of the latter to the former, or the 'apprehension' by the former of the latter, has assumed a paradoxical character which all sorts of theories had to be invented to overcome.
>
> (James, 1912, 52)

From the perspective of cognitive science, Jackendoff (1991) raises the same kind of question, which he also calls the Problem of Reality.[2]

> What is the relationship of the mind to the world, such that we can have knowledge of reality, such that we can have beliefs and desires about things in the world, and such that our sentences can be true or false?
>
> (Jackendoff, 1991, 411)

This way of framing the problem of reality, including the notions of truth and falsity, raises the question whether one can understand the problem in terms of correctness and incorrectness of certain states. Perhaps not all mental states are *truth*-apt, although other states may be accurate or inaccurate, or otherwise correct or incorrect. What would be crucial to a version of the problem of reality, though, is that this correctness or otherwise is determined by how things are with reality. So, for example, my belief that grass is green is true not only because grass is green, but because the belief is *about* grass. Or, my perception of the spoon in the water as being bent is inaccurate not only because the spoon is in reality straight, but also because the perception is *of* the spoon.

---

[2] Jackendoff distinguishes two versions of his problem: the "Philosophical" version, which I quote in the main text, and the "Psychological" version: 'How does the brain function as a physical device, such that the world seems to us the way it does, and such that we can behave effectively in the world?' (Jackendoff, 1991, 412). Jackendoff argues that we should favour the psychological version of the problem. He gives a series of examples where, he argues, the psychological version makes better sense than the philosophical version. His criticisms mostly turn on it not making sense to take various states as being *true* or *false*, and hence that the philosophical version of the problem does not make sense in these applications. Although, as can be seen, his own statement of the philosophical version of the problem is not the question of how *any* state gets to be true or false, but rather specifies only such a question for *sentences*. It is not clear, therefore, that his criticisms hit the mark by his own lights. In any case, I won't pursue this further here. My point is simply to indicate the importance and wide-ranging significance of the problem of reality. Note also: Jackendoff observes (p.413) that his view can be traced back to Kant.

OBJECTIVITY AND MODALITY   101

That said, I think we shouldn't frame the problem of reality simply as a problem of how states get to have correctness conditions in general, or how they get to be truth-apt. This would be to frame the problem too broadly. For we should leave open that there may be states that are not objective (not about the world), and so to which the problem of reality does not apply, but which nevertheless have correctness conditions of some kind. Later in this chapter, I will argue that there can be thoughts that are neither subjective nor objective, that lack correctness conditions determined by "reality", but that can nevertheless be held to other (logical) standards. I will also suggest that subjective thoughts are trivially correct, but not so as to imply that they have no correctness conditions (rather, one might think that their correctness condition—being thought—is trivially fulfilled). So, although when states that are about reality have correctness conditions determined by reality, we might use that as a way to highlight the problem of reality, we should not take that to be the problem itself. Note also that in the examples given, the puzzle that came out was not so much the *correctness or incorrectness* (truth or falsity) of the state, but rather the role that the states being *about reality* played. Although correctness conditions are part of the picture, and indeed will play a role in my argument, at heart the problem of reality is one of the relation between mind and world.

Our guiding question then is:

What is the relationship of the mind to the world such that our mental states are or can be about the world?

What makes this problem particularly difficult is that any attempt to explain the relation between mind and world seems already to presuppose a prior relation between mind and world, which is in turn what the question is asking us to explain.

We might think of the relation in two directions: how the world could present itself to the mind, or how the mind could reach out to the world. In the first case, we might think of the mind as passively receptive to the world, with reality 'impressing itself on our minds' (Gardner, 1999, 34). The question then is: how and why is the mind appropriately receptive to this input from the world? What accounts for the mind responding in the right way? There must be some features of minds that make them peculiarly suited to representing the world that impresses itself upon them, in distinction to other things which might also be in the presence of reality but *not* be so affected. (Bluntly put: a rock and a person might stand in the same—so far as we can tell—causal relations to a tree, but only the person, not the rock, ends up with a representation of the tree.)[3] It is then hard to see how

---

[3] Of course, a human person, unlike a rock, has all sorts of sense organs and brain structures, etc., which will be causally affected by the tree. But it is still (supposed to be) a mystery how those causal

102 THINKING OF NECESSITY

we might specify those special features without reference to the world or reality, i.e., without reference to the relation that the mind stands in to the world already. Indeed, one can see this idea emerging where some theories of how objective perception is possible make reference to the perceiver's *relation* to the world. For example, Susanna Siegel argues that the contents of object-seeing experiences include representation of subject-independence and perspectival connectness. That is, those contents *include* the conditionals '(SI) If S changes her perspective on *o*, then *o* will not thereby move', and '(PC) If S substantially changes her perspective on *o*, her visual phenomenology will change as a result of this change' (Siegel, 2006, 358). Those conditionals lay out a relation between the subject and the object of her perception.[4]

In the second case, we might think of the mind as actively reaching out to reality. The mind isn't some kind of inert wax tablet that waits for reality to come along and impress itself upon it, to make itself known; rather, the mind actively seeks out a world to represent. This might seem to solve the kind of problem sketched above; the mind is an active representer, where the rock is not. However, 'in order for our minds to reach out and read off the features of reality, we would have to know how to locate and read it—and again this condition could not be fulfilled unless reality were already an . . . object for us' (Gardner, 1999, 34). This time, the concern is that the mind won't be able to actively represent the world without some guidance or rules for what it is doing, if successful representation is going to be anything more than luck. Metaphorically speaking, the mind will need some kind of 'road-map' for getting in touch with reality in the right way. Again, it seems hard to see how we might understand this active capacity for representation without reference to some prior relation between mind and reality.

To sum up: the puzzle is how the mind is particularly suited to genuinely represent the world, and how the world is particularly suited to being represented by the mind. Any attempt to explain the relation between mind and world seems to presuppose a prior relation between mind and world, which itself calls for explanation.

So the problem of reality leads to an impasse: the broad ways we might seek to answer it seem already to presuppose a relevant relation between mind and world. Thus enters Kant's famous 'Copernican' hypothesis.

---

relations, in turn, make something (some neural structure, say) *about* the tree, as opposed to just standing in some causal relations. This is not to refute a causal theory of perception, just to articulate why one may find the general approach puzzling.

[4] See also, for example, Brewer (1997, 44): 'Although one does not figure as one object among many on a par with those one perceives in the normal way, their spatial relations with oneself are nevertheless displayed in perception. It is the actual spatial relations between the things one perceives *and oneself* which determine whether where they seem to be is where they really are. Thus, *it is in relation to oneself that things are perceptually presented* as determinately located' (latter emphasis added).

OBJECTIVITY AND MODALITY 103

> Hitherto it has been assumed that all our knowledge must conform to objects. But all attempts to extend our knowledge of objects by establishing something in regard to them *a priori*, by means of concepts, have, on this assumption, ended in failure. We must therefore make trial whether we may not have more success in the tasks of metaphysics, if we suppose that objects must conform to our knowledge.   (Bxvi)

Given the set up, the thought is a simple and natural one. If potential answers to the problem of reality presuppose a prior relation between mind and world—if the problem is insoluble, but also demands an answer—perhaps the lesson is that something went wrong in our posing of the problem in the first place. We ought not to assume an unbridgable 'epistemological chasm' (James, 1912, 67) between mind and world. The broad proposal here is to embrace the assumption that there is a prior relation between mind and world. We ought not to try to understand the mind and reality utterly independently, and then to inquire into how they come to be related. Instead, the way that we understand mind and world from the outset should already build in the relation between them.

There are two directions here, again. In following this broad proposal, one might think that we can require *either*, in our understanding of the mind, that the mind is already in touch with reality in some way, *or*, in our understanding of the nature of reality, that reality is inherently intentionally or epistemically accessible to the mind. If either one will do, one might then reasonably think that the former option is more plausible. That merely requires us to build into our philosophy of mind an account of mental states in terms of relations to reality, perhaps following approaches such as those we have already seen from Siegel (2006) and Brewer (1997). But the Kantian idea is stronger. It is that *both* putative directions are needed. We also need to understand reality as something that is in general epistemically accessible. Why? Suppose we start with the mind. We first consider the nature of our capacity for mental representation, and what conditions a mental state must fulfil in order for it to be objective; really about the world. But then, if that state is really about the world, the world must also be such that those conditions are necessary and sufficient for a representation to be about it. They turn out to be constraints *both* on the mind *and* reality. To give a brief example: we saw earlier that Siegel claims that certain conditionals be included in the content of objective perceptions, but note that the conditional (SI)—'If S changes her perspective on *o*, then *o* will not thereby move'—has consequences for the behaviour of objects (i.e., movement). And of course, Kant himself took conditions on possible objective cognition to also constitute conditions on what the world of which we can have cognition is like (B161).

The guiding idea, then, is to favour a conception of reality that already builds in intentional and epistemological considerations. The very notion of what it is to be part of reality, or an object (broadly understood), must include the possibility of

104 THINKING OF NECESSITY

our being able to think about it.[5] The sceptic might (and does) retort: 'it's perfectly plausible that there could be tracts of reality that, in fact, we really can't think about, so your epistemically loaded conception of reality is hopelessly impoverished'. However, such a sceptic faces their own challenges. First, to explain how it is that the bits of reality that we *can* think about come to be objects for us at all, that is, they still face the problem of reality for at least some of reality. Second, to untangle the paradox of how they seem to be thinking—even non-specifically—about parts of reality that cannot be thought about. In such a context, the Kantian suggestion that we should simply do away with a conception of reality as independent of our capacity for thinking about reality, and replace it with a conception that builds in an answer to the problem of reality, is—it seems to me—liberating. *Just don't worry* about the idea of a reality that we couldn't even think about in our wildest imaginings; how could that possibly be relevant to our understanding of and engagement with the world? This is not to say that purported thoughts "about" a reality that fails to conform to the conditions under which reality can be an object for us are *nonsense*. As introduced in Chapter 2, Kant allows that non-objective thoughts are still meaningful. We just shouldn't make the mistake of taking them to be objective, to be really about objects in reality, on pain of falling into serious error.

So, what must reality be like in order for us to be able to represent it? What must our mental states be like in order for them to count as objective? These questions, I have suggested, are two sides of the same coin. Kant's method was to start by considering the nature of our cognitive capacities and the conditions which a mental state would need to fulfil for it to be objective, and from there to conclude that reality—reality that can be an object for us—must be as those conditions require. The reader may be disappointed that my aim here is not to develop a full set of specific epistemic conditions for mind and world; that would be to attempt to recreate the first half of the *Critique of Pure Reason,* for which I have neither the space nor the capacity. For want of a better alternative, I will occasionally borrow Kant's conditions on objectivity to flesh out examples. These include conditions such as:

All objects are in space and time.

Every event has a cause.

---

[5] Note: the idea here is not that all concepts that can apply to reality explicitly build this in such that, for example, our concept *rock* becomes *thinkable-rock.* Rather, our conception of "the world" or "reality" must build in intentional considerations. One could say that our concept *reality* does become something like *thinkable-reality.* Or, one could say that a proper conception of reality should have been the latter concept all along.

OBJECTIVITY AND MODALITY   105

The one condition that I *will* seriously develop and defend is—unsurprisingly—a *modal* condition on objectivity.

Objective thoughts must be represented as being objective-possible.

This will be elaborated on in what follows.

In brief, Kant argues that objects must be presented to us in space and time, that they have a determinate part-whole structure, a determinate degree of their qualities (e.g., temperature, density, etc.), and conform to a framework of substances instantiating properties standing in causal and reciprocal relations. I will not attempt to defend or re-engineer these claims, but here is a sketch of why at least some similar conditions might seem plausible. What many of these conditions require is a certain kind of *unity* to the reality that we represent: objects are contained within a single unified spacetime, in a certain part-whole structure, and stand in causal and reciprocal relations to everything else, directly or indirectly. Could we make sense of a reality that was genuinely disjointed? One might think not, for two (reciprocal) reasons. First, if the mind is a unity, then to represent two distinct realities would be to represent them as at least somehow related.[6] (Compare how difficult it is genuinely to conceive of distinct spacetimes unconnected by any spatiotemporal distance, or to conceive of David Lewis's plurality of worlds as not like a universe of spatiotemporally related planets.)[7] Second, if we made sure to avoid this backdoor relation between realities, and achieved two genuinely unrelated thoughts of two genuinely unrelated realities, this would undermine the unity of the mind, which, I have argued, is a necessary condition of any thought at all (Chapter 3). So, our representations of reality—and hence, given the proposed framework, reality itself—must be unified in some way. Spatiotemporal, mereological, and causal relations seem to be plausible candidates for the kinds of relations that might unify reality.

In addition to these conditions, Kant also introduces modal conditions (otherwise this book would be very different): objects must be really possible, and their states must stand in necessary connections. As noted in my summary of Kant's views (Chapter 2), these conditions are strikingly "meta", making reference to the conditions of objectivity taken together. For an object to be really possible (for a concept to be of something really possible), it must to conform to conditions of objectivity; and for a state to be really (materially) necessary, is for it to follow from prior actual states, given conditions of objectivity. These state, in effect, that

---

[6] It doesn't follow that they are causally, spatiotemporally, or mereologically related—further argument would be required for that. But at least we have the starting point that there is a kind of unity to the reality that we can experience.

[7] According to Lewis (1986), possible worlds are sums of spatiotemporally related individuals. Worlds do not bear any spatiotemporal relations to each other.

106   THINKING OF NECESSITY

objective thoughts and the reality they are about must conform to conditions of objectivity. So far so unsurprising. However, Kant makes the stronger claim that we must be able to *represent* these modal conditions; we need to be able to represent things as possible and necessary as an *additional* condition on objective thought. (And on the other side, of course, reality also has these modal features.) The remainder of this chapter will build on the framework sketched so far, to mount an argument that we do indeed need certain modal concepts—and the ability to make modal judgments using those concepts—as a(nother) condition on objective thought.

We can combine this idea of conditions on objective thought with a general framework for defining relative modalities, to define modalities that are relative to conditions on objective thought. Recall, in general, one can define a relative necessity in the following way.[8]

Relative□   It is Φ-necessary that p iff $\exists\phi(\Phi\phi \wedge \Box(\phi \to p))$

It is Φ-necessary that p if and only if there are some suitable Φ-propositions which strictly imply p, i.e. which imply p as a matter of logical necessity. If we take the Φ-propositions to be propositions expressing conditions on objectivity, where '$O\phi$' means 'it is a condition (or conjunction of conditions) of objectivity that ϕ', then we can offer a definition of what I will call 'objective necessity' as follows.

Objective□   It is objective-necessary that p iff $\exists\phi(O\phi \wedge \Box(\phi \to p))$

There are two options for a formulation of the accompanying notion of objective possibility as a kind of relative possibility.

Objective◇   It is objective-possible that p iff $\neg\exists\phi(O\phi \wedge \Box(\phi \to \neg p))$

Objective◇*   It is objective-possible that p iff $\exists\phi O\phi \wedge \forall\psi(O\psi \to \neg\Box(\psi \to \neg p))$.

Either: it is objective-possible that p if and only if there are no conditions on objectivity that rule out p. Or: it is objective-possible that p if there are conditions on objectivity and none of them rule out p. For present purposes, we do not yet need to choose one formulation: we just need in view the idea of modalities defined relative to conditions on objectivity. There are further important details and complications yet to be worked out, which I will address in due course. For example, I have not yet clarified whether the conditions of objectivity are formal, material, general, or otherwise. My aim here is to motivate the importance of such modal concepts; in later chapters, I give a fuller account of them.

---

[8] See Chapter 2, section 2.4. See also the caveats on p.35, footnote 35, and further discussion in Chapter 10.

5.3 Objective, subjective, neither

So far in this chapter, I have been putting things broadly in terms of mental states. In what follows, I narrow my focus to consider *thoughts*. There are many different kinds of mental states, and I don't wish to make claims about them all. In particular, I wish to avoid debates about the objectivity of perception—how it is that perceptual states succeed in being about the world (although I still take the examples canvassed above to be helpful). I suspect the right kind of answer here is a complex mixture of philosophy and neuroscience that will take me far beyond my present aims. I also wish to avoid debates over the extent to which perceptions are, or depend upon, thoughts with conceptual content. My aim is to argue that a certain kind of conceptual ability is required for objective thought: it seems to me that this kind of claim, if applied to less intellectual states such as perception, is significantly more controversial. And I don't need to make an even *more* controversial claim than I'm already attempting. I take *thoughts* to be constituted by concepts unified into something like a propositional form. So, for example, there can be the thought that *modality is interesting*, but not the thought that *Socrates interesting man*. It is uncontroversial that thinking, in this sense, requires a set of conceptual abilities—thoughts contain concepts. My aim is to argue for certain conceptual abilities needing to be part of that package for objective thoughts: a conception of modality, via a conception of objectivity.

The first step of my argument is to argue that there is not an exhaustive distinction to be made between objective and subjective thoughts, but rather that some thoughts can fail to be either objective or subjective. Existing definitions of 'objective' usually define 'subjective' first, then 'objective' as 'otherwise', or vice versa. However, non-objective thoughts don't always have to be subjective, and non-subjective thoughts don't always have to be objective. There is something wrong with these definitions and the shared assumption that generates them.

Rather than defend one particular approach to defining objectivity or subjectivity, instead I will canvass a selection of influential and interesting accounts. We will see that they all allow for cases of non-subjective, non-objective thoughts.

In his discussion of Strawson on objectivity, Anil Gomes identifies two familiar candidate notions of objectivity, both of which take for granted an exhaustive distinction between subjectivity and objectivity.

Ontological: 'something is objective when it doesn't depend for its existence on minds, and subjective otherwise.'

Perspectival: 'whether or not something is objective turns on the extent to which it is tied to our point of view; things are objective to the extent that they are independent of a subject's point of view and subjective otherwise.' (Gomes, 2016, 947)

108 THINKING OF NECESSITY

Elsewhere, Peacocke takes an intuitive notion of *minimal objectivity* to be the following.

Minimal: 'A thinker's being in the state, or enjoying the event, does not in general make the content of the state or event correct.' (Peacocke, 2009, 739)

The definition is given in negative terms, contrasting with the case where a thinker's being in the state, or enjoying the event, *does* in general make the content of the state or event correct. This looks like a definition of subjectivity: a subjective thought is held to no "external" standard distinct from the thought itself, and so a thinker's having the thought is enough for it to be correct. Minimal objectivity, defined negatively against this, is then just a lack of subjectivity.

Eilan (1997, 238) notes that 'there are any number of conceptions of the subjective/objective distinction', and distinguishes in particular two (which she takes from Bernard Williams) which for our purposes line up approximately with the perspectival and minimal distinctions, as well as recognizing a third, *normative,* distinction.[9]

Normative: 'the realm of the subjective is the realm of the normative, the realm of meaning, value, and so forth ... the realm of the objective [is] the realm of the brute, meaning-free world.' (Eilan, 1997, 248)

The ontological definition, as applied to mental states or thoughts, is immediately puzzling, for surely *all* mental states, and in particular all thoughts, depend for their existence on minds. But the definition is not intended to render all states trivially subjective. One might clarify that it is the *content* of the thought that does or doesn't depend for its existence on minds. But again, it's not clear that this captures our intended distinction. Suppose, for the sake of argument, that the thought that *Port Talbot is in Wales* is objective, and the thought that *the Welsh countryside is beautiful* is subjective. In what sense does the *existence* of the latter content depend upon minds and the former not? Perhaps the answer is supposed to be something like: beauty is a property that things have entirely dependent on the reaction of certain kinds of minded beings, hence, if something is beautiful, that implies the existence of minds. Maybe so, but it's not clear that the *content,* rather than the *truth,* of the thought is what therefore depends upon minds. For, one might make all sorts of claims about minds and mind-related properties,

[9] Eilan mixes and matches conceptions of the subjective and the objective to answer her guiding question: 'how is objective knowledge possible from within the perspective of consciousness?' (Eilan, 1997, 236). She argues that the answer requires a combination of subjectivity understood in the perspectival and normative ways, and objectivity understood in terms of representations that are neither incorrigible nor evident. In a way, this can be read as agreement with my conclusion here, that we should not understand 'subjective' and 'objective' as mutually exhaustive and exclusive, insofar as she takes the key notions to be independently defined. However, she nevertheless appeals to three distinctions that *do* appear to be understood as exclusive and exhaustive.

without any of them ever being true. For example: *there are minded-creatures in the world, dogs have minds, there is beauty in the world,* and so on. And it seems that some of those claims should be understood as objective—such as the claim that there are minded-creatures—whether true or false. If it's really the *content,* and not the truth, of subjective thoughts that depends upon minds, then it seems we are led into a certain kind of account of content whereby claims about, say, beauty, which imply some kind of relation to minded-creatures, are not only dependent for their truth on the existence of minds, but would in fact be *meaningless* without the existence of minds to contribute to their content. This would imply that we can't even think subjective contents without there being minds to which we, or other things, bear certain relations. Given these difficulties and complications, from now on I will set the ontological version of the distinction to one side.

I am also hesitant to put too much weight on the normative version of the distinction. That would seem to build in a commitment to various philosophical positions about meaning and value. But we may wish to remain undecided about, for example, whether there is objective value in the world, whilst still being able to grasp what the issue is about, i.e., grasp a distinction between the objective and the subjective that doesn't already decide the debate. Henceforth, I shall focus on the perspectival and minimal distinctions as those that do best to capture *prima facie* plausible subjective/objective distinctions.

My main argument here is as follows. Given an intuitive and plausible sense of the target notions of objectivity and subjectivity, it seems plausible that a thought in general could fail to be objective and fail to be subjective. Moreover, read with this intuitive target notion in mind, both the perspectival and minimal versions of the distinction plausibly allow for thoughts that are neither objective nor subjective (as long as we give up the "subjective/objective otherwise" clause). As such, we should conclude that the distinction between the objective and the subjective is not an exhaustive one: there is a third case of neither objective nor subjective thoughts. For ease of reference, I shall call such cases 'nonjective'.[10]

David Wiggins also rejects defining 'subjective' and 'objective' in terms of each other.[11]

---

[10] See footnote 51 on p.48.

[11] Wiggins defines 'subjective' and 'objective' for a subject matter, not for a mental state, but this feature of his discussion is still interesting and instructive. He also includes the following pleasing historical note:

> *Historical note. The Oxford English Dictionary* under 'objective' says this. The scholastic philosophy made the distinction between what belongs to things *subjectivē* [Latin adverb] or as they are 'in themselves' (on the one hand) and (on the other) what belongs to them *objectivē* [Latin adverb] or as they are presented to consciousness. In later times the custom of considering the perceiving or thinking consciousness as pre-eminently 'the subject' brought about the different use of these words which now prevails in philosophy [and which prevails in our proposals]. According to this, what is considered as belonging to the perceiving or thinking self is called 'subjective' and what is considered as independent of the perceiving or thinking self is called in contrast 'objective'.
>
> So 'objective' and 'subjective', as it were, changed places!
>
> (Wiggins, 1995, 246, Wiggins's square brackets)

110 THINKING OF NECESSITY

> The opposite of 'objective' is 'non-objective'. It remains to be seen what the relation is of non-objective to subjective. (Wiggins, 1995, 244)

> Clearly the 'objective'/'non-objective' contrast and the 'non-subjective'/'subjective' contrast are two *different*, albeit connected, contrasts. (Wiggins, 1995, 247)

Although, the consequence that Wiggins notes is rather that the distinction may therefore fail to be *exclusive*.

> If we define 'objective' positively... and we define 'subjective' positively... then it will be an open question whether some moral question might be both subjective *and* objective. (Wiggins, 1995, 249)

My aim here is to argue that the subjective/objective distinction is not *exhaustive*. I am working under the assumption that it is probably exclusive, although I do not believe it would be a significant problem if it turned out that some thoughts are both objective and subjective—the key point for my argument is that some are *neither*.

Suppose that objective thoughts are in some sense "about" or "beholden to" the world, and subjective thoughts are in some sense to do with a subject. Considering first the perspectival option: it seems plausible that a thought could be independent of a subject's point of view without thereby succeeding in being objective in this rough and ready sense. The content of a thought may not be 'tied to our point of view', and yet *also* fail to say something about the world. For example, some philosophers think that so-called 'category mistakes' are neither true nor false because they fail to say something truth-apt about the world. Such a philosopher might not think that *The number 2 is rocky* is a subjective matter—it's not a matter of a subject's point of view—but, assuming it is a category mistake, neither is it the right kind of content to be true or false of the world.[12] However, it's also still an intelligible thought—we understand what it's supposed to mean, even if as a consequence of that we understand that it's making a particularly strange kind of claim. Conversely, a thought could surely lack whatever it takes for thoughts to be about the world without thereby becoming beholden to a particular point of view. Considering the same example: if certain kinds of category mistake debar a thought from representing the world as being a certain way without rendering it nonsensical, surely this doesn't also thereby turn it into something perspectival.

Turning to the minimal option: let us assume that thoughts have correctness conditions—conditions under which a thought counts as correct. The idea driving this argument is that objective thoughts have correctness conditions that are

---

[12] The point is not that thoughts about numbers are not objective, but that category mistakes are not, i.e., numbers just aren't the kinds of things that should be thought of as rocky or not rocky. This is not my considered view on category mistakes: it's just an example.

determined by how the world is. For example, the thought that *Wales is hilly* is correct or not depending on how things are with the world, i.e., depending on the terrain of Wales. And, plausibly, part of what it is for that thought to be *about Wales* is the fact that it is how things are with Wales that determines whether or not it is correct. Importantly, just thinking that Wales is hilly isn't enough for Wales to *be* hilly; these kinds of correctness conditions are not trivially fulfilled. This is then different to the correctness conditions of a subjective thought which *are* trivially fulfilled. For example, if you think that beauty is a subjective matter, then for a subject S to think that Wales is beautiful, if *Wales seems beautiful to S, is* sufficient for the correctness of the thought.[13] The key point I want to make here is that, *prima facie,* there is no reason to think that having correctness conditions that are not trivial is immediately to have correctness conditions that are determined by how the world is. Just because a thought is not *trivially* correct, this does not tell us anything about the nature of those non-trivial correctness conditions that it has instead. There are other kinds of correctness conditions that are not trivial, but equally are not obviously determined by the world. For example, candidate *logical* correctness conditions, such as being non-contradictory, or being logically true. If a thought had these kinds of correctness conditions and no others, then they need not be trivially fulfilled (I might have a contradictory thought, or a thought that is not logically true). But nor does their fulfillment seem to *require* any relation to how the world is (it may be logically true that *all unicorns are unicorns,* regardless of whether claims about unicorns are objective). Moreover, I have already argued that the laws of logic are laws of thought, so logical correctness conditions are not determined by the world.

Note: when I say that objective thoughts are "about the world", they could of course be about minds, or selves, and so on. What is important is that such thoughts treat what they are about as something intuitively "separate", about which one might get things wrong, even if it is a mind, or even one's own mind. There may be tricky cases here, but the main thrust of the point is that a thought may be neither objective nor subjective; I'm not claiming that the line between objective and subjective itself is clear cut.

It seems to me that taking the distinction between the objective and the subjective to be exhaustive betrays a problematic underlying assumption, namely, that thoughts (perhaps mental states more generally) *default to objectivity* if the threat of subjectivity is removed. But that would seem to imply that the objectivity of a thought—its making a claim about the world—does not require the satisfaction

---

[13] Examples of purported subjective thoughts need to be treated with care. I can entertain the proposition that *Wales is ugly* in thought without Wales being ugly. e.g., I might be thinking about how Wales might be if it was bulldozed and turned into a giant car park. A more developed account of the nature of subjective thinking needs to build in that, for example, such a thought is only subjective when Wales seems beautiful to one, or similar. I will not be able to offer that more developed account in detail here; my focus is on characterizing the objective and its distinction from the nonjective.

of positive, substantive conditions (beyond the negative condition of avoiding subjectivity). Subjectivity, on this assumption, is the only barrier to objectivity. However, on the contrary, one might think that objectivity is an *achievement*. Indeed, I already argued in section 5.2 that one attractive response to taking seriously the problem of reality is the view that thoughts must meet certain conditions in order to be objective. Those conditions might include or entail not being subjective, but it is unlikely that simply not being subjective is going to be enough of a condition on objective thoughts.

This kind of division will also have implications for our thinking about truth. Given the framework just sketched, it seems plausible to say that an objective thought is true just when it correctly represents the world. If this was all there was to truth, however, then nonjective and subjective thoughts couldn't be true, because they don't represent the world (for different reasons). However, subjective thoughts were not supposed to be false or not true; on the contrary, they are trivially true. And we may have reason to allow that some nonjective thoughts are true as well. All this is to say that, on the picture I am introducing, we will have to think about truth in a more inclusive way than correspondence with the facts of the world.

5.4 Objectivity and modality

Thus far, we have a series of kinds of thought which is more fine-grained than an exhaustive subjective/objective distinction. I will put it here in terms of correctness conditions rather than perspective. Briefly:

Subjectivity: Correctness of a thought is, in general, guaranteed by the thinking of the thought.

Non-subjectivity: Correctness of a thought is not in general guaranteed by the thinking of the thought.

Objectivity: Correctness of a thought depends upon whether the world is how the thought represents it to be.

Nonjectivity: Neither objective nor subjective.

If a nonjective thought is neither objective nor subjective, it follows that the correctness of the thought is not in general guaranteed by the thinking of the thought, and also that the correctness of the thought does not depend upon whether the world is how the thought represents it to be. I suggested that a remaining candidate for the correctness conditions of a nonjective thought might be logical conditions.

Nonjectivity*:   Correctness of a thought depends upon merely logical features of the thought.

To recall: I am not here taking 'thought' to be co-extensive with 'belief', where occurrent belief may be understood as a kind of thought which aims at the truth (or perhaps knowledge, which in turn entails truth). Thoughts, I noted earlier, are constituted by concepts unified into something like a propositional form. Such a characterization, in and of itself, does not specify any *attitude* towards that conceptual unity, nor one's aim in thinking it. Many thoughts might aim at the truth of their content (and so perhaps count as (occurrent) beliefs), but others may involve a different attitude towards the content. Perhaps in the minimal case of merely entertaining a proposition, one holds no attitude at all towards the content which one is thinking. Is ambivalence or non-commitment an attitude or a lack of attitude? I'm not sure. In any case, one might simply entertain that p (perhaps as a premise in speculative reasoning, perhaps as a disjunct or as part of a conditional), and thereby think that p without the mental equivalent of assertoric force. Nevertheless, if the thought is *objective*, then there is something about the *content* of the thought; it is correct only if it corresponds to reality in the right way. This is distinct from the correctness of an *attitude towards* a content, such as believing, disbelieving, supposing, etc. Quite obviously, if p, then S's belief that p is correct whereas T's disbelief that p is incorrect, even though both are thoughts of p. In this chapter, and in particular in the argument to follow, I'm concerned with correctness conditions as they connect to the *contents* of thoughts. We might—if we like—further distinguish between attitudes towards those contents in terms of further distinctions between correctness conditions for mental acts, rather than mental contents, but I'm not going to do that here.

The aim of this section is to argue that, whilst a two-way distinction between the objective and the subjective could be made and grasped non-modally, that is, without requiring the resources of modal concepts, we need modal concepts to make and grasp a three-way distinction that accommodates thoughts that are neither objective nor subjective, i.e., a distinction between the objective, the subjective, and the nonjective.

What kind of conceptual resources are required to grasp a two-way distinction between objectivity and subjectivity? Well, concepts of *objective* and *subjective*, one might glibly reply. Fair enough, if you find that answer satisfying. But the question is rather: what kind of conceptual leap would be required for a thinker, hitherto unable to grasp such concepts, to come to grasp them? The proposed answer is: something like a distinction between *actual* and *non-actual*, or *truth* and *falsehood*, or *appearance* and *reality*. Some conceptual resource that captures the idea that a thought may represent things as being a certain way, and yet things not be that way.

114 THINKING OF NECESSITY

I don't think one needs to describe the relevant conceptual resources further; one can make the same point with each example. Peacocke's approach to defining minimal objectivity nicely captures the idea that there is an important sense in which subjective states *can't be wrong*. If one thinks (subjectively) that *p*, then it is actually the case that *p*, or it is true that *p*; if it appears (subjectively) to be that *p*, then it really is that *p*. So, for example, if one thinks that the cake is delicious, or the cake appears to you to be delicious, that just is sufficient for the cake actually or really to be delicious.[14] *By contrast*, if we assume that non-subjectivity is sufficient for objectivity, objective states are *not* like that; they *can* be wrong. So, for example, if one thinks that this this is a chocolate cake, one may be mistaken (perhaps it looks like one, but is in fact parkin). In which case, one may think that this is a chocolate cake, but it is not actually so, or, one's thought is false; although it appears to you that the cake is chocolate, in reality it isn't. It is the *non-subjective* thoughts that risk this kind of error, and so in conceiving of non-subjectivity we need some kind of conceptual resource to capture that; to capture a difference between the actual and the non-actual, or the true and the false, or appearance and reality, or correctness and error.

One might also be tempted to conclude that those conceptual resources also already contain *modal* concepts. For the idea, it seemed, was that subjective states *can't*, objective states *can*, be wrong. And indeed, one might argue that the perspectival and minimal options for defining objectivity also—and unsurprisingly, if these resources are modal—draw on modal concepts, insofar as *dependence* and *making something so* can be construed as modal notions. Nevertheless, I think this is wrong. It is tempting, although misleading, to explain things modally. The key idea is that of *sufficiency*: in the subjective case, the thought is sufficient for its actuality or truth (appearance is sufficient for reality), whereas in the non-subjective case it is not sufficient. One can capture this sufficiency in terms of a conditional without requiring modal resources: *if one thinks (subjectively) that p, then it is actually the case that p, or it is true that p; if it appears (subjectively) to be that p, then it really is that p*. It is tempting to then define the non-subjective in terms of the *possibility* of error, but really all that is required, given the assumption of a dichotomy, is negation of the definition of subjective: non-subjective thoughts are thoughts for which their mere existence is insufficient for their correctness.

I conclude that in order to grasp a two-way distinction between the objective (non-subjective) and the subjective one needs to be able to grasp something like a distinction between actual and non-actual, or truth and falsehood, or appearance and reality.

But I have also argued that this two-way distinction is inadequate, resting on a faulty assumption. I have suggested instead that to properly capture the notion

---

[14] As noted earlier (footnote 13, p.111) such examples of subjective thought need to be treated with care.

of objectivity we need to acknowledge a *three-way* distinction between thoughts that are objective, those that are subjective, and those that are neither. However, the conceptual resources of a mere two-way distinction, as just discussed, are not going to be sufficient to capture this three-way distinction. Our question now, then, is this: what kind of conceptual leap would be required for a thinker, hitherto unable to grasp the concepts of *objectivity*, *subjectivity*, and *nonjectivity*, to come to grasp them? More particularly, the conceptual resources outlined above—actual/non-actual, etc.—are sufficient to grasp a distinction between the subjective and the non-subjective. For trivial correctness/actuality/truth/reality was what characterized the subjective, and so the negation of this captures the non-subjective. Our task then is to introduce the additional kind of conceptual resources required to further distinguish, amongst the non-subjective thoughts, the objective and the nonjective.

Returning to our rough and ready characterization of our target notions: objective thoughts succeed in being about the world, non-objective thoughts do not. What kind of difference is that? For one thing, you might suppose that whether an objective thought is correct or incorrect (true or false, if you like) depends upon whether the world is the way it represents the world to be, whereas whether a non-objective thought is correct or incorrect does not depend upon how the world is, because the thought does not succeed in making a claim about the world. At a first pass, then, we might say: objective thoughts *could be rendered correct by the world*, non-objective thoughts *could not*. Objective thoughts are the kind of thought that *can be* made correct by the world. This is, in effect, a modal way of cashing out the different kinds of correctness conditions of these different kinds of thoughts, in terms of the possibility of rendering a thought correct—what could render a certain kind of thought correct. Unlike the case of subjectivity above, though, that modal explication does not appear to be superfluous. Subjectivity was understood in terms of sufficiency. The proposal here is that objectivity is a matter of possibility. Part of the point arising from the subjectivity discussion was that, put one way, there's no need to grasp the idea of a subjective thought's *possible* correctness, for if it exists, it is correct. This is not so for non-subjective thoughts. If we just needed to classify them as the shadow of subjective thoughts, negatively, then we wouldn't need to introduce further conceptual resources. But once we need a more *positive* characterization of different kinds of non-subjective thought, this is where we need to introduce new—I suggest, *modal*—conceptual resources which capture that possibility of correctness or incorrectness and, in addition, the kinds of conditions that could make different non-subjective thoughts correct.

Are modal resources really needed here? Rather than saying that when we understand a thought to be objective, we understand that it *could be* true, perhaps we only need to say that when we understand a thought to be objective, we understand that it *is* true or false depending on how the world is. However, in a way, my point here is that taking a thought to be such *is* to draw on modal

116   THINKING OF NECESSITY

conceptual resources. There is a modal conceptual leap here. Why? Note that *objectivity* does not imply correctness (or truth) in particular, and it does not imply incorrectness (or falsity) in particular. It captures the idea that whether correct or incorrect, whatever the truth-value, this depends on how things are with the world (that the thought purports to represent). So it is not so much a categorical feature of the thought with which we are concerned here, e.g., its being true, but rather a range of alternatives for the thought. We might express this as a disjunction: 'it is true or false, depending on...'. It is perhaps better captured by our earlier gloss: '*whether* it is true or false depends on...'. Truth and falsity (correctness and incorrectness) are each *possibilities*, in some sense, for the thought, and which is actual depends upon how the world is. So although this way of framing our grasp of a concept of objectivity does not wear its modality on its sleeve, I contend that it nevertheless involves a modal conceptual leap: correctness is a possibility for the thought in an important sense.[15] If we are to take that leap, let us take it straightforwardly, and say that an objective thought could be true (of the world). It might appear that this ignores the possibility of falsehood, but in what follows we shall see that a certain kind of falsehood is not appropriate for objective thoughts. So it is just as well to leave it out of our grasp of objectivity.

There remains in this line of thought, however, a serious ambiguity. The phrase 'could be rendered correct by the world' has two very different readings. (1) A reading according to which it means 'the world determines whether the thought is correct'. So, for example, even if the thought expresses something impossible, such as $2 + 2 = 5$, it may still be the world that determines that this is incorrect, i.e., because of how the world is, the thought is false. (2) A reading according to which it means 'the thought could be true of the world'. So, for example, according to this reading, as the thought that $2 + 2 = 5$ could not be true of the world, the thought is not simply false, it is *not objective.*

I'm going to argue that we should opt for (2). First, notice that the modality introduced in (2)—a modality according to which a thought *could* or *could not* be true of the world—is just the notion of objective modality introduced in section 5.2, namely, a modality relative to conditions on objectivity. For objective thoughts conform to the conditions of objectivity, hence are not ruled out by those conditions, and so are objective-possible. And non-objective thoughts do not conform to the conditions of objectivity, and so are objective-impossible. To clarify: it is the *content* of thoughts that is objective or not, and so the content that is possible or not, relative to conditions on objectivity. So we end up with something like (2): the content of an objective thought is objective-possible; the

---

[15] 'Whether' is arguably a modal term, although I cannot defend this at length here. At least one entry for 'whether' in the OED defines it in terms of alternative possibilities: '*whether...or* = whichever of the alternative possibilities or suppositions be the case...' (OED). Lewis (1982) also takes a 'whether'-clause to present a set of alternatives captured in a possible worlds semantics.

content of a non-objective thought, and so in particular a nonjective thought, is not objective-possible.

The main bar, as I see it, to endorsing this view—that we grasp a distinction between objectivity and nonjectivity using objective-modal conceptual resources—is that it is a clear consequence that there is a class of impossible thoughts (thoughts with contents that are necessarily false) which are not merely not possibly true, but thereby *not objective*. But one might find this to be utterly wrong-headed: surely a necessarily false thought is, apart from anything else, *false,* and furthermore false because it misrepresents how things are, and *not* because it fails to represent how things are at all. Let us seriously consider this objection.

Begin by considering a thought that violates conditions on objectivity. For example, suppose that a condition on objective thought is that every event has a cause, and consider the thought that *there is an uncaused event.* It is tempting to say: the thought is about the world, but is false because it not only gets the world *wrong,* it gets it *very wrong.* It not only represents the world as being a way it *isn't,* but a way it *couldn't be.* However, if it truly violates conditions on objective thought, then it's a mystery how it can do this. How can the thought be about the world— and misrepresent it at all—if it conflicts with the very conditions under which a thought can be about the world?

This is reminiscent of some of Wittgenstein's remarks in the *Tractatus,* that a condition on a representation of reality (a picture) is that it shares its logical form with reality, and that it therefore depicts a possible combination of reality, i.e., a possible state of affairs.

> 2.18 What any picture, of whatever form, must have in common with reality, in order to be able to depict it—correctly or incorrectly—in any way at all, is logical form, i.e., the form of reality.
>
> 2.201 A picture depicts reality by representing a possibility of existence and non-existence of states of affairs.
>
> 2.202 A picture represents a possible situation in logical space.
>
> (Wittgenstein, 1921, 11–12)

The thought here is that a condition of a representation being about reality is that it shares something with reality; the possible forms that reality can take. Wittgenstein goes further in taking this also to be a condition on *thinkability* (3.02). That is unsurprising, if he takes the relevant notion of possibility here to be *logical* possibility, and if one further takes logic to be intimately connected to thinkability, as I also do. However, where I differ is in taking there to be *extra-logical* conditions also on representation of reality. So long as logical possibility is tied to thinkability, and some other kind of possibility is tied to objective representation, then a failure to cohere with this latter kind of possibility will not render something unthinkable; rather just (objective-)impossible.

118   THINKING OF NECESSITY

Perhaps what makes my proposal seem so puzzling—that necessarily false thoughts are not objective—is a background assumption that the only way a thought could be incorrect, or false, is by misrepresenting the world (and that the only way a thought could be true is by correctly representing the world).[16] If that were so, then taking a nonjective thought to be necessarily *false* would make no sense. But if we give up this assumption about falsity, things are less puzzling. Such a thought is false not because it represents the world as being a way it couldn't be; it is false because it fails to be objective in a particular way. If thoughts are true just when they correctly represent the world, and to be false is to be not true, then one can see that there are at least two ways to be false: to misrepresent the world, but also to fail to represent it at all (and *a fortiori* to fail to represent it correctly).

That said, it is not clear that all nonjective thoughts should count as false. Such thoughts, I have suggested, have logical correctness conditions of their own. One might think that certain logical forms are sufficient for truth or falsity, such as the form of a tautology, or the form of a contradiction. So, in principle, one might have a nonjective thought that otherwise met these correctness conditions. That said, to be nonjective it would have to conflict in some way with conditions of objectivity, and it is hard to think of an example of a logical or analytic truth that could do so. The thought that *there is an uncaused event* is, let us suppose, nonjective. It is false because it fails to represent the world correctly (in virtue of not representing the world at all), and moreover it does not meet any mere logical condition for truth (such as being a tautology). It makes a claim about the world that violates conditions on objectivity—that there are such things as uncaused events. However, consider: *if an event is uncaused, then it is uncaused.* Such a thought does not claim that there *are* uncaused events, and so does not seem to be in conflict with the condition that every event has a cause. And in general, logical and analytic truths tend not to make the kinds of claims that would be in conflict with such conditions.

This way of thinking about truth, falsity, and objectivity will have consequences for how we understand negation. There is a systematic connection between the correctness of p and *not-p*. For example, if it is true that p, it is not true that *not-p*. In light of the present discussion, it looks as though application of negation will also have consequences for the objectivity or otherwise of a thought. If the thought that p is (objective-)necessarily true, then its negation is necessarily false: application of negation will transform an objective thought into a non-objective thought. Conversely, if it is (objective-)necessarily false that p, then it should be true, indeed, *objective-necessarily true,* that *not-p*; if p is (necessarily) incorrect, *not-p* should be (necessarily) correct. But again, this implies that negation can

---

[16] This is also suggested in *Tractatus* 2.21: 'A picture agrees with reality or fails to agree; it is correct or incorrect, true or false.'

OBJECTIVITY AND MODALITY   119

transform a non-objective thought into something objective. Can that be right? Does negation have the power to make the objective non-objective, and to make the non-objective objective?

It shouldn't be news that negation is pretty powerful. For example, if you believe that logical truths make sense whilst contradictions are nonsensical, then you are committed to negation having a power to turn sense to nonsense (i.e., negating a logical truth results in nonsense). I don't endorse this view about contradictions myself, but it does draw out the power of negation to transform. It's uncontroversial that negation can transform necessary truth into impossibility: the negation of a necessary truth is itself impossible. Likewise, if some proposition has a special or important role, it should be no surprise that the negation of that proposition may take on a correspondingly different status. For example, if Alan promises that he will cook tomorrow, then the negation of that content—it is not the case that Alan cooks tomorrow—transforms into something (at least relatively) impermissible.

In light of such examples, if some proposition p plays a role in conditions on objectivity—if it itself expresses a condition on the possibility of objective thought—then we should expect negation to have a powerful transformative effect on p; the application of negation will transform a condition of objectivity into something that immediately violates conditions of objectivity, and hence into something that cannot itself be objective. If, moreover, it is necessary that p, the application of negation to p will have the familiar result of producing something impossible. Putting these two features of p together, the application of negation turns an objective necessary truth into a non-objective necessary falsehood. But these are entirely familiar examples of the power of negation to transform.

To sum up: What is the difference between objective and nonjective thoughts? The former conform to conditions on objectivity; the latter do not. Conformity to conditions on objectivity is a kind of relative possibility; non-conformity to those conditions is a kind of relative impossibility. So our key difference is a modal one: relative (objective) possibility vs. impossibility. We can now sketch a modified set of characterizations of the key terms of our distinction.

Subjectivity: Correctness of a thought is, in general, guaranteed by the thinking of the thought. Thinking of the thought is sufficient for its truth.

Non-subjectivity: Correctness of a thought is not in general guaranteed by the thinking of the thought. Thinking of the thought is not sufficient for its truth.

Objectivity: Correctness of a thought depends upon whether the world is how the thought represents it to be. The thought conforms to conditions of objectivity. The thought is objective-possible.

Nonjectivity: Neither subjective nor objective. Correctness of a thought depends upon merely logical features of the thought. The thought does not conform to conditions of objectivity. The thought is objective-impossible.

120   THINKING OF NECESSITY

These definitions sketched raise a question concerning the modal status of subjective thoughts. Subjective thoughts, insofar as they are not objective, do not conform to all conditions of objectivity. Does that mean they are therefore objective-impossible, such that things could not be that way? How can that be so, if subjective thoughts are, on the contrary, *guaranteed* to be true? This worry stems from a confusion about subjective thought. It is not that subjective thoughts are true, but trivially so, in the same way that objective thoughts are true. If, for example, it is subjective that *the cake is delicious,* this is trivially correct, but it is not *true of* the cake that it is delicious—that would be to make the thought objective. Being delicious, so the thought goes, is not a feature of the cake that we could get right or wrong, but is something to do with, and correct in virtue of, a subject's engagement with the cake. Moreover, if being delicious is, indeed, not an objective feature, then it is, after all, objective-impossible for the cake to be delicious: that isn't a way the cake can *be,* in contrast to a way the cake can *seem.*[17]

The conceptual leap required to grasp the three-way distinction between *subjective, objective,* and *nonjective,* I have argued, involves grasp of something like a distinction between actual and non-actual, or appearance and reality, *as well as* grasp of a modal distinction between what is and is not possible relative to conditions on objectivity. Modal concepts are implicated in our grasp of objectivity.

5.5 Objective thinking

Thus far, I have argued that in order to properly grasp a conception of objectivity, we must not only distinguish it from the subjective, but also from a third category that is neither objective nor subjective. I have further argued that modal conceptual resources are required to do so. In this section, I argue that a condition on our being able to have objective thoughts at all is that we grasp a conception of objectivity. Putting these steps together, the consequence is that in order to have objective thoughts at all, we need modal conceptual resources.

Thoughts have correctness conditions: this much is relatively uncontroversial.

> Thoughts, after all, have contents and, just like utterances, they can be said to be true or false, correct or incorrect, if their contents are. That thoughts have correctness conditions in this sense should, again, be rather uncontroversial.
>
> (Glüer and Wikforss, 2009, 38)

---

[17] We might also ask how to classify mixed-thoughts, made of logical complexes of different kinds of thought, such as *the cake is delicious and it took one hour to bake.* Is that subjective, because the first conjunct is, or objective, because the second conjunct is, or both, or neither (nonjective)? I have already noted that I make no claims to exhaustiveness, so there may be space here for hybrids. Such a thought seems to be *in part* about the world, and in part not, and to have correctness conditions that are likewise a mixture. But I will not pursue this issue in more detail here.

I argued in previous chapters that it is constitutive of thought (any thought) that it is evaluable in light of certain logical conditions, logical laws. These form a first stratum of correctness conditions for a thought. Moreover, I have argued in this chapter, different kinds of thoughts have different (additional) kinds of correctness conditions. Subjective thoughts have trivial correctness conditions. Nonjective thoughts have logical correctness conditions. And objective thoughts have correctness conditions that concern the world: for the content of some objective thought to be correct is, roughly, for it to correctly or truly represent reality, where this is usually a non-trivial achievement.[18]

To reiterate then: objective correctness conditions forge a link between an objective thought and how things are in reality. Our question now is: how does a thought—a mental state—come to have such correctness conditions, i.e., such a link to reality? This is, in effect, a version of the problem of reality introduced earlier in this chapter. The question is how this particular link between thought and reality—a certain kind of correctness condition—comes about. To simply presuppose such a link is to ignore a philosophically important question. We saw a sketch of an answer earlier: thoughts must meet certain conditions to be objective. This section will offer some detail on one condition: thoughts must be *represented as being objective/having objective correctness conditions* in order for them to have such correctness conditions and thereby to be objective. They must be represented as such by the thinker of the thought themselves. Hence, in order to have objective thoughts, a thinker must have a conception of objectivity with which to represent certain of their thoughts *as* objective. This condition is necessary, not sufficient: one might be mistaken about which of one's thoughts are objective. (Indeed, much of the *Critique of Pure Reason* is devoted to showing philosophers where they have gone wrong by mistaking non-objective thoughts for objective ones.)

There are many other questions we might ask about correctness conditions with which I shall not need to engage here. For example, there are differing views on the extent to which correctness conditions usher in a genuine kind of *normativity*. One might think that the very notion of *correctness* is already normative (e.g., Boghossian, 2003, 35), although Glüer and Wikforss (2009) contend that there are notions of correctness in good standing which are not normative.[19] My question here, however, is how a thought comes to have correctness conditions that relate to reality at all, not whether and how those conditions in turn relate to norms.

What, then, might explain how a thought comes to have objective correctness conditions? One might start by asking whether the causal history of a thought

---

[18] Note: the correctness conditions for subjective and nonjective thoughts are distinct. In order to be thoughts at all, both must be evaluable in light of laws of logic. Past that bar: subjective thoughts are true just in case they exist. Nonjective thoughts are true just in case they are logically true.

[19] For example, if thoughts have correctness conditions just when they can be sorted into categories, such as the true and the false, with no further "ought" arising.

122   THINKING OF NECESSITY

determines the kind of correctness conditions it has, for example, the thought must bear some causal relation to the reality which it is about. To properly assess causal theories of intentionality here would be a significant undertaking, going beyond the aims of this chapter. However, I shall offer some *prima facie* reasons to suggest that the causal story is unlikely to be successful.

It seems likely that a certain kind of cause will not be sufficient, and perhaps also not necessary, for a thought to be objective. If one wishes to allow that one can have objective thoughts about matters to which a thought cannot bear a causal relation, e.g., about abstract mathematical objects understood as existing acausally, then a causal condition will not be necessary for objective thoughts. That said, I've suggested that a plausible condition on objective thought, following Kant, might be some kind of causal principle, in which case this point would not stand.[20]

More importantly, it seems that a certain kind of causal condition is not sufficient for objective correctness conditions. First, note that subjective thoughts are also likely to bear causal relations to the part of reality that they concern. For example, if I find the joke funny, then I have (at least) witnessed the joke in some way, which would usually involve some kind of causal relation to it (hearing it, reading it, etc.). Benjamin Jarvis (2012) argues that causal connections are not enough to determine what a representation is of, and hence, what its correctness conditions are.

> Very plausibly, there must be some sort of causal connection between Eugene [a city in Oregon] and a piece of paper in order for the piece of paper to be a map of Eugene. However, the sort of causal connection required is not robust enough to distinguish between those pieces of paper that are maps of Eugene and those that aren't.   (Jarvis, 2012, 7–8)

Jarvis's point is that the difference between a piece of paper that is a map of Eugene and one that is not is teleological, i.e., that one has the end or telos of being a map (in this case, likely due to the intentions of whoever drew it) and one does not, and that the causal connections present are not sufficient to distinguish the two cases. For example, Jarvis sketches a case where Joe decides to draw a map of Eugene from memory, and José the city planner draws a plan for Eugene in which much of the city is to be left as it is. The map and the plan coincidentally turn out to be 'molecule-for-molecule duplicates'.

---

[20] It is an important and interesting question, which I will not be able to properly address here, how to think about the status of mathematical thoughts. On the one hand, it seems clear that they should count as objective: their correctness conditions go beyond mere logical correctness conditions (*pace* logicists), and mathematical truth is an objective, and not plausibly a subjective, matter. If that is so, but if there are also causal and spatiotemporal conditions on objects of thought, that suggests we should not be Platonists about mathematics, i.e., we should not believe in a realm of acausal, non-spatiotemporal entities which mathematics is about. There are many alternatives. Kant's philosophy of mathematics, for example, finds objective mathematical truth in the conditions of objectivity themselves.

> Both Joe's map and José's plan are causally sensitive to the features of Eugene. Indeed, to the extent that Joe's map would work as a map of Eugene, so would José's plan.... The two products are qualitatively identical, and thus could be swapped without making a difference. Nonetheless, the piece of paper Joe produces is a map while the piece of paper José produces is a plan. What fixes that Joe's product is a map while José's is a plan is the respective teloi of the two products.... The only causal properties that are particularly relevant here are the etiological properties—in particular, having been created with certain intentions—that fix the teloi of the products.   (Jarvis, 2012, 8)

In general, it is plausible that there are such cases where two things have similar qualities, and importantly, similar causal connections, but differ in their representational properties. Hence, causal connections are not sufficient to determine representational properties. This gives us strong reason to doubt that in the case of a mental state, the causal connection it bears to reality will be sufficient to determine its representational properties, in particular, whether it has objective correctness conditions.

The above gives us a clue to the next option, which is an *intentional* account: objective thoughts have correctness conditions that depend upon reality in the right way because we somehow *take* our thoughts to have such correctness conditions.[21] Consider the case of a barometer.[22] A working barometer represents atmospheric pressure; it is correct or incorrect, accurate or inaccurate, depending on whether and how well its states correspond in a predictable way to atmospheric pressure. The correctness conditions, that is, depend on something beyond the state of the barometer itself. However, there is nothing in and of itself that makes the barometer represent pressure in this way. The causal connection between pressure and the states of the barometer—the fact that the medium inside the barometer is caused to expand and contract by changes in local atmospheric pressure—is not sufficient to determine that the barometer is *representative of* pressure. (I assume the causal connection in this case is necessary.) The changes in the medium alone no more represent a change in pressure than, when I travel by aeroplane, my flimsy plastic water bottle does when it crumples during landing. What plausibly makes a difference is: the barometer represents atmospheric pressure *because and when we take it to*. At some point we noticed the relation between volume of medium and atmospheric pressure and exploited it to make devices that represent atmospheric pressure. (Similarly, there are circumstances where I may well take the crumpling of my bottle to represent a change in pressure.) We might offer a similar account about how our thoughts come to have

---

[21] *Pace* Jarvis (2012), who argues that intentions are not necessary for the teloses in terms of which he proposes an account of representation.

[22] See Leech (2021f, 11–12).

124 THINKING OF NECESSITY

correctness conditions that depend on something beyond the existence of those states themselves. Causal covariance with the environment is not enough. Our thoughts are objective *because and when* we in some sense take them to have objective correctness conditions.[23]

What about the conditions on objective thought that I introduced earlier, in response to the problem of reality? The thought there was that if we take seriously the problem of reality, we must acknowledge epistemic conditions on objects about which we can think and, by the same token, those conditions will constrain what thoughts are about reality. Conformity to these constraints will *allow* thoughts to be about reality; there is no longer the problem of how the mind and reality could be suited for one to represent the other. However, insofar as those conditions specify what reality must be like and must be represented to be like, e.g., causally integrated, they fail to answer the present question concerning how the representations come to have correctness conditions determined by reality. This final step, I contend, is to be offered by this intentional account. Thoughts that otherwise conform to conditions of objective thought are not barred from being objective, but they must *also* be *taken* to be objective.

Taking a thought that p to be objective, taking it to have objective correctness conditions, might be understood specifically or generally: as taking the thought that p to be correct *just when p*, or taking it to be correct *depending on how things are with reality*. I will argue for the latter. We should understand the conceptual resources required by taking a thought to have objective correctness conditions to be the *general* conceptual resources needed to think of objective correctness conditions.

It is plausible that grasping a thought involves either grasping or knowing or otherwise having some awareness of its correctness conditions. Even if correctness conditions are not constitutive of the meaning of a thought, they surely bear some close relationship to it. At the very least, as Boghossian puts it, 'whether one is thinking correctly depends upon what one is thinking, on the content of one's thought' (Boghossian, 2003, 35). In some cases, one might expect a thinker to grasp the specific correctness conditions of their thought. For example, it would be strange if one could think that *grass is green*, but have no grasp of the fact that whether this is correct depends upon how grass is, i.e., whether or not it is green. Think of it this way: to think that p is at least to be able to represent things as being such that p (even allowing for different attitudes towards p, e.g., supposing that p,

---

[23] Compare William Child on Davidson: 'Why should possession of beliefs require possession of the concept of objective truth? The central thought is that there is a crucial difference between a subject with beliefs and a system which simply interacts in complex causal ways with its environment—a mere information processor. And the idea is that the key difference between a system which has beliefs and one which merely processes information is that something with beliefs can itself make sense of the distinction between how things seem to it and how they really are' (Child, 1996, 16). Note that Davidson/Child go straight to an appearance/reality distinction here, which I have argued is inadequate to capture the notion of objectivity.

desiring that *p*). But to represent things as being such that *p* is just to represent how things would be if the thought that *p* was correct. It seems a mystery, then, how one could think that *p* without thereby grasping the correctness conditions of that thought. Note that this not only concerns the particular content of the thought that *p*, but quite generally: in grasping that *things being such that p* are the correctness conditions for one's thought, and not merely *thinking that p* (assuming that *p ≠ I think that p*), one thereby grasps that one's thought has correctness conditions that depend upon how things are with reality beyond one's own thoughts. So in grasping a thought, and in grasping its correctness conditions, one grasps that it has objective correctness conditions.

This story so far may seem reasonable in some cases, but difficulties arise with difficult-to-grasp contents, all in their own way connected to some kind of *externalism about content*. In such cases, it is unreasonable to expect a thinker to be able to fully or explicitly grasp the correctness conditions of their thought, and they therefore would not be able to take their thought to have its specific correctness conditions. However, if in possession of suitable conceptual resources, they would be able to take their thought to have objective correctness conditions *in general*. This move allows us to honour the considerations just adduced— that a thinker should have some kind of awareness of the correctness conditions of their thoughts—without rendering this requirement unreasonably and overly demanding. This is not to suggest that *all* mental content, or all thought content, is to be understood as external (or "wide"). Nor will I engage in detail with the vast literature on externalism about mental content. My focus here will be on three key kinds of examples.

Externalism about mental content is the view that in order to have certain kinds of mental representations, one must bear a suitable relation to the environment.[24] There are many more specific varieties and applications of externalism. I will be drawing on examples connected to three different varieties: *natural kind externalism, social externalism,* and what I will call *infinite externalism*.

Natural kind externalism is the view that the content of our natural kind concepts depends upon the features of the natural kinds to which we refer with those concepts, features which require empirical investigation to discover. Such a view as applied to natural kind *terms* was made famous by Kripke and Putnam.[25] But one can transpose the familiar examples to illustrate the view as applied to thoughts and concepts.[26] According to such a view, a natural kind concept such as *gold* has as its content the chemical substance picked out by that concept. That substance is the element with atomic number 79. But one can perfectly well, it seems, grasp the concept *gold*, and think of gold as being a yellow metal, without grasping that it is an element with atomic number 79. (Indeed, whenever I write about this example

---

[24] See Lau and Deutsch (2019).   [25] See, e.g., Putnam (1975); Kripke (1980).
[26] See, e.g., McGinn (1977).

I always need to double-check the atomic number, let alone when I used to think about gold before I learned enough chemistry to understand anything about the difference between elements and compounds, and atomic numbers.) Given that the content of the concept is *element with atomic number 79,* thoughts containing the concept *gold* will include this in their correctness conditions. For example, if I think that *this ring is made of gold,* that thought is correct just when this ring is made from the element with atomic number 79. But, as noted, I may well think this thought without grasping that particular correctness condition, if I am ignorant about the chemical composition of gold. This may bar me from being able to grasp the *particular* correctness conditions of my thoughts about gold.[27] But it is left open that I could grasp that my thoughts about gold—at least the objective ones—have correctness conditions that depend upon how things are with reality, e.g., with what the ring is made of.

To clarify: sometimes we contrast the external content of a natural kind term with something like an internal "conceptual" content. So, e.g., the concept that accompanies my use of the word 'gold'—a word that refers to (samples of) the element with atomic number 79—might be *yellow metal.* The meaning of the word might mismatch with some of the ways we (perhaps mistakenly) tend to think about gold. My suggestion here is not to overrule this picture and change what we say about the conceptual accompaniment of the use of natural kind terms. Rather, I present a mental analogue, where we have thoughts about gold, understood as *that stuff,* where its true nature may require empirical discovery. There are interesting questions concerning how this concept relates to our concept of *gold as a yellow metal* and to the word 'gold', but these are not my concern here. The crucial point is that some of our concepts have external (or wide) content.

Second, *social externalism* is the view that the content of some of our concepts depends upon how they are used by other thinkers in our social context, and not just on ourselves and our own minds. The most obvious cases are those where the content of a concept is determined by some kind of theoretical expertise which is not available to all thinkers in the community. The classic example originates with Burge (1979). The concept *arthritis* is of a condition of the joints only, but a

---

[27] One could respond: I can very well grasp that my thought that *this ring is made of gold* is correct just when this ring is made from gold, relying upon the externally determined content of my concept *gold* to provide an accurate grasp of the correctness conditions of this thought. It seems to me, however, that if such a response is successful to this extent, then it simply raises difficult problems elsewhere. e.g., placed on Twin Earth, I may be able to exploit this externally determined content in order to correctly ascribe to myself the thought that *this is a gold ring,* even though a corresponding concept in the minds of Twin Earthers, expressed by the word 'gold', picks out a substance UVW rather than element 79. But I wouldn't, in an important sense, know what thoughts I was thinking—thoughts about element 79 or thoughts about UVW. I might be guaranteed grasp of the correctness conditions of my thoughts, and accurate self-ascriptions of my thoughts, at the cost of really knowing which thoughts I'm thinking at all. In any case, I will suggest that the thinker doesn't *need* to grasp the particular correctness conditions of their thoughts; we can go general. So we can avoid problems arising from this option, such as they are. Thank you to Bill Brewer for discussion.

non-expert thinker may think that she has arthritis in her thigh, thereby assuming that arthritis can also affect the thigh (bone and muscle). It doesn't seem reasonable to think that such a thinker fails to think about arthritis *at all*: it is just that she doesn't know very much about the details of the condition, perhaps beyond that it causes a certain kind of musculoskeletal pain, not knowing the particulars of how it affects joints (and only joints). When consulting a doctor who explains that the pains can't be arthritic, a perfectly reasonable response from our thinker would be: 'Oh, I thought I could have arthritis in the thigh as well, but I was wrong. I've learned something new today about arthritis'. She might *also* realize that in thinking about the pain in her thigh, she's thinking of something that isn't arthritis, but that doesn't exclude that she was *also* thinking about arthritis. Again, we have a kind of case where a thinker can think thoughts using a concept—*arthritis*—without being able to grasp the correctness conditions of those thoughts. Before her trip to the doctor, our thinker did not grasp that her thought that *I have arthritis in my thigh* would be correct just in case she had a certain condition of the joints in her thigh (which is not the case, so the thought is incorrect). Nevertheless, it is open that she grasped that the correctness of her thought depends on how things are with reality, e.g., how things are with her thigh.

Third, a slightly different case arises from Kripkensteinian rule-following considerations. I can't summarize the general point better than Lau and Deutsch (2019).

> Roughly, the argument is that our usage of any linguistic expression must be finite in that the term has only been applied to a finite range of cases. But the meaning of a term prescribes its correct application in infinitely many other novel situations that we have not encountered before. A skeptic can therefore come up with different theories of what we mean by the term, theories that accord with our past usage, but whose prescriptions in the novel situations diverge from one another. According to Kripke's Wittgenstein, all physical facts about our limited linguistic dispositions or cognitive capacities are finite in character. They are not sufficient to determine which of the skeptic's theory gives the correct meaning of the term we use. This goes to show that there are no intrinsic facts that determine the meaning we associate with the term. If this argument is valid, the same is true of the contents of our thoughts and concepts. According to Kripke, this skeptical argument shows that we cannot "speak of a single individual, considered by himself and in isolation, as ever meaning anything." Instead, it is argued that meaning and content can only be justifiably ascribed to an individual when considered as a member of some linguistic community.

So, for example, suppose that some thinker Mark, like us all, has only ever had a finite number of thoughts about (what we shall assume for now is) addition. Let us suppose he's had all of the thoughts concerning sums of two numbers under 100.

128　THINKING OF NECESSITY

And let's suppose they've all been correct. So, for example, he's (purportedly) thought that *two plus two is four*, and that *five plus seven is twelve*, but not that *one hundred plus two hundred is three hundred*. Are all of these thoughts of Mark's, along with the fact that they were all correct, sufficient to determine that he was thinking about *addition*, rather than some other function, say, *schmaddition*, according to which any "sum" (schmum?) concerning at least one number greater than or equal to 100 makes 100?[28] In general, we can cook up any number of spurious functions that *might* be picked out by the concept *plus* in Mark's thoughts, depending on which cases he has and hasn't yet encountered. The problem is that it seems that no finite amount of thinking about adding—which is all Mark can do, being a finite being—is enough to determine exactly which function he's thinking about, i.e., which correctness conditions apply to Mark's thoughts. The proposed general solution is again externalist in flavour: it is the linguistic and conceptual community in which Mark finds himself that determines which rules are in play, which correctness conditions apply to Mark's utterances and thoughts about addition. But again, the details of this community may not be immediately apparent to a competent thinker within that community. So, it may be that Mark is a perfectly competent thinker of thoughts about addition (not schmaddition or quaddition), without grasping the infinite detail of the correctness conditions of these thoughts. But again, it is open that Mark takes these thoughts to have correctness conditions that depend upon reality in general.

I have sketched three cases where the content of a concept—and so the correctness conditions of certain thoughts containing it—depends upon external factors that may not be known to a competent thinker, i.e., a thinker who is still able to think thoughts using such concepts. Rather than demanding that thinkers be able to grasp the correctness conditions of such thoughts—and thereby undermining the externalist intuitions in these cases, or the ability of thinkers to think these thoughts—we can allow a weaker condition: Thinkers don't need comprehensive knowledge of external content, but only to be able to take their thoughts to have a certain kind of correctness condition in general. That is, they take the thought to be correct or not depending on how things are with reality, beyond their simply having the thought. As a consequence, just having the thought is not sufficient to make the thought correct; hence, one accesses a distinction between thoughts that are, and are not, correct, given conditions beyond the having of the thought.

So, I have suggested so far that objective thoughts are objective in part because we take them to have objective correctness conditions, and that this involves a general, and not always a specific, grasp of those conditions. Taking a thought to be objective is a necessary, but not a sufficient, condition for the thought to

---

[28] I've used 'schmaddition' rather than 'quaddition' because I've changed the example from the classic Kripkensteinian one.

OBJECTIVITY AND MODALITY   129

be objective. For there are other conditions on objective thought, as we saw in a response to the problem of reality. This means that taking a thought to be objective is defeasible: there may be cases where a thinker takes their thought to be objective but they are mistaken, because the thought violates some other condition of objectivity. And after all, it seems reasonable that we are not omniscient about what matters are objective or not.

Is taking the thought that p to be objective itself a distinct objective thought, i.e., the thought that p *is objective*? If so, regress threatens. For, in order to be an objective thought, it must itself be taken to be objective by means of a further objective thought, which must itself be taken to be objective, by means of yet another objective thought, and so on.

If taking the thought that p to be objective is any kind of distinct thought, it's hard to see how it could fail to be objective. For, as we just saw, one can be correct or incorrect about whether the thought is objective, depending on how things are with the thought. There is no trivial correctness, so it is not subjective, and these correctness conditions are not merely logical, so it is not nonjective.

Is the regress vicious? Mere regress, in and of itself, is not necessarily a bad thing. However, I fear in this case it would be. We are dealing with finite thinkers here. Such thinkers just aren't capable of thinking an infinite number of thoughts each time they want to think a single objective thought.

The problem here stems from assuming that taking a thought to be objective is a *separate* mental act to thinking the thought itself. If each objective thought takes *itself* to be objective, then no regress threatens. There is just one thought. I propose to cash this out as follows: objective thoughts are not of the form p, but of the form *it is objective that p,* where the prefix *it is objective that* captures the idea that whether or not it is the case that p depends on how things are in reality. We might equally express the prefix as *it is (objective-)possible that p.*

To this it may well be objected: we *don't*, usually, think *it is objective that p*: we just think that p. We don't, as a matter of fact, constantly have explicit thoughts about objectivity. I think this is exactly right. We must then temper the view: it is not that all thoughts *do* include as a prefix *it is objective that*, but rather that we have the *ability* to add to any objective thought: *it is objective that....* It will not have escaped the reader's notice that this is very similar to Kant's 'I think'; Kant's claim is not that we *always and explicitly* prefix our thoughts with *I think*, but rather our ability to do this is constitutive of the unity of our thoughts. Likewise, an ability to prefix our thoughts with *it is objective that* is constitutive of our tacitly taking those thoughts to have objective correctness conditions, and hence that ability is a necessary condition of those thoughts being objective.

A further question: I have proposed that a necessary condition of a thought being objective is that it be taken to be objective, but *taken to be objective by whom*? I have assumed that this would be by the thinker themselves, and indeed, to avoid regress I have folded this into the content of the thought itself. But could

130   THINKING OF NECESSITY

the thought instead be taken to be objective *by others*? For example: *S's thought T is objective only if S is reasonably interpretable by others as thinking a thought T with objective correctness conditions.* Perhaps this is a natural extension of the externalism considerations above: if the content of Sally's thoughts about arthritis is in part determined by medical experts, then why not take other features of her thinking also to be determined by the conceptual and linguistic community in which she lives?

In a way, this proposal isn't at cross purposes with my primary aim here. My aim is to implicate certain modal concepts in our capacity for objective thought. If *others* must take a thinker's thoughts to be objective, as a necessary condition for them to be objective, then those others still require these modal concepts in order to do so. So a conceptual community in which there is objective thought would require there to be thinkers with modal concepts, and the crucial link here is preserved: no objective thought without modal concepts. Nevertheless, I prefer the approach according to which the thinker must take her own thoughts to be objective.

First, there remains the potential for a regress. Suppose S_1 must be taken by an interpreter S_2 to be thinking objectively. In turn, surely S_2's taking S_1 to be thinking objectively will be in turn another objective thought (about S_1), and hence require that someone—either S_1, or someone else, S_3—take S_2 to be thinking objectively, which in turn requires that they are interpreted as thinking objectively, and so on. We can avoid such a regress by modalizing: just as in the individual case, I remarked that we need only have the *ability* to prefix our thoughts with *it is objective that*, so in the communal case we need only say that the thinker is interpret*able* in a certain way: not that an actual interpreter is present and interpreting each thought episode. What this doesn't solve, however, is a lingering strangeness that what makes a thought objective is not so much the content of the thought, as external attitudes towards that thought. In the individual case, this strangeness was avoided along with my response to the threat of regress: the objectivity condition is itself included in the content of the thought. On an interpretationist view, however, that condition—involving as it does interpreters distinct from the thinker—must lie outside of the content of the thought. This is not to say that all of our thoughts won't in fact be available to an ideal interpretator—it's not to say that we have radically private thoughts—but it allows that what explains in part the objectivity of a thought is a matter of the content of the thought, and the attitude of its own thinker.

Second, briefly, my motivation here for the plausibility of this intentional account was that it makes sense that a thinker must have some grasp of the correct conditions for their thoughts. This is a motivation for the individual version, not the communal version. If only others needed to be able to grasp the correctness conditions of a thinker's thoughts, then that would allow for non-senient information systems, potentially, to be objective thinkers (e.g., I can grasp the correctness conditions of the barometer's states).

One final consideration: one might worry that objective thought, on my proposed view, requires some quite advanced conceptual machinery (a capacity to conceive of objective correctness conditions, and hence to employ modal concepts). How, then, should we think about the capacity to think in developing minds, such as those of children?[29] The account I propose here is intended to be applicable to mature minds, but there are nevertheless substantial questions how we get there and what capacities we have at each stage. To adequately address development questions here would be too great a task, but I shall offer one initial response, namely, that it is not clear to me how demanding the conceptual requirements here really are. The condition on objective thought proposed is that a thought must be taken to be objective, where this requires a capacity to conceive of a thought being correct or not in light of how things are with reality, beyond the thinking of the thought. Now, one might, for example, take the development of capacities such as *object permanence* to manifest a capacity to grasp such concepts, or at least an important step on the road towards such a capacity. Even very young children are thought to show object permanence (even if there is disagreement over when this normally develops), which may suggest that even very young children have the building blocks in place to be able to conceive of objectivity in the way required here.[30]

In conclusion: we should take the problem of reality seriously and acknowledge that there are substantive conditions on objective thoughts. One of those conditions is that we must take our objective thoughts to be objective, where this is understood as the ability to prefix those thoughts with *it is objective that....* We must thus be in possession of a concept of objectivity and have the ability to use that concept. I have also argued that the concept of objectivity is modal: in order to distinguish the objective both from the subjective and from the nonjective, we need modal conceptual resources. Those modal conceptual resources can be specified as relative to conditions on objectivity. We can thus conclude: the possession of and ability to use *modal concepts* of a certain kind is a necessary condition on objective thought.

---

[29] Thank you to an anonymous reader for pressing this question.

[30] See, for example, Gopnik (1988), in which the development of object permanence is connected to the development of a theoretical conception of objecthood.

6

What Is Metaphysical Necessity?

What is metaphysical necessity? What is metaphysical possibility? Philosophers talk and write about metaphysical modality all the time. We make claims about what is metaphysically necessary or metaphysically possible, and we compare metaphysical modalities to other kinds of modality, such as logical, physical or normative modality (perhaps, for example, in order to claim that some particular phenomenon or claim is necessary in one sense, but merely contingent in another). All of this is premised on the assumption that we know what we're talking about when we refer to metaphysical necessity or possibility. But do we?

In this chapter, I offer an account of metaphysical necessity, drawing on the notion of objective necessity that emerged in the previous chapter. In order to do so, I will first set out what one might hope to achieve in giving such an account. I start by distinguishing two levels of the question 'what is metaphysical necessity?'. What is our target notion? And what metaphysical account should we give of the target notion? Next, I set out my proposals for how to understand the target notion of metaphysical necessity: that we should be neutral over the extension of the notion and, to some extent, its logical behaviour; and that the notion is best captured as 'the strictest real necessity'. I argue that objective necessity fits the bill for being the strictest real necessity and hence earns the title 'metaphysical necessity'.

6.1 Metaphysical necessity as a target notion

There are (at least) two levels to the question: What is metaphysical necessity?

(A)   What is the target notion? Do we have a clear enough sense of what we're looking for, independent of a metaphysical account?

(B)   What metaphysical account should we give of that target notion?

The first level is methodological or conceptual: it concerns clarification of the topic of inquiry. The second level is metaphysical: it concerns the development of a metaphysical account of the target notion which was clarified at the first level. At the second level, we may go beyond clarification to provide a metaphysical theory of the phenomenon of interest. For example, we might agree on the target notion of a *whole* as something constituted by parts, but go on to disagree on a metaphysical

---

Thinking of Necessity: A Kantian Account of Modal Thought and Modal Metaphysics. Jessica Leech,
Oxford University Press. © Jessica Leech 2023. DOI: 10.1093/oso/9780198873969.003.0006

account of what it takes for some parts to constitute a whole (contact? fusion? anything? nothing?).

A similar way of dividing two levels of the question is suggested by Gideon Rosen.

> We might imagine it asked by an up-to-date philosopher who grasps the concept well enough but wants to know more about *what it is* for a proposition to hold of metaphysical necessity. Alternatively, we might imagine it asked by a neophyte who's never heard the phrase before and simply wants to know what philosophers have in mind by it.   (Rosen, 2006, 13)

This is certainly getting at the same idea, although question A need not be asked only for the neophyte. Philosophers sometimes need to take a step back to clarify the questions they are asking as well. Rosen sets up the search for something like an answer to A (for the neophyte) as the search for an 'informal elucidation' of the concept of metaphysical necessity. It is a refinement of his proposed informal elucidation that I shall be defending later in this chapter.

It seems reasonable to suppose that, as far as possible, it is better when we can give separate answers to A and B, that is, if we can first get a clear sense of a target notion, and then engage in substantive debate over the metaphysics of that target notion. For example, we can all agree on what a table—in general—is supposed to be.[1] But we can then disagree on the metaphysics—particles arranged table-wise, three-dimensional, four-dimensional, essentially wooden, and so on. It may well be that in some cases A and B will blur together, or collapse, perhaps in cases of highly technical notions. However, given the great diversity of metaphysical accounts of metaphysical necessity, and yet a persisting impression that everyone is trying to give an account of more or less the same thing, I remain optimistic that there is something to be said about the target notion of metaphysical necessity independent of a substantial metaphysical theory of its nature.

An answer to A might be provided by a definition. If one is sceptical about the prospects for successful definitions of concepts,[2] then one can still accept the distinction between A and B, but with a weaker expectation of an answer to A, such as a specification of a core of the target notion, or important aspects of the cluster of concepts associated with it, or plausible implications of the notion, or a bunch of core examples, and so on.

One might wonder if an inquiry into A should be a largely hermeneutic investigation into how the term 'metaphysical necessity' is actually employed and understood, or a reformist project recommending the best way to understand the

---

[1] Well, there will be difficult cases. Is a large packing crate put into service underneath a family dinner a dining table or not? But by and large everyone knows what a table is.
[2] e.g., Fodor (1998).

134 THINKING OF NECESSITY

term. My intention here is the former kind of project, although I will not carry out an empirical linguistic investigation into actual usage of the term. Rather, my arguments here are based on what seems to me to be the fairly uncontroversial observation that there is a great diversity of metaphysical accounts of metaphysical necessity in the literature, accompanied by a widely held assumption that there is some kind of genuine disagreement between these accounts, and hence a shared target notion the metaphysics of which is at issue. My aim is to draw out an understanding of that target notion that leaves room for—and thereby also makes sense of—that genuine disagreement.

6.2 Extensional neutrality

It is not uncommon for metaphysical necessity to be introduced by way of example. For example, Alvin Plantinga begins his book on necessity with the following remarks.

> But what exactly do these words—'necessary' and 'contingent'—mean? What distinction do they mark? Just what is supposed to be the difference between necessary and contingent truths? We can hardly explain that p is necessary if and only if its denial is impossible; this is true but insufficiently enlightening. It would be a peculiar philosopher who had the relevant concept of impossibility well in hand but lacked that of necessity. Instead, *we must give examples and hope for the best.* (Plantinga, 1978, 1, my emphasis)

This passage concerns unqualified modalities, 'necessity' and 'contingency', rather than any particular kind of necessity or contingency. As such, Plantinga may well be right that we can't explain modal notions without appeal to other modal notions. So much should be accepted by anyone who isn't in the business of reducing the modal to the non-modal. However, Plantinga goes on to give examples that he claims lie between logical necessity on the one hand, and causal or natural necessity on the other. So this passage has been taken as a comment on the prospects for defining or clarifying a notion of *metaphysical* necessity.[3]

What is the typical list of examples? Nowadays, one can expect most of the following to appear in a selection of introductory examples for metaphysical necessity:

- Logical and conceptual necessities. e.g., logical truths, laws of logic, analytic truths. These necessities are not usually thought of as *distinctively*

---

[3] e.g., Sider (2011, 266–7); Clarke-Doane (2021, 1862–3).

metaphysical, but they should be included, for if they are not metaphysically necessary, then their negations are metaphysically possible, and that would be implausible.

- Mathematical necessities. e.g., $2 + 2 = 4$.
- "Laws of metaphysics". e.g., laws of classical mereology, principles governing determinates and determinables.
- Kripkean *a posteriori* necessities. These include *object identities*, e.g., 'Hesperus is Phosphorus'; *theoretical kind identities*, e.g., 'water is H_2O', 'gold is the element with atomic number 79'; *essentialist claims*, e.g., *essentiality of kind* ('Socrates is human'), *essentiality of origin* ('Elizabeth II has George VI as a parent'), and *essentiality of constitution* ('Kripke's lectern is made from wood, not ice').

Such lists of examples may serve a helpful heuristic or pedagogical purpose, in getting someone (perhaps our neophyte) started thinking about the right kind of area. But if this is supposed to be a way to determine *what the target notion of metaphysical necessity is*, then we need to do better.

The main problem with the way of example is that it rules out large-scale disagreement over *what is metaphysically necessary*, i.e., disagreement over the extension of *metaphysical necessity*. There *is* existing disagreement over many of these cases, and in at least some of those debates the dispute is genuinely over whether or not something is metaphysically necessary, and not over the very notion of metaphysical necessity. Sometimes disputes over the extension of some concept C *are* at heart a dispute over the very meaning or content of C. For example, arguably, when Elizabeth Barnes (2014) argues that certain topics in feminist philosophy are a part of metaphysics, she is not merely applying a universally shared conception of metaphysics and noting that these topics fall into its extension; she is arguing that our concept of metaphysics ought to be such that these topics fall under it, and hence that the concept of metaphysics should not mandate that metaphysical topics only concern what is fundamental. I do not want to rule out the existence of such disputes, nor that sometimes this might be what's going on in debates about metaphysical necessity. But at least sometimes the debate really is just about extension. For example, Mackie (2006) lays out a clear and widely held definition of an essential property as a necessary property,[4] but, on those terms, argues against the gamut of essentialist claims.

Aside from the fact that there *is* such disagreement over the extension of *metaphysical necessity*, we anyway ought to allow that there *can be*. It would be a strange philosophical debate, it seems, where there is no question, once a term is defined, what falls under it. If the term is nicely defined, it might be fairly

---

[4] a is essentially F just when necessarily, if a exists, then a is F. See Mackie (2006, 6).

136 THINKING OF NECESSITY

straightforward to work out to what it applies. But we don't in general define key terms of art by just giving a list. If we can find a suitable definition of the target notion of metaphysical necessity, then, so much the better.

I contend that an elucidation of the target notion of metaphysical necessity should remain neutral over the extension of the notion. Does this mean that the elucidation should allow for *some* variation over extension, or for *total* variation? Must *some* of the typical list be included for a notion to count as *metaphysical necessity*, or could one develop an account of metaphysical necessity, perfectly in line with the target notion, that turned out to yield *none* of the typical examples as metaphysically necessary? In the latter case, there are two options: could there be some metaphysical necessities *all* of which were different to the usual list; and could there be *no* metaphysical necessities at all?

I do want to allow for an *empty* extension. I see no reason why we couldn't have a perfectly respectable concept of necessity and then discover that nothing is necessary (everything is contingent) in that sense. For example, one might argue that even though there is a concept of necessity in good standing, everything, including the laws of logic, is revisable.[5] If there are no necessities at all, then *a fortiori* there are no metaphysical necessities. I don't think such a view is *true*, but I don't see why it should be ruled out by a merely conceptual requirement that the concept of necessity be non-empty.

A different view would be that there are no *distinctively* metaphysical necessities (where a kind of necessity □ is distinctive just when there is no distinct sense of necessity ■ such that $\Box\phi \leftrightarrow \blacksquare\phi$). Again, I see no problem with articulating a clear concept of a kind of necessity only to find out that it is not distinctive. If, for example, one developed a view according to which it is naturally necessary that *p* if and only if it is metaphysically necessary that *p*, surely this should count as something substantive and interesting, and not an indictment of the very concept of metaphysical necessity.[6] Even if, as a result, we decide to proceed using only the concept of natural necessity, I don't see why this renders a concept of metaphysical necessity defective (rather than merely surplus to requirement).

One might respond that sometimes we do consign empty theoretical concepts to the scrapheap, such as *phlogiston* or *aether*. If our notion of metaphysical necessity turns out to be empty or non-distinctive, should it not also be scrapped? Maybe so. My point here is rather: the meaning and meaningfulness of the target notion should not depend upon its having a non-empty and/or distinctive extension. The constraint of extensional neutrality preserves the possibility of genuine disagreement over cases and, moreover, the possibility of discovering that the notion itself

---

[5] Such a view might be inspired by Quine's work, although there are reasons to think that even Quine doesn't take the laws of logic to be revisable. See, e.g., Shapiro (2000).

[6] See, e.g., Schaffer (2005) vs. Wilson (2013).

is useless.[7] The point is that we shouldn't be able to show that *metaphysical necessity* is, or is not, like *phlogiston* just by virtue of understanding.

Could the extension of *metaphysical necessity* be non-empty and distinctive, yet contain none of the typical examples? I can think of positions one might take on many of the entries on the typical list according to which they are metaphysically contingent. Many philosophers deny essentialist necessity claims, and one can use counterpart theory to avoid necessary identities. The modal status of many claims of metaphysics is under debate.[8] Logical, conceptual, and mathematical cases, however, are more difficult to deny. Even if one thinks that some logical truths are contingent (e.g., some logical truths concerning an actuality operator), it is hard to claim that *all* logical truths are contingent, unless one is denying a modal status to logical truths altogether.[9] And even if one could coherently deny all of these cases, there is a serious question *what else* could be metaphysically necessary if none of these? Given the difficulties here, by 'extensional neutrality', then, I mean that a target notion of metaphysical necessity should allow that many of the typical examples of metaphysical necessity could turn out not to be metaphysically necessary after all, and that the notion of metaphysical necessity may turn out to have an empty extension, or to be co-extensive with other distinct modal notions.

6.3 The space between

Another approach to introducing a target notion of metaphysical necessity locates it "between" logical and conceptual necessity on the one hand, and natural or physical necessity on the other. For example,

> Many philosophers take there to be a non-epistemic veridical notion of necessity which is *metaphysical necessity*.... This notion is supposed, in particular, to be distinct from both analytic necessity and physical necessity. That is, there are things that are metaphysically necessary, but not analytically necessary. (Presumably it cannot go the other way around). And there are things that are metaphysically necessary but not physically necessary, or vice versa.
>
> (Priest, 2021, 3)[10]

---

[7] The notion of discovery here is rather different to that in the natural sciences. The sense in which one might 'discover' that there is no metaphysical necessity is that one might conclude this on the basis of philosophical argument, which is different to the way we discovered that there is no phlogiston. All the same, the point stands, that such a philosophical conclusion should not be prejudged just by understanding the concept of metaphysical necessity, without further metaphysical work.

[8] See Miller (2010).

[9] For example, the Tarskian. See Chapter 3, section 3.1.

[10] There is an important sense in which if it is metaphysically necessary that p, then it is also physically necessary that p. Otherwise, it could be metaphysically necessary that p, yet physically possible that not-p, which seems implausible. I take it that here Priest means that there are things that are metaphysically necessary but not *distinctively* physically necessary. e.g., if it is metaphysically necessary that Socrates is human, then it is physically necessary that Socrates is human, but not because this is required particularly by the laws of physics.

This is also a feature of Plantinga's use of introductory examples (he uses the term 'broad logical necessity' rather than 'metaphysical necessity').

> ... we must give examples and hope for the best. In the first place, truths of logic ... are necessary in the sense in question. Such truths are logically necessary in the narrow sense; .... But the sense of necessity in question—call it 'broadly logical necessity' is wider than this. Truths of set theory, arithmetic and mathematics generally are necessary in this sense, as are a host of homelier items such as
>
> No one is taller than himself
>
> Red is a colour
>
> ...
>
> ... So the sense of necessity in question is wider than that captured in first order logic. On the other hand, it is narrower than that of causal or natural necessity.
>
> Voltaire once swam the Atlantic
>
> for example, is surely implausible. Indeed, there is a clear sense in which it is impossible. Eighteenth-century intellectuals (as distinguished from dolphins) simply lacked the physical equipment for this kind of feat.... These things are impossible for us; but not in the broadly logical sense. (Plantinga, 1978, 1–2)

The result is a picture of nested modalities, where metaphysical modality is identified by its position in that nested structure.

According to this nested structure, if it is logically necessary that p then it is metaphysically necessary that p, but not always vice versa. If it is metaphysically necessary that p then it is naturally necessary that p, but not always vice versa.

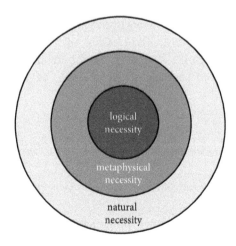

And if it is naturally possible that p then it is metaphysically possible that p, but not always vice versa. If it is metaphysically possible that p then it is logically possible that p, but not always vice versa.

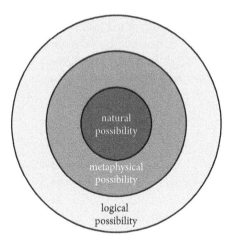

If we admit a variety of kinds of necessity, such as (narrow) logical necessity, metaphysical necessity, natural necessity, and so on, then it may well turn out that they stand in these relationships. But do we want to assume this, as a constraint on the very notion of metaphysical necessity?

As with the way of example, this would rule out a range of metaphysical debates that should remain genuine and substantive. For example, debates concerning whether the laws of nature are metaphysically necessary or contingent (yet naturally necessary) could be viewed, in at least some cases, as debates over whether metaphysical and natural necessity have the same extension. For example, suppose that it is naturally necessary that p if and only if the laws of nature entail that p.[11] But suppose that all and only the laws of nature are metaphysically necessary. Assuming a plausible principle that whatever follows logically from a metaphysical necessity is also metaphysically necessary,[12] this would collapse metaphysical and natural necessity together. However, this is ruled out by the picture sketched above, where the very notion of metaphysical necessity lies *between* logical and natural necessity. In other words, extensional neutrality rules out the "space between" approach to isolating a target notion of metaphysical necessity, for this approach assumes that metaphysical necessity has a distinctive extension.

---

[11] With some caveats. See Leech (2016); Hale and Leech (2017).

[12] Suppose the contrary, that it could be metaphysically necessary that p, metaphysically contingent that q, and q follow logically from p. Put in terms of a worlds semantics: p is true in all (metaphysically possible) worlds. The laws of logic hold at all metaphysically possible worlds. So q must also be true at all metaphysically possible worlds. But if q is contingent, there must be at least one such world at which it is not true. Contradiction.

140 THINKING OF NECESSITY

Moreover, even if these modalities do in fact exhibit this relational structure, such an approach arguably gets the direction of explanation the wrong way around. One might think that we should start with our conceptions of various kinds of necessity and then determine their logical relations, rather than starting with logical relations between some purported kinds of necessity and taking those to be definitive of those kinds.[13] One could introduce a range of necessities in this way, but one should not straightforwardly expect them to line up with existing modal notions without further examination or argumentation.

6.4 The strictest real necessity

How can we do better? I now turn to what Rosen (2006) calls an 'informal elucidation' of metaphysical necessity: metaphysical necessity is *the strictest real necessity*.[14]

Rosen introduces his informal elucidation as something for the neophyte, initially involving examples and more.

> If we do not begin with a definition, we must offer some sort of informal elucidation.... The neophyte is presented with a battery of paradigms and foils, ordinary language paraphrases (with commentary), and bits and pieces of the inferential role of the target notion, and then somehow as a result of this barrage he cottons on. (Rosen, 2006, 14)

He then outlines the idea of metaphysical necessity as the strictest real necessity. Such a definition has three parts: *strictest*, *real*, and *necessity*.

---

[13] Even a philosopher such as Williamson, who takes modal logic to be a guide to modal metaphysics, starts with a target notion of metaphysical necessity which he then wants to capture with the most appropriate logical system: 'We must first articulate the pre-theoretic standard we want theorems of the logic of metaphysical modality to meet' (Williamson, 2013, 92). That is: 'The necessity at issue here is metaphysical. What is metaphysically necessary is what could not have been otherwise, what would have obtained whatever had obtained; not even the laws of physics can be assumed to be metaphysically necessary in this sense. But whether anyone could have known or thought or said that the circumstance at issue obtained is irrelevant' (Williamson, 2013, 3).

[14] Divers (2018, 10) also introduces a 'weaker' conception of metaphysical necessity, 'A-necessity', as 'a necessity that is alethic, objective and absolute, and which tolerates the inclusion of a posteriori cases'. This is more or less the same as Rosen's informal elucidation, where 'objective' and tolerance of *a posteriori* cases corresponds to *real* necessity, and 'absolute' corresponds to *strictest*. I will continue with Rosen's version here, however, as Divers (2018) is more concerned with finding a practical use for such a notion of necessity, rather than defending this as a *characterization* of metaphysical necessity. Although of course I take the function question to be important! It is interesting to note that Divers distinguishes A-necessity from a stronger notion, 'M-necessity', which is 'enhanced by some further substantive 'metaphysical' component' (2018, 10). This A-necessity/M-necessity distinction may correspond roughly with my distinction between levels A and B, although I shall not pursue this comparison here.

Necessity: First and obviously, although crucially, metaphysical necessity is a kind of necessity: 'To say that *P* is metaphysically necessary is to say that *P must* be the case' (Rosen, 2006, 14).

Real: Second, it is a 'real' necessity. This is to say, it is alethic (if it is metaphysically necessary that *p*, then *p*), non-epistemic, and—to distinguish it from logical and conceptual necessities which are also (arguably) alethic and non-epistemic— 'substantive'.

The 'non-epistemic' clause needs careful clarification. The intention is to rule out modalities defined in terms of what is known (either by some agent, or by everyone), or in terms of *a priori* knowledge. Such kinds of necessity are factive, since if it is known that *p*, then *p*. However, accompanying kinds of possibility may allow for the epistemic possibility of logical impossibilities. For example, there is a sense in which some as yet unproven, perhaps undecidable, logical falsehood may be *possible for all we know*, and possible given what is known *a priori*, yet logically impossible. Arguably, such epistemic modalities are orthogonal to the kinds of modalities of interest here. The intention, however, is *not* to rule out other kinds of modality that might be thought of as epistemic in another way, for example, as concerning or relating to epistemic conditions on our capacity to represent the world. This will be spelled out more soon.

The crucial ingredient to get clear on is being 'substantive'. Rosen remarks,

> At this point the usual procedure is to invoke an epistemological distinction along with certain crucial paradigms. One says: 'Unlike the various logical and semantic species of necessity, metaphysically necessary propositions are sometimes *synthetic* and *a posteriori* ...'. (Rosen, 2006, 15)

This, then, is real modality: 'any modality that is alethic, non-epistemic, and sometimes substantive or synthetic' (Rosen, 2006, 16).

One *can* perhaps supplement this sketch of real modality with examples or paradigms, as Rosen suggests. Such examples might help the neophyte to 'cotton on', but, I have argued, they should play no role in properly determining the target notion. And insofar as it is these 'crucial paradigms' and examples that seem to be bringing in syntheticity and *a posteriority*, extensional neutrality leaves us in need of an alternative way to delineate the real necessities.

Without appealing to paradigms and examples, one might nevertheless think that that epistemic necessity is allied to the *a priori*, and conceptual and logical necessities to the analytic, such that we can distinguish real necessity from each by specifying that (some) real necessities are *a posteriori* and synthetic. However, a concern remains that this violates extensional neutrality. Impressive as the advent of the necessary *a posteriori* has been, the recognition that metaphysical necessity, and so at least some real necessity, might not be *a priori* is a relatively new idea

142 THINKING OF NECESSITY

in philosophy, and it is not uncontested.[15] As such, it seems unwise to write *a posteriority* into the very target notion. That real necessities might be synthetic is an idea with a longer heritage,[16] but again, it has not survived uncontested.[17] In general, the task to distinguish metaphysical from logical, conceptual, and epistemic necessity is one that must be approached with care, if we are not to violate extensional neutrality, i.e., by ruling out collapse of metaphysical into one of these necessities. We want a *conceptual distinction* that need not entail an *extensional distinction*.

My proposed starting point is the idea that what is distinctive of the notion of real, as opposed to logical or conceptual, modality, is that it concerns *how the world could have been different*.[18] There is a sense in which logical and conceptual notions of modality also concern how the world could have been different: logical modalities, such as *necessarily, it's raining or it isn't raining*, can be about the world and the things in it, i.e., *rain*. Indeed, this much could be said of pretty much *any* modality. e.g., if it's epistemically possible that it rains, or if it is morally permissible that it rains, these modalities concern something worldly, namely, rain.[19]

The crucial difference, however, is the *source* of the modality. A call for an account of the source of necessity has been typically understood as a call for an explanation of necessity (where explanation is to be understood as metaphysical, not causal or epistemic, explanation).[20] Roughly, it is the question of where necessity "comes from". A straightforward way to understand this is as asking what the truth-conditions are of true statements of necessity, e.g., what are the truth conditions of 'Necessarily, $2 + 2 = 4$'? However, Blackburn (1993) argues that this is too narrow, since it assumes that the function of modal discourse is to describe modal facts. As we have seen (in Chapter 1), this is an assumption that we ought not to make without further support. Instead, we can understand a call for an account of the source of necessity as an explanation of necessity, more broadly conceived, which allows for explanation in terms of, for example, the function of modal discourse rather than truthmakers for modal truths. My suggestion is that the notion of real necessity is to be understood in terms of the kind of source it has, i.e., a constraint on the kind of explanation that would be appropriate for real necessities.

---

[15] See Leech (2019) for more on the discovery of the necessary *a posteriori.*

[16] Most notably, in Kant's *Critique of Pure Reason.*   [17] e.g., Ayer (1936).

[18] For a review and rebuttal of several other options see Clarke-Doane (2021).

[19] Clarke-Doane (2021) argues that we cannot distinguish logical from real modality in this way, because, 'such notions [of logical possibility] explicitly concern *how the world could have been*—not, e.g., how it might be for all we know, or how it normatively may be' (Clarke-Doane, 2021, 9). But as explained, this is not the sense in which real modalities are distinctively about the world.

[20] See Blackburn (1993) and Hale (2002b) on the source of necessity. Metaphysical explanation does not depend upon our particular interests or what we happen to understand.

The target notion of *real modality* is a notion of a modality that *has its source in something to do with the world.*[21] An explanation of a real necessity, for example, must be given in terms of something explicitly to do with the world, and so not, for example, just in terms of knowledge, or norms, and so on. I'm deliberately leaving 'something to do with the world' fairly open, because it is there that the scope for substantive metaphysical disagreement opens up (and after all, if the target notion was supremely clear in the first place, there might be a bit less disagreement over what to make of it). Is it the essential natures of things in the world? Their dispositional properties? Or something else? Not all options need be realist.[22] Perhaps the source is the conceptual scheme through which we are able to experience the world. Perhaps it has its source in semantic norms governing language used to talk about the world.[23] Perhaps, even, real necessity is a kind of epistemic necessity, suitably understood, based in epistemic conditions on experience of the world. Even such a view would count as being of real necessity, so long as the target notion of necessity in question was not understood simply in terms of what we know, but importantly in terms of conditions of knowing *the world.* (This is also a reason to drop the 'non-epistemic' clause of real necessity; the important work to rule out problematic cases is done instead by the specification of source.) Note also that real modality is a general variety of which there may be many species. For example, natural modality, if it has its source in the laws of nature, will to that extent have its source in something to do with the world, i.e., its natural laws.

How does the source account help? Let us compare real to logical necessity to illustrate. At the heart of the target notion of logical necessity is the idea that it is that necessity distinctive of the relationship between premises and conclusion in a logically valid argument, where logical validity is in turn determined by the

---

[21] 'The world' is not intended in a technical sense, e.g., 'the actual world', but rather as a catch all for what we might call 'reality', or 'whatever it is we have knowledge and experience of', or similar. So, for example, if one favoured a possibilist metaphysical account of real necessity, according to which modal facts are determined in part by the existence of non-actual possibilia, my proposal would not result in the incompatible claim that the source of this necessity is in the actual world; in such a case *something to do with the world* at level A would be cashed out at level B as *what possibilia exist in reality.*

[22] Can you have an anti*realist* account of *real* modality? The terminology here is unfortunate, but not contradictory. The 'real' in 'realist' arguably means something different to the 'real' in 'real necessity'.

[23] e.g., Thomasson (2020). The semantic norms at the heart of her view are, or depend upon, 'world-regarding' rules. 'Clearly not all rules of a language can be given simply by giving definitions in other terms of the language, or else the language would not be learnable at all—there would be no "way in," so to speak. There must be some "semantically basic" terms, the rules for which are introduced in other ways if language is to be learnable at all. Rules for introducing semantically basic terms may instead take the form of *world-language* rules. Such *world-regarding* rules are set up at least in part by (explicit or implicit) ostensive definitions. . . . Acknowledging the presence of semantic rules of many different forms, including *world-language* rules, is crucially important. For it enables us to handle the challenges raised by Kripkean cases of *de re* and a posteriori necessities . . .' (2020, 67–8, some emphasis added). There are some interesting parallels between Thomasson's view as briefly presented here, and Martha Kneale's 1938 account of *a posteriori* metaphysical necessities, which also relies crucially on the nature and role of ostensive definition to account for *a posteriori* necessities. See Kneale (1938) and Leech (2019) for discussion.

laws of logic.[24] At the level of target notions (level A), this distinguishes logical necessity from real necessities: absent a further account, the notions of logical validity and logical laws do not imply a particular kind of relation to the world. Now, one might take a metaphysical view (level B) according to which logical necessity has its source in the world because, for example, the laws of logic are grounded in the nature of logical entities.[25] In that case, since logical necessity is metaphysically explained in terms of the nature of worldly things, logical modality would turn out to be a kind of real modality after all. This is indeed what certain philosophers mean to claim: because logical necessity has its source in the natures of logical entities, it is a subspecies of metaphysical (and hence real) necessity. My proposal allows for this to be a *substantive claim about* metaphysical necessity (as a kind of real necessity) and logical necessity. For the thought is that *the target notion* of metaphysical necessity has written in that it is a real necessity, and so that it has a source in the world; the target notion of logical necessity does not. But there is then huge scope to disagree further over the nature and source of logical validity and laws at level B. By clearly distinguishing definitions or elucidations at level A from debates at level B, we can avoid collapse of the notions (A) of real necessity and logical necessity. Compare: if the claim that logical necessity has its source in the world was at the conceptual level (A), then one might expect the claim that all logical necessity is a kind of real necessity to be analytic or trivial in some way. But that seems hugely implausible. Separating a target notion from a metaphysical account allows us to accommodate non-trivial, informative claims about the relations between these different modalities.

This proposal also helps to explain why it is likely to turn out that real modalities are sometimes synthetic and *a posteriori*. Insofar as the source of these modalities is worldly, the relevant worldly facts are likely in at least some cases to be synthetic or *a posteriori*, although there is still room for this to be disputed.

Finally, one might worry that this account of metaphysical necessity as real necessity is in tension with extensional neutrality, for one might read the source condition as distinctive of some but not other metaphysical accounts of metaphysical necessity. However, the idea of a source in something to do with the world is deliberately permissive enough to capture all the candidate views, realist or antirealist, possibilist or actualist, as sketched above. Is it *too* permissive? I don't have a knockdown argument that it's not, but the distinction between questions A and B can go a long way to dispelling potential worries. For any metaphysical account of a kind of modality such that it has its source in something to do with the world, we can always ask whether that source is plausibly part of the shared target notion over which there is, presumably, philosophical disagreement concerning

---

[24] See Chapter 3, section 3.1.

[25] See, e.g., Vaidya (2006); Hale (2013), but also Keefe and Leech (2018); Leech (2022b); and Chapter 4, section 4.3.2.

its nature. It is *real* modality that has this kind of source written into the shared target notion: other target notions either don't specify a source at all, or a different kind of source, appealing to, for example, logical laws, conceptual relations, states of knowledge, or courses of action. Whilst these latter might ultimately be given a place in the world, that is not part of the conceptual content that makes it into the target notion. For example, it is not part of the concept of a logical law that it have an explanation in terms of the essence of logical functions, even though that might feature in a metaphysical account of logical laws, and so understanding a target notion of logical necessity in terms of logical laws would not include the idea of a source in the world.

Strictest: Thirdly, we must distinguish metaphysical necessity from other putative kinds of real necessity:

> the various causal or nomic modalities: physical necessity, historical inevitability, technical impossibility (as in: 'It's impossible to fabricate an artificial liver'), and so on. (Rosen, 2006, 16)

The final part of the proposal is thus that metaphysical necessity is the *strictest* real necessity (and metaphysical possibility is the least restrictive real possibility):

> If it is metaphysically necessary that p, then there is no real sense of possibility according to which it is possible that $\neg p$.[26]
>
> If it is possible that p in any real sense of possibility, then it is metaphysically possible that p.[27]

Does this preserve extensional neutrality? One might think that requiring metaphysical necessity to be the strictest of the real necessities verges into the forbidden territory of the space between. However, as long as the target notion of metaphysical necessity is understood as the strictest real necessity, and the target notion of physical necessity is understood differently (perhaps in connection with laws of physics), then it will be a substantive matter to consider the relation between these two necessities. Once again, we gain clarity by distinguishing between levels A and B: it is at level B that we might discover co-extension, with no harm done to a conceptual distinction at level A. For example, we may discover (at level B) when giving a metaphysical account of physical necessity, perhaps understood

---

[26] Alternatively: If p is metaphysically necessary, it is necessary in every real sense (Rosen, 2006, 16). The formulation in terms of a lack of competing possibility is preferable when defining logical necessity as the strictest necessity and metaphysical as relative: see Chapter 10.

[27] What is the modal status of these conditionals? Insofar as I am taking these to spell out part of the target notion of metaphysical necessity, they will have something like the status of conceptual necessities.

146 THINKING OF NECESSITY

(at level A) as that necessity distinctive of the laws of physics, that if p is physically necessary then there is no real sense of possibility according to which it is possible that $\neg p$, rendering physical necessity the strictest real necessity and hence co-extensive with metaphysical necessity. But, as explained, this is a metaphysical discovery which is informative precisely because there is a conceptual distinction between the two target notions.

To summarize: I have argued that we should distinguish between (A) saying what the target notion of metaphysical necessity is, and (B) giving a further metaphysical account of that notion. I have also argued that we should remain neutral to a great extent over the extension of the notion of metaphysical necessity when attempting task (A). I then defended a version of the claim that metaphysical necessity is the strictest real necessity, drawing on the notion of *source* to characterize real necessity.

Before moving on, I want to address two further points. Firstly, some readers may be surprised that I have not mentioned counterfactuals in my account here. One might think that the notion of metaphysical necessity is closely allied to everyday counterfactual thinking, namely, where metaphysical necessities *would be true, no matter what were the case.*[28] However, I do not believe that counterfactuals belong in the target notion of metaphysical necessity. In brief, it is plausible that everyday counterfactual thinking may operate against a range of different kinds of modality. Compare, for example, 'no matter what you try, nothing would travel faster than the speed of light' (a sensible pronouncement against a background of physical necessity), or 'no matter what you did to this, it wouldn't have been edible' (a comment on a particularly bad dish, against a background of culinary modality). At least *prima facie,* it seems that we need a notion of metaphysical necessity to pick out metaphysical-modal counterfactuals, rather than vice versa.

Secondly, the proposed target notion is deliberately designed as common ground in disagreements over the metaphysics of metaphysical necessity. But once we all agree that metaphysical necessity is the strictest real necessity, and we agree on extensional neutrality, what is left to make sense of and fuel disagreement at the metaphysical level? The short answer is: 'plenty'. We may have wider metaphysical commitments that feed into our disagreements, such as views on existence, properties, realism, and more. And indeed, even though I have argued for extensional neutrality when elucidating the target notion, one may well have good reasons for taking the accommodation of some examples to be important at the metaphysical level. For example, if one has other reasons for thinking that individuals have essential properties, one will want to honour such cases in one's metaphysics of necessity.

---

[28] See, e.g., Williamson (2007).

6.5 Objective necessity is the strictest real necessity

Recall the definition of objective necessity that was introduced in the previous chapter (p.106):

Objective□ It is objective-necessary that p iff $\exists \phi (O\phi \wedge \Box(\phi \to p))$

That is, it is objective-necessary that p just when there are some conditions of objectivity that logically necessarily imply p. I will now argue that objective necessity is the strictest real necessity. I take it for granted that objective necessity is a kind of necessity. What remains to be shown is that it is *real*—that it is *alethic*, and has its *source in something to do with the world*—and that it is the *strictest* such necessity.

Objective necessity is alethic. In answer to the problem of reality (see Chapter 5, section 5.2), reality is inherently intentionally or epistemically accessible to the mind. So all reality must conform to conditions of objectivity that specify the conditions under which the mind can represent reality. Hence, the conditions of objectivity—and their logical consequences—are universally true of the world. Since it is objective-necessary that p just when p follows from some conditions on objectivity, and since those conditions are true, it follows that it is also true that p.

Objective necessity has its source in something to do with the world. The explanation of objective necessity is given in terms of the conditions under which we are able to think objectively, i.e., the conditions under which our thoughts get in touch with the world. Hence, in tandem with the previous point, this means that objective necessity is a real necessity. The conditions of objectivity concern the conditions under which reality can be represented by the mind, and the conditions under which the mind can represent reality. Hence they are something to do with the world: conditions on a representable world.

Objective necessity is the strictest *real necessity*: if it is objective-necessary that p, then there is no real sense of possibility according to which it is possible that $\neg p$.

If it was possible that $\neg p$ in some real sense, and yet objective-necessary that p, then some real sense of possibility would concern matters beyond reality, i.e., beyond how things are with the world. If it were true that $\neg p$, the conditions of objectivity would not hold. But earlier I argued that any reality that can be represented is subject to conditions on objectivity, and moreover, that we should respond to the problem of reality by embracing the idea that what it is to be part of reality must include the possibility of our being able to represent it. So everything in reality—everything in the world—conforms to conditions on objectivity.[29] Real necessity and possibility have their source in something to do with the world, i.e.,

---

[29] Chapter 5, section 5.2.

148   THINKING OF NECESSITY

an explanation of a kind of real possibility must be given in terms of something explicitly to do with the world. So the source of real possibility conforms to conditions of objectivity, i.e., is objective-possible. At best there is a strange tension here, between a purported kind of possibility that is compatible with objective-impossibilities, but which has its source in something that must conform to conditions on objectivity. This tension is dissolved if we accept that objective-necessity is the strictest real necessity, i.e., that if it is objective-necessary that p, then there is no real sense of possibility according to which it is possible that $\neg p$.

This is not a knock-down argument, but the onus lies with my opponent to provide a plausible example where (a) a kind of modality is plausibly a real modality; (b) there are real possibilities in this sense which are incompatible with conditions on objectivity, and yet (c) there is a clearly specified source of the modality which is compatible with conditions on objectivity. I myself struggle to find examples to meet all of these conditions. For example, one might define "cheese-dream modality" as having its source in something to do with the world, namely, the interaction between neurophysiology and consumption of cheese at bedtime. Eating a lot of cheese at bedtime, and certain interactions with one's neurophysiology, is surely objective-possible. This may give rise to the possibilities of dreams, which, let us suppose, fly into the realms of the objective-impossible. So we get the combination of objective-possible source with objective-impossibilities. But of course cheese-dream modality isn't a real modality because it isn't *factive*.

Suppose that other kinds of real necessity are relative, i.e., defined in terms of a class of propositions, e.g., laws of biology for biological necessity. Then, in cases where there are conditions on objectivity, but there exist none of the relevant kind of propositions (e.g., there are no laws of biology), it will not be the case that if it is metaphysically necessary that p, it is biologically necessary that p, since the existential clause for the latter kind of necessity (there are laws of biology) would be false. Nevertheless, the strictest real necessity is defined in terms of competing real possibilities, i.e., *if it is necessary that p in the strictest real sense, there is no real sense of possibility according to which it is possible that $\neg p$*. In the case where there are no laws of biology, nothing is possible relative to laws of biology, just as nothing is necessary relative to laws of biology. So there is no sense of real possibility, i.e., biological possibility, according to which it is possible that $\neg p$. I postpone a fuller discussion of this to Chapter 10, where the issue arises again in relation to logical and metaphysical modality.

One might object that objective-necessity isn't the strictest real necessity, because it does not concern all of reality, it covers only reality *about which we can think objectively*. There is surely then a kind of necessity which concerns *all* of reality, regardless of what we can represent, which is stricter. However, as I have already noted, the response to this appeals to the problem of reality and the proposed solution: the problem is solved precisely by giving up the notion of a reality understood independently of what we can think of objectively. So if one

WHAT IS METAPHYSICAL NECESSITY? 149

takes the problem of reality seriously; and if one follows the recommendation to introduce conditions on objective thought as a solution to that problem; and if one also defines a kind of necessity relative to those conditions; one will see that this kind of necessity is the strictest real necessity. I realize that these are big "if"s, but they are proposed in response to serious philosophical questions. To reject these proposals, then, one will incur the challenge to answer these questions in a different way.

The target notion of metaphysical necessity is to be understood as the strictest real necessity. But we have now seen that objective necessity is the strictest real necessity. At the very least, objective necessity and metaphysical necessity are therefore co-extensive. I propose we should go further: we can use the notion of objective necessity to provide an account of metaphysical necessity, i.e., an answer to question B: metaphysical necessity is objective necessity, that is, metaphysical necessity should be understood as a kind of necessity that is relative to conditions of objectivity. To give an account of metaphysical necessity, we need to provide an account of the strictest real necessity. The account of objective necessity does that: it gives an account of a necessity that is relative to conditions of objectivity, and explains why such a kind of necessity would be the strictest real necessity.

One might object that there are competing accounts of necessities that have equal claim to being the strictest real necessity. For example, suppose you give an account of a kind of necessity that has its source in the essential natures of things; so it is necessary that p in this sense if and only if it is true in virtue of the natures of all things that p. Such a kind of necessity is arguably real: it has its source in something to do with the world (essential natures of things) and is factive (trivially: if it is true in virtue of the natures of all things that p, then it is true that p). Is it the strictest real necessity? Since, let us grant, objective necessity is also a strictest real necessity, it would have to be that all and only those propositions true in virtue of the natures of things would also follow from conditions of objectivity. It would be strange if that was a brute fact. So, either the conditions of objectivity would have to be constrained by the essential natures of things, or the essential natures of things would be in some way determined by conditions of objectivity. The former option faces the question why the essences of things should constrain our very capacity for objective thought. Of course, what things are like will determine the truth and falsity of our thoughts; if Socrates is essentially human, then it is true to think that Socrates is human, and false to think that Socrates is a boiled egg. But why should this constrain the very conditions under which our thoughts can even be about the world?[30] If we then turn to the latter option, where essence is determined by conditions on objectivity, then we don't have an alternative to objective-necessity after all; the strictest real necessity is objective-necessity, where we have reason to

---

[30] I made a similar point with respect to thought and essence in Chapter 4, section 4.3.2.

150 THINKING OF NECESSITY

include in conditions on objectivity something to do with essence.[31] The argument generalizes to other alternative proposals for the strictest real necessity: either we face an implausible constraint on objective thought, or the alternative is subsumed under objective-necessity.

So: metaphysical necessity is objective-necessity. Earlier, I argued that possession of a concept of objective modality is a condition on our capacity for objective thought. Given our distinction between levels A and B, we cannot quite conclude that possession of the concept *metaphysical necessity*, understood as the concept *strictest real necessity* is a condition on a capacity for objective thought, but we can conclude that possession of a modal concept that provides an account of metaphysical necessity *is*. This is good enough for me. Indeed, it may go some way to explaining why philosophers often assume that the concept of metaphysical necessity is a philosophical invention, removed from everyday thought and talk. Perhaps that concept (at level A) strictly speaking *is*, but there is a very closely related concept that, I have argued, is implicated in our capacity to think objectively. It is closely related insofar as it is the concept of the kind of necessity that is the strictest real necessity.

6.6 Metaphysical necessity is objective necessity

We thus arrive at our Kant-inspired account of metaphysical necessity: metaphysical necessity has its source in conditions of objective thought, i.e., metaphysical necessity is relative to conditions of objectivity. Let's label this view 'Modal Transcendentalism'.[32] This is strikingly similar to the kind of view given by Kant in the *Postulates of Empirical Thinking* (see Chapter 2, section 2.3) although we have arrived here via a slightly different route (albeit a route with recognizably Kantian scenery). This account now raises many important questions, to be addressed over the course of the final chapters of this book.

What is the relation between logical and metaphysical necessity? We will revisit the relation between these two key kinds of modality, which have been the focus of this book. Metaphysical necessity is a *relative necessity*; logical necessity is *absolute*.

What is metaphysically necessary? Which, if any, of the typical cases of metaphysical necessity are counted as such according to Modal Transcendentalism? This concerns to a great extent the nature of the conditions of objective thought.

---

[31] See Chapter 9, section 9.2.3 for a suggestion of how essentialist necessities might be accommodated by my proposed approach.

[32] Thank you to Mark Textor for the label.

For example, if they are general, one might expect that metaphysical necessities should also therefore be general. We must then ask:

How, if at all, does the account accommodate *de re* necessities?   This will lead to questions concerning necessary and contingent existence of individuals, as well as essentialist necessity claims. *De re* and essentialist necessities are often thought to be *a posteriori*. So:

How, if at all, does the account accommodate *a posteriori* necessities?   This question introduces wider epistemological issues, not least:

How, if at all, are we able to know metaphysical modal truths?   This book is not primarily a treatise on modal epistemology, but we should have something to say about the prospects for addressing the epistemological question.

What is the formal framework for metaphysical modality?   We have a formalization of objective necessity, but this needs to be expanded and some consequences considered. In particular, we will consider the best formalization for metaphysical *possibility*; the prospects for *iteration* of metaphysical modals; and whether and how this non-worlds metaphysical account can be reconciled with a modal logic employing a possible worlds semantics.

In brief, metaphysical necessity is *relative*, logical necessity *absolute*. This relation allows us to explain the commonality between different kinds of modality. Metaphysical necessity is relative to *general* conditions on objective thought. This will have consequences for *de re* and *a posteriori* necessities. *Knowledge* of metaphysical necessity involves a philosophical investigation into the conditions of objective thought. This may help to shed light on the notion of conceivability, and its relation to possibility. Metaphysical necessity can be captured in a formal system with a familiar normal logic, where metaphysical necessity and possibility are not captured by simple modal operators, but by complex formulas. This complexity allows us to clarify how to think about duality and iteration with respect to metaphysical modalities, and thence to consider the validity of familiar modal schemas.

Appendix: In defence of *metaphysical necessity*

It is not unusual to encounter criticisms of the very notion of metaphysical necessity. My proposals in this chapter can also be applied in defence of the notion against these complaints. In this additional section, I'll briefly consider three key challenges to the target notion of metaphysical necessity: that there's no

152   THINKING OF NECESSITY

such philosophically interesting and unambiguous target notion; that the notion is empty; and that the notion is disjunctive and picks out at best an unnatural division in reality.

First, some philosophers have complained that there isn't a single, clear notion of metaphysical necessity. Rather, we seem to have, at best, a ragbag of otherwise interesting metaphysical notions. I will consider in particular Rosen's objection to the informal elucidation of his that I've adopted here.

Rosen (2006) argues that the informal elucidation is consistent with two different conceptions of metaphysical necessity and is hence ambiguous.

> [I]t is universally assumed that a question about the metaphysical modal status of any given proposition is clear and unambiguous, at least as regards the predicate. We may not be able to say what metaphysical necessity really is in its inner most nature. But thanks to the informal elucidation sketched above or something like it, we know enough about it to ask unambiguous questions about its nature and its extension. . . . I shall suggest that the informal explanation sketched above is consistent with two distinct conceptions of necessity and possibility. . . . Questions about metaphysical necessity are ambiguous, and where divergent resolutions of the ambiguity yield different answers, the modal question as we normally understand it has no answer.   (Rosen, 2006, 17)

Rosen introduces two competing conceptions: the Standard Conception (SC) and the Non-Standard Conception (NSC).

(SC) P is metaphysically necessary when it holds in every (Non-Standard) possible world in which the actual laws of metaphysics also hold, where the basic laws of metaphysics are the truths about the form or structure of the actual world.

(NSC) P is metaphysically necessary when its negation is logically incompatible with the natures of things.

The substance of Rosen's argument is that there are cases over which these disagree, such that it is metaphysically necessary that p according to SC but not according to NSC. For example,

(Pairing)   For any things x and y, there exists a set containing just x and y.

By Rosen's argument, this is SC-necessary because the pairing axiom is an actual law of metaphysics, but NSC-contingent because its negation is logically compatible with the natures of things.

I will not delve into the details here, for my response is general. It is simply that, given the distinction between (A) target notion and (B) metaphysical account, we should not view the difference between SC and NSC as reflecting *an ambiguity in the target notion*, but rather as *a disagreement over the metaphysical account* of metaphysical necessity. It is surely to be expected that different metaphysical accounts of metaphysical necessity will disagree on the extension of metaphysical necessity. Viewed in this way, SC and NSC do not expose any ambiguity in the target notion, they simply disagree over the further metaphysical account. SC takes 'the source in something to do with the world' to be *the actual laws of metaphysics*; NSC takes it to be *the natures of things*. As such, they deliver different results in some cases. But they conform to the same target notion.

Even if one insisted on taking SC and NSC to be supplementing the target notion, it is not straightforward to conclude that the notion of metaphysical necessity is therefore ambiguous. Suppose you take SC to be in part definitive of metaphysical necessity. Then you might acknowledge that there are some metaphysical necessities the negations of which are logically compatible with the natures of things, but you won't accept that there is any real sense in which those negations are therefore possible. Suppose you take NSC to be in part definitive of metaphysical necessity. You may then acknowledge some notion of necessity defined in terms of the actual laws of metaphysics, but you'll deny that this is metaphysical necessity. The dispute between SC and NSC in these terms would simply be a disagreement over the meaning of 'metaphysical necessity', and not evidence of an ambiguity in the word. Even so, I see no reason to allow this extra content to be built into the target notion, for it straightforwardly violates the constraint of extensional neutrality.

In short, the target notion of metaphysical necessity has not been shown to be ambiguous. The dispute between the standard and non-standard conceptions is better understood as a dispute at level B, not level A. But even if it were a dispute at level A, the content of the target notion of metaphysical necessity would go beyond the strictest real necessity and would also not imply the ambiguity of the term— just a disagreement over its proper (unambiguous) meaning.

The second challenge is that the notion of metaphysical necessity is empty. Graham Priest professes scepticism about metaphysical necessity. As we saw earlier, he introduces the notion of metaphysical necessity as lying in the space between analytic and physical necessity. He then asks: 'Do we have good reasons for supposing there to be such a notion?' (Priest, 2021, 3). I have already argued that 'the space between' is the wrong way to define metaphysical necessity. In any case, Priest's line of argument is not to claim that there is something incoherent or ambiguous in the notion of metaphysical necessity, but rather to show that it is *empty*; that there are no things that are distinctively metaphysically necessary. For example, part of his strategy is to cast doubt on Kripkean necessities.

My response to this kind of challenge is straightforward. I have already argued for extensional neutrality. Developing a view according to which the notion of metaphysical necessity is empty would not immediately undermine its good standing; it would be an interesting philosophical proposal. There is a *notion*

154 THINKING OF NECESSITY

of metaphysical necessity. It is distinct from notions of analytic necessity and physical necessity. But this leaves open the possibility for surprising metaphysical conclusions. If one had reason to conclude that the notion is empty, there would be a further question whether to stop using the notion for theoretical purposes— perhaps it should be scrapped like *phlogiston*, or perhaps it would still be useful like *frictionless plane*—but there wouldn't cease to be a meaningful notion.

I take the final challenge to arise from the work of philosophers such as Ted Sider and Ross Cameron. Sider (2011) denies that modal notions 'carve at the joints', and offers what he calls a 'Humean' reduction of modality.

> To say that a proposition is necessary, according to the Humean, is to say that the proposition is i) true; and ii) of a certain sort.   (Sider, 2011, 269)

The necessities are either true propositions of a certain sort (e.g., mathematical axioms, principles of classical mereology), or logical consequences of those propositions, where logical consequence in turn is given a non-modal treatment.[33] The notion of metaphysical necessity is therefore disjunctive: *to be metaphysically necessary is to be a mathematical truth, or an analytic truth, or a natural kind identity,* .... If, like Sider, you think that metaphysics should focus on natural distinctions that carve nature at the joints, then so much the worse for metaphysical necessity.

Cameron proposes a similar 'neo-conventionalism' about metaphysical modality.

> [I]t is not true by convention that $2 + 2 = 4$, but rather a matter of convention that this truth is a necessary truth. The idea is that there is not something special (some glow of necessity) that the proposition $<2 + 2 = 4>$ has that the proposition <there are monkeys> lacks; it is simply that the conventions governing our modal language pick out the former and not the latter as a necessary truth.... There is nothing special about the truths of maths, or analytic truths, or natural kind identities, etc., that we are latching on to when we single them out as necessary truths, it's just that we consider such propositions important, and so we use our modal language to accord them special status.   (Cameron, 2009, 14)

His key thought is that the distinction between the metaphysically possible and impossible, between the metaphysically necessary and contingent, is *unnatural*.

> [M]aybe our modal vocabulary isn't latching on to some natural distinction between the possible and the impossible; maybe we're latching on to some highly

---

[33] See also Sider (2005).

WHAT IS METAPHYSICAL NECESSITY?   155

> unnatural distinction, and there is nothing more to a world's being a possible world than that it falls on one side of this unnatural distinction and not the other. This is what the neo-conventionalist thinks.   (Cameron, 2010, 148)

This perhaps goes further even than Sider, insofar as the distinction need not even be natural enough to correspond to a tractable disjunction.

One might understand modal Humeanism and neo-conventionalism either as claims at level A (the target notion is disjunctive/unnatural) or level B (the class of metaphysical necessities is unnatural). If we understand them in the first way then my earlier arguments suggest that the Humean/neo-conventionalist is wrong. There is a clear and well-motivated non-disjunctive and not obviously unnatural notion of metaphysical necessity: *the strictest real necessity*. If we understand them in the second way, then for all I've said here, one may well discover that a metaphysical account of the strictest real necessity reveals that it draws an unnatural division in reality. This would be an interesting metaphysical discovery about a notion that remains in good standing.

However, perhaps this is too quick. One element of the target notion I have defended is *necessity*. It is arguably this that is under attack from Sider and Cameron: all there is to the notion of necessity is a list of various kinds of proposition.

> *Why* are logical (or mathematical, or analytic, or . . .) truths necessary? The Humean's answer is that this is just how our concept of necessity works. One can give no deeper answer to this question than to the question of why a water glass counts as a cup (assuming that it does). There are many possible meanings we could have chosen for 'cup' ; some include glasses, some don't; none carve nature at the joints better than any others; the meaning we have in fact chosen includes glasses; and that's all there is to it. Likewise for 'necessary'.
>
> (Sider, 2011, 289)

It is no good replying to this that all the relevant truths are real necessities, because the claim here is that there is nothing more to being necessary than appearing on the list. An answer to this would seem to demand no less than a defence of the very concept of necessity (metaphysical or otherwise). That is what I have attempted to do in the previous chapters, in arguing that there are modal concepts written into our capacities for thought and objective thought. In particular, in Chapter 5 I argued that grasp of a notion of objective modality is a condition of our capacity for objective thought. In this chapter I have argued further that this fits the bill for being metaphysical necessity. Hence, metaphysical necessity is saved from the jaws of non-substantiality: our (metaphysical) modal concepts are more than simply a conventional list.

7

Relative and Absolute Necessity

7.1 Relative and absolute necessity

The conclusion of the previous chapters is that metaphysical necessity is relative to conditions of objectivity.

Metaphysical□ It is metaphysically necessary that p iff $\exists\phi(O\phi \wedge \square(\phi \rightarrow p))$

That is, it is metaphysically necessary that p just when there are some conditions of objectivity that logically necessarily imply p. Metaphysical necessity is *relative to* conditions of objectivity, and it is also a *relativization of* logical necessity.

A kind of necessity is absolute if it is the strictest kind of necessity, or necessity unrestricted. More precisely:

A□1 It is absolutely necessary that p iff $\neg\exists \Diamond (\Diamond\neg p)$

It is absolutely necessary that p if and only if there is no sense of (alethic, non-epistemic) possibility (here represented by '$\Diamond$') such that it is possible that it is not the case that p.[1] For example, we might think that it is absolutely necessary that everything is self-identical. What this means, according to the definition, is that there is no (alethic, non-epistemic) sense in which it is possible for something to fail to be self-identical. And that seems right: surely nothing could be distinct from itself. Contrast this with, for example, the necessity of the laws of nature. It is physically necessary that force equals mass times acceleration. But couldn't things have been such that this was false, and in fact force and mass had a quite different relationship, such that force *plus* mass equalled acceleration? It seems plausible that things *could* have been that way, had the laws of nature been different. In which case, it isn't *absolutely* necessary that force equals mass times acceleration, but rather necessary only relative to our laws of nature, say.

This definition is put in terms of an *alethic, non-epistemic* sense of possibility. As earlier (p.141), 'epistemic' here is understood in terms of what we know, rather than in terms of something like epistemic conditions. There may be some

---

[1] I am here using a quantifier over kinds of possibility to capture the claim that 'there is no sense of possibility . . .'. Such a kind of quantification belongs only to the meta-language as a shorthand to help express such claims.

Thinking of Necessity: A Kantian Account of Modal Thought and Modal Metaphysics. Jessica Leech, Oxford University Press. © Jessica Leech 2023. DOI: 10.1093/oso/9780198873969.003.0007

RELATIVE AND ABSOLUTE NECESSITY   157

absolute necessities that, *for all we know*, could be false. For example, let us suppose that a given unproven logical proposition L is true. Suppose also that any logical proposition, if true, is logically necessarily true, and thereby absolutely necessarily true. So L is logically necessarily true. However, there is a sense of possibility according to which it is possible that $\neg L$: L is thus far unproven, so the *epistemic possibility* remains that $\neg L$. But this doesn't have any bearing on the absolute necessity of L, only on our *knowledge* of L. The only relevant senses of possibility for this definition of absolute necessity are thus alethic, non-epistemic, senses, i.e., senses of possibility which *conflict with* the purported absolute sense of necessity. For example, it can be absolutely necessary that p, whilst epistemically, doxastically, or perhaps even legally possible that p. But it can't be absolutely necessary that p and at the same time physically or biologically possible that p. From now on, I will omit the cumbersome 'alethic, non-epistemic' qualification, but unless otherwise specified, this is intended throughout.

$A\square 1$ tells us what absolute necessity is. In similar terms, we can define (mere) relative necessity as a kind of necessity for which *there is* a competing sense of possibility.

$R\square 1$ It is relatively necessary that p iff $\boxdot p \wedge \exists \lozenge (\lozenge \neg p)$

Where '$\boxdot$' stands for some kind of alethic, non-epistemic necessity.

Earlier, I provided a schema for a formulation of relative necessities:[2]

$Relative\square$ It is Φ-necessary that p iff $\exists \phi (\Phi\phi \wedge \square(\phi \rightarrow p))$

It is Φ-necessary that p just when there is a proposition ϕ, falling under a condition Φ, and it follows absolutely necessarily from ϕ that p. i.e., it is necessary that p relative to Φ-conditions of some kind. I take logical necessity to be absolute necessity, hence '$\square$' represents logical necessity, and 'following absolutely necessarily' is following logically.[3] But even leaving open the question of what kind of

---

[2] See Chapter 2, section 2.4.

[3] Hale (1996) presents a proof that logical necessity is absolute necessity, adapted from McFetridge (1990). The necessity in question is identified as logical via a set of assumptions governing the necessity operator $\square$ (Hale, 1996, 96). Assume for *reductio* that it is logically necessary that if A then B ($\square(A \rightarrow B)$), and that there is a(n arbitrary) alethic, non-epistemic sense of possibility according to which it is possible that A and not-B ($\blacklozenge(A \wedge \neg B)$). By strengthening (If $\square(\phi \rightarrow \psi)$ then $\square((\phi \wedge \chi) \rightarrow \psi)$) it follows that $\square((A \wedge \neg B) \rightarrow B)$. Trivially, $\square(\neg B \rightarrow \neg B)$ (since in all cases, $\square(\phi \rightarrow \phi)$). By strengthening, it follows from $\square(\neg B \rightarrow \neg B)$ that $\square((A \wedge \neg B) \rightarrow \neg B)$. But then it follows that $\square((A \wedge \neg B) \rightarrow (B \wedge \neg B))$ (since if $\square(\phi \rightarrow \psi)$ and $\square(\phi \rightarrow \chi)$ then $\square(\phi \rightarrow (\psi \wedge \chi))$). Since it is possible that A and not-B, $\blacklozenge(A \wedge \neg B)$, it is therefore also possible that B and not-B, $\blacklozenge(B \wedge \neg B)$ (since if $\blacklozenge\phi$ and $\square(\phi \rightarrow \psi)$ then $\blacklozenge\psi$). But $\neg\blacklozenge(B \wedge \neg B)$: no contradiction is possible in any relevant sense of possibility. Therefore, by *reductio*, $\neg\blacklozenge(A \wedge \neg B)$. If $\square(A \rightarrow B)$, then there is no sense of (alethic, non-epistemic) possibility according to which it is possibly not the case that $A \rightarrow B$. Hale then defends two lemmas which allow us to generalise the result to all cases, not just conditional formulas. *Lemma 1:* $\square p$ iff $\square((p \rightarrow p) \rightarrow p)$. *Lemma 2:* $\blacklozenge\neg p$ iff $\blacklozenge((p \rightarrow p) \wedge \neg p)$. 'Now if $\square p$, then by

158 THINKING OF NECESSITY

necessity is absolute, *Relative*□ captures the key idea that relative necessities can be expressed as a relativization of absolute necessity. According to this schema, absolute necessities trivially count as relative in virtue of following from any propositions whatsoever. A schema for *mere* relative necessities simply adds the specification that it is not absolutely necessary that p.

Relative□* It is *merely* Φ-necessary that p iff $\exists \phi(\Phi\phi \wedge \Box(\phi \to p))$ and $\neg \Box p$

One can also define absolute necessity in similar terms to *Relative*□, i.e., as a kind of necessity which follows logically from *any* proposition. So we have, for example:

A□2 It is absolutely necessary that p iff $\forall \phi \Box(\phi \to p)$[4]

Note in *A□2* it no longer matters what kind of propositions p follows from, i.e., whether or not $\Phi\phi$, as p follows from all and any propositions. Indeed, we could just write '$\Box p$', where this expresses that it is logically necessary that p.

Hale (2013) presents a proof that these two definitions of absolute necessity—what he calls maximally absolute necessity (*A□1*) and limit-absolute necessity (*A□2*)—are logically equivalent.[5] We can sketch the argument informally here. If it is necessary that p, and there's no competing sense of possibility according to which possibly $\neg p$, then there is not any proposition which rules out p. Otherwise it would be possible, relative to the truth of that proposition, that $\neg p$. Vice versa, if p follows from every proposition, then how could we define a kind of possibility according to which $\neg p$ was possible? No matter what, it is the case that p.

7.2 Metaphysical necessity is relative necessity

The view that metaphysical necessity is relative necessity might seem surprising at best. Metaphysical necessity is often taken to be distinctively absolute. For example, Hale (1996) writes of the friends of metaphysical necessity that,

> they would want to hold that when it is metaphysically necessary that p, there is no good sense of 'possible' (except, perhaps, an epistemic one) in which it is possible that not-p. Metaphysical necessities hold true at all possible worlds without qualification or exception (in contrast, perhaps, with e.g. physical necessities, which are true of all physically possible worlds...). (Hale, 1996, 95)

Lemma 1, $\Box((p \to p) \to p)$, whence by McFetridge's thesis, $\neg\blacklozenge((p \to p) \wedge \neg p)$ for any sense of $\blacklozenge$, so that $\neg\blacklozenge\neg p$, by Lemma 2. Thus we have: (*Generalised McF*): If $\Box p$ then there is no sense in which $\blacklozenge\neg p$' (Hale, 1996, 98, notation adapted for consistency).

[4] See also Hale (2013, 101).

[5] See Hale (2013, 110–12). Hale does not assume that the necessity operator in the definition for limit-absolute necessity is a logical necessity operator, but this does not affect this proof—the lack of assumption is important elsewhere for him.

Similarly, Williamson writes:

> What is metaphysically necessary is what could not have been otherwise, what would have obtained *whatever* had obtained.
>
> (Williamson, 2013, 3, emphasis added)

But logical necessity is plausibly stricter than metaphysical necessity: there are metaphysical necessities that are not logically necessary (e.g., Socrates is human), but not vice versa. So how can metaphysical necessity be absolute?

One might employ the broad strategy to downgrade logical necessity and possibility as not concerning *how things could be,* but as rather constrained by considerations of *expressive resources.* Metaphorically speaking, metaphysical possibility marks the outer boundaries of possibility, but we can purport to travel beyond those bounds due to the impoverished expressive resources of various logics. So, for example, suppose that it is metaphysically necessary that Socrates is human. There is no sense in which this could genuinely fail to be the case (so the thought goes). But it is not a logical truth in any familiar logic. Compare: it is a logical truth according to classical predicate logic that $\exists x(x = x)$, but this is logically contingent according to classical propositional logic. Indeed, it can only be expressed in the latter as p. Hence, metaphysical necessity is absolute necessity because it is the strictest *genuine* necessity, and we can ignore stricter logical necessities as not genuine, but rather due to poverty of expressive resources.

> [T]hose 'possibilities'—such as the austerely logical possibility that there are male vixens—are possibilities *in name only*, not *real* or *genuine* possibilities at all. There is, to be sure, no overt—or first-order extractable—contradiction involved in the supposition (so expressed) that there are male vixens. But while absence of first-order—or more generally, purely proof-theoretic—inconsistency is certainly a *necessary* condition for real possibility, it is clearly insufficient. It affords no guarantee that there could be a situation in which the supposition would be realised.   (Hale, 1996, 100)

This approach does not sit well with the view developed in this book. Logical necessity is more than an artefact of expressive resource or proof theory; it has its source in the laws of thought. And metaphysical necessity is to be understood as relative to conditions on objectivity, in line with an answer to the problem of reality. However, on such a view, it is perfectly possible to fully accommodate the relevant intuitions: i.e., that mere logical possibility is not a way things 'genuinely' could be, and that metaphysical necessity is in some sense absolute, because it concerns the most general features or conditions of being.

Recall, according to the proposed account, all of reality that can be an object for us is (all objects of objective thought are) subject to conditions of objectivity.

160 THINKING OF NECESSITY

Metaphysical possibility is a matter of compatibility with these conditions. Hence, *there can be no* metaphysically impossible object or real thing. Nevertheless, one can still maintain that logical necessity is solely absolute, and that logical possibility, whilst not having the same kinds of consequences for real objects as metaphysical modality, still has a vital role to play. Even though on this view metaphysical necessity is not *absolute*, it is *the strictest real* necessity. It is this feature which allows the view to accommodate the intuition that metaphysical necessity is at least as strong as any other kind. It does not have this strength *tout court*, but it is nevertheless the strongest *real* necessity, the strongest kind of necessity which yields the widest kind of possibility for the world. This is clearly an important status for a necessity to have. This should satisfy those who think that metaphysical necessity is absolute because mere logical possibilities do not seem to be a good guide to how reality could be. The Modal Transcendentalist does not claim that they are.

Nevertheless, metaphysical necessity is a merely relative necessity. We can explain how it is the strictest real necessity in terms of the significant status of the propositions to which it is relative: conditions of objectivity. However, the ultimate source of the resulting modal force—the mysterious "oomph"—of metaphysical necessity (indeed, any relative necessity) is borrowed from the absolute necessity of which it is a relativized form, logical necessity. The ultimate source of alethic modality is thus in constitutive norms for thought.

If logical necessity is understood as having its source in constitutive norms for *thought*, then *of course* one wouldn't expect logical possibility to give a straight-forward guide to how real things might be: the possibilities for what we can think shouldn't be taken to determine what can be. There are further constraints to be taken into account if we want to consider what could really be the case. We have seen that those are conditions on our capacity for *objective* thought. However, it is a mistake to think that this demotes the status of mere logical possibility to something that is not 'genuine', to possibility 'in name only'. It is not a problem that logical possibility itself does not tell us how the world of real objects can be—possibility and necessity are restricted to the real world by an appropriate relative base.

What *is* a more significant challenge here is to draw a line, amongst the various layers of putative logical modalities, between 'genuine' logical possibilities and possibilities in name only. Absolute necessity should not be *too* restrictive. For example, it is necessary according to first order predicate logic that $\forall x(Fx \vee \neg Fx)$. But there is a sense of possibility—that defined by propositional logic—according to which it could be false. The suggested response here is in terms of expressive resource. Rather than claiming that the field of, e.g., propositional logical necessity is genuinely wider than that of first order predicate logical necessity, one can claim that there is *one* space of absolute possibilities, but differences in which vocabularies can *express* which of those possibilities.

The difference between the necessities of propositional logic and those of first-order logic is not a difference in the ranges of possibilities throughout which they hold. At the linguistic level, it is simply a difference in the kind of vocabulary required for their adequate expression. (Hale, 2013, 114–15)

Logical necessities 'in central and basic cases' are characterized, or identifiable, as 'absolute necessities expressible by sentences which essentially involve only logical words' (Hale, 2013, 145). Propositional logical necessities, for example, would then be understood as absolute necessities expressible by sentences which essentially involve only the vocabulary of propositional logic.

This doesn't help us to draw a particular line around the absolute necessities. But it gives us the resources to explain away putative 'stricter' necessities. The debate must come down to positive reasons to take one kind of necessity to be absolute rather than another. Here, I refer the reader back to the arguments of Chapters 3 and 4. There I defended an account of the function and source of logical necessity as tied to our capacity to think. As already noted, this kind of necessity should not be understood merely in terms of expressive resources. It is an important modal notion in its own right, and one that plays a foundational role in our ability to think and reason. As such, it is not appropriate to *explain away* these logical necessities. Rather, whatever propositions are required to count as logically necessary in line with the laws of thought will constitute the outer boundary of absolute necessity. We can then treat any stricter notions of necessity, allied with alternative logical systems, in terms of expressive resources.

What, then, *is the One True Logic* that aligns with the laws of thought, and which thereby gives us absolute necessity? I cannot answer that question here. I have gestured towards some likely starting points in Chapter 3.[6] There is undoubtedly further work to be done on this, which I cannot complete here. However, I shall close this section by responding to one common objection.

The objection, as it is often put to me, is 'What would Graham Priest think?'. There are a great variety of different logical systems with different rules few, if any, of which are shared by all. If only one of these is the One True Logic, then what should we say about the status of all the rest? And if the One True Logic concerns constitutive norms for thought, and is something in the vicinity of classical logic, then how is it that otherwise ostensibly excellent thinkers such as Graham Priest profess to be thinking in line with very different logical laws, such as those of a paraconsistent logic?

There are several points that can be made in response. First, I'm happy to leave it as a matter of open inquiry which logical system captures the laws of thought. Perhaps it will turn out that Graham Priest is right. I, myself, have moments of sympathy with relevant logic (Leech, 2020). That we do not know which logical

---

[6] I also discuss this further in Leech (2020).

162 THINKING OF NECESSITY

system is privileged in this way does not show that none has this status. Second, there are reasons to think that any logical system will at least need a certain minimal set of rules governing, for example, the conditional and universal generalization.[7] Third, even paraconsistent logics are not as wild as one might think. For example, Priest's Logic of Paradox (*LP*) (Priest, 1979), does in fact validate the Law of Non-contradiction. For suppose $\neg(A \wedge \neg A)$ was false for some A. Then $A \wedge \neg A$ would be true. So both A and $\neg A$ would be true. But given the semantics for $\neg$, this is impossible: if A is true then $\neg A$ is false. So $\neg(A \wedge \neg A)$ must be true. Even if A and $\neg A$ were *true-and-false*, as is allowed in *LP*, this would only mean that $A \wedge \neg A$ and $\neg(A \wedge \neg A)$ would both be *true-and-false* as well. Importantly, $\neg(A \wedge \neg A)$ would not be plain *false*. So it is possible that there be contradictions which are *true-and-false*, but there is no room for contradictions which are plain *true*. Just because a logic can tolerate contradiction without explosion, does not mean that it has to violate the Law of Non-Contradiction.

Finally, I find it helpful to draw a distinction between a plurality of logics, which are formal mathematical systems worthy of study, and a single logic which tells us the logical rules for thinking of minds like ours. Mathematical logical systems may have many interesting properties and applications, but given that the very idea of logic has come out of the study of reasoning and valid forms thereof, we might retain the idea that the study of logic and logical necessity should maintain a link to a logical system as a system of reasoning. Systems falling short may be mathematically interesting, but are not relevant for the determination of absolute necessity.

7.3 Relative necessity: arguments from linguistics and similarity

In the previous section, I have clarified and briefly defended the claims that logical necessity is absolute and that metaphysical necessity is relative. But there are also positive reasons in favour of treating one as a relativization of the other. In this section, I rehearse what I call the *argument from linguistics* and the *argument from similarity*. Both are intended to lend support to what I call *the relative modality view*. This is the view that as far as possible we should treat kinds of modality as related by relativization.[8]

7.3.1 The argument from linguistics

Most arguments in the literature in favour of relative modality of some form are to be found in linguistics and philosophy of language, regarding the nature of modal *terms*. The main argument comes from the plethora of different modals of the same force, i.e., different 'must's and 'can's. There is such a great variety of modals to be

---

[7] See Chapter 4, section 4.2.2. [8] These arguments are developed in Leech (2020).

found in the linguistic data that it is implausible to think they are entirely different words with different meanings (such that words such as 'must' are ambiguous in a similar way to 'bank').[9] Furthermore, all these different 'must's and 'can's do seem to have a similar kind of meaning, or overlap to some extent in what they mean. It makes better sense to assume that, rather than ambiguous words with many meanings, we have univocal words with one meaning along with something like parameters to be determined by context.

Lycan (1994) motivates the view by considering the many different and subtle changes in modals in everyday use, concluding that,

> everyday English is shot through with restricted alethic modalities whose restrictions are almost capriciously diverse, rarely aligned with any easily specifiable modal concept known to logicians, and irreparably vague—yet calculated on the spot by ordinary human speakers/hearers with hardly a conscious thought.
>
> (Lycan, 1994, 176)

Having considered similar data, Kratzer (1977) argues that,

> All this leaves us with many different 'must's and 'can's. What can we do with them? We could give them different names. Numbers have been proposed. Let's have
>
> 'must$_1$', 'must$_2$', 'must$_3$',...
> 'can$_1$', 'can$_2$', 'can$_3$',...
>
> But we might not have enough numbers. How many bits of knowledge are there, to which we can refer? How often does the Queen change her mind?... How many kinds of duties can we take into consideration? And even if we had enough numbers, it would not be very sensible to use them here. In everyday conversation we do not use subscripts when we use the words 'must' and 'can'. Somehow we do without them. And even quite easily. There must be another way by means of which we make ourselves understood using these words.
>
> (Kratzer, 1977, 339–40)

For Kratzer, the explanation of this other way is a common core of meaning—'must-in-view-of', 'can-in-view-of'—relativized to different parameters. Lewis (1979) also appears to be convinced by this kind of argument.

> The "can" and "must" of ordinary language...usually...express various relative modalities.... That suggests that "can" and "must" are ambiguous. But on that hypothesis, as Kratzer has convincingly argued, the alleged senses are altogether too numerous. We do better to think of our modal verbs as unambiguous but relative. (Lewis, 1979, 354)

---

[9] i.e., land bordering a river vs. financial institution.

164   THINKING OF NECESSITY

This may be a widely accepted view regarding modal terms, but these are arguments concerning pieces of language, and the current project is concerned with the *metaphysics* of modality. Conclusions regarding how modal language works do not immediately tell us how reality is. However, two arguments for a metaphysical thesis of relative modality—that most kinds of modality are in fact merely relative forms of another, fundamental, kind of modality—can be formulated on the basis of these arguments concerning modal language.

The first argument is an appeal to take the account of modal language seriously as a guide to modal reality. If we speak about a plentiful variety of kinds of modality, and we say something true, then we should be prepared to accept that there are many such kinds of modality in the world. And, if we take seriously the claim that our modal terms are univocal but relative, this suggests that we ought to take seriously the idea that there is one core type of modality, to which the others are relative.

Consider things from another direction. Suppose we agree that modal terms are univocal but relative. If we also claim that in reality different kinds of modality are not relative to one fundamental kind, but independent, then it seems that we will have to say something like: for each (or most) relativization(s) of a modal term in our language, there is a kind of modality in the world corresponding to it, but which is not itself relative in the manner described. This seems strange. Apart from anything else, why would we use the same word, with a constant meaning, to refer to so many different things? If, e.g., the 'must's in '2 + 2 must equal 4' and 'Every effect must have a cause' denote genuinely distinct and unrelated modalities in the world, how can we explain using the same word with the same core meaning? Indeed, what could that core meaning be, if not a basic kind of modality?

One might object here that there is a significant disanalogy between the linguistic case and the metaphysical case: the linguistic accounts claim that there is a common core to all modal terms with a parameter to be fixed, whereas the metaphysical account argues that there is a fundamental kind of modality, to which other kinds of modality are relative. e.g., the core element 'must-in-view-of x' is supposed to be common to logical necessity and physical necessity alike, in both cases being fleshed-out with a specification of the conditions in view of which something is necessary. In contrast, the metaphysical view takes, e.g., physical necessity to be a form of logical necessity, relative to some conditions. Doesn't this disanalogy make it difficult to use the linguistic considerations as an aid to the metaphysical view? No. Consider, there must be some kind of limiting case for 'must-in-view-of', where the set of conditions in view of which something is necessary is minimal, perhaps empty.[10] What kind of modality might this express? Surely a kind of necessity which is relative to no conditions is not properly

---

[10] Kratzer (2012, 49) allows that this parameter 'can be filled by the empty conversational background'.

described as relative at all. It seems to me that this limiting case of necessity on the linguistic view corresponds to absolute necessity on the metaphysical view, to which other kinds of necessity are relative.

One might also object to the account of modal terms as relative. Vetter and Viebahn (2016) argue, to the contrary, that modals do not share a single core meaning with differences accounted for in terms of *context-sensitivity*, but rather that modals are *polysemous*: they have related meanings, such as, for example, 'healthy' in the sense that a salad is healthy and in the sense that a dog is healthy. In their view, for example, 'may' has (at least) an epistemic meaning and a deontic meaning, and 'can' has (at least) a deontic meaning and a dynamic meaning, where dynamic modalities are understood as relating to abilities and, more broadly, real alethic modalities. Such a view does not *prima facie* lend support to the relative modality view, although it does still lend broad support to the idea that we need to account for similarities between modalities, insofar as this is reflected in similarities in modal terms. However, that said, Vetter and Viebahn allow for context-sensitivity *within* what they call different 'modal flavours'. For example, within the modal flavour of dynamic modality for 'can', one can account for variation in terms of context sensitivity such that, e.g., relative to Aristotle's rational capacities as a human he can use an iPad; relative to the state of technology at the time he was living Aristotle cannot use an iPad. In the present chapter I am only attempting to defend the relative modality view as applied to alethic, non-epistemic modalities. In which case, the polysemy account of the meaning of modal terms is not, after all, a threat. The linguistic evidence to which I am appealing is arguably within one modal flavour.

All told, leading linguistic accounts of modal terms lend some support to the relative modality view. However, this is not particularly strong support. There are all sorts of cases in which language is misleading, where it might not be a good guide to reality. For example, it is generally taken to be a bad idea to introduce an ontology of *sakes* just because we use phrases such as 'For heaven's sake!'. So I do not place too much weight on this argument. It is perhaps enough to note that the linguistic theories are in line with the relative modality view. There is a better argument, along similar lines, that does not tie itself so closely to linguistics.

7.3.2 The argument from similarity

Consider the variety of different kinds of necessity. They have many differences. Even so, they are alike in an important way. They are *necessities*. That may sound obvious, but if they are given entirely different accounts, it may seem a mystery why they seem to have something so distinctive in common, that they concern a way in which things *must* be so. That different necessities and possibilities have something in common demands explanation. One plausible explanation that

166 THINKING OF NECESSITY

meets this need is that all modalities can be expressed as relativizations of one basic kind of modality in the world (or as that kind itself).

In particular, we answer the call for explanation if all non-logical necessities can be expressed as relativizations of logical necessity. Recall the formulation of relative necessity.

Relative□   It is Φ-necessary that p iff $\exists\phi(\Phi\phi \wedge \Box(\phi \to p))$

All kinds of necessity formulated in this way share a core relation to the necessity captured by '□'. They have in common that they are relativizations of logical necessity. We can draw from this a stronger or a weaker conclusion. The stronger conclusion is that the modal force in any such relative necessity *just is* the modal force of logical necessity; relative necessity inherits its modal "oomph" from logical necessity. The weaker conclusion is that the fact that it is possible to formulate a kind of necessity as relative to logical necessity shows a certain kind of commonality between the kinds of necessity. Even if relative necessity does not strictly speaking inherit its modal force from logical necessity, it must be sufficiently closely related to allow for the relative necessity formulation to apply. I happen to prefer the stronger view, but either way relativization provides an answer to the call for explanation.

Given such a formulation, we can also say that logical necessity, as expressed by '□', is at least as strong as all relative necessities defined in terms of it. Trivially, if it is logically necessary that p ($\Box p$), then (as long as there are some Φ-propositions)[11] it is also relatively necessary that p,[12] and so there is no sense of relative possibility such that it is possible that $\neg p$.

This argument is not quite an argument to the best explanation, but rather an argument to a plausible explanation: there is a phenomenon to be explained, and treating modalities as relative provides a fairly simple and plausible explanation. Let us briefly consider one alternative that might seem just as good. The core idea is that we can explain what different kinds of modality have in common by the fact that they can be expressed as *derivative of* a shared kind of necessity. Relativization is one way to derive one modality from another. But what about other modes of derivation, such as restriction? Perhaps one could account for similarity because one kind of modality is a *restriction* of another, i.e., the physical possibilities might be a subset of the metaphysical possibilities, or the logical necessities a subset of the metaphysical necessities. More precisely, we might say that Φ-necessity is a restriction of Ψ-necessity just when it is Φ-necessary that p if and only if it is

---

[11] I will have more to say about this qualification in Chapter 10.

[12] If it is logically necessary that p, then for any proposition q, $\Box(q \to p)$. So in particular, this will hold for the case where q is any Φ-proposition.

Ψ-necessary that p and Δp, where Δp expresses some additional condition on Φ-necessities.[13]

Let me offer one reason why relativization may be more appealing than restriction. In order to explain important similarities between different kinds of *necessity* in terms of restriction, one will need a very wide notion of necessity to restrict. For example, let us suppose that the realm of physical necessity is narrower than the realm of human necessity (there are human necessities not physically necessary, such as not running 100m in less than 5 seconds, but no physical impossibilities are humanly possible). If one were to apply a restrictive strategy here, the physical necessities would simply be a subclass of the human necessities. In order to accommodate all the different kinds, the widest kind of necessity is going to be something very weak; hardly an ideal paradigm from which to explain how it is that, e.g., physical necessities are necessary. In contrast, relativization does not need the basic kind of modality to somehow "contain" all the others. This allows us to take a stronger and more intuitively robust kind of modality as the basic kind.

One might reply: there is no such problem if we proceed by restriction of *possibility*, for the widest and weakest possibilities are often taken to be of a plausibly basic kind, such as logical possibilities. Even so, relativization has the advantage of being able to take the same basic kind of modality, whether starting with necessity or possibility. For example, suppose we begin with a general formulation of relative possibility. Either:

Relative$\diamond$ It is Φ-possible that p iff $\neg \exists \phi (\Phi \phi \wedge \neg \diamond (\phi \wedge p))$

That is: it is Φ-possible that p just when there's no Φ-proposition that rules out p. Or:

Relative$\diamond$*   It is Φ-possible that p iff $\exists \phi (\Phi \phi \wedge \forall \psi (\Phi \psi \rightarrow \diamond (\psi \wedge p)))$

That is: it is Φ-possible that p just when there are some Φ-propositions, and all of them are compatible with p. These formulations are based on the same variety of base modality, logical possibility ($\diamond$). I could have just as easily formulated them in terms of logical necessity ($\Box$), i.e., $\neg \exists \phi (\Phi \phi \wedge \Box (\phi \rightarrow \neg p))$ or $\exists \phi (\Phi \phi \wedge \forall \psi (\Phi \psi \rightarrow \neg \Box (\psi \rightarrow \neg p)))$. The fact that taking necessity or possibility first makes

---

[13] For example, according to some essentialists, logical necessity is a restriction of metaphysical necessity in the sense that it is metaphysically necessary that p just when it is true in virtue of the natures of *all* things that p, and logically necessary that p just when it is true in virtue of the natures of *some things, namely the logical things,* that p. One could capture this in the form suggested as: it is logically necessary that p if and only if it is metaphysically necessary that p and it is true in virtue of the natures of logical things that p.

168 THINKING OF NECESSITY

no difference to the variety of base modality suggests that this kind of derivation is more robust than restriction.[14]

7.3.3 Modal differences

In response to the call for an explanation of similarity between different modalities, an opponent might reply that a relative theory of modality cannot account for important *differences* between the most significant kinds of modality. This is one of Fine's complaints when he discusses treating natural necessity as a relative kind of necessity.[15] He suggests that different modalities have a distinctive 'modal force' which is lost when they are treated as relative modalities.

> One might wish to press the objection further and claim that no definition stated entirely in terms of metaphysical necessity could capture the peculiarly modal force of truths that are naturally necessary yet metaphysically contingent. Just as it has been supposed that there is a conceptual barrier between normative and non-normative concepts, so one might think that there is a conceptual barrier, not merely between modal and non-modal concepts, but also between different 'grades' of modality.   (Fine, 2005, 247–8)

Fine suggests that a naturally necessary truth, say, is necessary in a peculiar way that cannot be captured in terms of a relativization of another kind of necessity. He then goes further in proposing that there might be a *conceptual barrier* between different fundamental kinds of modality, making it impossible for us to be able to understand one in terms of another.

What is this 'modal force' that Fine claims is peculiar to each fundamental kind of modality? One might understand this in terms of principles obeyed by a kind of modality, e.g., we might explain the difference between metaphysical and normative modal force in terms of the fact that the former kind of necessity implies truth (is factive), the latter not. But this doesn't help with Fine's distinction between the peculiar modal forces of metaphysical and natural necessity, which are both factive. Perhaps these modalities obey the same principles (e.g., perhaps they are both captured by an S5 system). Perhaps not (e.g., perhaps metaphysical necessity is captured in an S5-system, natural necessity in an S4-system). However, the general point to be made is that a difference in *logical strength* does not immediately imply a difference in *kind*. A necessity operator is still a

---

[14] What about epistemic and non-alethic modalities? Can the relative necessity view be extended to necessities more widely construed? That will not be my concern here. But see Leech (2020) for discussion.

[15] He also raises a more complex objection, to which I respond in Leech (2016).

necessity operator, whether it be defined in an S4-system, an S5-system, or any other system.

What about a difference in scope? Fine claims that metaphysical necessity is *de re*, whereas natural necessity is *de dicto*. However, this is no good as an indicator of peculiar modal force, as he also claims that normative necessity is *de dicto* and fundamentally distinct from natural necessity. The combination of factivity and scope is more promising: for Fine, natural necessity is *de-dicto-factive*, metaphysical necessity is *de-re-factive*, and normative necessity is *de-dicto-non-factive*. But this still leaves Fine unable to distinguish in this way between, e.g., logical, conceptual and metaphysical necessities. Accordingly, these necessities are taken to be of a kind. On Fine's view, logical necessity and conceptual necessity are restrictions of metaphysical necessity, and thereby have the same peculiar modal force. i.e., metaphysical necessity is understood as truth in virtue of the nature of all things, and then logical necessity and conceptual necessity are understood as truth in virtue of the nature of some things in particular, i.e., logical concepts and concepts respectively. However, it still seems strange to claim that natural necessity is *so very different* that, not only does it have a different kind of modal force to logical, conceptual and metaphysical necessity (where these three are moreover of the same kind), but there may even be some kind of *conceptual barrier* between natural necessity and the others.

Fine explicates the idea of peculiar modal force further.

> There appears to be an intuitive difference to the kind of necessity attaching to metaphysical and natural necessities (granted that some natural necessities are not metaphysical). The former is somehow 'harder' or 'stricter' than the latter. If we were to suppose that a God were capable of breaking necessary connections, then it would take more of a God to break a connection that was metaphysically necessary than one that was naturally necessary.   (Fine, 2005, 259)

The idea is that metaphysically necessary connections are 'harder to break' than naturally necessary connections. But this doesn't make the notion of modal force any less mysterious. First, as already noted, the relation between strength and modal force is not clear. Why not say that natural necessity is a kind of necessity with the same *kind* of modal force as metaphysical necessity, but with different *strength*? Second, this difference in strength can be explained without appeal to the obscure notion of 'modal force'. e.g., if metaphysical necessity is relative to principles governing all things, but natural necessity is relative to principles governing physical objects and processes, it might seem natural to conclude that metaphysical necessity will be the stronger kind given its wider subject matter, but not due to a different modal force.

The attempt to explicate the idea in terms of a 'conceptual barrier' between natural and metaphysical necessity, analogous to the conceptual barrier between the modal and non-modal, highlights a potential misrepresentation of a relative modality view. Fine presses his objection against a definition of natural necessity 'stated entirely in terms of metaphysical necessity'. It seems unsurprising that if we only have the concept of metaphysical necessity at our disposal, we will be unable to represent much more than metaphysical necessity. Likewise, if we only have the concept of logical necessity at our disposal, we will be unable to represent anything else. Granted, if a definition of relative necessity were phrased *entirely* in terms of another kind of necessity, this might pose a problem. But this isn't the case. The formulations proposed importantly include a class of propositions to which a kind of necessity is relative, and an operator capturing important features of those propositions (e.g., that they are conditions of objectivity). The formulations are only partially in terms of logical necessity; they are also in terms of a key set of propositions of a certain kind. The simple answer to Fine's challenge is thus that the 'peculiarity' of each kind of modality is parasitic upon them being related to different kinds of propositions.

These considerations combine to suggest that we should think of different kinds of alethic modality as relative to a basic modality. This coheres with our linguistic practices. It allows us to explain what it is that these different kinds of necessity have in common. The modal force of different alethic necessities can be found in one and the same source: the modal force of the basic modality. And we can account for important differences between kinds of modality by appeal to the different things to which they are relative, i.e., laws of physics, as opposed to laws of biology. Most importantly for present purposes, this applies to metaphysical necessity as much as anything. We can explain the similarities between metaphysical and logical necessity: metaphysical necessity is logical necessity relativized. But we can also explain the differences. Whilst logical necessity concerns only laws of thought, metaphysical necessity is relative to conditions on objective thought.

8

What Is Metaphysically Necessary?

Metaphysical Necessity and *De Re* Necessity

According to Modal Transcendentalism, metaphysical necessity is relative to conditions of objectivity. What is metaphysically necessary according to Modal Transcendentalism? In these final chapters, my aim is to develop a general framework, i.e., to draw out some general consequences of Modal Transcendentalism and apply them to important types of cases and common claims about metaphysical necessity. In particular, are (any) metaphysical necessities *de re*? Are (any) metaphysical necessities *a posteriori*? Can Modal Transcendentalism accommodate any essentialist claims, such as essentiality of kind or essentiality of origin? Does anything exist necessarily, or is existence contingent?[1] First, in this chapter we shall consider: are (any) metaphysical necessities *de re*?

In addition to providing a more detailed framework for metaphysical necessity, addressing such questions serves two further aims. First, although I earlier argued that metaphysical necessity should not be completely beholden to typical cases, since such cases are so commonly associated with metaphysical necessity, it is still worthwhile to explain the extent to which Modal Transcendentalism can accommodate them, and if not, why not.[2] Second, and relatedly: one might take the inability of Modal Transcendentalism to honour some such case to constitute a counterexample to the account. Hence, again, it is worthwhile treating such cases in more detail to forestall this line of objection.

I shall proceed as follows. First, I argue that conditions on objectivity are general, which has consequences for how and the extent to which metaphysical necessities are *de re*. Next, I explore further the purported connection that is widely assumed to hold between metaphysical necessity and *de re* necessity. In doing so, I will rehearse Quine's concerns about the intelligibility of *de re* modality, which arguably pose a threat to Modal Transcendentalism. I then sketch how *de re* modalities can be accommodated in the framework of Modal Transcendentalism, before arguing that Quine's objections can be answered.

---

[1] This framework could then be fleshed out with a comprehensive account of the conditions of objectivity. Given the length and complexity of such a further project, this is left for future work.

[2] See Chapter 6, section 6.2.

Thinking of Necessity: A Kantian Account of Modal Thought and Modal Metaphysics. Jessica Leech, Oxford University Press. © Jessica Leech 2023. DOI: 10.1093/oso/9780198873969.003.0008

8.1 Conditions on objectivity are general

The first and central point to be discussed concerns what conditions of objective thought are like. Conditions on objectivity were introduced as a solution to the problem of reality; the problem of how mental states get to be about reality. Without endorsing a detailed list of such conditions, I sketched some examples from Kant; objects must be presented to us in space and time, have a determinate part-whole structure, a determinate degree of their qualities (e.g., temperature, density, etc.), and conform to a structure of substances instantiating properties standing in causal and reciprocal relations. These conditions broadly require the reality that we represent to be unified: objects are contained within a single unified spacetime, in a certain part-whole structure, and stand in causal and reciprocal relations to everything else, directly or indirectly.

The one condition of objectivity that I did discuss in more detail was a modal condition: we need objective modal concepts—of metaphysical modality—and the ability to make modal judgments using those concepts as a(nother) condition on objective thought. More precisely, we must take our objective thoughts to be objective, where this is understood as the ability to prefix those thoughts with *it is objective that....* The concept of objectivity involved in this prefix is modal, and can be specified as modality relative to conditions on objectivity. There are several consequences to draw from this.

First, any condition on objectivity trivially counts as metaphysically necessary, insofar as it folllows logically from conditions on objectivity. So, for example, if it is a condition on objectivity that objects be spatiotemporal, then it is metaphysically necessary that objects are spatiotemporal. Moreover, if, as I have argued, it is a condition on objectivity that *if a subject is able to think objectively, then they possess (and have the ability to use) metaphysical modal concepts*, then it is metaphysically necessary that *if a subject is able to think objectively, then they possess (and have the ability to) use metaphysical modal concepts*. Note, this doesn't require the existence of any thinkers, only that *if* there are objective thinkers, they must have this capacity. This seems to me to be an interesting metaphysical necessity about thought.

Second, conditions on objectivity are plausibly *general,* not particular. That is to say, they do not concern particular individuals, such as, for example, *Socrates is human,* but rather general claims, such as, for example, *everything is temporal.* The example in the previous paragraph, concerning objective thought, is also of general form: i.e., $\forall x(Ox \rightarrow Px)$.[3] Given the role that conditions on objectivity are intended to play, it is greatly implausible that they would concern particular individuals.

---

[3] Where 'Ox' stands for 'x is able to think objectively' and 'Px' stands for 'x possesses metaphysical modal concepts'. One could offer more complex formalizations, e.g., $\forall x(Ox \rightarrow \exists y(My \land Pxy))$, where '$My$' stands for '$y$ is a metaphysical modal concept' and 'Pxy' means 'x possesses y'. But the point stands: the more complex suggestions are still general.

For that would imply that the existence of those particular individuals, or facts about them, are necessary conditions on objective thought. But what individuals could they be? They would need to be individuals written into the very fabric of objective thought. The notion of conditions on objectivity concerns what reality, and our representations of reality, must be *like* in order for the latter to be about the former. There is nothing to suggest that this must involve the existence of some particular things rather than others, beyond constraints on what those things must be like.

If some conditions on objectivity turn out to concern generic claims about individuals, e.g., that something of such-and-such type must exist, this does not introduce particular individuals in a problematic way. For example, suppose that *if everything is spatiotemporal, then spacetime must exist*, such that it is a condition on objectivity that spacetime exists. The plausible reading of this is not that *the very spacetime we live in, this one*, must exist, i.e., that it is a condition on objectivity that $\exists x(x = s)$, where 's' rigidly designates actual spacetime. There's no clear reason why *this* spacetime should exist, beyond the claim that *some spacetime or other, perhaps very much like this one*, must exist. That is, the plausible reading here is that it is a condition on objectivity that $\exists x Sx$, where 'Sx' means 'x is (a) spacetime'.[4]

Another potential route to particular conditions might go via necessitism. If you hold that everything that exists exists necessarily (and that there couldn't be any other things than what actually exists), then to think objectively of anything will necessarily involve thinking of some of the particular things that exist. There could be no other objects of thought beyond those already available. If you are a necessitist, then this may be a fact about objective thought: any thoughts of objects must be about a or b or $c \dots$ (where a, b, $c \dots$ name all the actual objects). However, this is not a *condition on objective thought* in the sense required by the problem of reality. Those are a special set of necessary conditions on thought which provide an account of how thought can be about the world. Perhaps one might say: conditions on objectivity would explain how a subject could *think about a* or b or c at all. They would not include a specification that a, b, $c \dots$ are the objects; just a generic specification of how thought about objects in general is possible.

Metaphysical necessity is therefore relative to *general* conditions on objectivity.

8.2 *De re* modality and metaphysical modality

If metaphysical necessity is relative to general conditions on objectivity, then one might assume that, *prima facie*, all metaphysical necessities are *de dicto*. Can Modal Transcendentalism accommodate *de re* necessity? Does it need to?

---

[4] I'm not arguing here that the existence of spacetime is metaphysically necessary. This is just an example to illustrate the point.

174 THINKING OF NECESSITY

Informally speaking, *de re* claims pertain to *things*, whereas *de dicto* claims pertain to 'dicta' or 'sayables'. 'De dicto' is associated with things such as propositions, sentences, and statements. 'De re' is associated with the things that propositions, sentences, and statements are about. More formally, *de re* modality is standardly understood as the case where a (rigid) constant or free variable occurs within the scope of a modal operator. *De dicto* modality is accordingly understood as the case where any variable in the scope of a modal operator is bound within the scope of the operator. For example, '$\Box Fa$' and '$\exists x \Box Fx$' are *de re* whereas '$\Box \exists x Fx$' is *de dicto*. The idea is that, if it is necessary that Jane is human, then this is understood as being a *de re* necessity applying to *Jane*. Similarly, if there is *something* such that necessarily *it* is human, this is also understood as a *de re* necessity for *it*. By contrast, if it is necessary that there is something which is human, then there is no *thing* this possibility attaches to, it is simply a necessary proposition. It is true if it is necessary that there is *something or other* which is human; there need be no particular individual which is necessarily human.

The question of whether and how Modal Transcendentalism can accommodate *de re* necessity is not just one of intellectual curiosity; metaphysical necessity is often taken to have a close relationship to *de re* necessity. For example, Fine writes:

> All forms of *de re* necessity (and of essence) will be fundamentally metaphysical, even though some forms of *de dicto* necessity may not be.   (Fine, 2002, 243)

If one takes metaphysical necessity to have its source in the identities or essences of things, then the rationale is clear. Such a kind of necessity, thus understood, primarily concerns *the things themselves* and not features of how we refer to those things. As such, they will primarily, if not exclusively, generate *de re* necessities. *De dicto* metaphysical necessities would presumably only arise if the things themselves and their essences make true some generalizations.

The connection between *de re* necessity and metaphysical necessity need not arise only from a commitment to an essentialist metaphysics of modality. This is also a feature of Quine's famous attack on *de re* modality. Quine distinguishes 'three grades of modal involvement' (Quine, 1953). The first grade is metalinguistic: a modal predicate is applied to the name of a (closed) sentence. For example,

'p' is necessary.

The second grade is no longer metalinguistic: a modal operator that is part of the object language is applied to a (closed) sentence. This kind of modal operator is captured in familiar modal logics by box and diamond symbols. For example,

It is necessary that p.

$\Box p$

The third grade allows modal operators to apply to predicates or open sentences. This grade allows for 'quantifying in', i.e., quantifying into the scope of a modal operator. For example,

Everything is necessarily F.

$\forall x \Box Fx$

Such formulas involve the application of a condition that includes a modal operator to a variable. In this case, the condition '$\Box F$' is applied to a free variable 'x', which is then bound outside of the scope of that modal condition. We might informally read this condition as saying that x is necessarily F. In cases of *de re* modality which involve a name (constant) rather than a variable, we have the same kind of modal condition. For example, in '$\Box Fa$' the modal condition of being necessarily F is predicated of the individual a.

Quine's objection to the third grade is, in brief, as follows. In some cases, substitution of purportedly co-referential terms in modal contexts can lead to a change of truth-value. For example,

Necessarily, 8 is greater than 7.

is true. '8' and 'the number of planets' purport to be co-referential, i.e., they appear to pick out the same thing (the number 8). But,

Necessarily, the number of planets is greater than 7.

is, plausibly, false. It is plausible that there could have been fewer than 7 planets orbiting the sun. Therefore, concludes Quine, modal contexts are referentially opaque. According to Quine, this is due to (a) the kind of necessity at issue, and (b) the understanding of quantification in play.[5] The kind of necessity at issue is logical necessity. This is a kind of necessity that is sensitive to the way that things are represented. For example, whilst it is logically necessary that *if Cicero is wise, then Cicero is wise* (as an instance of $p \rightarrow p$), it is not logically necessary that *if Cicero is wise, then Tully is wise*, even though Cicero is Tully. The understanding of quantification in play is what Quine calls quantification 'ordinarily understood', that is, objectual quantification. It is,

---

[5] I am here closely following the interpretation of Divers (2017). See also Ballarin (2012).

176 THINKING OF NECESSITY

> quantification over what he [Quine] would call extensional entities: these include
> the objects of folk theory (people, tables, tigers, mountains, stars...) and the
> objects, both concrete and abstract, of science (electrons, spacetime points,
> sets...). (Divers, 2017, 221)

Here, then, is the problem. In a *de re* modal predication, because quantification is
understood objectually, as ranging over objects and not (exclusively) linguistic or
semantic entities, the modalized condition (e.g., 'is necessarily greater than 7') is
predicated of *a thing* (e.g., *the number 8*, or the value of *x*), not of a linguistic expression (e.g., '8' or 'the number of planets'). However, the kind of modality that is
ascribed—logical necessity—is dependent on the particular linguistic expression.
Thus put, *de re* modal predication is unintelligible, insofar as it attempts to apply a
kind of language-dependent modality to a language-independent kind of thing. It
is just incomprehensible what it would be for some individual object, Cicero, say,
to be *logically necessarily* thus and so. This is the disease, and paradoxes such as
the number of planets example are a symptom.

What is the cure? If Quine is correct in his diagnosis, then, broadly speaking,
we can either change the kind of quantification, or change the kind of modality,
or give up on *de re* modality. The first strategy aims 'to make sense of *de re* modal
predication by: (i) reconceiving the domain over which we quantify, and with a
view to (ii) making the domain combine safely with the (intended) linguistic—
analytic—character of the modality' (Divers, 2017, 222). This strategy requires
quantification over something that is sensitive to differences in how something
is represented; something like quantification over Fregean senses. Apart from
Quine's objections to such an approach,[6] I take it that such an understanding of
quantification is not broadly attractive: we want to be able to quantify over things,
not (only) different modes of presentations of things.

The second strategy is, broadly speaking, Smullyan's well-known response to
Quine (Smullyan, 1947, 1948). Problematic cases such as the number of planets
example are dealt with by recognizing that definite descriptions are not singular terms, but rather devices of quantification, in line with Russell's theory of
descriptions. So, for example, the substitution of the name '8' in the true sentence
'Necessarily, 8 is greater than 7' with the description 'the number of planets' is
disallowed.[7] However, since this second option retains our ordinary objectual
understanding of quantification, it requires one to make sense of a kind of modality
that properly applies to things rather than to modes of presentation. This, then,

---

[6] See Divers (2017, 223).

[7] For a masterfully clear and detailed account of the ways in which a semantics for definite descriptions makes a difference in our treatment of extensional and nonextensional sentential connectives, see
Neale (1995). Crucially, one may allow substitution of singular terms, even in nonextensional contexts,
without also having to endorse various substitution principles governing definite descriptions, such as
that which is operative in the number of planets example.

is why Quine famously objects to *de re* modality as involving a commitment to essentialism. Quantified modality,

> complicates the logic of singular terms; worse, it leads us back into the metaphysical jungle of Aristotelian essentialism.   (Quine, 1953, 174)

Hence, we can see how from a quite general point of view, *de re* modality leads to a conception of modality that is distinct from logical modality, that concerns things in reality rather than our representations of them. This starts to look a lot like metaphysical modality.

> The reconception of the modality is as a language-independent, non-analytic but still strict (not-merely-causal) modality, that applies to ordinary things independently of any considerations about how they are specified. . . . *metaphysical modality.*   (Divers, 2017, 224)

This digression further motivates our interest in *de re* modality in the present context, but it also raises the question of whether my proposed account, if it is to accommodate *de re* modality, can avoid Quine's objections. The question is pressing because the basic modal operator in terms of which relative necessities are defined is a logical modality operator. I will first propose how *de re* modality can fit into the account, and then return to reconsider Quine's challenge.

8.3 *De re* modality and relative necessity

Let us grant that the conditions of objectivity are general. Most, if not all, will be expressible in terms of a universal quantification, i.e., $\forall x \Phi(x)$.[8] Some might be generic existential claims, i.e., $\exists x \Phi(x)$. At first blush, one would expect only generalities to follow from generalities. After all, if our only assumption is that everything is Φ, without any further assumption about what things there are, it is hard to see how we could yield any conclusion that any particular thing, a, say, is Φ. Similarly, even if we assume that something is Φ, that only tells us that *something or other* is Φ; it doesn't tell us anything about *which thing* is Φ. So, if only generalities follow from generalities; if conditions of objectivity are general; and if metaphysical necessities follow from conditions of objectivity; then all metaphysical necessities are general. The most obvious cases of these general, *de dicto* metaphysical necessities are those of the conditions of objectivity themselves, which are trivially metaphysically necessary in virtue of entailing themselves.

---

[8] More generally, $\forall x_1, \ldots, x_n \Phi(x_1, \ldots, x_n)$.

178 THINKING OF NECESSITY

However, there are also *instances* of generalities. These will be treated differently according to different background logics. For example, in classical logic, in the absence of any further assumptions concerning particular individuals, both universally and existentially quantified formulas allow us to introduce a constant, i.e., to infer $\Phi(a)$.

> From $\forall x \Phi(x)$ infer $\Phi(a)$, where a already occurs in the proof, or if there are no constants, a is new.
>
> From $\exists x \Phi(x)$ infer $\Phi(a)$, where a is new.

So one might take general conditions of objectivity to thereby yield *de re* metaphysical necessities. For example, grant that it is metaphysically necessary that p just when $\exists \phi (O\phi \wedge \Box(\phi \rightarrow p))$, and suppose that $O(\forall x Fx)$, i.e., that it is a condition on objectivity that everything is F. Given a plausible conversion of the proposed $\forall$-elimination rule, we have that $\Box(\forall x Fx \rightarrow Fa)$. Putting this together entails that $\exists \phi (O\phi \wedge \Box(\phi \rightarrow Fa))$, i.e., we have a *de re* metaphysical necessity: it is metaphysically necessary that Fa.

Nevertheless, note that what turns out to be *de re* metaphysically necessary, on such a view, will depend upon what the general conditions of objectivity are. And the source of such *de re* necessities will lie in the general conditions of objectivity, not in any independent distinctive features of the individual entities concerned. For example, in this schematic example, the necessity of Fa is derived from the general condition on objectivity that (and hence the general metaphysical necessity of) $\forall x Fx$.

Later (in Chapter 9, section 9.1.2) I will offer reasons to favour a free logic over classical logic. In a free logic, the implications just sketched fail in the absence of an additional assumption to the effect that a exists. So we need alternative rules for the quantifiers. For example,

> Take $\mathfrak{E}$ to be an existence predicate. Then:
>
> From $\forall x \Phi(x)$ infer $\neg \mathfrak{E}a \vee \Phi(a)$, where a already occurs in the proof, or if there are no constants, a is new.
>
> From $\exists x \Phi(x)$ and $\mathfrak{E}a$ infer $\Phi(a)$, where a is new.[9]

Note: the existence predicate '$\mathfrak{E}a$' can be cashed out in various ways to the same effect, e.g., as '$\exists x\, x = a$'.

With these alternative rules we can yield a similar result. Grant, again, that it is metaphysically necessary that p just when $\exists \phi (O\phi \wedge \Box(\phi \rightarrow p))$, and suppose that $O(\forall x Fx)$. Given a plausible conversion of the free $\forall$-elimination rule,

---

[9] See Priest (2008, 290–1).

WHAT IS METAPHYSICALLY NECESSARY? 179

we have that $\Box(\forall xFx \rightarrow (\neg\mathfrak{E}a \vee Fa))$, or equivalently, $\Box((\forall xFx \wedge \mathfrak{E}a) \rightarrow Fa)$. Putting this together again entails a *de re* metaphysical necessity: $\exists\phi(O\phi \wedge \Box(\phi \rightarrow (\neg\mathfrak{E}a \vee Fa)))$. It also entails something else, which will be of importance very soon, namely: $\exists\phi(O\phi \wedge \Box((\phi \wedge \mathfrak{E}a) \rightarrow Fa))$. Therefore, given a background free logic as well, we can yield *de re* metaphysical necessities. As before, they are derived from general conditions on objectivity, and do not have their source in particular features of individual things.

The upshot of this is that the core cases of metaphysical necessity, according to Modal Transcendentalism, are general conditions on objectivity and hence *de dicto* necessities. But given plausible assumptions about instances of generalities, there is an associated class of derivative *de re* necessities.

The foregoing discussion brings out an interesting further point. In the case of a background free logic, we saw that an existence assumption plays an important role. Where we have universally general conditions on objectivity, those *together with the assumption that a exists,* yield an instance of the generality: e.g., $\exists\phi(O\phi \wedge \Box((\phi \wedge \mathfrak{E}a) \rightarrow Fa))$. Even in the case of classical logic there is a covert assumption of a similar kind, namely, that as long as there are already constants in use, they should be used to provide instances of the universal generality ('from $\forall x\Phi(x)$ infer $\Phi(a)$, *where a already occurs in the proof*'). Informally speaking, this says something like: if everything is Φ, and if you already have a handle on a, then a is Φ. If you take a universal generality together with any extant individuals, then you can conclude that those individuals are also instances of the generality.

This leads us towards the notion of a kind of conditional metaphysical necessity, relative to conditions on objectivity *and* the actual individual facts, i.e., particular actual truths about individuals. Recall, in the case where a exists, together with conditions on objectivity that include that everything is F, this gave us:

$$\exists\phi(O\phi \wedge \Box((\phi \wedge \mathfrak{E}a) \rightarrow Fa))$$

We can generalize this: if we take into account all of the actual facts about individuals (which will include facts about what exists, such as $\mathfrak{E}a$), as well as general conditions on objectivity, we will yield the same consequence:

$$\exists\phi\exists\psi(O\phi \wedge T\psi \wedge \Box((\phi \wedge \psi) \rightarrow Fa))$$

where '$T\psi$' says that ψ is an actual truth about individuals. Assuming that it is an actual truth that $\exists xx = a$, then given the Modal Transcendentalist definition of metaphysical necessity, and the assumption that $O(\forall xFx)$, we yield that it is necessary that Fa relative to *conditions on objectivity and the actual facts*.

We thus have in view a kind of relative necessity that is related to, but not exactly the same as, metaphysical necessity, namely, necessity relative to conditions on objectivity as well as all the actual individual truths.

180 THINKING OF NECESSITY

Take $O\phi$ to state that ϕ is a condition on objectivity. And take $T\psi$ to state that ψ is an actual individual truth. At first blush, we might take *conditional metaphysical necessity* to be captured by the following:

CMN* $\quad \exists\phi\exists\psi(O\phi \land T\psi \land \Box((\phi \land \psi) \to p))$

Unfortunately, this has the displeasing result that any actual individual truth is conditionally metaphysically necessary, even where the truth does not appear to be an instance of any general metaphysical necessity, i.e., in the case where ψ is p.[10] One way to remedy this is simply to add the condition that p does not follow from ψ alone, i.e.:

CMN $\quad \exists\phi\exists\psi(O\phi \land T\psi \land \Box((\phi \land \psi) \to p) \land \neg \Box(\psi \to p))$

This additional clause ensures that the general metaphysical necessity is making some contribution to the implication of p.[11]

I think this notion of conditional metaphysical necessity gets the following kind of case right. Suppose that it is metaphysically necessary that all humans are rational. Then, for instance, if Socrates is a human, he is rational. But it is not the case that it is metaphysically necessary that Socrates is rational. Socrates might not have been a human, for all we've said so far. And he might not have existed at all. Nevertheless, we *can* say that it is conditionally metaphysically necessary that Socrates is rational: conditional on a general metaphysical necessity and the actual facts about Socrates, such as the fact that he is human.

It is also striking that CMN mirrors Kant's account of material necessity.[12] Recall, he argued that existence could not be cognized *a priori,* and hence that real necessity would not apply unconditionally to objects of experience. Nevertheless, *relative to certain aspects of the actual world,* he defined a kind of material necessity that was appropriate for cognition. Via a different route, we have ended up at a similar destination: metaphysical necessity is primarily general and so, in the absence of further assumptions about what exists, does not apply directly to individual things, but we can recognize a kind of necessity that applies conditional on what is actual.

---

[10] Assume that p is an actual individual truth, so Tp. But since $\Box(p \to p)$, it will also be true that $\Box((\phi \land p) \to p)$, for any ϕ, and in particular if ϕ is a condition on objectivity. So if there are conditions on objectivity, it will be true that $\exists\phi\exists\psi(O\phi \land T\psi \land \Box((\phi \land \psi) \to p))$, just because p entails itself.

[11] This is also the reason why I have been careful to say "actual individual truth". The conditions of objectivity are also actually true, so we don't want the additional clause here to rule out cases where p follows from conditions of objectivity! By "actual individual truth", I mean an actual, non-modal, truth, that makes reference to particular individuals, such as $\exists x\, x = a$ or Fa. If one wanted to allow for conditions of objectivity that concern particular individuals, this would need to be amended.

[12] See Chapter 2, sections 2.4 and 2.5.2.

WHAT IS METAPHYSICALLY NECESSARY? 181

In this section I have focused on statements of *de re* necessity that involve the use of constants. The other kind of formulation of *de re* necessity involves 'quantifying in', i.e., into name position, e.g., $\forall x \exists \phi(O\phi \wedge \Box(\phi \to Gx))$ or $\exists x \exists \phi(O\phi \wedge \Box(\phi \to Gx))$. We have already seen why we wouldn't expect metaphysical necessity claims primarily to concern particular individuals: metaphysical necessities for particular individuals must be derived as instances of general necessities. This goes also for quantified-in claims that are derived from particular instances, e.g., where $\exists x \exists \phi(O\phi \wedge \Box(\phi \to Gx))$ results from quantification into $\exists \phi(O\phi \wedge \Box(\phi \to Ga))$, if such quantification in is permitted. If the conditions of objectivity are general, and so do not imply anything about particular individuals, beyond instances of those generalities, equally, there will be no particular individual such that the conditions of objectivity imply anything about it.

Quite generally, there may well be *de re* relative necessities of kinds other than metaphysical necessity, depending on the kinds of propositions to which they are relative. For example, one could define Barack-necessity relative to a list of facts about Barack Obama, including 'Barack is a US citizen'. From this one can clearly yield genuine *de re* Barack-necessities, such as the trivial 'Barack-necessarily, Barack is a US citizen', and the generalization 'Something is Barack-necessarily a US citizen'.[13]

Having seen how Modal Transcendentalism might accommodate *de re* necessary modal claims, we can now return to see whether Quine's challenge bites.

8.4 Relative necessity and Quine's challenge

8.4.1 Quine's challenge again

Look again at the proposed formulations of metaphysical necessity as relative necessity, with a *de re* modal predication included: here are two examples, one with a name, one with quantification into name position.

$$\exists \phi(O\phi \wedge \Box(\phi \to Fa))$$
$$\exists x \exists \phi(O\phi \wedge \Box(\phi \to Fx))$$

Both involve quantifying into sentence position in the scope of a modal operator— $\dots \exists \phi \dots \Box \dots \phi \dots$ —as, indeed, does any statement of relative necessity on the proposed formulation. Both are also *de re* with respect to the name or variable (in name position) in the scope of the modal operator: $\dots \Box \dots a \dots, \exists x \dots \Box \dots x \dots$.

---

[13] i.e., $\Box_B Cb$, $\exists x \Box_B Cx$, treated as relative necessities respectively as $\exists \phi(B\phi \wedge \Box(\phi \to Cb))$ and $\exists x \exists \phi(B\phi \wedge \Box(\phi \to Cx))$.

182   THINKING OF NECESSITY

Let us set aside substitution cases such as 'the number of planets' and '8'; these issues are satisfactorily addressed by recognizing that definite descriptions are devices of quantification and not singular terms.[14] However, it is important to recognize that this response only goes halfway. The challenge remains to make sense of a combination of logical modality and quantification ordinarily understood. As Roberta Ballarin puts the point, 'according to Quine, the Russellian analysis of descriptions eliminates *at most* problems of substitution, not of quantifying in' (Ballarin, 2012, 243). To address Quine's worries, we need to consider the nature of the modal predications involved, as well as the nature of the quantification.

The modal operator here, '□', is a logical necessity operator. I agree with Quine that the meaning of such an operator is intimately related to the notion of logical validity (Quine, 1953), however, I disagree with the consequences he draws from this. Quine argues that since 'is valid' is a metalinguistic predicate that applies to arguments and sentences (e.g., " 'p' is valid"), so is the semantic predicate 'Nec', which can be applied to the name of a sentence to say, in so many words, that the sentence is valid (e.g., "Nec 'p' "). If we then introduce a statement operator into our object language, 'nec', or '□', which reflects the behaviour of 'Nec', it should not do anything that a metalinguistic predicate could not do, such as admit of quantifying in. For Quine, since it is illegitimate to quantify into quotation marks (for example, from " 'Cicero is wise' is valid" to "$\exists x$'x is wise' is valid"), it is therefore illegitimate to quantify into the scope of the statement operator (as in '$\exists x \square x$ is wise').

I think we can reply to Quine on his own terms (to be explained soon). But in any case, I argued earlier (Chapter 3) that logical necessity is to be understood as *that necessity that is distinctive of logical validity*; it is not itself *the same as* logical validity. We might understand the rule of necessitation—from $\vDash \phi$ one may infer $\vDash \square\phi$—as somehow capturing that transition from metalinguistic validity predicate to object language necessity operator.[15] If one rejects a modal understanding of validity, then this way to understand logical necessity is not available. But I already committed myself to a modal understanding of validity earlier.[16] I am thus not constrained to understand the necessity operator as covertly metalinguistic. To reiterate: the operator expresses a kind of necessity that is distinctive of logical validity, and thus far should be expected to behave in related ways (e.g., such that logical truths come out as necessary), but insofar as the operator captures the necessity distinctive of validity and not validity itself, it need not conform to the exact same constraints as a validity predicate.

Quine's unintelligibility challenge is that it doesn't make sense to apply modal predicates directly to things. We can now see more clearly why. The point is more

---

[14] See Smullyan (1947, 1948); Neale (1995).

[15] Similarly, if $\phi \vDash \psi$ then, via a semantic deduction theorem, we can infer $\vDash \phi \to \psi$, and thence $\vDash \square(\phi \to \psi)$.

[16] See Chapter 3, section 3.1.

WHAT IS METAPHYSICALLY NECESSARY? 183

easily understood if we first put it in terms of a distinction between object language and metalanguage, as would normally be found in a presentation of a formal logic. *Validity* is a notion that belongs to the metalanguage: a validity symbol such as '⊨' does not belong to the vocabulary of the formal object language, but is used to express semantic properties and relations of formulas of the object language, for example, that one formula is validly entailed by another ($\phi \vDash \psi$). Quine takes the graduation from the first to the second grade to involve the addition of a statement operator into the object language, i.e., our '□', or his 'nec'. But for Quine this operator in the object language, '□' or 'nec', is a kind of covert version of the metalinguistic predicate, '⊨' or 'Nec'. Thus understood, it just doesn't make sense to say, for example, that Jimmy is validly male (as in '□(Jimmy is male)'), or, indeed, that *anything* is validly male (as in, for example, '$\exists x \square(x$ is male)', because we are effectively confusing two different languages; the object language in which we quantify, and the metalanguage in which we express notions such as validity. We are effectively saying something like '$\exists x \vDash (x$ is male)'. But that is obviously ill-formed. Hence, *de re* modalizing involves a mishmash of languages that was forgiveable when we applied the modal operator to a closed sentence (such as '□(all bachelors are male)'), because that is in line with comparable uses of the metalinguistic validity predicate ("'All bachelors are male' is valid"), but disastrous if we try to apply it to an open sentence. Given Quine's understanding of 'nec', to say that something is nec-male is about as meaningful as any attempt to mix languages. For example, while you probably understand what I mean by 'The cow jumped sur la lune', it is not a sentence of either English or French. The distinction between object language and metalanguage is not as clear-cut when we consider examples in natural rather than formal languages. For example, 'is valid' is an English predicate as much as 'Jimmy is male' is an English sentence. However, I think this language-mixing interpretation does best at capturing the *unintelligibility* claim. Otherwise, it's very hard to see, as I will shortly discuss, why we should not conclude that *de re* modal formulas are just false, rather than nonsense.

Moving away from the metalinguistic reading of the logical necessity operator means that the strength of the unintelligibility charge is diminished. There is no longer a mishmash of languages, or something akin to such a mishmash. Rather, we have the challenge to make sense of the application of logical modal predicates that properly belong to the object language. Insofar as logical necessity is understood to derive in some way from logical validity, it might seem strange to apply such modal predicates directly to things. However, it is no longer obviously *unintelligible*. A purportedly inappropriate predication such as 'Something is logically necessarily male' seems strange because we expect logical necessity to hold of sentences (or arguments) that are logically valid, or whatever those sentences stand for, not of the things over which our ordinary quantifiers range. At worst, *de re* modalizing involves a kind of category mistake. But category mistakes are

184 THINKING OF NECESSITY

false, not unintellgible.[17] Compare: 'The number 2 is pink' is false, but I know full well what it means; that is how I can recognize its falsity.

Let us set aside the worry that *de re* modal claims are *unintelligible*. A significant aspect of Quine's challenge remains. It is still the case that category mistakes guarantee that a range of claims will be false. For example, numbers are not the kind of thing that can have a colour, so any attempt to predicate colours of numbers is going to go wrong (and turn out false). Similarly, the Quinean may retort, there remains something defective about *de re* modality even if it is strictly speaking intelligible, for any such modal predication is guaranteed to end in falsity.

There's a serious problem lurking here. If all *de re* modal predicates are equally inapplicable to the objects of ordinary quantification, then sentences of the form 'a is necessarily-F' and 'a is possibly-non-F' will be equally false. Suppose duality: $\Box Fa$ if and only if $\neg \Diamond \neg Fa$. If it is guaranteed to be false that $\Box Fa$, then assuming a standard semantics for negation, it is guaranteed to be true that $\neg\Box Fa$. But then by duality it is true that $\Diamond\neg Fa$. So this is a true *de re* modal predication after all. If that is also guaranteed to be false due to a category mistake, we are led into contradiction, and something in the foregoing line of reasoning must be abandoned. The deeper issue is that it isn't clear how negation should interact with such operators, if their *de re* use always ends in falsity.

Less formally, if all *de re* modal claims are false, one might remark that there's hardly any point in making such claims. If you think that there are some true *de re* modal predications to be made, then one may well happily venture into the Aristotelian jungle in order to do so. One reinterprets the modal operator so that modal predicates appropriately apply to things. I'm less keen to be able to make true *de re* modal claims. Nevertheless, it is a substantive metaphysical question, over which there are interesting and substantive metaphysical debates, whether any such claims are true—a question which should not be answered immediately merely by the form in which such claims are made.

Our challenge is now: how can we make sense of logical modal predications, such that they are not immediately classified as category mistakes and thereby guaranteed to be false (or otherwise automatically rendered false)?

8.4.2 Quantification into sentence position

First, let us consider quantification into sentence position in the scope of the modal operator (as it appears in the formulation of relative necessity: $\exists \phi \ldots \Box (\ldots \phi \ldots)$). This does not raise the kind of quantifying-in problems just discussed. As should by now be clear, logical modal predicates apply perfectly well to sentence-like

---

[17] See, e.g., Magidor (2009).

things. Even Quine should be able to stomach this. Nevertheless, one might baulk (with Quine) at the appearance of this kind of quantification in general. This is not the place for a treatise on higher-order quantification. But let me briefly explain how I am understanding it in this context, in which I am following Prior (1971).

In general, when we quantify into the position of a certain kind of expression, the variable takes on something like the role of that kind of expression. So, for example, in familiar first-order quantification into name position, given that names 'stand for' individual objects, we can take the variable to range over a domain of individual objects.

> The variable may be said, in the first place, to stand for a name . . . in the sense that we obtain an ordinary closed sentence by replacing it by a name. . . . The variable 'x' may be said, in a secondary sense, to 'stand for' individual objects . . . in the sense that it stands for . . . any name that stands for (refers to) an object.
>
> (Prior, 1971, 35)

Whatever it is that predicate expressions or relational expressions do, if we quantify into these positions, the way those variables work will be at least in part determined by that role. And whatever it is that (closed-)sentences do, if we quantify into sentence position, the way those variables work will be at least in part determined by the role of sentences. It is only if, for example, predicate expressions stand for objects, or if sentences stand for objects, that we will be able to take such higher-order variables to range over special kinds of objects, such as universals or propositions.

> If we now consider the open sentence 'Peter φ's Paul', it is equally easy to say what 'φ' . . . 'stands for' in the first sense—it keeps a place for any transitive verb, or any expression doing the job of a transitive verb. . . . The question what it 'stands for' in the second sense, i.e. what would be designated by an expression of the sort for which it keeps a place, is senseless, since the sort of expression for which it keeps a place is one which just hasn't the job of designating objects. Similarly with the two variables in 'If p then q', or the one in 'James believes that p'. The variables here stand for, i.e. keep places for, sentences; but since it is not the job of sentences to designate objects, there is just no question what objects these variables 'stand for' in the second sense.   (Prior, 1971, 35)

In sum, I am not taking the quantification into sentence position to introduce an ontology of propositions. It simply allows us to make sense of relative modalities as relative to certain conditions.

Any talk of propositions, e.g., Φ-propositions, can be understood in a deflationary sense, also in line with Prior. He takes propositions to be 'logical constructions'. This does not mean that propositions are a special kind of object; a 'logically

186 THINKING OF NECESSITY

constructed' object. Rather, sentences that seem to be about propositions are about something else, and only seem to be about propositions due to a particular kind of logical construction used in the sentence.

> 'Propositions are logical constructions' is an assertion about language, but it isn't an assertion that propositions are themselves bits of language, but rather an assertion about sentences that are ostensibly about propositions, to the effect that they are not in reality about propositions but about something else.... Part of what it says may be, e.g., that the sentence 'The proposition that the sun is hot is true' means no more and no less than the sentence 'The sun is hot', i.e., the sentence 'The proposition that the sun is hot is true' is not in reality about the proposition that the sun is hot, but about the sun. Similarly 'The proposition that the sun is hot would be true even if unasserted' means the same as 'The sun would be hot even if no one said so', and is not about the proposition that the sun is hot but about the sun. (Prior, 1971, 12)

So a sentence of the form '$\exists\phi(O\phi \wedge \Box(\phi \to p))$' may appear to be about the existence of some propositions. However, if we follow Prior's suggestion, it is in fact about the conditions under which it is true that p. For example, 'There are some propositions that are conditions of objectivity that logically necessarily imply that every event has a cause' would be understood, not as being in reality about the existence of these propositions, but rather as being about the conditions under which every event has a cause.

8.4.3 Quantification into name position

What can we say about quantifying into name position? And more generally, any *de re* modalizing, whether it concerns a name or a free variable?

Quine thinks that *de re* modality leads us into the jungle of Aristotelian essentialism because it requires an understanding of modality that is impervious to differences in the way that we refer to things. For him, this means that the source of the modality must lie in the object.

> An object, of itself and by whatever name or none, must be seen as having some of its traits necessarily and others contingently, despite the fact that the latter traits follow just as analytically from some ways of specifying the object as the former traits do from other ways of specifying it. (Quine, 1961, 155)

The crucial requirement is that a modal predicate applies *no matter how we refer to an object*. However, this leaves open two options. (1) The modal predicate applies no matter how we refer to the object, because it captures something about how the object is independent of how we refer to it; the source of the modality is in the object. (2) The modal predicate applies no matter how we refer to the object, because it applies universally (no matter the object, and no matter the mode of referring to it). In the first case, the way we specify the object doesn't make a difference because the modal property inheres in the object. This is the metaphysical jungle of Aristotelian essentialism. In the second case, the way we specify the object doesn't make a difference because the modal predicate applies (or not) universally. There may then be a range of reasons why the modal predicate behaves in this way.

For example, the predicate 'is such that everything is wise or not wise' applies truly to any object, no matter how we specify the object. e.g., 'Socrates is such that everything is wise or not wise' is true. This is not because everything— including Greek philosophers—has written within its nature logical truths such as '$\forall x(Fx \lor \neg Fx)$'. Rather, it is because we can construct predicates out of sentences— 'x is such that ϕ', or simply '$\phi(x)$'—and in particular out of logical truths 'y is such that $\forall x(Fx \lor \neg Fx)$'. If the sentence is true, then the predicate will apply truly to everything. If the sentence is necessarily true, then the predicate will necessarily apply truly to everything.

Fine (2005) puts the point in terms of *logical satisfaction*.[18] We are familiar with a distinction between truth and logical truth, where the latter is determined by logical form. i.e., sentences with a particular logical form, such as '$\forall x(Fx \lor \neg Fx)$', are guaranteed to be true. Similarly, Fine suggests, we can by analogy understand a distinction between satisfaction and logical satisfaction. We understand the idea that an object, a, may, or may not satisfy a condition '$\varphi(x)$'. For example, Socrates (the man) satisfies the condition 'is wise', but not 'is Incan'. By analogy with logical truth, we can also understand the idea that an object may satisfy a condition on the basis of logical form. For example, Socrates satisfies the condition '$Fx \lor \neg Fx$', not because of anything in particular about Socrates, but due to the logical form of the condition.

> Logical truth is truth that can be determined on the basis of logical form. Logical satisfaction is therefore satisfaction that can be determined on the basis of logical form.   (Fine, 2005, 108)

> A condition will be satisfied by an object and, in general, by a sequence of objects just in case it can be determined to be so satisfied on the basis of the logical form of the condition alone.

---

[18] Ballarin (2012, 239) frames Quine's challenge in similar terms: 'It is incoherent, not just false, to say about an object directly, i.e., independently of any characterization, that it is analytically, logically, provably, or a priori blue or self-identical. The underlying suggestion seems to be that while there are clear notions of logical, provable, or even analytic *truth,* there are no clear corresponding notions of logical, provable, or analytic *satisfaction*'.

188 THINKING OF NECESSITY

> On such a conception, many conditions will be logically satisfied; for example, a condition of the form '$Fx \lor \neg Fx$' will be logically satisfied by any object.
>
> (Fine, 2005, 109–10)

Therefore, there are many predicates that necessarily apply truly to things, regardless of how we refer to those things.[19]

On this basis, we can recognize a family of logical modal predicates, some of which are true of everything, some of which are false of everything, and some of which differentiate between things. Let us take x *logically satisfies condition* '$\varphi(x)$' to be equivalent to x *satisfies condition* '$\Box\varphi(x)$' (just as we earlier took '$\Box\phi$' to capture the modal element of '$\vDash \phi$').[20]

First, we have logical modal predicates that apply truly to everything. For example, since everything logically satisfies 'everything is wise or not wise', everything satisfies 'x is necessarily such that everything is wise or not wise'. In particular, Socrates is necessarily such that everything is wise or not wise.

Second, we have predicates that do not apply truly to anything, regardless of how we refer to it. For example, nothing logically satisfies 'x is snub-nosed.' So nothing satisfies 'x is necessarily snub-nosed.' The laws of logic give us no reason to think that anything is snub-nosed, unlike the case of everything necessarily being such that $\forall x(Fx \lor \neg Fx)$.

Third, we can also account for modal predicates that are true of some but not other things. We have already seen that nothing is necessarily snub-nosed. By the same token, no matter how we refer to things, everything is not-necessarily-snub-nosed.[21] That is: nothing satisfies 'x is necessarily snub-nosed,' so everything satisfies 'x is not necessarily snub-nosed.' But Socrates *is* snub-nosed. Since Socrates is snub-nosed but not necessarily snub-nosed, he is contingently snub-nosed. Whilst everything satisfies the condition 'x is not necessarily snub-nosed,' only those things that are snub-nosed, such as Socrates, satisfy the condition 'x is snub-nosed and not necessarily snub-nosed.' So 'Socrates is contingently snub-nosed' is true, as is 'Something is contingently snub-nosed'. However, it is open to say that the source of these truths is not solely in Socrates's nature. Yes, it is Socrates and what he is like that accounts for the truth of 'Socrates is snub-nosed'. But it is the logical

---

[19] I have presented here what Fine calls the 'object blind' account of logical satisfaction, according to which satisfaction is determined by the logical form of the condition alone, and not the logical form of the objects.

[20] See also Fine (2005, 107): 'instead of saying 'x satisfies $\Box\psi(x)$', we may use a relational idiom and say 'x necessarily fulfils $\psi(x)$'.

[21] Are you worried that if we refer to Socrates as 'the snub-nosed philosopher', then it must be logically necessary that the snub-nosed philosopher is snub-nosed, hence, there is one way that we refer to Socrates, namely, as the snub-nosed philosopher, according to which he is necessarily snub-nosed after all? This kind of case is resolved by the Smullyan-style response to distinguish between singular terms and definite descriptions, the latter of which are not devices of reference but devices of quantification.

form of the condition, along with the laws of logic, that accounts for the modal element. That is, the laws of logic require of nothing that it be snub-nosed. This, in conjunction with Socrates's being snub-nosed, accounts for the contingency of Socrates's snub-nosedness.

How does this help us with Quine's challenge? It gives us an alternative to Aristotelian essentialism. We can make sense of a range of modal predicates that apply, or not, to objects, regardless of how we refer to those objects. But this is not because those objects have necessary and contingent properties, understood in a metaphysically deep way, as creatures lurking within the Aristotelian jungle. Rather, it is because those predicates correspond to conditions the satisfaction of which is determined by the logical form of the condition alone, independently of the object and how we refer to it. In some hybrid cases, such as contingency predicates, the modal element is explicable by the same means. Moreover, this all concerns a logical modality operator. We can perfectly well understand the application of logical modal predicates directly to objects without falling into unintelligibility.

One might worry, as does Hale, that this approach does not allow for any non-trivial *de re* modalities. The underlying notion of a logically satisfied condition is all or nothing: the logical form of the condition ensures that either everything is necessarily such that φ, or nothing is.

> A true singular proposition, $\Box A(t)$, will be a non-trivial *de re* necessity only if what it says holds by necessity of its object, t, and is not, as a matter of necessity, true of all objects whatever—that is, only if it is not the case that $\Box \forall x A(x)$.... According to the linguistic conception, the only propositions which are *de re* necessarily true are those whose universal closures are necessarily true ... there can be no non-trivial *de re* necessities. If that is right, anyone who wishes to claim that there are non-trivial *de re* modalities *must* reject the broadly linguistic conception of necessity. (Hale, 2020, 47–8)

For Hale, this is a reason to favour a metaphysical understanding of the modal operator. In the context of Modal Transcendentalism, triviality is not problematic. We have already seen that we do not expect to yield straightforward non-trivial *de re* metaphysical modalities. Our challenge was primarily to make intelligible the combination of logical modality and ordinary objectual quantification. Hale does not question intelligibility here, hence we can set this worry aside. That said: note that we were also able to accommodate some non-trivial *de re* modalities: not necessities, but contingencies.

In sum, we can accept that *de re* modal claims involve a direct predication of a modal predicate to an individual (hence, we do not need to reinterpret objectual quantification). We can also accept that modal predicates apply independently of how we refer to an object. However, this does not force us to change our

190   THINKING OF NECESSITY

understanding of the modality involved. Modal predicates, understood in terms of a distinctively *logical* modality, may apply independently of how we specify objects, not because the objects have modal properties, but because those predicates apply indiscriminately for other reasons. We thus have an answer to Quine's challenge, combining logical modality and ordinary quantification without entering the metaphysical jungle of Aristotelian essentialism.

What is the upshot of this for the present account of metaphysical necessity? According to Modal Transcendentalism, the modal predicates that apply in *de re metaphysical* modal predications (to individuals) will all be of a complex conditional form such as 'x is (logically) necessarily F-if-ϕ'. Take a purported *de re* metaphysical modal formula such as '$\exists x \exists \phi (O\phi \wedge \Box(\phi \to Fx))$'. The first clauses of this formula do not lie within the scope of the modal operator. The modal operator here applies to the open sentence '$\phi \to Fx$', i.e., 'x is F-if-ϕ'. Hence, we end up with the complex conditional modal predication: 'x is (logically) necessarily F-if-ϕ'. In this case, it is specified that ϕ is a condition on objectivity.

In conclusion: it is plausible that the conditions of objectivity are general. This means that there are unlikely to be any distinctive *de re* metaphysically necessary truths, beyond instances of *de dicto* metaphysical necessities. Nevertheless, *de re* modalizing is intelligible. And indeed, there will be some fairly trivial cases of *de re* necessities, constructed from predicates that apply regardless of how we refer to anything, i.e., logically satisfied conditions. Since these are logical necessities, they will also be metaphysical necessities, but not distinctively so.

9

Essence, Existence, and Modal Knowledge

Modal Transcendentalism can, in principle, intelligibly accommodate *de re* metaphysical necessities. We are now in a position to consider some notable examples. I will consider in turn necessary and contingent existence, essentialist claims of necessity, and the necessary *a posteriori*. The latter consideration will invite some promissory remarks on modal knowledge and conceivability.

Although I have argued that metaphysical necessity should not be beholden to typical cases, such cases are nevertheless commonly associated with metaphysical necessity, and so it is worthwhile to explain the extent to which Modal Transcendentalism can accommodate them. Moreover, one might take the inability of Modal Transcendentalism to honour some such case to constitute a counterexample. Hence, it is worthwhile treating such cases in more detail.

9.1 Necessary and contingent existence

9.1.1 Necessary existence

One might think that it is a fairly plausible and uncontroversial assumption to hold that some things exist contingently, whilst some things exist necessarily. That is, of all the things that exist, some of them could have failed to exist, whilst others could not have failed to exist. One might also think that there could have existed some things other than those that actually exist. Typical examples of contingent objects might be human beings, trees, rivers, and telephone directories. Typical examples of necessary objects might be mathematical objects, such as numbers and sets, and other kinds of purported abstract object, such as universals and propositions. Some people believe that there is a necessarily existing being they call 'God'. Any account of metaphysical necessity should be able either to accommodate these assumptions about necessary and contingent existence, or have a good reason why those assumptions should be given up.

Immediately, we can see that Modal Transcendentalism is unlikely to yield any metaphysically necessary existence, because the conditions on objectivity to which metaphysical necessity is relative are general. Therefore, it is hard to see how they could imply claims about the existence of particular things. For example, consider the following attempts to capture the claim that Socrates metaphysically necessarily exists.

Thinking of Necessity: A Kantian Account of Modal Thought and Modal Metaphysics. Jessica Leech,
Oxford University Press. © Jessica Leech 2023. DOI: 10.1093/oso/9780198873969.003.0009

$\exists \phi(O\phi \wedge \Box(\phi \rightarrow \text{Socrates exists}))$

or

$\exists \phi(O\phi \wedge \Box(\phi \rightarrow \exists x(x = \text{Socrates})))$

The notion of necessary existence here is not unintelligible. It is just that nothing satisfies that condition, so long as the conditions on objectivity are general. Even if the conditions of objectivity included something like the requirement that *something* exist, that would not yield the necessary existence of *particular individuals*.[1]

What about mathematical and abstract objects? Aren't they metaphysically necessary beings? How can we account for our intuitions that things such as numbers and sets exist necessarily? These questions could only be properly answered in the context of a detailed discussion of the philosophy of mathematics, more detailed than I can offer in what remains of this book. Hence, I will offer just a few comments.

For Kant, mathematics has its source in the conditions of objectivity; more particularly, for him, in the forms of sensibility, space and time. According to some interpretations of Kant, on his view we can understand geometry as concerning the structure of space and arithmetic in terms of the structure of time. We can have *a priori* knowledge of mathematics because it concerns the *a priori* structure of sensibility. And we can be assured of the meaningfulness and objective applicability of our mathematical concepts and proofs because we can construct instances of them in intuition.[2] On this kind of view, we no longer consider particular individual objects, such as the number 2, but rather mathematical structures that, for example, include a point or node corresponding to what we think of as the number 2. Such structures apply to our world, but we can learn about them *a priori*, since they have their source in our capacity for objective representation of the world. It seems to me that there is scope to develop an account of mathematics that is consonant with the present account of modality on this basis. There are, strictly speaking, no necessarily existing mathematical entities. However, we can explain away our intuitions (not in the Kantian sense) concerning such things in terms of the structures involved in the conditions of objectivity. Some of those structures are mathematical, i.e., the number structure. Some might be more metaphysical, e.g., one might take the category of *substance and inherence* to be contributing a general structure of particular and universal to

---

[1] For example, suppose the conditions on objectivity include $\exists x(x = x)$, i.e., something exists. At best *de re* instances of this condition would simply be the self-identity of anything that does exist, e.g., Socrates = Socrates, rather than the necessary existence of those things.

[2] See Hintikka (1967); Parsons (1969).

the world we experience, hence accounting for our intuitions (not in the Kantian sense) concerning the necessary existence of universals.[3]

Another central case of necessity existence, as briefly mentioned, concerns belief in God understood as a necessary being. Whether or not one endorses such a belief, one might think that it is intelligible, or at the very least intelligible to those who hold the belief. How, on the proposed view, could a theist make sense of their belief, if any claim of necessary existence is guaranteed to be false? There are several options:[4] here is one relatively simple example. Recall, one could retain the framework of Modal Transcendentalism, but flesh out what the conditions of objectivity are in different ways. Perhaps, one might argue, the existence of God is a condition of objectivity, since without God nothing in reality would have been created, and so objective thought is not possible without God and their creative powers. Therefore, there is at least one particular existential claim amongst the conditions of objectivity concerning God, which may accordingly filter through into the metaphysically necessary existence of God.

In summary, whether Modal Transcendentalism allows for metaphysically necessary beings depends upon the kinds of principles that are included in the conditions on objectivity to which, it is proposed, metaphysical necessity is relative. I have argued that those conditions are general; hence, nothing exists necessarily.

9.1.2 Contingent existence

Therefore, everything that exists, exists contingently.

However, there is a complication for any account of metaphysical necessity when it comes to contingent existence. There is an argument arising from a putative theorem of quantified modal logic for the view that everything that *could* exist *must* exist. The Barcan Formula and Converse Barcan Formula together imply that everything that could exist, does exist, and that everything that does exist, exists necessarily. I have argued that nothing exists metaphysically necessarily. One would hope that this would leave us with some contingent beings, if we want to have anything left in our ontology at all. So, if we want to hold on to the idea that there are contingent beings, we need to respond to this argument. In the case

---

[3] There is an extensive literature on structuralism in the philosophy of mathematics, and on Kantian philosophy of mathematics. That is why a proper discussion and defence of the tentatively sketched strategy would require more space than is available here. At least, this approach would require an understanding of structures that did not simply reify them into a special kind of object. For an overview of structuralism in the philosophy of mathematics see Reck and Schiemer (2020). For more on the relation between structuralism and Kant see Parsons (2007).

[4] A Kant-inspired option may seek to classify thoughts about God as nonjective, and attempt to account for belief in God in relation to practical and moral reasoning. See Leech (2021g) for some limited discussion of thoughts about God.

194 THINKING OF NECESSITY

of metaphysical necessity, I will argue that the fact that metaphysical necessity is relative blocks the relevant proofs. In the case of logical necessity, we will be led to give up the assumption that at least one thing exists, and hence to favour the adoption of a free logic rather than classical logic. Such a move, we shall see, is in line with taking the laws of logic to have their source in laws of thought.

Modal logics are usually developed by adding modal vocabulary to an existing logic. For example, Propositional Modal Logic arises from the addition of modal operators $\Box$ and $\Diamond$ to the Propositional Calculus. Quantified Modal Logic involves the addition of these operators to Predicate Logic. Once these operators have been added, the logician then needs to consider how to extend the semantics of the logic to accommodate and interpret these new modal formulas, and also to investigate what new formulas are now theorems of the logic.

The inception of Quantified Modal Logic raised the question, amongst others, of how these new modal operators interact with the quantifiers. Ruth Barcan Marcus famously proved two propositions concerning this interaction.

Barcan Formula (B) $\quad \forall x \Box \Phi(x) \rightarrow \Box \forall x \Phi(x)$

(equivalent to $\Diamond \exists x \Phi(x) \rightarrow \exists x \Diamond \Phi(x)$)

Converse Barcan Formula (CB) $\quad \Box \forall x \Phi(x) \rightarrow \forall x \Box \Phi(x)$

(equivalent to $\exists x \Diamond \Phi(x) \rightarrow \Diamond \exists x \Phi(x)$)

What is striking about these formulas is that they together entail that everything that could possibly exist necessarily exists. As Hale (2013) explains,

> (CB) asserts that if it is necessary that every object satisfies a certain condition, then it is true of each object that it necessarily satisfies that condition. It is a theorem of standard first-order quantification theory + identity that $\forall x \exists y x = y$. By the rule of Necessitation, it is a theorem of quantified K + identity that $\Box \forall x \exists y x = y$. Given (CB), it follows that $\forall x \Box \exists y x = y$. (CB) thus requires that every object necessarily exists.   (Hale, 2013, 207)

Moreover, (B) states (in its equivalent form) that if it is possible that something fulfil a certain condition, then there is something that possibly fulfils that condition. So, for example, suppose that it is possible that there is something identical to Pegasus (although we assume, for the time being, that there is no such thing as Pegasus). By (B), it follows that *there is* something that is possibly Pegasus.

> Thus (B) and (CB) together require that the objects which do exist are all the objects there could be, and that none of them could fail to exist—they rule out both contingent existence and contingent non-existence.   (Hale, 2013, 208)

ESSENCE, EXISTENCE, AND MODAL KNOWLEDGE   195

What are the consequences of this for Modal Transcendentalism? First: (B) and (CB) are not directly valid for metaphysical necessity, because metaphysical necessity is defined as a relative kind of necessity.

Consider (B) and (CB) for an arbitrary kind of relative necessity.

(B$_R$) $\forall x \Box_R \Phi(x) \rightarrow \Box_R \forall x \Phi(x)$

(CB$_R$) $\Box_R \forall x \Phi(x) \rightarrow \forall x \Box_R \Phi(x)$

Expanded out, these become:

(B$_R$) $\forall x \exists \phi (R\phi \wedge \Box(\phi \rightarrow \Phi(x))) \rightarrow \exists \phi (R\phi \wedge \Box(\phi \rightarrow \forall x \Phi(x)))$

(CB$_R$) $\exists \phi (R\phi \wedge \Box(\phi \rightarrow \forall x \Phi(x))) \rightarrow \forall x \exists \phi (R\phi \wedge \Box(\phi \rightarrow \Phi(x)))$

Are these longer, more complex, formulas valid? More carefully, suppose we add to first-order quantified modal logic a definition of a relative necessity modal operator $\Box_R$, such that $\Box_R A =_{df.} \exists \phi (R\phi \wedge \Box(\phi \rightarrow A))$. Would we expect either (B$_R$) or (CB$_R$) to be theorems of such a system? No.

Firstly, we could have a case where, for each thing x, there are some R-propositions that imply that condition Φ is true of x, but no R-propositions imply the general truth that condition Φ is true of everything. For example, consider a world in which everything is green. This world contains only two objects, a and b. At this world, there are two (and only two) R-propositions, (1) that a is green, and (2) that b is green.[5] There is no R-proposition that states that everything is green, and no R-proposition that states that there is nothing other than a and b. In such a case, for each thing, the R-propositions imply that it is green: if it is a, then (1) implies that it is green, if it is b, then (2) implies that it is green, and there is nothing other than a and b. However, (1) and (2) do not together entail that everything is green. For that they would need the additional premise that everything is either identical to a or b. Hence, we have a counterexample to (B$_R$). In general, then, we would not expect (B$_R$) to be valid in a simple system including relative necessity operators.

(B$_R$) does not hold in general for relative necessities. But perhaps a version of (B) might hold for particular kinds of relative necessity, given the specific behaviour of the kinds of propositions to which the necessity is relative. As such, we now need to consider metaphysical necessity as defined according to Modal Transcendentalism. It may turn out that peculiar features of the propositions to which metaphysical necessity is relative—conditions on objectivity—give us other reasons to expect its version of the Barcan Formula to hold. So consider:

---

[5] This argument does not depend on contingentism about propositions. i.e., there may exist many more propositions, and indeed, perhaps all of the propositions that could exist do exist, but only two of them are R-propositions at this world.

196   THINKING OF NECESSITY

(B$_M$) $\forall x \exists \phi (O\phi \wedge \Box(\phi \rightarrow \Phi(x))) \rightarrow \exists \phi (O\phi \wedge \Box(\phi \rightarrow \forall x \Phi(x)))$

This says that if everything is such that the conditions on objectivity imply that it satisfies condition Φ, then the conditions of objectivity imply that everything satisfies Φ. To show that this is not valid, we need a case where the antecedent is true, but the consequent is false. I argued in Chapter 8 (section 8.3) that particular metaphysical necessities for individuals would only be generated as instances of general necessities. For example, if it is a general metaphysical necessity that everything exists in time, then if Socrates exists, Socrates exists in time. So according to Modal Transcendentalism, if there are cases where the antecedent of (B$_M$) comes out true, that will be precisely because there is also a general necessity (such as the necessity of $\forall x \Phi(x)$) of which we have instances, i.e., that will be because the consequent of (B$_M$) is true. In short, nothing is such that the conditions on objectivity alone distinctively imply that it, specifically, satisfies some condition. So we must look elsewhere for a counterexample.

Consider cases where the antecedent is true because it follows from a logical necessity. For example, it is logically necessary that $\forall x(Fx \vee \neg Fx)$, i.e., $\Box \forall x(Fx \vee \neg Fx)$. By (CB), $\forall x \Box(Fx \vee \neg Fx)$ But then, if there are conditions on objectivity, it follows that $\forall x \exists \phi (O\phi \wedge \Box(\phi \rightarrow (Fx \vee \neg Fx)))$. Such cases will generate true antecedents for (B$_M$). But by the very same token they will also generate true corresponding consequents. For these cases were based on an initial logical necessity such as $\Box \forall x(Fx \vee \neg Fx)$. From which it follows that $\exists \phi (O\phi \wedge \Box(\phi \rightarrow \forall x(Fx \vee \neg Fx)))$. There is no counterexample here, but the argument turned on whether the Barcan formulas are valid for '$\Box$'.

Let us now turn to (CB$_R$). We can again describe a counterexample. In general, we can have cases where the R-propositions entail a general truth that everything x satisfies condition $\Phi(x)$, without entailing, for each thing, that it satisfies this condition. For example, the conditions on objectivity, as I have characterized them, may imply that everything is in time. But they do not thereby imply that each particular thing, for example Socrates, is in time, unless we add the assumption that Socrates exists. Again, this is just what we expect of Modal Transcendentalism. The conditions on objectivity generate primarily general necessities, not particular necessities for individuals. The latter is only possible with additional assumptions about the existence of those individuals. As our counterexample to (CB$_R$) is effectively a counterexample to the special case (CB$_M$), we don't need to consider this latter in more detail. It is simply false. If (CB$_M$) is not valid for metaphysical necessity, then the necessitist argument does not straightforwardly go through: actual existence does not imply metaphysically necessary existence via (CB$_M$).

However, our work is only half done. For the Barcan formulas are supposed to hold of $\Box$ directly. This has potentially troublesome consequences for Modal Transcendentalism. Most notably, it will be the case that everything that exists,

ESSENCE, EXISTENCE, AND MODAL KNOWLEDGE   197

exists *logically* necessarily. Therefore, since logical necessity implies metaphysical necessity (as long as there are some conditions on objectivity), everything that exists, exists *metaphysically* necessarily as well, after all.[6]

At the heart of the problem is how logic—and by association logical modality—smuggles in an existence assumption. If we can avoid the existence assumption, then we avoid the problems just raised. Hale (2013, 208–10) presents candidate proofs of the standard Barcan and Converse Barcan Formulas, and identifies the problematic steps as those that import questionable existence assumptions.

Converse Barcan:

1	(1)	$\Box\forall x\Phi(x)$	*assumption*
1	(2)	$\forall x\Phi(x)$	$1\times\Box\text{-}elimination$
1	(3)	$\Phi(a)$	$2\times\forall\text{-}elimination$
1	(4)	$\Box\Phi(a)$	$3\times\Box\text{-}introduction$
1	(5)	$\forall x\Box\Phi(x)$	$4\times\forall\text{-}introduction$
	(6)	$\Box\forall x\Phi(x) \rightarrow \forall x\Box\Phi(x)$	$1-5\times\rightarrow\text{-}introduction$

Barcan:

1	(1)	$\forall x\Box\Phi(x)$	*assumption*
1	(2)	$\Box\Phi(a)$	$1\times\forall\text{-}elimination$
1	(3)	$\Phi(a)$	$2\times\Box\text{-}elimination$
1	(4)	$\forall x\Phi(x)$	$3\times\forall\text{-}introduction$
1	(5)	$\Box\forall x\Phi(x)$	$4\times\Box\text{-}introduction$
	(6)	$\forall x\Box\Phi(x) \rightarrow \Box\forall x\Phi(x)$	$1-5\times\rightarrow\text{-}introduction$

At the crucial step, the Converse Barcan proof moves from $\forall x\Phi(x)$ to $\Phi(a)$ with no previous occurrence of 'a' in the proof. A similar move is made in the Barcan proof, from $\forall x\Box\Phi(x)$ to $\Box\Phi(a)$ with no previous occurrence of 'a'. Hale challenges this kind of step:

> The premise from which $\Phi(a)$ is inferred—viz. $\forall x\Phi(x)$—says only that every object satisfies the open sentence $\Phi(x)$; it says nothing whatever about *which* objects exist—in particular it does not imply that the object a exists. But $\Phi(a)$ may well express a proposition which cannot be true unless a exists. Step (3) [of the Converse Barcan proof] illicitly smuggles in that assumption.
>
> (Hale, 2013, 209)

He concludes that we should reject the standard classical rule of universal quantifier elimination, according to which one can introduce a new constant to form

---

[6] Suppose that $\Box\forall x\exists y(x = y)$. Then $\exists\phi(O\phi \wedge \Box(\phi \rightarrow \forall x\exists y(x = y)))$. But then by (CB), $\exists\phi(O\phi \wedge \forall x\Box(\phi \rightarrow \exists y(x = y)))$. So everything is such that it follows from conditions on objectivity that it exists.

198 THINKING OF NECESSITY

an instance, in favour of a rule that requires an instance to make use of 'a supplementary premise to the effect that *a* exists' (ibid.).[7]

From the point of view of the various theses defended in this book, such an existence assumption is indeed illicit. I argued earlier that logic and logical necessity have their source in the laws of thought, and that there are *additional* conditions on objective thought. The conclusion that logic commits us to the existence of something (in the case of first-order classical logic), and the further consequence for its extension into quantified modal logic that everything that exists exists necessarily, fly in the face of the separation of logic and ontology that has been built up by considerations of the purpose and nature of logical and metaphysical modalities. One might take this to be a *modus tollens* for the background framework that I have defended; I prefer to take this to show that something has gone wrong in our toleration of the existence assumption of classical logic. So this is one departure from classical logic that I do need to, and want to, endorse.

In this, I am following Hale (2013), who endorses a negative free logic in his response to the Barcan formula proofs. A free logic is 'free' in the sense that it is free of existential assumptions. A free logic allows that singular terms may fail to refer and lacks the classical assumption that there exists at least one thing. A negative free logic holds that a necessary condition on the truth of a simple predication $F(t_1, \ldots, t_n)$ is that the terms $t_1, \ldots, t_n$ refer to existing objects.[8]

I will end this section with some remarks on what, roughly, this shows about the relation between the modal metaphysical questions that I have been considering and the endorsement of a free logic.

It is notable that my approach to modal metaphysics stands in significant opposition to the essentialist approach of Hale. Where he takes the source of logical and metaphysical modalities to lie in the nature of things (the natures of logical functions for logical necessity, and the natures of all things for metaphysical necessity), I have urged us to take the source of logical and metaphysical modalities to lie in thought (thought in general for logical necessity, and objective thought for metaphysical necessity). It is by no means a shared *metaphysical picture* that lies behind our preferences for free logic. Rather, at least in this context, it is a commitment to the idea of *contingent existence* that has driven the move to a negative free logic. In my case, it is also the conviction that logic should have no consequences for existence. Moreover, the laws of logic and logical modalities arising from them should not be existentially committing—it is only the conditions on objective thought that have direct implications for what there might be in reality. Recall, metaphysical necessity is the strictest real necessity. Hence, if logic alone makes claims about existence, we should not take these seriously, and seek to expunge them as illegitimate.

---

[7] See also Chapter 8, section 8.3, for discussion of these quantifier rules.
[8] See Hale (2013, 209).

9.2 Essentialism

9.2.1 Essential preliminaries

The next class of typical cases to be considered are essentialist claims.

There are different kinds of statements of essence. For example,

Objectual essence: It's essential to Socrates to be a human.

Generic essence: It's essential to being a human to be a rational animal.

Factual essence: It's essential to Socrates's being a human that he be a rational animal.[9]

Statements of objectual essence are perhaps most recognizable: they attribute an essential property, such as being human, to an object or individual, such as Socrates. Examples of typical objectual essentialist claims include essentiality of kind, essentiality of origin, and essentiality of constitution.

Essentiality of kind: if a is of kind K, then a is essentially of kind K.

For example, Socrates is human, and so Socrates is essentially human (and not a boiled egg).

Essentiality of origin: if a has origin O, then a essentially has origin O.

For example, Queen Elizabeth I is the daughter of King Henry VIII, so Elizabeth I is essentially the daughter of Henry VIII (and not William Shakespeare).

Essentiality of constitution: if a is composed of chunk of material M, then a is essentially composed of M.

For example, my desk is composed of a particular chunk of particleboard, so my desk is essentially composed of that chunk of particleboard (and not, for example, some wooden planks).

Statements of generic essence should also be familiar as capturing cases of purported type identities and Aristotelian real definitions. For example, it's essential to being water to be H_2O, and it's essential to being human to be a rational animal. The former kinds of case are familiar from Kripke's *Naming and Necessity,* where he was interested in the necessity of *a posteriori* identities largely concerning theoretical or scientific types, such as heat, water, and tigers. I also include here Aristotelian

---

[9] See Correia and Skiles (2019, 649).

real definitions, for it seems to have been these kinds of generic essentialist claims that Aristotle himself intended to make. Whilst he clearly endorses, for example, taking the real definition of *human* to be *rational animal*, he warns us against trying to define *individuals* rather than *kinds*.

> When one of the definition-mongers defines any individual, he must recognize that his definition may always be overthrown; for it is not possible to define such things. (Aristotle, *Metaphysics*, VII, 15)

Statements of factual essence are perhaps less familiar. They can be understood as a generalization of objectual and generic cases. If Socrates is essentially a human, then it is essential to the fact that something is Socrates, that that thing is human; or if it is essential to being human to be a rational animal, then it is essential to the fact that Socrates is human that Socrates is a rational animal.

Essentialist claims are typically taken *to be*, or *to entail*, metaphysical necessity claims. In the first case (which I call 'modalism'), essentialist claims are straight-forwardly understood as *de re* metaphysical necessity claims.[10] In the second case (which I call 'm-essentialism'),[11] essentialist claims are taken to be claims about *essences* or *natures* of things (whether 'essence' is taken to be a primitive notion or understood in further terms).[12] M-essentialists take metaphysical necessities to have their source in essence. For example, the necessity of Socrates's being human has its source in the nature of Socrates: because it is part of what it is to be Socrates that he be human, he *couldn't* have failed to be human and still exist. For present purposes, I do not need to engage with the dispute between modalists and m-essentialists about essence.[13] We need only consider the extent to which Modal Transcendentalism accommodates any essentialist necessity claims.

We must further distinguish between individual essences and shareable essences. The former are properties taken to be both necessary and (necessarily) sufficient for the existence of an individual. One might take the property of originating from a particular pair of gametes to be both necessary *and* (necessarily) *sufficient* for the existence of a particular human. So, for example, anything that ever originated from the gametes that I actually originated from would be me, and I could only exist if I originated from those gametes.[14] By contrast, it has also been argued that things have their kinds essentially, e.g., I am human, so I couldn't

---

[10] See, e.g., Wiggins (2001); Mackie (2006).

[11] Short for 'essentialism about modality'. Not to be confused with 'essentialism' in the sense of an endorsement of some essentialist claims, such as the essentiality of kind. Hence the 'm-'.

[12] See, e.g., Fine (1994, 1995); Hale (2013). Some m-essentialists further explicate the notion of essence in other terms, for example, real definition, grounding, or generalized identity. This still counts as m-essentialism as long as they do not appeal to metaphysical modality in their account of essence.

[13] Elsewhere I cast doubt on the prospects for m-essentialism. See Leech (2018, 2021c, 2022b).

[14] This is ignoring the possibility of monozygotic twins, which is by no means a trivial simplification. This is also assuming that I am a human (and not merely, for example, contingently constituted by one).

ESSENCE, EXISTENCE, AND MODAL KNOWLEDGE   201

have existed without being human. The view is obviously not that being human is *sufficient* for my existence, otherwise all other humans would be me (which they are not!). Rather, the view is only that kind properties are *necessary*. I will not be concerned with sufficiency claims, i.e., whether Modal Transcendentalism can accommodate individual essences. More pressing are simply the necessity claims, which are shared by individual and shareable essences alike.

9.2.2 Essentiality of kind and a general problem for essentialism

In this section, I lay out a general problem for accommodating familiar essentialist claims, such as the essentiality of kind and origin, in a straightforward way in the proposed account of metaphysical necessity. In the following section, I propose an alternative approach which, as well as benefitting from independent virtues, comfortably accommodates the possibility of essentialist claims within Modal Transcendentalism. I will first focus on the essentiality of kind as an instructive example, then generalize the problem that arises. The root of the problem is that essentialist claims are not sufficiently general. This is, in many ways, unsurprising. They are, after all, supposed to concern the special properties of different things.

We have seen that Modal Transcendentalism is unlikely to directly generate *de re* metaphysical necessities, such as *it is metaphysically necessary that Socrates is human.* So we can immediately assume that essentialist claims such as the essentiality of kind are not to be straightforwardly accommodated. This is what we should expect if we wish to take the source of modality not to lie in the things themselves, but in our capacities for thinking about things in general. It is, however, still open at this point that there may be *general* necessities from which we can derive particular instances and conditional metaphysical necessities. Let us therefore consider the prospects for this strategy.

Take the essentiality of kind. And consider the case of Socrates being metaphysically necessarily human. Suppose that this is an instance of a general metaphysical necessity. *Which one?* It is not, for example, metaphysically necessary that everything is human. We need something that plausibly is among, or follows from, conditions on objectivity.

Sortal essentialists take sortal concepts to be indispensible to our capacity to identify and reidentify particulars. Wiggins (2001), for example, has argued that since identification and reidentification of particulars is possible only through application of sortal concepts, particulars therefore fall under their sortals necessarily. Here there appears to be scope to build essentialism into Modal Transcendentalism. Conditions on objectivity concern our capacity to think about objects. That, plausibly, includes a capacity to individuate and to reidentify things.[15]

---

[15] See chapter 2 of Strawson (1959) and the commentary of Evans (1985) for an exploration of this line of thought.

202 THINKING OF NECESSITY

If these latter capacities require in turn the possession and deployment of sortal concepts, then it may be that Modal Transcendentalism yields some necessities of kind.

What is a sortal concept?

> Although [the notion of a sortal concept] has been employed in slightly different ways, a common thread is provided by the idea that sortal concepts have a special role in *individuation*: they are concepts that provide *criteria of identity* or *principles of individuation* for the things that fall under them.
>
> (Mackie, 2006, 120)

Intuitively, sortal concepts (or the properties that things have when they fall under sortal concepts) give us ways to count. For example, we can count cats, mountains, and loaves of bread, but not reds, talls, or louds (compare: we can count, for example, red *postboxes*, tall *giraffes*, loud *bangs*).[16] Amongst the sortal concepts are *substance sortals*: these are connected to the identity and persistence conditions of things. That is to say, a substance sortal concept provides a principle determining identity at a time and over time for things falling under it. For example, if *human* is a substance sortal concept, and Socrates is human, then his being human (his falling under the concept *human*) determines the conditions under which he is the same as or distinct from humans at a time (amongst other things, he is distinct from humans that are spatially unconnected to him), and the conditions under which he is the same as or distinct from humans at other times (i.e., one might expect some kind of continuity of biological processes to hold between the same human at different times). Not all sortals are substance sortals. To give another example, whilst both *kitten* and *cat* are sortal concepts—we can count kittens and we can count cats—it is *cat*, not *kitten*, that is the more plausible substance sortal. For, quite obviously, Tiger the cat can grow up from being a kitten to an adult cat without ceasing to exist. In what follows, I will be concerned with substance sortals. Hence, from now on, by 'sortal' I will mean 'substance sortal' unless specified otherwise.

So, the idea is that sortals are required for individuation and reidentification. There are two potential consequences of this. First, sortals correspond to *permanent properties*, that is, if an individual a is S, where S is a property corresponding to a sortal concept, then a is *always* S. Since being S is what determines what is the same as or distinct from S over time, if a lost the property

---

[16] As well as count nouns such as 'cat' and 'mountain', mass nouns such as 'gold' and 'water' also count as sortal terms. Although we cannot count golds and waters (in the intended sense), we can, as it were, measure the amount of such a mass. As Lowe (2009) puts it, in the case of count nouns it makes sense to ask 'how many?', in the case of mass nouns it makes sense to ask 'how much?', e.g., how much gold exists in the safe? For the sake of simplicity, I will focus my argument on sortals expressed by count nouns.

ESSENCE, EXISTENCE, AND MODAL KNOWLEDGE   203

of being S, then that would no longer be a. This, crucially, is *not* the claim that *necessarily, a is S*. It is the claim that, *given that a is S, a could not survive becoming non-S*. I am inclined to think that both claims (of necessity and permanence) are false, but this is not the main point here. So let us grant that sortal concepts may, indeed, play such a role in individuation and reidentification, and hence that they correspond to permanent properties.[17]

The second potential consequence is that, since sortals play this role, they are therefore necessary properties, i.e., if a is S, then necessarily a is S. This is the move that ushers in the essentiality of kind.

Here is our statement of the essentiality of kind.

If a is K, then necessarily, a is K.

Modal Transcendentalism would formulate this directly as follows:

If a is K, then $\exists\phi(O\phi \wedge \Box(\phi \rightarrow a \text{ is } K)$.

We already know this isn't going to work. General conditions on objectivity alone are not going to logically imply that a is K. However, earlier we saw that one can generate conditional metaphysical necessities.[18]

CMN $\exists\phi\exists\psi(O\phi \wedge T\psi \wedge \Box((\phi \wedge \psi) \rightarrow p) \wedge \neg\Box(\psi \rightarrow p))$

In this case, this would require some general conditions, plus some actual truths about a, that would together entail that a is K. We are looking for something of the form:

$\Phi(a)$.

General conditions on objectivity.

Therefore, Ka.

What kind of facts about a might feed in here? The obvious choice is: that a is K. After all, this is the antecedent in the statement of essentiality of kind. The thought there is: given that a is K, it is necessarily so. However, it is equally obvious that this will not help us here. If we already assume that a is K, the general conditions make no contribution at all.

Alternatively, we might appeal to the fact that a exists. We then seek to yield 'a is K' as an instance of a general necessity. However, this again doesn't work. For it would seem to require the general necessary that *everything is K*. i.e., the thought would seem to be that Ka is an instance of $\forall x Kx$, but for that to give us the

---

[17] But see Campbell (2006); Hazlett (2010); Leech (2018).   [18] See Chapter 8, section 8.3.

204　THINKING OF NECESSITY

metaphysical necessity of Ka, it would have to be a condition on objectivity, and hence a metaphysical necessity, that $\forall x Kx$. But that is hardly plausible if we have in mind examples such as 'Socrates is human' or 'Tiger is a cat'. For it's not the case that everything is human, or that everything is a cat!

A more plausible general metaphysical necessity would be,

$$\exists \phi (O\phi \wedge \Box(\phi \rightarrow \forall x(x \text{ has a sortal property})))$$

i.e., it is metaphysically necessary that everything has a sortal property (everything falls under a sortal concept), because it follows from the conditions on objectivity, which include general conditions under which we can individuate things. However, even if this is true, it only guarantees that everything has some sortal property or other, not that anything has a particular sortal property. In light of the fact that a exists, we could yield the conditional metaphysical necessity that a has a sortal property. We may even learn that a is K. But there's nothing here to show that a couldn't have had a different sortal property to K. For example, we might establish that, given that Socrates exists, he must have some sortal property. And indeed, he does; he is human. But this does not rule out the possibility of his having had a different sortal property, e.g., he could have been a donkey.

Is there a way to strengthen this, to add that everything has its sortal property *necessarily*? Let us reformulate the previous general necessity more carefully:

$\Box$**SP**　$\exists \phi (O\phi \wedge \Box(\phi \rightarrow \forall x \exists F(S(F) \wedge Fx)))$

i.e., it is metaphysically necessary that everything x is such that there is a property F that is sortal $(S(F))$, and x is F. This, if true, gives us the result that everything has some sortal property or other (since metaphysical necessity is factive).

SP　$\forall x \exists F(S(F) \wedge Fx)$

What the essentialist seeks is that everything has its sortal property metaphysically necessarily, i.e., using '$\Box_M p$' as shorthand for 'It is metaphysically necessary that p':

SP$\Box$　$\forall x \exists F(S(F) \wedge \Box_M Fx)$

Cashed out according to Modal Transcendentalism this becomes:

SP$\Box$*　$\forall x \exists F(S(F) \wedge \exists \phi (O\phi \wedge \Box(\phi \rightarrow Fx)))$

Thus spelled out, we can immediately see a familiar problem arising for SP$\Box$*. We've already seen that conditions on objectivity are unlikely to imply specific features of specific individuals (i.e., of the form 'Fx'), unless they are instances of general necessities. Certainly, there's no reason to think that *everything* is such that the conditions on objectivity will imply that *it* has some specific and distinctive sortal feature. The additional complications do not solve the basic problem: *conditions on objectivity are general, and do not imply that particular individuals have some particular properties that distinguish them from others.*

I will shortly argue that a similar problem applies generally to other kinds of essentialist claims. But first, let me set aside a potential line of argument. One might simply say: Modal Transcendentalism cannot accommodate essentiality of kind (and perhaps also other essentialist claims), but *so what*? The essentiality of kind is wrong anyway. If Modal Transcendentalism can't accommodate such a claim, so much the better for Modal Transcendentalism.

As it happens, I do indeed disagree with most essentialist claims. This is in part because I am convinced by the comprehensive criticisms of essentialism made by Mackie (2006).[19] If you also agree that we simply don't need to accommodate essentialist claims, that's all well and good. But I acknowledge that—even given my earlier arguments for extensional neutrality[20]—the idea that *de re* essentialist claims are distinctive of metaphysical necessity holds powerful sway over many a philosopher's intuitions about metaphysical necessity. As such, simply ruling out essentialist metaphysical necessities because they do not fit in with my unconventional proposal—that metaphysical necessity is relative to conditions on objective thought—may be seen by many to show that the proposal is incorrect. Therefore, I'll continue to explore how the approach considered in this section cannot help to accommodate essentialist necessities. But in the following section, I'll show how another approach *can*. Hence, Modal Transcendentalism does not automatically exclude a core class of typical cases of metaphysical necessities (although there remains scope to exclude these cases for other reasons).

Here is the general problem. First, for objectual essences. These all concern properties (including relational properties) predicated of particular individuals, e.g., of Socrates, Elizabeth I, and my desk. Those properties are also not universal properties that everything has just in virtue of existing, i.e., being human, being a daughter of Henry VIII, being made of particleboard. If we grant that the conditions on objectivity are general, and do not concern either particular individuals, such as Socrates, nor the particular similarities and differences between individuals, such as being human or not, then there are not going to be any metaphysical necessities of the required kind. There will be no true cases of the form:

$$\exists \phi (O\phi \wedge \Box(\phi \rightarrow Fa))$$

Where 'Fa' is some purportedly essential predication (such as 'Socrates is human').

---

[19] See also Leech (2018).　　[20] See Chapter 6, section 6.2.

206 THINKING OF NECESSITY

Moreover, there are not going to be any suitable general metaphysical necessities from which the essentialist necessities could follow as conditional metaphysical necessities. Because the essential features are not universal, we cannot combine a general metaphysical necessity that *everything is F*, with the actual truth that *a* exists, to yield the result that *a* is *F*. (I can't see that appeal to any *other* actual truths could help either. The formulation of CMN—$\exists\phi\exists\psi(O\phi \wedge T\psi \wedge \Box((\phi \wedge \psi) \rightarrow p) \wedge \neg\Box(\psi \rightarrow p))$—was designed to ensure that conditions on objectivity made a non-trivial contribution to conditional necessities, which means that appeal to the actual fact that *a* is *F*, e.g., that Socrates is human, won't yield the conditional metaphysical necessity of *Fa*, since this follows from *Fa* alone.) Where there is a plausible general metaphysical necessity in the vicinity, it is not suitable to yield the particular necessities we are seeking. For example, we have seen that even if it is plausible that it is metaphysically necessary that everything has a sortal property, it does not follow that anything has its actual sortal property necessarily. Similarly, even if there were reasons to think that necessarily everything has an origin,[21] or necessarily everything is composed of something,[22] that would not show that anything has its actual origin necessarily, or that anything has its actual composition necessarily.

The problem extends to generic essence claims as well. There is a question how best to formulate such claims.[23] Setting aside such considerations for now, it suffices to make the observation that familiar and central cases of generic essence claims concern matters too specific to plausibly belong to, or follow directly from, general conditions on objectivity. For example, there's no reason to think that conditions on objectivity would have anything in particular to say about animals or water. Even if one tried to shoehorn some of these cases into our conceptual repertoire, such that generic essentialist claims were treated as a kind of conceptual necessity, that still wouldn't help. Even if it is plausible to think that our capacity for thinking, and for thinking objectively, is constrained by what concepts we possess and the relations between those concepts, our possession of some rather than other concepts (such as *blue* and *water*, rather than *grue* and *twater*), is not plausibly part of the conditions on objectivity. There might be some concepts that come along with a capacity for objective thought. Indeed, I've argued that a concept of modality is one of them.[24] However, these are not at all the kinds of cases the essentialists have in mind. And there's no reason I can think of why the possession of the concept *human*, or the concept *water*, should be a part of the conditions on a capacity for objective thought at all.

---

[21] Perhaps if there were reasons to think that nothing exists eternally?

[22] Perhaps if there are reasons to think that there are no atomic simples?

[23] For example, should 'It's essential to being a human to be a rational animal' be understood as involving claims about properties, e.g., the essence of the property *human*, or as involving general claims, e.g., that everything that's a human is a rational animal, or something else? See Correia (2006) for discussion.

[24] See Chapter 5.

9.2.3 Essence and identity

In the previous section, I argued that typical cases of metaphysical necessities associated with essentialist claims cannot be accommodated in Modal Transcendentalism by taking them to directly follow from conditions on objectivity, nor by building essentialist principles into the conditions on objectivity. In this section, I propose an alternative strategy, namely, to accommodate essentialist claims by adopting an understanding of them in terms of *generalized identity*, conjoined with the necessity of identity.[25]

Identity is a familiar notion. The usual conventions for the identity sign '=' in predicate logic allow that it is grammatical to flank the identity sign with constants or variables standing for objects in the domain, e.g., '$x = a$'. But it is not usually permissible to flank the identity sign with predicates or sentences, e.g., '$F = G$', '$Fa = Gb$'. Rather, in these latter cases, we use expressions to otherwise capture equivalence, such as co-extension (e.g., '$\forall x(Fx \leftrightarrow Gx)$', everything is F if and only if it's G) or material equivalence (e.g., '$Fa \leftrightarrow Gb$', a is F if and only if b is G). As such, identity is usually taken to distinctively concern objects.[26]

Recently, there has been a developing interest in a broader notion of *generalized identity*.[27] This is a notion often captured by our everyday use of the phrase 'just is', as in 'Water *just is* H_2O'. We say that water *is identical to* H_2O in some sense that is not obviously to do with the identity of particular individuals. Further typical examples of statements of generalized identity include:

(1) For a thing to be a bachelor *is* for it to be an unmarried adult male.

(2) For a thing to know a proposition *is* for it to truly, justifiably believe that proposition.

(3) For the Atlantic Ocean to be filled with water *is* for it to be filled with H_2O molecules.

(Correia and Skiles, 2019, 643)

We can express generalized identity using an equivalence sign as follows.[28] In the most general case, it can be flanked by propositional constants.

$p \equiv q$

To be read: For it to be the case that p *is* for it to be the case that q.

---

[25] Some of the exposition and discussion in this section closely follows that of Leech (2021c).
[26] See Frege (1979, 120).   [27] See, e.g., Rayo (2013); Dorr (2016); Correia and Skiles (2019).
[28] Here I follow Correia and Skiles (2019, 644).

208 THINKING OF NECESSITY

Then, we can specify the form of cases where we want to capture the generalized identity of properties of things.

$Fx \equiv_x Gx$

To be read: For a thing to be F is for it to be G.

This is a special case of the more general formulation:

$p \equiv_{x,y,\dots} q$

To be read: For some things $x, y, \dots$ to be such that p is for them to be such that q.

The generalized identity operator '$\equiv$' has many of the typical features of the standard identity operator. According to Correia and Skiles, it is reflexive, symmetric and transitive. Importantly, it can be understood to conform to a version of Leibniz's Law. Leibniz's Law for (objectual) identity says that if x is identical to y, then x and y have all and only the same properties.

LL= $\quad \forall x \forall y((x = y) \rightarrow (\Phi(x) \leftrightarrow \Phi(y)))$

By analogy, Leibniz's Law for generalized identity says that if for it to be the case that p *is* for it to be the case that q, then p and q have all and only the same substitutional features (roughly speaking). More carefully:

LL$\equiv$ If $p \equiv_v q$ and Φ, then $\Phi[q//p]$, where $\Phi[q//p]$ results from sentence Φ by replacing one or more occurrences of p by q, with the condition that no variable that is free in $p \equiv_v q$ is bound in Φ or $\Phi[q//p]$.

(Correia and Skiles, 2019, 645). So, for example, if *for the Atlantic Ocean to be filled with water is for it to be filled with H_2O molecules*, and *either the Atlantic ocean is filled with water or I'm an armadillo*, then *either the Atlantic ocean is filled with H_2O molecules or I'm an armadillo.*

What does this have to do with essentialism? Correia and Skiles (2019) propose an analysis of essentialist statements in terms of generalized identity statements. A statement of essence might state the essence of something *in full* or *in part*. If there is nothing more to the essence of being human than being a rational animal, then we can state the essence of being human *in full* by saying: 'It's essential to being human to be a rational animal'. We can also state the essence of being human *in part* by saying: 'It's essential to being human to be rational'. Correia and Skiles (2019, 649) treat statements of *full generic essence* straightforwardly as statements of generalized identity:

ESSENCE, EXISTENCE, AND MODAL KNOWLEDGE

Being F is what it is to be G *in full* if and only if $Gx \equiv_x Fx$.

Statements of *partial generic essence* are slightly more complicated. The basic idea is that in making a statement of partial essence we are leaving something out of one side of a generalized identity. Hence, in a statement of partial essence we are stating part of a conjunction that would amount to a statement of the full essence.

> Being F is *partially* what it is to be G if and only if there is some H such that $Gx \equiv_x Fx \wedge Hx$.

So, in this case, being F is *a conjunctive part of* what it is to be G.[29] Correia and Skiles introduce further notation to capture this:

$$Fx \subseteq_x Gx$$

Having presented a treatment of generic essence, we can treat statements of objectual essence as a special case of generic essence. For example, 'Tiger is essentially a cat' becomes 'Being a cat is part of what it is to be Tiger', and so 'cat$(x) \subseteq_x x =$ Tiger'.[30]

In sum, one can treat essentialist statements as various kinds of statements of generalized identity. Now we are in a position to develop a way to accommodate essentialism within Modal Transcendentalism. Modal Transcendentalism can accommodate the necessity of identity. Moreover, there is an analogue of the necessity of identity for generalized identity. Hence, we can potentially capture the necessities associated with essentialist claims via the necessity of generalized identity.

Ruth Barcan Marcus famously presented a proof of the necessity of identity, later taken up by Kripke.[31]

(1) $\forall x \forall y ((x = y) \rightarrow (\Phi(x) \rightarrow \Phi(y)))$ LL=

(2) $\forall x \Box (x = x)$ Necessity of self-identity

(3) $\forall x \forall y ((x = y) \rightarrow (\Box(x = x) \rightarrow \Box(x = y)))$ 1

(4) $\forall x \forall y ((x = y) \rightarrow \Box(x = y))$ 2,3

Leibniz's Law tells us that if x is identical to y, then if some condition is true of x, it is also true of y: x and y have all and only the same properties. Everything is

---

[29] It is easiest to understand partial generic essence in the simple case where F and H are *genus* and *differentia*, providing a *species* G, such as: to be human just is to be rational and animal. However, note that Correia and Skiles allow for cases where H could simply be G. For example, to be human just is to be human, hence to be human just is to be rational and human.

[30] See Correia and Skiles (2019, 649–50).

[31] Barcan (1947); Kripke (1971). See also Leech (forthcoming).

210 THINKING OF NECESSITY

necessarily self-identical, that is, x is necessarily identical to x. So, given Leibniz's Law, it must also be that y is necessarily identical to x. That is, if $x = y$, then, necessarily $x = y$. Identity is necessary.

We can modify this proof to show the necessity of generalized identity.[32]

(1) If $p \equiv q$ and Φ, then $\Phi[q//p]$ LL$\equiv$
(2) $\Box(p \equiv p)$ Necessity of self-g-identity
(3) $p \equiv q \rightarrow (\Box(p \equiv p) \rightarrow \Box(p \equiv q))$ 1
(4) $p \equiv q \rightarrow \Box(p \equiv q)$ 2,3

Leibniz's Law for generalized identity tells us that if for it to be the case that p *just is* for it to be the case that q, then if Φ is true, Φ will remain true under any replacement of one of more occurrences of p by q in Φ.[33] Everything is necessarily self-identical in the sense of generalized identity, that is, necessarily, for it to be the case that p *is* for it to be the case that p. But then, given Leibniz's Law, we can replace one occurrence of p with q with the result that necessarily, for it to be the case that p *is* for it to be the case that q. That is, if $p \equiv q$, then, necessarily $p \equiv q$. Generalized identity is necessary.

Both proofs crucially rely on a principle of substitutivity at step (1), and the assumption that this holds even for modal contexts, such as are introduced by step (2).[34] These together license the substitution at step (3). This interacts in important ways with our assumption about the kind of necessity involved. It is plausible that self-identity is logically necessary, but then one may worry that allowing a derivation of (3) effectively allows substitution of co-referential terms into an opaque context. To give a well-worn example, whilst it may well be logically necessary that Hesperus is Hesperus, it does not seem right to say that it is *logically* necessary that Hesperus is Phosphorus. But if we accommodate this concern by insisting that the modal operator at step (3) expresses metaphysical modality, and hence so does the modal operator throughout the proof (to avoid equivocation), we face the challenge to accommodate these claims of necessity within our preferred account of metaphysical modality, in this case, in Modal Transcendentalism.[35]

Let us begin by considering first the necessity of identity: plain objectual identity. How does the necessity of identity fit into Modal Transcendentalism? Let us begin by supposing that self-identity is logically necessary. Hence, it is also metaphysically necessary.[36] There are then three potential options for how to accommodate specific identities as *conditionally* necessary in some sense.

---

[32] See Leech (2021c).
[33] With the condition that no variable that is free in $p \equiv q$ is bound in Φ or $\Phi[q//p]$.
[34] See, e.g., Burgess (2014) for discussion.
[35] Thank you to an anonymous reader for pressing this issue.
[36] Since, trivially, all logically necessities follow logically from any proposition, and so *a fortiori,* from conditions of objectivity.

ESSENCE, EXISTENCE, AND MODAL KNOWLEDGE   211

First, in Chapter 8 (section 8.3), I proposed an account of how to accommodate in Modal Transcendentalism instances of general necessities. In short, if we add to conditions of objectivity a stock of actual truths, such as specific actual identities (e.g., that $a = b$), then we may expect to yield the conditional metaphysical necessity of these instances. However, recall the definition of conditional metaphysical necessity:

CMN $\exists\phi\exists\psi(O\phi \wedge T\psi \wedge \Box((\phi \wedge \psi) \rightarrow p) \wedge \neg\Box(\psi \rightarrow p))$

This was designed to ensure that the conditions of objectivity made a contribution to the conditional necessity. However, in the case of the necessity of identity, they do not appear to do so. Suppose the logical necessity of self-identity, and also that actually $a = b$. If we grant the proof of the necessity of identity for logical necessity, we yield the result that $\Box a = b$. This will also follow trivially from conditions of objectivity and the actual truths together, but the conditions of objectivity themselves play no non-trivial role, and so CMN is not satisfied.

Second, then, rather than a conditional metaphysical necessity, we might say we have a *conditional logical necessity*. We begin with the necessity of identity.

$$\forall x \forall y(x = y \rightarrow \Box(x = y))$$

And let us suppose a particular case of identity.

$$a = b$$

Given this assumption, we can apply the rule of $\forall$-elimination to yield:

$$a = b \rightarrow \Box(a = b)$$

Given our assumption that $a = b$, we also yield:

$$\Box(a = b)$$

However, importantly, we have not discharged our assumption that $a = b$. More formally:

	(1)	$\forall x \forall y(x = y \rightarrow \Box(x = y))$	necessity of identity
1	(2)	$a = b$	assumption
1	(3)	$a = b \rightarrow \Box a = b$	$\forall$Elim 1,2
1	(4)	$\Box a = b$	MPP 2,3

212 THINKING OF NECESSITY

What we have is a *conditional* necessity. It is merely conditionally necessary that $a = b$, on the assumption that $a = b$. But this, after all, seems right. As already noted, we don't want it to be a straightforward matter of logical necessity that, for example, Hesperus is Phosphorus, not least since Venus might have failed to exist. All that we had in mind was the claim that, should Hesperus and Phosphorus exist, they could not fail to be identical. So it seems fair to say that, on the assumption that Hesperus is Phosphorus, we can conclude that necessarily, Hesperus is Phosphorus.[37]

Thirdly, then, how does this notion of conditional logical necessity relate to metaphysical necessity? As long as there are conditions of objectivity, then any logical necessity will also be metaphysically necessary. So, if $a = b$ is logically necessary given that actually $a = b$, it should also follow that $a = b$ is metaphysically necessary given that actually $a = b$.

So much for the necessity of identity. Let us now consider *generalized identity*. One might further extend the resources of Modal Transcendentalism to include generalized identity. If this move is defensible, then we can reason similarly. We begin by granting that generalized self-identity is logically necessary: for example, it seems a plausible axiom of any formal system of generalized identity that $p \equiv p$. If it is logically necessary, then it is also metaphysically necessary. And in general, the necessity of generalized self-identity just seems overwhelmingly plausible: surely it's necessary that for it to be the case that p *just is* for it to be the case that p. What else could it be? We have seen a proof to extend the necessity of generalized self-identity to the necessity of any generalized identity. But since, if Correia and Skiles are right, essentialist claims are just disguised claims of generalized identity, then we have here the resources to include within Modal Transcendentalism metaphysical necessities associated with familiar essentialist principles. For example, if what it is to be Socrates is, in part, to be human, and this is a generalized identity, then by the line of thought just presented, it is *necessary*. In brief: *Socrates is necessarily human.*

In more detail: as earlier, in the case of (non-generalized) identity, we can recognize conditional logical necessities, *mutatis mutandis* for generalized identity, and thence for essence. Begin with the necessity of generalized identity.

$$p \equiv q \rightarrow \Box(p \equiv q)$$

And let us suppose a particular case of generalized identity.[38]

---

[37] I discuss this kind of reading of conditional logical necessity of identity in Leech (2021c), pp.905–6.

[38] The necessity of generalized identity is not presented in quantified form, but as a schema. Hence particular cases are instances of the schema.

$$p_0 \equiv q_0$$

Given this assumption, we can instantiate the general schema of the necessity of generalized identity to yield:

$$p_0 \equiv q_0 \rightarrow \Box(p_0 \equiv q_0)$$

Given our assumption that $p_0 \equiv q_0$, we also yield:

$$\Box(p_0 \equiv q_0)$$

However, importantly, we have not discharged our assumption that $p_0 \equiv q_0$. We have a *conditional* necessity. It is merely conditionally necessary that $p_0 \equiv q_0$, on the assumption that $p_0 \equiv q_0$. But this, after all, seems right. We don't want it to be a matter of logical necessity that, for example, what it is to be swimming in water is what it is to be swimming in H_2O. It seems fair to say that, conditional on the actual facts, which include that fact that what it is to be water is to be H_2O, it is necessary that what it is to be swimming in water is what it is to be swimming in H_2O.

As before, it will also follow that there is a sense in which generalized identities (and the essentialist claims that they may capture) are conditionally metaphysically necessary. As long as there are conditions of objectivity, then any logical necessity will also be metaphysically necessary. So, if $p_0 \equiv q_0$ is logically necessary given that actually $p_0 \equiv q_0$, it should also follow that $p_0 \equiv q_0$ is metaphysically necessary given that actually $p_0 \equiv q_0$.

In Leech (2021c) I discuss the prospects for using the necessity of generalized identity to give an account of how essentialist claims might imply necessity claims, as required by m-essentialists, i.e., essentialists about modality. I argue that it can't help the m-essentialist, given their particular commitments and aims.[39] But here I am putting the proposal to different use. Take the source of necessity to lie not in essences, but in laws of thought. The necessity of generalized identity, plus an account of essentialist statements in terms of generalized identity, opens up the option to accommodate the necessity of essentialist statements, if one should so wish. My proposal here then turns on whether one takes the relevant class of generalized identity claims to be *true*. If they are true, then they are (in some sense) necessary. And we get the essentialist necessities. But one might deny their truth. For example, I disagree that it is part of what it is to be Socrates to be human, so I would also deny that Socrates is essentially human, and accordingly deny that Socrates is necessarily human.

---

[39] In short, if an m-essentialist also wants to give an account of logical necessity in terms of essence, then they can't appeal to the logical necessity of self-identity as part of an account of how essence can imply necessity without begging the question. See Leech (2021c).

214 THINKING OF NECESSITY

One final point. One might worry that the necessity of identity and the necessity of generalized identity generate the same kind of problems that we saw earlier for *de re* necessities. These necessities of identity are *de re*. Hence, as before, we should expect that no particular identities are necessary. For example, it is true that Cicero is identical to Tully. But if this were straightforwardly logically or metaphysically necessary, then this would threaten to clash with our intuition (and the result from earlier) that Cicero is a contingent being. For how can it be true no matter what that Cicero is Tully, if there is no such thing as Cicero?[40] Or, suppose it is true that what it is to be Socrates is, in part, to be human. Is this logically necessary? This is clearly no logical truth, nor does it resemble one. However, the worry is misplaced. I have argued that these cases are of a kind of conditional necessity. *Given the actual facts about (generalized) identity,* there are necessary (generalized) identities, but they do not stand alone.

9.3 The necessary *a posteriori*

It was once assumed that necessity, *a priority*, and analyticity on the one hand, and contingency, *a posteriority*, and syntheticity on the other hand, were of a kind and so co-extensive. This assumption has been subject to some famous challenges, most notably Kant's synthetic *a priori*,[41] and Kripke's necessary *a posteriori* and contingent *a priori*.[42] At least in part as a result of these challenges to the co-extension assumption, a significant strand of modal epistemology has concerned itself with whether and how modal knowledge is *a priori* or *a posteriori*. Part of the legacy of Kripke's *Naming and Necessity* is that it is often taken to be a commonplace that many metaphysical necessities are *a posteriori*. Given my proposed treatment of *de re* modalities and essentialist modalities, we are in a position to indicate where *a posteriori* knowledge is likely to enter into an account of knowledge of these modalities. However, as we will see, this does not really get to the heart of the challenge to explain our knowledge of modality.

First, what do '*a priori*' and '*a posteriori*' mean? We might be tempted to say that *a posteriori* knowledge is knowledge that requires experience, while *a priori* knowledge is knowledge independent of experience. But even Kant saw the problem with this.[43]

---

[40] Recall: according to a negative free logic it is a necessary condition on the truth of a sentence that the singular terms refer. So if 'Cicero' doesn't refer, then 'Cicero is Tully' is false.

[41] Kant (1998). Stang (2011) also argues that, despite appearances, Kant also does not take necessity and *a priority* to be co-extensive.

[42] Although see Kneale (1938) for an earlier advent of the necessary *a posteriori*, and Leech (2019) for discussion.

[43] I will here discuss the *a priori* in terms of knowledge that has a kind of independence from experience. There is a growing literature exploring an additional metaphysical conception of the *a priori*, evident in many places in Kant's work, involving knowledge "from the grounds". See, for example,

ESSENCE, EXISTENCE, AND MODAL KNOWLEDGE   215

> There is no doubt whatever that all our cognition begins with experience; for how else should the cognitive faculty be awakened into exercise if not through objects that stimulate our senses and in part themselves produce presentations, in part bring the activity of our understanding into motion to compare these, to connect or separate them, and thus to work up the raw material of sensible impressions into a cognition of objects that is called experience?   (B1)

Arguably, experience is a condition of all knowledge; for we can hardly come to know anything while unconscious. Nevertheless, we can draw a distinction between different roles that experience plays in knowledge. As Kant puts it,

> although all our cognition commences **with** experience, yet it does not on that account all arise **from** experience.   (B1)

Timothy Williamson draws an illuminating distinction between *enabling* and *evidential* roles of experience in knowledge: experience plays an evidential role in knowledge that p if it provides evidence for believing that p; experience plays an enabling role if it provides the opportunity to acquire concepts required to grasp p. When experience plays an enabling role, it 'awakens the cognitive faculty into exercise'; when it plays an evidential role, our knowledge 'arises from' experience.

> Experience is held to play an evidential role in my visual knowledge that this shirt is green, but a merely enabling role in my visual knowledge that all green things are coloured: I needed it only to acquire the concepts *green* and *coloured*, without which I could not even raise the question whether all green things are coloured.
>
> (Williamson, 2007, 165)

In terms of this distinction, we can understand experience to be *merely enabling* in cases of *a priori* knowledge; *a priori* knowledge is compatible with experience playing an enabling role, but not with experience playing an evidential role. By contrast, experience plays a *strictly evidential* role in cases of *a posteriori* knowledge. In what follows, I will adopt this as my background conception of *a priori* and *a posteriori* knowledge. Note that Williamson does not take this to be an exhaustive distinction: he takes there to be a kind of 'armchair' knowledge in which experience plays more than a merely enabling, but less than a strictly evidential, role.[44]

Smit (2009). Since the present section focuses on the contemporary discussion of modal epistemology, I will here set aside this alternative understanding of the *a priori*. See Stephenson (forthcoming) for discussion of the co-extension assumption in light of this metaphysical understanding of the *a priori*.

[44] Indeed, this is where he seats his account of modal knowledge. Briefly: Williamson takes knowledge of metaphysical modality to have its source in knowledge of counterfactuals, which in turn

216   THINKING OF NECESSITY

Many philosophers agree that there is an important class of metaphysical necessities that are knowable only *a posteriori*. This might mean one of two things.

1. There are cases where it is metaphysically necessary that *p*, but it is not knowable *a priori* that *p*; it is only knowable *a posteriori* that *p*.
2. There are cases where it is metaphysically necessary that *p*, but it is not knowable *a priori* that *necessarily p*; it is only knowable *a posteriori* that *necessarily p*.

The first case concerns how we can come to know something that is necessary; the second concerns how we can come to know that something is necessary.

Both claims are typically made of the kinds of examples presented by Kripke (1980), and of other essentialist claims, such as *(Necessarily) Hesperus is Phosphorus*; *(Necessarily) Gold is the element with atomic number 79*; *(Necessarily) Cats are animals*; *(Necessarily) Water is H₂O*; *(Necessarily) Socrates is human*. With respect to (1), these examples concern facts that can only be discovered through empirical methods. These are facts that science or experience has taught us. However, there are reasons for thinking that they are nevertheless necessary. For example, 'Hesperus' and 'Phosphorus' both refer to the same thing, and one thing could not have been two things, so it is necessary that Hesperus is identical to Phosphorus. It might have been that when the names were first coined they were used differently, such that they referred instead to two different objects. However, this would not be a case of Hesperus no longer being Phosphorus—of one thing being two things— but rather a case of the names 'Hesperus' and 'Phosphorus' being used differently. So, once it happened that, in the actual world, 'Hesperus' and 'Phosphorus' were coined to refer to one and the same thing, it could not have been that Hesperus was not identical to Phosphorus. That said, it took some empirical work to discover that the names did indeed pick out the same thing: that the star shining in the morning sky and the star shining in the evening sky, which were thusly named, are in fact both the planet Venus. I have put this in terms of names, because we tend to use names to refer to things, but the more general point is that we might pick out one thing in two different ways, and mistakenly believe that we have two things when we have one, such that although the 'two' things picked out are necessarily identical, that they are identical will be a matter of an empirical discovery that these two different ways of picking things out pick out one and the same thing.

With respect to (2), Kripke (1971) and others have employed a *deduction model* to explain knowledge of necessity. According to such a model, the relevant

---

involves a kind of simulation in imagination. He takes this simulation to be informed by experience in a way that is more than merely enabling, but experience still does not play a strictly evidential role in our counterfactual knowledge. Hence, this kind of knowledge is not to be comfortably classified as either *a priori* or *a posteriori*.

knowledge is deduced from a non-modal truth and an *a priori* modal conditional.[45] For example,

(1) If Hesperus is Phosphorus, then necessarily, Hesperus is Phosphorus.
 [*A priori* conditional]

(2) Hesperus is Phosphorus. [Non-modal truth]

Therefore,

(3) Necessarily, Hesperus is Phosphorus.

In general,

(1) $P \to \Box P$

(2) P

Therefore,

(3) $\Box P$

Knowledge that it is necessary that p, according to this model, depends upon some *a priori* inferential knowledge: that (3) follows from (1) and (2). Whether the knowledge that it is necessary that p is entirely *a priori* or not further depends upon how we come to know the premises, (1) and (2). In many cases, knowledge of the non-modal premise, (2), is plausibly *a posteriori*, e.g., discovery that Hesperus is the same celestial body as Phosphorus via astronomy. This is enough to render our knowledge of (3) *a posteriori* overall, since even if our knowledge of so-called 'Kripke-conditionals', (1), is *a priori*, our knowledge of (3) still depends upon the *a posteriori* methods needed for knowledge of premise (2).

In general, deduction models explain why knowledge that something is necessary may be *a posteriori,* in terms of an *a posteriori* contribution to a more complex overall account of how such knowledge is come by. Moreover, note that this *a posteriori* contribution corresponds to knowledge of the proposition that is necessary. i.e., *a posteriori* knowledge that p, where p is necessary, makes a contribution to *a posteriori* knowledge that it is necessary that p.

Departing from the letter of deduction models, we can see how *a posteriori* knowledge enters into a more complex picture of the epistemology of *de re* and essentialist modalities. First, consider conditional metaphysical necessities. In Chapter 8, *de re* conditional necessities were taken to follow from general conditions on objectivity plus the actual facts about individuals.

---

[45] See, e.g., Hale (2013, 259) and Mallozzi et al. (2021).

218 THINKING OF NECESSITY

CMN It is conditionally metaphysically necessary that p if and only if $\exists\phi\exists\psi(O\phi \wedge T\psi \wedge \Box((\phi \wedge \psi) \rightarrow p) \wedge \neg\Box(\psi \rightarrow p))$

In order to know that $\exists\phi\exists\psi(O\phi \wedge T\psi \wedge \Box((\phi \wedge \psi) \rightarrow p) \wedge \neg\Box(\psi \rightarrow p))$, for some specific p, we would need to know (1) that p follows as a matter of logical necessity from some ϕ and ψ, where (2) $O\phi$ and (3) $T\psi$, and (4) that $\neg\Box(\psi \rightarrow p)$. Analogously to the standard deduction model, we can ask how we come to know each of these elements. (1) and (4) appear to require *a priori* logical inferential knowledge. (2) raises the question of how we come to know what the conditions on objectivity are. (3) is the likely seat of *a posteriority*: it is plausible that our knowledge of the actual facts about individuals, e.g., that a exists, or our knowledge of other actual truths about a, is *a posteriori*. In cases where it is *a posteriori*, that will introduce an *a posteriori* element into our overall knowledge of the conditional necessity. Modal Transcendentalism can therefore accommodate *a posteriori* conditional metaphysical necessity.

Second, consider essentialist claims. I have proposed that Modal Transcendentalism might accommodate essentialist claims by adopting an approach according to which they are a kind of generalized identity claim. This gives us a version of the deduction model as follows.

(1) $p \equiv q \rightarrow \Box(p \equiv q)$

(2) $p \equiv q$

Therefore,

(3) $\Box(p \equiv q)$

(1) is known via *a priori* logical reasoning about identity. (3) is deduced from (1) and (2). The interesting step is (2): how might we come to know a generalized identity? Sometimes, *a posteriori*. Those cases of generalized identity that align with familiar Kripke cases such as *water is H_2O*, and objectual identities such as *Hesperus is Phosphorus*, we have already allowed as *a posteriori*. However, cases of generalized identity corresponding to other essentialist claims, such as the claim that Socrates is essentially human, are less straightforward. This, according to the proposal, is understood as the claim that being human is part of what it is to be Socrates. But how might we come to know *that*? It is an *a posteriori* matter to find out that Socrates *is* human, just as it is to find out that Socrates is a philosopher. But how might we learn that being human features in the generalized identity of *what it is to be* Socrates, whilst being a philosopher does not? This requires nothing less than an epistemology of essence.[46]

---

[46] The essentialist who takes essential truth to ground necessary truth has another route via a similar deduction model: (1) If it is essential to x that it is F, then it is necessary that x is F. (2) It is essential

I am not going to look further into the epistemology of essence, but will make two remarks. First, it is important to note that the deduction model only takes us a small way towards knowledge of essentialist necessity claims. At bottom, an epistemology of essence is still required. Second, what we are left with here is a framework for the development of Modal Transcendentalism. If one wishes to include essentialist claims, then the generalized identity approach may provide a way to do so. If one wishes to explain the epistemology of essentialist necessity claims, the deduction model highlights the need for a thoroughgoing epistemology of essence.

9.4 Two kinds of conceivability

I want to close this chapter by offering some promissory remarks about how a fuller picture of modal epistemology might go for the metaphysics of modality proposed in this book. In the previous section, I left open what might have seemed to be the most important question: whence knowledge of general metaphysical necessity? I will suggest that knowledge of conditions on objectivity is achieved by what is often called 'transcendental philosophy', and sketch how this might allow us to shed some light on the slippery notion of *conceivability* and its role in modal knowledge. I'll propose that we should distinguish between conceivability understood in terms of what is *thinkable* and conceivability understood in terms of what is *objectively thinkable*. Logic helps us to explore the first kind; transcendental philosophy helps us to explore the second.

Conceivability approaches to modal epistemology take conceivability to be a guide to possibility and necessity. Conceivability is taken either to provide evidence for (Yablo, 1993), or to entail (Chalmers, 2002), possibility, and conversely, inconceivability is taken to provide evidence for or to entail impossibility (and thereby necessity via negation). Conceivability, roughly speaking, concerns a capacity of beings that can conceive of things: it concerns what we, or perhaps idealized minds, are able to conceive of. This is supposed to provide a guide to what there might have been.

It is a tricky matter to say what conceivability is. If one's conception of conceivability is overdemanding, then lots of plausibly conceivable scenarios will not count as conceivable. If conceivability is underdemanding, then this will correspond to too weak a kind of possibility to be of any interest. Conceivability is often taken to align with what is conceptually possible and/or compatible with one's *a priori* knowledge. So, in line with many of our intuitions, logical and conceptual impossibilities are inconceivable, but typical examples of metaphysical

to x that it is F. Therefore, (3) it is necessary that x is F. See Hale (2013); Mallozzi et al. (2021). Since I reject m-essentialism, I will not consider this model further here.

220 THINKING OF NECESSITY

impossibilities, such as water failing to be H_2O, or Socrates failing to be human, are perfectly well conceivable. As such, conceivability accounts that wish to accommodate these kinds of necessities must do some additional work either to explain why their negations are conceivable, or to make them inconceivable after all.[47]

This brief introduction to conceivability approaches allows us already to raise two important questions, which Mallozzi et al. (2021) call 'The Connection Question' and 'The Scope Question'.

> **The Connection Question:** ... How is conceivability connected to possibility? Given that metaphysical modality is an objective modality that is mind-independent, while conceivability is subject-sensitive and mind-dependent, how are the two connected such that conceivability may entail, or at least provide evidence for possibility? Answering the Connection Question should thus clarify how mind-dependent conceivability may provide one with justification for believing that something is mind-independently possible.
>
> **The Scope Question:** This question further specifies the Connection Question, by asking how conceivability can effectively cast light on matters of *metaphysical* possibility, as opposed to *logical-conceptual* possibility. Remember that primary conceivability is a purely *a priori* exercise based on considerations of (ideal) logical and conceptual coherence of a described scenario. What ensures that conceivability exercises so constrained successfully capture metaphysical modality?
>
> (Mallozzi et al., 2021)

The Connection Question challenges us to explain how a mental capacity to conceive of or imagine things relates to how things might be. The Scope Question reinforces this challenge, by asking how we could expect such mental capacities to provide a guide to a real modality such as metaphysical modality.[48]

The accounts of the nature and source of logical and metaphysical modality presented in this book invite the following sketch of answers to the Connection Question and the Scope Question.

Logical necessity has its source in the laws of thought, which are constitutive norms for thought. What is conceivable is what is consistent with the laws of thought (perhaps also including some conceptual connections). As the laws of thought are normative, we are still able to think in violation of those laws. But recall: the laws of logic are rationally indubitable.[49] We can understand conceivability in terms of whether we can *rationally doubt* something, rather than whether

---

[47] See, for example, Roca-Royes (2011) on why this is difficult to achieve without smuggling in assumptions about essentialist knowledge.

[48] See Chapter 6, section 6.4 on real modality.

[49] See Chapter 4, section 4.2.2.

we can *think* it. Conceivability, thus understood, provides a guide to logical possibility.[50] This provides the core of an answer to the Connection Question.

By contrast, metaphysical necessity is relative to conditions of objectivity, that is, conditions on our capacity for objective thought. Kant's method for discovering such conditions is transcendental philosophy.

> I call all cognition transcendental that is occupied not so much with objects but rather with our mode of cognition of objects insofar as this is to be possible *a priori*. A **system** of such concepts would be called **transcendental philosophy**.
>
> (A11–12/B25)

Here is not the place for an extended discussion of the nature, practice, and potential for success of transcendental philosophy. However, here is one way to understand the idea, as developed in Schafer (2020). Transcendental philosophy begins with our self-conscious rational capacities, i.e., our capacities to engage in reasoning and objective conceptual thought. Such capacities are governed by principles, i.e., the rules or laws by which they function properly. Since they are self-conscious, we also have the capacity to make those principles explicit via reflection on our capacities.

> [T]he idea here is that, simply in engaging in a rational activity like judgment or inference, I must have a basic awareness of both this activity and the principles that govern it. Thus, rather than involving a receptivity to something external to our rational capacities, the self-consciousness at issue here arises because, in performing these acts, these capacities must make these acts and their underlying principles available to consciousness.... (Schafer, 2020, 11)
>
> It is the work of the critical philosophy to give us this sort of explicit consciousness of these basic principles. (Schafer, 2020, 12)

A special kind of reflection on our own rational capacities, such as our capacity for objective thought, allows us to develop explicit awareness of the principles governing the exercise of such a capacity. This kind of reflection is possible because the capacities are themselves self-conscious in the right kind of way. Such reflection may also provide a starting point for further exploration of these capacities. For example, from here we may engage in transcendental arguments: arguments that start from some assumed premise and argue regressively to consider the necessary conditions of the possibility of the truth of the premise. Such an argument might, for example, begin with a basic principle of objective thought made explicit, and

---

[50] Whether we take this to be defeasible evidence for logical possibility, or to entail logical possibility, depends upon how robust we take the phenomenon of rational indubitability to be. I will leave this open here.

222 THINKING OF NECESSITY

then proceed to develop further necessary conditions of the possibility of a rational capacity governed by such a principle.[51]

There is scope here for an account of our knowledge of conditions of objectivity, and thereby of metaphysical necessities, via transcendental philosophy understood as a special kind of reflection on our capacity for objective thought, which makes explicit principles that were implicit in our use of this capacity. For example, one might understand the arguments of Chapter 5 as doing just that: reflecting on what it takes to think objectively and isolating some necessary conditions of having such a capacity. One can understand this special kind of reflection as a kind of conceiving: we explore what is conceivable, constrained by and given principles of objective thought. Since metaphysical necessity is relative to conditions on objective thought, this kind of conceivability provides a clear guide to metaphysical possibility. If we understand conceivability within the constraints of the principles of this rational capacity in terms of compatibility with those principles, then since compatibility with conditions on objectivity entails metaphysical possibility, whatever is conceivable in this sense will be metaphysically possible. Therefore, an answer to the Connection Question here trades on the links between metaphysical modality and conditions on objectivity on the one hand, and links between conditions on objectivity and this kind of conceivability—as outlined in terms of transcendental philosophy—on the other. An answer to the Connection Question, according to Mallozzi et al. (2021), should 'clarify how mind-dependent conceivability may provide one with justification for believing that something is mind-independently possible'. The trick here is that, for the Kantian, metaphysical possibility is not strictly speaking mind-independent, since it is connected to conditions on objective thought. The answer to the Scope Question is that a kind of conceivability distinctively tied to conditions on our capacity for *objective thinking* will provide a guide to that kind of modality that is relative to such conditions, namely metaphysical modality.

We saw earlier in this section that it is a challenge to understand conceivability in the right kind of way to adequately capture all and only the possibilities one wants. The suggestion here is that distinguishing between *thought* and *objective thought,* and the laws or conditions that govern these two capacities, as I have urged elsewhere in this book, may have a further pay-off when it comes to modal epistemology. We may then distinguish between conceivability understood in terms of what is *thinkable* and conceivability understood in terms of what is *objectively thinkable.* Logic helps us to explore the first kind; transcendental philosophy helps us to explore the second.

---

[51] See Schafer (2020, 10). For more on transcendental arguments in general, see, e.g., Stern (1999); Pereboom (2016).

10

Metaphysical Necessity in a Formal System

In this final chapter, my aim is to address some issues that arise for the beginnings of a formal system for metaphysical necessity. I consider, in particular, the conjunction property, duality, iteration of modality, and the use of possible worlds semantics. I will not present a full formal system of metaphysical necessity here. Rather, my aim is to draw out some of the more philosophically important and interesting issues that will need to be addressed as part of that larger formal project.

Let us assume as a starting point a standard propositional modal logic, plus resources for propositional quantification, plus axioms for metaphysical necessity. I will not set out the full formal details of such a logic here, but rather make some remarks on the more important aspects of the system. Note: I will not extend my discussion to consideration of a system for metaphysical necessity that takes quantified modal logic as its background logic. The main points that I have to make on this have already been made in Chapters 8 and 9, regarding a treatment of *de re* modalities, necessity of identity, and the Barcan Formulas.

The language of the system includes modal operators $\Box$ and $\Diamond$. These are interpreted as logical necessity and possibility respectively, the correct logic for which, we shall assume, is S5. As such, all models assume an unrestricted accessibility relation between worlds. I discuss the use of possible worlds semantics in the final section of this chapter.

The system includes the following definitions of metaphysical necessity ($\Box_M p$) and metaphysical possibility ($\Diamond_M p$).

$\Box\mathbf{M}$ $\quad \Box_M p =_{df} \exists \phi (O\phi \wedge \Box(\phi \to p))$

$\Diamond\mathbf{M}$ $\quad \Diamond_M p =_{df} \exists \phi O\phi \wedge \forall \psi (O\psi \to \neg\Box(\psi \to \neg p))$

There are two important features of these definitions that I want to highlight and further explain: whether $\Box_M$ has the conjunction property, and why $\Box_M$ and $\Diamond_M$ are not duals.

Thinking of Necessity: A Kantian Account of Modal Thought and Modal Metaphysics. Jessica Leech,
Oxford University Press. © Jessica Leech 2023. DOI: 10.1093/oso/9780198873969.003.0010

224 THINKING OF NECESSITY

10.1 The conjunction property

The definition of metaphysical necessity, $\square$M, involves quantification over a single propositional variable.[1] This invites the question of whether metaphysical necessity has the conjunction property, namely,

Conjunction property: $\quad \square_M A, \square_M B \vdash \square_M (A \wedge B)$.

This is a desirable property for metaphysical necessity to have. For it would seem strange at best to say, for example, that it is metaphysically necessary that every event has a cause, and metaphysically necessary that everything is in time, but not metaphysically necessary, and so metaphysically *contingent*, that *every event has a cause and everything is in time*.

There are (at least) two ways to ensure that metaphysical necessity has the conjunction property. One option, adopted for formulations of relative necessity in general in Hale and Leech (2017), is to replace the single quantifier with a finite string of quantifiers:

$$\square\mathbf{M}^* \quad \square_M p =_{df} \exists \phi_1, \ldots, \exists \phi_n (O\phi_1 \wedge \ldots \wedge O\phi_n \wedge \square((\phi_1 \wedge \ldots \wedge \phi_n) \rightarrow p))$$

This does the job, although it raises issues to be resolved. First, we need to consider that the proper language of metaphysical necessity would now seem to include resources for numerical indices. Second, there is a question whether the limitation to a *finite* string is subject to potential counterexamples, for example, if there are plausible cases where a proposition is necessary relative to an *infinite* set of relevant propositions.[2]

An alternative option is to assume that a conjunction of conditions on objectivity is itself a condition on objectivity, i.e., $OA, OB \vdash O(A \wedge B)$. This allows us to then conjoin distinct propositions p, q such that $Op \wedge \square(p \rightarrow A)$ and $Oq \wedge \square(q \rightarrow B)$ to yield $O(p \wedge q) \wedge \square((p \wedge q) \rightarrow (A \wedge B))$, from which it follows that $\exists \phi (O\phi \wedge \square(\phi \rightarrow (A \wedge B)))$. In Hale and Leech (2017) we cautioned against taking this approach for relative necessities *in general*, however, in the present context it does not seem unreasonable. If it is a condition on objectivity that p, and it is a condition on objectivity that q, I find it hard to justify nevertheless claiming that it is *not* a condition on objectivity that $p \wedge q$. For if it were not, that would seem to imply that one could think objectively whilst $p \wedge q$ did not hold true. But then one of p or q would have to be false. But, by hypothesis, they are both conditions on objectivity, so if there is objective thinking going on, they had better

---

[1] For some remarks on how I am understanding propositional quantification, see Chapter 8, section 8.4.

[2] See Hale and Leech (2017, 18) and Roberts (2020).

METAPHYSICAL NECESSITY IN A FORMAL SYSTEM   225

both be true! To conclude otherwise, one would need to argue that conditions on objectivity have some additional extra status that is not guaranteed to be shared by conjunctions of them, such as a kind of logical non-complexity. But I see no reason to think that. As such, I will continue to endorse the simpler formulation of metaphysical necessity, $\Box$M, under the assumption that the operator O has the conjunction property, and thereby confers that property onto metaphysical necessity itself. If one prefers, the first option remains open.

10.2 Metaphysical possibility, absolute necessity, and duality

The second point of note is the complexity of $\Diamond$M. There are two reasons for this. Firstly, the informal intuitive idea of relative modality is that something is possible or necessary *relative to* something else. So, for example, if we take physical modality to be relative to the laws of physics, the idea is that *relative to the laws of physics, some things are possible, others necessary.* Now, that doesn't make much sense if we allow that sometimes things might be physically possible or necessary *even if there weren't any laws of physics.* In short: we should take seriously the idea that *both* relative necessity *and* relative possibility *require there to be* a relevant group of propositions.

This means that we cannot simply take the obvious dual of a kind of relative necessity to define a corresponding kind of relative possibility. i.e.,

$\Box$M-dual $\Diamond_M p =_{df} \neg \exists \phi (O\phi \wedge \Box(\phi \rightarrow \neg p))$

For this can be true when there are no conditions on objectivity at all. A second option would simply shift the first negation inwards, i.e.,

$\Diamond$M* $\Diamond_M p =_{df} \exists \phi (O\phi \wedge \neg \Box(\phi \rightarrow \neg p))$

This is to say that it is metaphysically possible that p just when there are some conditions on objectivity and they don't rule out p. This ensures that there are some conditions of objectivity against which metaphysical possibility is determined, however, it allows that there might be some *other* conditions of objectivity that *do* rule out p. The proposed formulation in $\Diamond$M specifies that there are conditions on objectivity and that *no* such conditions rule out p.

$\Diamond$M $\Diamond_M p =_{df} \exists \phi O\phi \wedge \forall \psi(O\psi \rightarrow \neg \Box(\psi \rightarrow \neg p))$

We in effect add the existential claim as a conjunct to $\Box$M-dual.

The second motivation for $\Diamond$M is that it allows one to avoid a problem of compatibility with our understanding of absolute necessity.

226 THINKING OF NECESSITY

A□1   It is absolutely necessary that p iff $\neg\exists \lozenge (\lozenge\neg p)$

It is absolutely necessary that p if and only if there is no sense of (alethic, non-epistemic) possibility such that it is possible that it is not the case that p.[3] Logical necessity is absolute necessity. Therefore,

If $\square p$ then $\neg\exists \lozenge (\lozenge\neg p)$

This goes for notions of relative possibility as well. So, in particular, we should be able to infer,

If $\square p$ then $\neg \lozenge_M \neg p$.

If it's logically necessary that p, then it's not metaphysically possible that not-p.

This is confirmed by $\lozenge$M. For suppose that $\square p$ but $\lozenge_M \neg p$. Then $\exists\phi O\phi \wedge \forall\psi(O\psi \rightarrow \neg\square(\psi \rightarrow p))$. Let us take an instance $O\phi_1 \wedge \forall\psi(O\psi \rightarrow \neg\square(\psi \rightarrow p))$, and so $O\phi_1 \wedge \neg\square(\phi_1 \rightarrow p)$. But since $\square p$, it must be that $\forall\phi\square(\phi \rightarrow p)$, and therefore $\square(\phi_1 \rightarrow p)$. Contradiction. Therefore, if $\square p$ then $\neg \lozenge_M \neg p$.

However, if we define absolute necessity in a different way, trouble threatens. Sometimes absolute necessity is defined as the *broadest necessity*, i.e., if it is absolutely necessary that p, then it is necessary that p in all other alethic, non-epistemic senses of necessity. Since logical necessity is absolute necessity, that would imply:

If $\square p$ then $\forall\boxed{\square}(\boxed{\square}p)$

And in particular:

If $\square p$ then $\square_M p$.

But that will be false in circumstances where there are no conditions of objectivity. In general, logical necessity ($\square p$) will not imply relative necessity ($\square_\Phi p$) in circumstances where there are none of the relevant kinds of propositions (Φ-propositions).[4]

Roberts (2020) raises this as an objection to the relative necessity formulation developed in Hale and Leech (2017) and adopted here. Assume that absolute necessity is the broadest necessity, such that $\forall\phi(\square\phi \rightarrow \square_\Phi\phi)$ for any relative

---

[3] I am here using a quantifier over kinds of possibility and necessity, quantifying into operator place, in order to capture claims about different senses of possibily and necessity. Such a kind of quantification belongs only to the meta-language as a shorthand to help express such claims.

[4] Note: this does not require contingentism about propositions. If you think all propositions exist necessarily, then it may still be contingent whether a given proposition is a Φ-proposition.

necessity. Let $\top$ be the tautology $\forall \phi(\phi \rightarrow \phi)$. $\top$ is true in all worlds in all models, and therefore so too is $\Box\top$. However, in a world with no Φ-propositions, $\Box_\Phi\top$ is false. For the existential clause, $\exists\phi\Phi\phi$, is not true if there are no Φ-propositions. Hence in this world $\forall\phi(\Box\phi \rightarrow \Box_\Phi\phi)$ is false, and hence is not valid. However, if one assumes that this just is how absolute necessity is properly defined, we can no longer make sense of a distinction between absolute and relative necessity.

The answer to this problem lies in the fact that relative possibility is not defined as the dual of relative necessity, as is evident from $\Box$M and $\Diamond$M. This means that the two candidate definitions of absolute necessity—one in terms of other senses of possibility, one in terms of other senses of necessity—are not equivalent. For example, it may be the case that $\Box p$, and that there are no senses of possibility such that $\Diamond_\Phi\neg p$, i.e., for all senses of possibility, $\neg \Diamond_\Phi\neg p$. But if we give up the principle that $\Box_\Phi p \equiv \neg \Diamond_\Phi\neg p$, then we cannot also infer from this that $\Box_\Phi p$. Since these two definitions—*no competing possibility, broadest necessity*—are not equivalent, we must choose one. It is the definition in terms of there being no competing possibility that, I contend, better captures the spirit of absolute necessity. For, if it is *absolutely necessary* that p, the implication is that it couldn't be but that p, such that it is *absolutely impossible* that $\neg p$: $\neg \Diamond \neg p$. As such, competing senses of possibility should be ruled out. What really gives Roberts's objection its bite, in my view, is not so much the falsity of $\Box_\Phi\top$, but the fact that this is taken to imply $\Diamond_\Phi\bot$,[5] where *any* possibility of a contradiction may seem abhorrent. By contrast, the mere *lack* of necessity is not so obviously bad. For, on the present view, to say that $\neg \Box_\Phi\top$ is just to say that there are no Φ-propositions from which it follows that $\top$, which may be true just because there are no Φ-propositions. This would only be a clearly *bad* consequence if it implied that, therefore, $\Diamond_\Phi\bot$. But according to $\Box$M and $\Diamond$M (taken as exemplars of relative necessity and possibility), it does not.

The result of all this is that $\Box_M$ and $\Diamond_M$ are not duals (similarly for any relative possibility and necessity defined in terms of the same Φ-propositions). It is not the case that $\Box_M p \equiv \neg \Diamond_M\neg p$. However, there is something like duality in the vicinity, namely, *if* there are some conditions on objectivity, *then* metaphysical possibility and necessity are duals: $\exists\phi O\phi \rightarrow (\Box_M p \equiv \neg \Diamond_M\neg p)$.[6] This seems entirely right. If there are no conditions on objectivity, then there is no such thing as metaphysical modality, as I have defined it here. However, if there are any such conditions, then

---

[5] If $\Box_\Phi\top$ is false, then by a standard semantics for negation, $\neg \Box_\Phi \top$ is true. By duality, $\Box_\Phi A \equiv \neg \Diamond_\Phi \neg A$, it follows that $\Diamond_\Phi\neg\top$, and the negation of a tautology, $\neg\top$, is a contradiction, $\bot$.

[6] *Necessity to possibility direction*: Suppose $\exists\phi O\phi$, $\exists\phi(O\phi \wedge \Box(\phi \rightarrow p))$ but $\neg\neg[\exists\phi O\phi \wedge \forall\psi(O\psi \rightarrow \neg \Box (\psi \rightarrow \neg\neg p))]$, i.e., $\exists\phi O\phi \wedge \forall\psi(O\psi \rightarrow \neg \Box (\psi \rightarrow p))$. So $\forall\psi(O\psi \rightarrow \neg \Box (\psi \rightarrow p))$, hence $\neg\exists\psi\neg(O\psi \rightarrow \neg \Box (\psi \rightarrow p))$. But from this it follows that $\neg\exists\psi(O\psi \wedge \neg\neg\Box (\psi \rightarrow p))$, i.e., $\neg\exists\psi(O\psi \wedge \Box (\psi \rightarrow p))$. Contradiction. *Possibility to necessity direction*: Suppose $\exists\phi O\phi$ and $\neg[\exists\phi O\phi \wedge \forall\psi(O\psi \rightarrow \neg \Box (\psi \rightarrow p))]$, but $\neg\exists\phi(O\phi \wedge \Box (\phi \rightarrow p))$. Since the first conjunct is true, $\neg\forall\psi(O\psi \rightarrow \neg \Box (\psi \rightarrow p))$, hence $\exists\psi\neg(O\psi \rightarrow \neg \Box (\psi \rightarrow p))$, and so $\exists\psi(O\psi \wedge \neg\neg\Box (\psi \rightarrow p))$. This implies $\exists\psi(O\psi \wedge \Box (\psi \rightarrow p))$. Contradiction. We conclude that $\exists\phi O\phi \rightarrow (\Box_M p \equiv \neg \Diamond_M\neg p)$. No special use was made of the meaning of O, so we may generalize this to any relative modalities defined similarly to $\Box$M and $\Diamond$M.

228 THINKING OF NECESSITY

there is metaphysical modality, and it behaves as one would expect, i.e., possibility and necessity are duals.

Importantly, this has no consequences for $\Box$ and $\Diamond$: they remain duals as in a standard modal logic. Moreover, it is important to emphasize that $\Box_M$ and $\Diamond_M$ are not simple modal operators, but are constructed out of a combination of quantifier and modal clauses. As such, we can rest assured that the background modal logic may remain normal and familiar in other ways. Anything we do depends upon the rules for $\Box$, $\Diamond$, and the propositional quantifiers. These are all operators that admit of duals. And I do not deny that one can define a dual for each of $\Box_M$ and $\Diamond_M$: but given their complexity, we have further options for which formulas we take to adequately capture the concepts of interest. Supposing we agree that $\Box M$ captures adequately the concept of metaphysical necessity. We may now ask: in capturing the concept of metaphysical *possibility*, should we aim for a dual of the whole formulation of $\Box_M$, or should we consider its constituent parts, or should we take a different approach altogether? We have seen that simply taking the dual of $\Box_M$ to define metaphysical possibility causes trouble. Metaphysical possibility also requires the existence of conditions of objectivity, but the dual of $\Box_M$ precisely *negates* this existential claim. So some version of the existential clause from $\Box_M$ must be retained. As a consequence, we should conclude that to align with the notions that we are trying to capture, $\Diamond_M$ is not a true dual of $\Box_M$.[7]

10.3 Modal principles and iteration

What modal principles will hold for metaphysical necessity and possibility in a formal system? Principles of particular interest are:

T $\quad \Box_M A \rightarrow A$

B $\quad A \rightarrow \Box_M \Diamond_M A$

4 $\quad \Box_M A \rightarrow \Box_M \Box_M A$

5 $\quad \Diamond_M A \rightarrow \Box_M \Diamond_M A$

T is built into the target notion of metaphysical necessity as alethic and so is validated. However, counterexamples to B (Dummett on unicorns) have been used as an argument against S5 being the logic of metaphysical necessity.[8] And there are well-known attacks on the validity of 4 for metaphysical necessity.[9] I will not engage in the detail of these debates here, but rather chart out the consequences of the proposed account of metaphysical necessity for these principles.

---

[7] Thank you to Carlo Nicolai for extensive discussion of the issues in this section.
[8] See Dummett (1993); Reimer (1997).   [9] Perhaps most famously Salmon (1981).

METAPHYSICAL NECESSITY IN A FORMAL SYSTEM   229

T is easy. Since $O\phi$ is factive,[10] so is $\square_M\phi$. For suppose that $\exists\phi(O\phi \wedge \square(\phi \to p))$. Take the instance $O\phi_1 \wedge \square(\phi_1 \to p))$. Since $O\phi_1$, ϕ_1 is true. Given that $\square(\phi_1 \to p)$, it follows that p is true as well. So $\exists\phi(O\phi \wedge \square(\phi \to p)) \to p$.

Note, however, that, given the failure of duality, $\square_M p \to p$ is not equivalent to $p \to \Diamond_M p$.[11] A simple counterexample is provided by a world where there are no conditions on objectivity but it is true that p. In such a world, $\square_M p \to p$ is true, since the antecedent is false (because the existential clause that there are conditions on objectivity is false). But $p \to \Diamond_M p$ is false, since by hypothesis it is true that p, but by the same token as before, it is false that $\Diamond_M p$. However, as with duality, the equivalence holds under the condition that there are conditions of objectivity, i.e., $\exists\phi O\phi \to ((\square_M p \to p) \leftrightarrow (p \to \Diamond_M p))$.[12]

All of the other principles of interest involve iteration of modality. They therefore invite the general question of how to make sense of iterations of metaphysical modality, understood as a kind of relative necessity. Let us consider two iterated phrases (since these occur in B, 4, and 5): $\square_M\square_M p$ and $\square_M\Diamond_M p$. Cashed out fully, these should read as:

$\square_M\square_M$: $\exists\phi(O\phi \wedge \square(\phi \to \exists\psi(O\psi \wedge \square(\psi \to p))))$

i.e., there are some conditions on objectivity that logically necessarily imply that there are some conditions on objectivity that logically necessarily imply that p. And,

$\square_M\Diamond_M$: $\exists\phi(O\phi \wedge \square(\phi \to (\exists\psi O\psi \wedge \forall\chi(O\chi \to \neg\square(\chi \to \neg p)))))$

i.e., there are some conditions on objectivity that logically necessarily imply that there are some conditions on objectivity none of which logically imply that $\neg p$.

What would it take for such iterated modalities to be true? It all depends on what we understand as being included in and implied by conditions on objectivity. Most clearly, if these iterations are to be true, it must be that conditions on objectivity imply something *explicit* about conditions on objectivity. That is, each iteration includes within it the claim that conditions on objectivity imply that there are conditions on objectivity, i.e., $\exists\phi(O\phi \wedge \square(\phi \to \exists\psi O\psi))$. This, on its own, is—

---

[10] See Chapter 6, section 6.5.

[11] Compare: Assume T for $\square$, i.e., $\square A \to A$. And suppose in particular $\square\phi \to \phi$ but $\neg(\phi \to \Diamond\phi)$. Then $\phi \wedge \neg\Diamond\phi$. Assuming duality for $\square$ and $\Diamond$, it follows that $\square\neg\phi$. But by T, it follows that $\neg\phi$. Contradiction.

[12] Assume T for $\square_M$, i.e., $\square_M A \to A$. Suppose in particular $\exists\phi O\phi$ and $\square_M p \to p$ but $\neg(p \to \Diamond_M p)$. Then $p \wedge \neg\Diamond_M p$. Since $\exists\phi O\phi$, $\square_M p \equiv \neg\Diamond_M \neg p$ (see footnote 6). So it follows that $\square_M\neg p$. But then by T, $\neg p$. Contradiction $(p \wedge \neg p)$. Therefore, $\exists\phi O\phi \to ((\square_M p \to p) \to (p \to \Diamond_M p))$. Now assume T for $\Diamond_M$, i.e., $A \to \Diamond_M A$. And suppose in particular that $\exists\phi O\phi$ and $p \to \Diamond_M p$ but $\neg(\square_M p \to p)$. Then $\square_M p \wedge \neg p$. By T, it follows that $\Diamond_M \neg p$. Since $\exists\phi O\phi$, $\square_M p \equiv \neg\Diamond_M \neg p$ (see footnote 6). So it follows that $\neg\square_M p$. Contradiction $(\square_M p \wedge \neg\square_M p)$. Therefore, $\exists\phi O\phi \to ((p \to \Diamond_M p) \to (\square_M p \to p))$.

230   THINKING OF NECESSITY

perhaps surprisingly—what we should expect, given the arguments of Chapter 5. There I argued that in order to have objective thoughts we need to possess a conception of objectivity and to be able to represent some thoughts as being objective, which in turn required the possession of a concept of modality relative to conditions on objectivity. So, conditions of objectivity, on this view, include the conceptual resources to express claims such as 'there are some conditions of objectivity'. Moreover, insofar as we have any objective thoughts, and thereby represent the thought as compatible with conditions on objectivity, this includes within it the assumption that there are some conditions on objectivity. So at least part of these iterated claims can be defended: $\exists\phi(O\phi \wedge \Box(\phi \rightarrow \exists\psi O\psi))$.

What of the rest? The remainder of these iterated modalities says something further: not just that there are conditions on objectivity, but that there are conditions on objectivity *that imply p*, or *none of which imply ¬p*. To address this, we need to consider the modal principles more fully. Take 4, for instance, as it would cash out for metaphysical necessity.

$$\mathbf{4}_M \quad \exists\phi(O\phi \wedge \Box(\phi \rightarrow p)) \rightarrow \exists\phi(O\phi \wedge \Box(\phi \rightarrow \exists\psi(O\psi \wedge \Box(\psi \rightarrow p))))$$

This says that *if* there are conditions on objectivity that imply p, then there are conditions on objectivity that imply *that there are conditions on objectivity that imply p*. Thus far, I have suggested that it might be written into the conditions on objectivity that there are conditions on objectivity *in general*. But this principle takes it further. Suppose, for the sake of argument, that it follows from conditions on objective thought that everything is temporal. The 4 principle requires that, moreover, it follows from conditions on objective thought *that there are conditions on objective thought that imply that everything is temporal*. But why should that be so? This comes down to the issue of what, precisely, is included in the conditions on objective thought, and that's a question that I've not fully answered. So far, conditions on objectivity have been characterized as general, and as placing constraints on our capacity to represent the world as well as on what the world that we represent is like. Plausibly, we might expect such conditions to concern general features of the world, such as, for example, things being in time, or things being causally related. It is not obvious why we should expect any *further* constraints on what the conditions on objectivity might be. At least we can see what would be required to defend 4: an account of why conditions on objectivity include further content that ensures these consequences.

Rather than pursue this line of thought, it is worth pausing to ask *why* we want principles such as 4 to come out as valid. 4 says that if something is necessary, it is *necessarily* necessary. Presumably, the worry here is that, if it was necessary that p, but contingently so, then it could have been that it wasn't necessary that p. And if it had been that it wasn't necessary that p, then it would have been possible for it not to be the case that p after all. The failure of 4 seems to undermine the strength of the necessity claim. But note: this line of thought also relies upon an iterated modality: it presumes that if $\neg\Box_M\Box_Mp$, then $\Diamond_M\neg\Box_Mp$, and then $\Diamond_M\Diamond_M\neg p$. As such, this line of thought trades on unqualified applications of duality. It is not, we have seen, in general valid to infer $\Diamond_M\neg\Box_Mp$ from $\neg\Box_M\Box_Mp$, for in the case where there are no conditions on objectivity, it may for this reason be true that $\neg\Box_M\Box_Mp$, and for the same reason be false that $\Diamond_M\neg\Box_Mp$. So the general line of reasoning fails.

Even so, if there are conditions on objectivity, then under that assumption (that $\exists\phi O\phi$) the inference does hold. And indeed, the antecedent of 4, $\Box_Mp$, entails that there are. So we should assess the truth of the consequent under the assumption that the antecedent is true, and hence under the assumption that $\exists\phi O\phi$. The issue then turns on whether or not it is true that $\Box_M\Box_Mp$. For if it is not, because the conditions on objectivity do not fully specify what conditions on objectivity there should be, then even though it will therefore be true that $\neg\Box_M\Box_Mp$, it will be perfectly acceptable that also $\Diamond_M\neg\Box_Mp$. For this also says, in effect, that none of the conditions on objectivity specify what conditions on objectivity there should be, in particular, that there be none that necessitate p. In short: the unqualified line of thought is illegitimate. Properly qualified, the failure of 4 and its equivalents make coherent sense.

In short: we may or may not defend 4 for metaphysical modality. If, for the reasons discussed in this section (concerning what is in included in conditions on objectivity), we decide against 4, the line of thought rehearsed just now will not serve to undermine those reasons, for this response rests on making claims about conditions on objectivity that will have already been rejected.

The upshot of this is ultimately that one should not assume that the rejection of a modal principle that includes iteration, such as 4, allows for implausible iterated modal claims. For example, $\neg(\Box_Mp \rightarrow \Box_M\Box_Mp)$ need not imply $\Box_Mp \wedge \Diamond_M\neg\Box_Mp$. The implication in general is blocked by the failure of duality for $\Box_M$ and $\Diamond_M$. Even under the assumption that $\exists\phi O\phi$, which reintroduces a form of duality, if one chooses to reject the truth of (almost) any iterated modality due to the content or nature of the conditions on objectivity, this does not undermine one's uniterated modal claims in a problematic way. If we take this path, then we cannot assure ourselves that what is metaphysically necessary is metaphysically necessarily so. However, we also should not worry that therefore it is metaphysically contingently so. We may rest content with simple metaphysical modalities, and save iteration for the logical modalities and perhaps, depending on the details, for other relative modalities.

232 THINKING OF NECESSITY

10.4 Possible worlds semantics

The formal system the beginnings of which I have sketched here assumes a possible world semantics. The system promises to capture the behaviour of the logical modalities ($\Box$ and $\Diamond$) and the metaphysical modalities ($\Box_M$ and $\Diamond_M$). However, the metaphysical account of logical and metaphysical modalities that I have developed in this book appeals, not to worlds, but to our capacities for thought and objective thought and the laws and constraints governing these capacities. To what extent, then, is my assumption of possible world semantics legitimate?

We can distinguish between a *pure* and an *impure* conception of the semantics.[13] A pure possible worlds semantics is poorly named, since the so-called 'worlds' are not (yet) interpreted as such.[14] A pure semantics is a formal, mathematical, algebraic conception that takes no steps towards interpreting its machinery in terms of worlds, circumstances, alternatives, possibilities, etc., and takes no steps towards interpreting the $\Box$ and $\Diamond$ operators as expressing any prior notion, including any distinctively *modal* notions. By contrast, an impure semantics *does* introduce an element of interpretation. The present employment of possible worlds semantics is not pure, for we are taking the $\Box$ and $\Diamond$ operators to express logical modalities, and also $\Box_M$ and $\Diamond_M$ operators, defined in terms of a further interpreted operator O, to express metaphysical modalities.

What commitments does an impure modal theory with a worlds semantics incur? The semantics involves quantification over a domain (of so-called 'worlds'). The orthodoxy is that we are ontologically committed to those things that need to exist for the truth of those quantified statements that we take to be true. For example, if we are committed to the truth of $\exists x F x$, then we are committed to the existence of something that is F, for the formula is true only when there exists something in the domain of quantification that falls under the predicate 'F'. Similarly, if we are committed to the truth of some modal statements, and if the semantics of those modal statements is given in terms of quantification over worlds, then we are likewise committed to the existence of worlds to the extent that the semantics requires.

But do we need to take quantification over worlds seriously? The purpose in introducing them here is primarily inferential. The value in providing a formal system for logical and metaphysical modality lies in making exact and explicit the formulation of such modal claims and their logical connection to other claims. For example, we have seen in this chapter how to accommodate the T schema, and the issues that accompany further modal schemas that involve modal iteration.

---

[13] Plantinga (1978); Divers (2016).

[14] For this reason, Divers (2016, 3) calls the uninterpreted logics QUIDO or IDO logics, and their semantics QUIDO or IDO structures: 'They are so labelled because they are various proof-theoretic enhancements of **QU**antified non-modal logic with **I**dentity that are **I**ntensional with respect to the box ("$\Box$") of our **D**ual **O**perators.'

It is therefore tempting to say that the possible worlds semantics underlying such a formal system doesn't need to be taken seriously: the metaphysics and truth-conditions of modal claims have already been dealt with earlier; a formal system with a worlds semantics now serves only to clarify and to model our modal reasoning, independent of our account of what it takes for modal claims to be true.

However tempting this may be, it is hard to defend. Divers (2016, 24–5) presents a stepwise account of different types of elucidation that may be intended by use of an impure theory. Let us consider the first three levels of elucidation.

1. *Heuristic.* Interpretation of the semantics in terms of worlds is 'a way of thinking and speaking that is attractive, but not in itself of any logical or philosophical cash value.'
2. *Instrumental.* A worlds-interpretation has logical and philosophical cash value, namely, by 'providing techniques or methods that we are entitled to use in order to reach conclusions about validity: about which modal conclusions do and which do not, follow from which modal premises.'
3. *Literal.* A theory with a worlds-interpretation 'tells the (literal) truth about semantic features of modal expressions.' In some way or other, we take the semantics seriously as a guide to the truth-conditions of modal statements.

Divers articulates two further levels where the semantics is taken to be increasingly explanatory, but these three suffice for present purposes.

Since, as I have already stated, the primary purpose of a formal system is to elucidate modal inferences, (1) is insufficient; we hope to gain some logical cash value from the semantics. As such, the second, instrumental level looks attractive. We can help ourselves to the philosophical and logical cash value of understanding modal reasoning in terms of worlds, without incurring a commitment to taking worlds as featuring in the literal truth-conditions of modal statements. However, the instrumental level is unstable.

> The glaring challenge that any such instrumentalist must confront is to say something about why the first-order methods are reliable. And then a dilemma looms. On one hand, the would-be instrumentalist might then be drawn into making deeper claims about the impure semantics, in which case she is no longer just an instrumentalist.... On the other hand, the would-be instrumentalist might point out the following truth: the completeness of various logics, as guaranteed by the pure semantics, is available to her as a guarantor of the safety of the first-order methods. But in that case, we need have here nothing that requires the play with impure semantic theory. What we may have is no more than the combination of a user-friendly idiom whose philosophical cash value does not derive from its content, even minimally construed. This dilemma fuels the suspicion that that such instrumentalism about a genuinely impure

234 THINKING OF NECESSITY

> possible-worlds semantic theory of validity may be an untenable position that is set to collapse under minimal scrutiny. (Divers, 2016, 25)

The challenge is that we need to say why thinking of the semantics of our formal system in terms of *possible worlds* does anything to help our purposes; understanding modal reasoning. And that requires us to say something more substantial about the truth-conditions of modal statements, and hence takes us onto the third level. The alternative is to appeal to the pure features of the semantics without the worlds interpretation, in which case we are no longer dealing with impure theory. Since it is clear that I am appealing to impure theory, we must take on the explanatory challenge and hence ascend to level three.

The lesson here is thus: if we want to exploit the valuable resources of a modal logic with a possible worlds semantics, and if we want to understand them as such—as modal, and as a worlds semantics—then we cannot avoid taking seriously the implication that the truth-conditions of our modal formulas involve quantification over things called 'possible worlds', and therefore the potential for ontological commitment to worlds. To close, then, I shall explain how this is compatible with the non-worlds-based metaphysical account.

There is nothing in this level of elucidation that determines the precise nature of these worlds; just that they are in our domain of quantification and that they have something to do with modal truth. As such, we need not include anything like David Lewis's pluriverse. An ersatz account that understands worlds in terms of already acceptable actual (kinds of) things will be satisfactory. Ersatz accounts of worlds are often accused of failing to give a reductive account of modality, but since I have from the outset dismissed the aim of reduction, that is no problem in this context.[15]

Why should we take quantification over worlds, even ersatz worlds, to be suitable for modelling modal reasoning? Here is a sketch of how such a worlds semantics coheres with the metaphysical account. Take the formulation of a claim of metaphysical necessity: $\exists\phi(O\phi \wedge \Box(\phi \rightarrow p))$. This gives us a recipe for building possible worlds out of sets of propositions or sentences. For it in effect tells us that it is true that p in all worlds composed out of or otherwise corresponding to the logical closure of a set of conditions of objectivity + a set of actual facts compatible with those conditions. Thus understood, it seems reasonable to understand modal reasoning in terms of such sets, since they are already operative in our understanding of modal claims, such as our metaphysical necessity claim.

---

[15] See Chapter 1, section 1.1.

Concluding Remarks

In this book, I have set out to develop a Kant-inspired theory of modality, driven by a methodology which takes seriously questions about the function of modal judgment as a guide to a metaphysics of modality. I have argued that we need logical modal concepts as a condition on our ability to think, and metaphysical modal concepts as a condition on our ability to think objectively. Concordant with this, I have argued that logical necessity has its source in the laws of thought and that metaphysical necessity is relative to conditions on objective thought. I then further developed this account of metaphysical necessity, which I termed "Modal Transcendentalism".

The book makes many bold and controversial claims, and leaves more questions unanswered. But I hope that the approach and the proposals will serve as a prompt for further debate. For example, this is just one way to carry out an investigation into modal metaphysics via the function-based methodology. It would be interesting to see other, less Kantian, developments of this methodology. Much of the discussion of the function of modal judgment is underpinned by the claim that the distinction between *objective* and *subjective* is not exhaustive: it seems to me that this claim, and its consequences, are worthy of further exploration. As a final example, my focus in this book was on the *metaphysics* of modality, and its connection to our capacity for thinking, but I did not devote as much space to the *epistemology* of modality. The suggestion that conceivability approaches to modal epistemology could be enhanced in relation to an account of transcendental philosophy has scope for further development, and perhaps provides a nice example of how looking back through the history of philosophy can reinvigorate more recent debates in surprising and potentially fruitful ways.

Bibliography

Allais, L. 2015. *Manifest Reality: Kant's Idealism and his Realism*. Oxford: Oxford University Press.

Allison, H. E. 2004. *Kant's Transcendental Idealism: An Interpretation and Defense*. New Haven and London: Yale University Press.

Aristotle. 360 BCE. *Metaphysics*. http://classics.mit.edu/Aristotle/metaphysics.7.vii.html. Translated by W. D. Ross.

Ayer, A. J. 1936. *Language, Truth and Logic*. London: Penguin Books.

Baldwin, T. 2002. "The Inaugural Address: Kantian Modality." *Proceedings of the Aristotelian Society, Supplementary Volumes* 76:1–24.

Ballarin, R. 2012. "Quine on Intensional Entities: Modality and Quantification, Truth and Satisfaction." *Journal of Applied Logic* 10:238–49.

Barcan, R. C. 1947. "The Identity of Individuals in a Strict Functional Calculus of Second Order." *Journal of Symbolic Logic* 12:12–15.

Barnes, E. 2014. "Going beyond the Fundamental: Feminism in Contemporary Metaphysics." *Proceedings of the Aristotelian Society* CXIV:335–51.

Beall, J. and Restall, G. 2016. "Logical Consequence." In Edward N. Zalta (ed.), *The Stanford Encyclopedia of Philosophy*. Winter 2016 edition.

Blackburn, S. 1993. "Morals and Modals." In *Essays in Quasi-Realism*, 52–74. Oxford: Oxford University Press.

Boghossian, P. A. 2003. "The Normativity of Content." *Philosophical Issues* 13:31–45.

Boyle, M. 2009. "Two Kinds of Self-Knowledge." *Philosophy and Phenomenological Research* 78:133–64.

Brewer, B. 1997. "Foundations of Perceptual Knowledge." *American Philosophical Quarterly* 34:41–55.

Burge, T. 1979. "Individualism and the Mental." In T. F. Uehling, Peter A. French, and H. K. Wettstein (eds.), *Midwest Studies in Philosophy IV: Studies in Metaphysics*, 73–121. Minneapolis: University of Minnesota Press.

Burgess, J. P. 2014. "On a Derivation of the Necessity of Identity." *Synthese* 191:1567–85.

Cameron, R. 2009. "What's Metaphysical about Metaphysical Necessity?" *Philosophy and Phenomenological Research* 79:1–16.

Cameron, R. 2010. "On the Source of Necessity." In Bob Hale and Aviv Hoffman (eds.), *Modality: Metaphysics, Logic, and Epistemology*, 137–51. Oxford: Oxford University Press.

Campbell, J. 1994. *Past, Space, and Self*. Cambridge, MA: MIT Press.

Campbell, J. 2006. "Sortals and the Binding Problem." In F. MacBride (ed.), *Identity and Modality*, 203–18. Oxford: Clarendon Press.

Chalmers, D. 2002. "Does Conceivability Entail Possibility." In T. S. Gendler and J. Hawthorne (eds.), *Conceivability and Possibility*, 145–200. Oxford: Clarendon Press.

Child, W. 1996. *Causality, Interpretation, and the Mind*. Oxford: Oxford University Press.

Clarke-Doane, J. 2021. "Metaphysical and Absolute Possibility." *Synthese* 198:1861–72.

Conant, J. 1992. "The Search for Logically Alien Thought: Descartes, Kant, Frege, and the *Tractatus*." *Philosophical Topics* 20:115–80.

BIBLIOGRAPHY

Correia, F. 2006. "Generic Essence, Objectual Essence, and Modality." *Nous* 40:753–67.

Correia, F. and Skiles, A. 2019. "Grounding, Essence, and Identity." *Philosophy and Phenomenological Research* 98:642–70.

Davidson, D. 1974. "On the Very Idea of a Conceptual Scheme." *Proceedings and Addresses of the American Philosophical Association* 47:5–20.

Divers, J. 2002. *Possible Worlds*. London and New York: Routledge.

Divers, J. 2004. "Agnosticism about Other Worlds: A New Antirealist Programme in Modality." *Philosophy and Phenomenological Research* 69:660–85.

Divers, J. 2010. "Modal Commitments." In B. Hale and A. Hoffman (eds.), *Modality: Metaphysics, Logic, Epistemology*, 189–219. Oxford: Oxford University Press.

Divers, J. 2016. "Philosophical Issues from Kripke's 'Semantical Considerations on Modal Logic.' " *Principia* 20:1–44.

Divers, J. 2017. "De Re Modality in the Late Twentieth Century." In M. Sinclair (ed.), *The Actual and the Possible: Modality in Modern Philosophy*. Mind Occasional Series. Oxford: Oxford University Press.

Divers, J. 2018. "W(h)ither Metaphysical Necessity?" *Aristotelian Society Supplementary Volume* XCII:1–25.

Divers, J. and Elstein, D. 2012. "Manifesting Belief in Absolute Necessity." *Philosophical Studies* 158:109–30.

Divers, J. and González-Varela, J. E. 2013. "Belief in Absolute Necessity." *Philosophy and Phenomenological Research* 87:358–91.

Dorr, C. 2016. "To Be F Is to Be G." *Philosophical Perspectives* 30:39–134.

Dummett, M. 1993. *The Seas of Language*. Oxford: Clarendon Press.

Eilan, N. 1997. "Objectivity and the Perspective of Consciousness." *European Journal of Philosophy* 5:235–50.

Etchemendy, J. 1990. *The Concept of Logical Consequence*. Cambridge, MA: Harvard University Press. Reissued by CSLI Publications and Cambridge University Press, 1999.

Etchemendy, J. 2008. "Reflections on Consequence." In D. Patterson (ed.), *New Essays on Tarski and Philosophy*, 263–99. Oxford: Oxford University Press.

Evans, G. 1985. "Things without the Mind—A Commentary upon Chapter Two of Strawson's *Individuals*." In Antonia Phillips (ed.), *Collected Papers*, 249–90. Oxford: Oxford University Press.

Fine, K. 1994. "Essence and Modality." *Philosophical Perspectives* 8:1–16.

Fine, K. 1995. "Senses of Essence." In W. Sinnott-Armstrong, D. Raffman, and N. Asher (eds.), *Modality, Morality and Belief: Essays in Honor of Ruth Barcan Marcus*, 53–73. Cambridge: Cambridge University Press.

Fine, K. 2002. "Varieties of Necessity." In Tamar Szabo Gendler and John Hawthorne (eds.), *Conceivability and Possibility*, 253–81. Oxford: Oxford University Press.

Fine, K. 2005. *Modality and Tense: Philosophical Papers*. Oxford: Clarendon Press.

Finn, S. 2021. "Limiting Logical Pluralism." *Synthese* 198:4905–23.

Fodor, J. A. 1998. *Concepts: Where Cognitive Science Went Wrong*. Oxford: Oxford University Press.

Frege, G. [1884]1950. *The Foundations of Arithmetic*. J.L. Austin (trans.). Oxford: Blackwell.

Frege, G. 1956. "The Thought: A Logical Inquiry." *Mind* 65:289–311.

Frege, G. 1979. "Comments on Sense and Meaning." In Friedrich Kambartel Hans Hermes and Friedrich Kaulbach (eds.), *Gottlob Frege: Posthumous Writings*, 118–25. Chicago: University of Chicago Press.

Gardner, S. 1999. *Routledge Philosophy Guidebook to Kant and the Critique of Pure Reason*. London and New York: Routledge.

Geach, P. 1958. *Mental Acts*. London: Routledge & Kegan Paul.

Geach, P. 1969. "What Do We Think With?" In *God and the Soul*. London: Routledge & Kegan Paul.

Glüer, K. and Wikforss, Å. 2009. "Against Content Normativity." *Mind* 118:31–70.

Gomes, A. 2016. "Unity, Objectivity, and the Passivity of Experience." *European Journal of Philosophy* 24:946–69.

Gomes, A. and Stephenson, A. 2016. "On the Relation of Intuition to Cognition." In D. Schulting (ed.), *Kantian Non-Conceptualism*, 53–79. London: Palgrave Macmillan.

Gopnik, A. 1988. "Conceptual and Semantic Development as Theory Change: The Case of Object Permanence." *Mind and Language* 3:197–216.

Hale, B. 1996. "Absolute Necessities." *Nous Suppliment: Philosophical Perspectives, 10, Metaphysics* 30:93–117.

Hale, B. 1999. "On Some Arguments for the Necessity of Necessity." *Mind* 108:23–52.

Hale, B. 2002a. "Basic Logical Knowledge." *Royal Institute of Philosophy Supplement* 51: 279–304.

Hale, B. 2002b. "The Source of Necessity." *Philosophical Perspectives* 16:299–319.

Hale, B. 2013. *Necessary Beings: An Essay on Ontology, Modality, & the Relations between Them*. Oxford: Oxford University Press.

Hale, B. 2020. *Essence and Existence: Selected Essays*. Oxford: Oxford University Press.

Hale, B. and Leech, J. 2017. "Relative Necessity Reformulated." *Journal of Philosophical Logic* 46:1–26.

Hazlett, A. 2010. "Brutal Individuation." In A. Hazlett (ed.), *New Waves in Metaphysics*, 72–90. Palgrave Macmillan.

Hintikka, J. 1967. "Kant on the Mathematical Method." *The Monist* 91. Reprinted in C. Posy (ed.), *Kant's Philosophy of Mathematics: Modern Essays* (Dordrecht, The Netherlands: Kluwer, 1992).

Hogan, D. 2021. "Thing in Itself (*Ding an sich selbst*)." In J. Wuerth (ed.), *The Cambridge Kant Lexicon*, 454–7. Cambridge: Cambridge University Press.

Humberstone, I. L. 1981. "Relative Necessity Revisited." *Reports on Mathematical Logic* 13:33–42.

Humberstone, I. L. 2004. "Two-Dimensional Adventures." *Philosophical Studies* 118:17–65.

Hume, D. 1739, 1740. *A Treatise of Human Nature*. London: Penguin (1969).

Jackendoff, R. 1991. "The Problem of Reality." *Nous* 24:411–33.

James, W. 1912. *Essays in Radical Empiricism*. New York: Longmans, Green, and Co.

Jarvis, B. W. 2012. "Norms of Intentionality: Norms That Don't Guide." *Philosophical Studies* 157:1–25.

Kant, I. 1992. *Lectures on Logic*. Translated and edited by J. Michael Young. New York: Cambridge University Press.

Kant, I. 1997a. *Critique of Practical Reason*. Translated by Mary Gregor, introduction by Andrews Reath. Cambridge: Cambridge University Press.

Kant, I. 1997b. *Lectures in Metaphysics*. Translated and edited by K. Ameriks, and S. Naragon. Cambridge: Cambridge University Press.

Kant, I. 1998. *Critique of Pure Reason*. Translated and edited by Paul Guyer and Allen W. Wood. New York: Cambridge University Press.

Kant, I. 1999. *Correspondence*. Translated and edited by A. Zweig. Cambridge: Cambridge University Press.

Kant, I. 2000. *Critique of the Power of Judgment*. Edited by Paul Guyer; translated by Paul Guyer and Eric Matthews. Cambridge: Cambridge University Press.

Kant, I. 2004. *Prolegomena to Any Future Metaphysics*. Translated and edited by G. Hatfield. Cambridge: Cambridge University Press.

240 BIBLIOGRAPHY

Keefe, R. and Leech, J. 2018. "Essentialism and Logical Consequence." In Ivette Fred-Rivera and Jessica Leech (eds.), *Being Necessary: Themes of Ontology and Modality from the Work of Bob Hale*. Oxford: Oxford University Press.

Kimpton-Nye, S. 2018. *Common Ground for Laws and Metaphysical Modality*. Ph.D. thesis.

Kitcher, P. 2017. "A Kantian Critique of Transparency." In Anil Gomes and Andrew Stephenson (eds.), *Kant and the Philosophy of Mind: New Essays on Consciousness, Judgement, and the Self*. Oxford: Oxford University Press.

Kneale, M. 1938. "Logical and Metaphysical Necessity." *Proceedings of the Aristotelian Society* 38:253–68.

Kratzer, A. 1977. "What 'Must' and 'Can' Must and Can Mean." *Linguistics and Philosophy* 1:337–55.

Kratzer, A. 2008. "The Notional Category of Modality." In P. Portner and B. H. Partee (eds.), *Formal Semantics: The Essential Readings*. Oxford: Blackwell.

Kratzer, A. 2012. "The Notional Category of Modality." In *Modals and Conditionals*. Oxford: Oxford University Press.

Kripke, S. 1971. "Identity and Necessity." In Milton K. Munitz (ed.), *Identity and Individuation*, 135–64. New York: New York University Press.

Kripke, S. 1980. *Naming and Necessity*. Oxford: Blackwell.

Lau, J. and Deutsch, M. 2019. "Externalism about Mental Content." In Edward N. Zalta (ed.), *The Stanford Encyclopedia of Philosophy*. Metaphysics Research Lab, Stanford University, Fall 2019 edition.

Leech, J. 2012. "Kant's Modalities of Judgment." *European Journal of Philosophy* 20:260–84.

Leech, J. 2014. "Making Modal Distinctions: Kant on the Possible, the Actual, and the Intuitive Understanding." *Kantian Review* 19:339–65.

Leech, J. 2015. "Logic and the Laws of Thought." *Philosopher's Imprint* 15:1–27.

Leech, J. 2016. "The Varieties of (Relative) Modality." *Pacific Philosophical Quarterly* 97:158–80.

Leech, J. 2017a. "Judging for Reasons: On Kant and the Modalities of Judgment." In Anil Gomes and Andrew Stephenson (eds.), *Kant and the Philosophy of Mind: New Essays on Consciousness, Judgement, and the Self*. Oxford: Oxford University Press.

Leech, J. 2017b. "Kant's Material Condition of Real Possibility." In M. Sinclair (ed.), *The Actual and the Possible: Modality in Modern Philosophy*. Mind Occasional Series. Oxford: Oxford University Press.

Leech, J. 2017c. "Nicholas F. Stang, Kant's Modal Metaphysics Oxford: Oxford University Press, 2016." *Kantian Review* 22:341–46.

Leech, J. 2017d. "The Normativity of Kant's Logical Laws." *History of Philosophy Quarterly* 34:291–311.

Leech, J. 2018. "Essence and Mere Necessity." *Royal Institute of Philosophy Supplements* 82 (Metaphysics):309–32.

Leech, J. 2019. "Martha Kneale on Why Metaphysical Necessities Are Not *A Priori*." *Journal of the American Philosophical Association* 5:389–409.

Leech, J. 2020. "Relative Necessity Extended." *Journal of Applied Logics* 7:1179–1200.

Leech, J. 2021a. "Apodictic (*apodiktisch*)." In J. Wuerth (ed.), *The Cambridge Kant Lexicon*, 38–40. Cambridge: Cambridge University Press.

Leech, J. 2021b. "Assertoric (*assertorisch*)." In J. Wuerth (ed.), *The Cambridge Kant Lexicon*, 51–2. Cambridge: Cambridge University Press.

Leech, J. 2021c. "From Essence to Necessity via Identity." *Mind* 130:887–908.

Leech, J. 2021d. "Kant on the Necessity of Necessity." *History of Philosophy and Logical Analysis* 25:66–94.

Leech, J. 2021e. "Problematic (*problematisch*)." In J. Wuerth (ed.), *The Cambridge Kant Lexicon*, 347–9. Cambridge: Cambridge University Press.

Leech, J. 2021f. "The Function of Modal Judgment and the Kantian Gap." *Synthese* 198:3193–212.

Leech, J. 2021g. "The Significance of Kant's Mere Thoughts." *Inquiry* 1–31.

Leech, J. 2022a. "A Transcendental Argument for the Principle of Possibility." In Karl Schafer and Nicholas F. Stang (eds.), *The Sensible and Intelligible Worlds: New Essays on Kant's Metaphysics and Epistemology*. Oxford: Oxford University Press.

Leech, J. 2022b. "Logical Essence." *Argumenta* 7:415–37.

Leech, J. forthcoming. "The Necessity of Identity." In Elke Brendel, Massimiliano Carrara, Filippo Ferrari, Ole Hjortland, Gil Sagi, and Gila Sher (eds.), *The Oxford Handbook of Philosophical Logic*. Oxford: Oxford University Press.

Leech, J. and Textor, M. forthcoming. "Kant and Lotze on Substance and Causation." In Anil Gomes and Andrew Stephenson (eds.), *The Oxford Handbook to Kant*. Oxford: Oxford University Press.

Lewis, D. 1973. *Counterfactuals*. Oxford: Blackwell.

Lewis, D. 1979. "Scorekeeping in a Language Game." *Journal of Philosophical Logic* 8:339.

Lewis, D. 1982. " 'Whether' report." In Tom Pauli et al. (eds.), *Philosophical Essays Dedicated to Lennart Åqvist on his Fiftieth Birthday*. Filosofiska Studier. Reprinted in D. Lewis (1998) *Papers in Philosophical Logic*. Cambridge: Cambridge University Press.

Lewis, D. 1986. *On the Plurality of Worlds*. Oxford: Blackwell.

Longuenesse, B. 1998. *Kant and the Capacity to Judge*. Translated by Charles T. Wolff. Princeton: Princeton University Press.

Lowe, E. J. 2009. *More Kinds of Being: A Further Study of Individuation, Identity, and the Logic of Sortal Terms*. Oxford: Wiley Blackwell.

Lycan, W. G. 1994. *Modality and Meaning*. Dordrecht, The Netherlands: Kluwer.

Mackie, P. 2006. *How Things Might Have Been: Individuals, Kinds, and Essential Properties*. Oxford: Clarendon Press.

Mackie, P. 2020. "Can Metaphysical Modality Be Based on Essence?" In Dumitru Mircea (ed.), *Metaphysics, Meaning, and Modality: Themes from Kit Fine*. Oxford: Oxford University Press.

Magidor, O. 2009. "Category Mistakes Are Meaningful." *Linguistics and Philosophy* 32:553–81.

Mallozzi, A., Vaidya, A., and Wallner, M. 2021. "The Epistemology of Modality." In Edward N. Zalta (ed.), *The Stanford Encyclopedia of Philosophy*. Metaphysics Research Lab, Stanford University, Fall 2021 edition.

Marcus, E. 2009. "Why There Are No Token States." *Journal of Philosophical Research* 34:215–41.

Marshall, C. 2010. "Kant's Metaphysics of the Self." *Philosopher's Imprint* 10:1–21.

McFetridge, I. 1990. "Logical Necessity: Some Issues." In John Haldane and Roger Scruton (eds.), *Logical Necessity and Other Essays*, volume 11 of *Aristotelian Society Series*, chapter VIII, 135–54. Aristotelian Society.

McGinn, C. 1977. "Charity, Interpretation, and Belief." *Journal of Philosophy* 74:521–35.

McLear, C. 2021. "Kantian Conceptualism/Nonconceptualism." In Edward N. Zalta (ed.), *The Stanford Encyclopedia of Philosophy*. Metaphysics Research Lab, Stanford University, Fall 2021 edition.

Miller, K. 2010. "Three Routes to Contingentism in Metaphysics." *Philosophy Compass* 5:965–77.

BIBLIOGRAPHY

Montague, M. 2013. "The Access Problem." In U. Kriegel (ed.), *Phenomenal Intentionality*, 27–48. Oxford: Oxford University Press.

Moran, R. 2001. *Authority and Estrangement: An Essay on Self-Knowledge*. Princeton: Princeton University Press.

Mouton, D. L. 1969. "Thinking and Time." *Mind* 78:60–76.

Neale, S. 1995. "The Philosophical Significance of Gödel's Slingshot." *Mind* 104:761–825.

Newton, A. 2015. "Kant on the Logical Origin of Concepts." *European Journal of Philosophy* 23:456–84.

Nolan, D. 2010. "Response to John Divers." In B. Hale and A. Hoffman (eds.), *Modality: Metaphysics, Logic, Epistemology*, 220–6. Oxford: Oxford University Press.

OED-Online. 2020. "whether, pron., adj. (and n.), and conj."

Parsons, C. 1969. "Kant's Philosophy of Arithmetic." In C. Posy (ed.), *Kant's Philosophy of Mathematics: Modern Essays*, 43–80. Dordrecht, The Netherlands: Kluwer, 1992.

Parsons, C. 2007. *Mathematical Thought and its Objects*. Cambridge: Cambridge University Press.

Peacocke, C. 1992. *A Study of Concepts*. Cambridge, MA: MIT Press.

Peacocke, C. 2009. "Objectivity." *Mind* 118:739–69.

Pereboom, D. 2016. "Transcendental Arguments." In T. S. Gendler, H. Cappelen, and J. Hawthorne (eds.), *The Oxford Handbook of Philosophical Methodology*. Oxford: Oxford University Press.

Plantinga, A. 1978. *The Nature of Necessity*. Oxford: Oxford University Press.

Priest, G. 1979. "Logic of Paradox." *Journal of Philosophical Logic* 8:219–41.

Priest, G. 2008. *An Introduction to Non-Classical Logic: From If to Is*. Cambridge: Cambridge University Press, second edition.

Priest, G. 2021. "Metaphysical Necessity: A Skeptical Perspective." *Synthese* 198:1873–85.

Prior, A. N. 1971. *Objects of Thought*. Oxford: Clarendon Press.

Putnam, H. 1975. "The Meaning of Meaning." In *Philosophical Papers Vol. II: Mind, Language, and Reality*. Cambridge: Cambridge University Press.

Quine, W. V. 1936/1976. "Truth by Convention." Reprinted in *The Ways of Paradox*. Cambridge, MA: Harvard University Press.

Quine, W. V. 1953. "Three Grades of Modal Involvement." *Proceedings of the XIth International Congress of Philosophy* 14:65–81. Reprinted in *The Ways of Paradox and Other Essays*, revised edition (Cambridge, MA: Harvard University Press, 1976), 158–76.

Quine, W. V. 1961. "Reference and Modality." In *From a Logical Point of View*, 139–59. New York: Harper and Row.

Quine, W. V. 1963/1976. "Carnap and Logical Truth." Reprinted in *The Ways of Paradox*. Cambridge, MA: Harvard University Press.

Rayo, A. 2013. *The Construction of Logical Space*. Oxford: Oxford University Press.

Reck, E. and Schiemer, G. 2020. "Structuralism in the Philosophy of Mathematics." In Edward N. Zalta (ed.), *The Stanford Encyclopedia of Philosophy*. Metaphysics Research Lab, Stanford University, Spring 2020 edition.

Reimer, M. 1997. "Could There Have Been Unicorns?" *International Journal of Philosophical Studies* 5:35–51.

Roberts, A. 2020. "Relative Necessity and Propositional Quantification." *Journal of Philosophical Logic* 49:703–26.

Roca-Royes, S. 2011. "Conceivability and *De Re* Modal Knowledge." *Nous* 45:22–49.

Rosen, G. 2006. "The Limits of Contingency." In F. MacBride (ed.), *Identity and Modality*. Mind Association Occasional Series, 13–39. Oxford: Oxford University Press.

Routley, R. and Routley, V. 1980. "Human Chauvinism and Environmental Ethics." In M. A. Mannison, D. McRobbie, and R. Routley (eds.), *Environmental Philosophy*, 96–189. Canberra: Australian National University, Research School of Social Sciences.

Rumfitt, I. 2010. "Logical Necessity." In B. Hale and A. Hoffman (eds.), *Modality: Metaphysics, Logic, Epistemology*, 35–64. Oxford: Oxford University Press.

Russell, B. 1919. *Introduction to Mathematical Philosophy*. London: Allen and Unwin.

Salmon, N. 1981. *Reference and Essence*. Princeton: Princeton University Press.

Schafer, K. 2020. "Transcendental Philosophy as Capacities-First Philosophy." *Philosophy and Phenomenological Research* online first:1–26.

Schaffer, J. 2005. "Quiddistic Knowledge." *Philosophical Studies* 123:1–32.

Sellars, W. 1969. "Language as Thought and as Communication." *Philosophy and Phenomenological Research* 29:506–27.

Shapiro, S. 2000. "The Status of Logic." In P. Boghossian and C. Peacocke (eds.), *New Essays on the A Priori*, 333–66. Oxford: Oxford University Press.

Sidelle, A. 1989. *Necessity, Essence, and Individuation: A Defense of Conventionalism*. Ithaca: Cornell University Press.

Sidelle, A. 2009. "Conventionalism and the Contingency of Conventions." *Nous* 43:224–41.

Sider, T. 2005. "Reductive Theories of Modality." In Michael J. Loux and Dean W. Zimmerman (eds.), *The Oxford Handbook of Metaphysics*. Oxford: Oxford University Press.

Sider, T. 2011. *Writing the Book of the World*. Oxford: Oxford University Press.

Siegel, S. 2006. "Subject and Object in the Contents of Visual Experience." *Philosophical Review* 115:355–88.

Smit, H. 2009. "Kant on Apriority and the Spontaneity of Cognition." In Samuel Newlands and Larry M. Jorgensen (eds.), *Metaphysics and the Good: Themes from the Philosophy of Robert Adams*, 188–251. Oxford: Oxford University Press.

Smullyan, A. F. 1947. "The Problem of Interpreting Modal Logic by W. V. Quine." *Journal of Symbolic Logic* 12:139–41.

Smullyan, A. F. 1948. "Modality and Description." *Journal of Symbolic Logic* 13:31–7.

Stalnaker, R. 2012. *Mere Possibilities: Metaphysical Foundations of Modal Semantics*. Princeton and Oxford: Princeton University Press.

Stang, N. F. 2011. "Did Kant Conflate the Necessary and the A Priori?" *Nous* 45:443–71.

Stang, N. F. 2016. *Kant's Modal Metaphysics*. Oxford: Oxford University Press.

Stephenson, A. forthcoming. "Kant and Kripke: Rethinking Necessity and the A Priori." In James Conant and Jonas Held (eds.), *The Palgrave Handbook of German Idealism and Analytic Philosophy*. London: Palgrave Macmillan.

Stern, R. (ed.). 1999. *Transcendental Arguments: Problems and Prospects*. Oxford: Clarendon Press.

Strawson, P. F. 1959. *Individuals*. London and New York: Routledge.

Szabó, Z. G. 2013. "Compositionality." In Edward N. Zalta (ed.), *The Stanford Encyclopedia of Philosophy*. Fall 2013 edition.

Thielke, P. 2006. "Fate and the Fortune of the Categories: Kant on the Usurpation and Schematization of Concepts." *Inquiry* 49:438–68.

Thomasson, A. L. 2013. "Norms and Necessity." *Southern Journal of Philosophy* 51:143–60.

Thomasson, A. L. 2020. *Norms and Necessity*. New York: Oxford University Press.

Vaidya, A. J. 2006. "The Metaphysical Foundation of Logic." *Journal of Philosophical Logic* 35:179–82.

van Fraassen, B. 1980. *The Scientific Image*. Oxford: Oxford University Press.

Vetter, B. 2015. *Potentiality: From Dispositions to Modality*. Oxford: Oxford University Press.

244 BIBLIOGRAPHY

Vetter, B. and Viebahn, E. 2016. "How Many Meanings for 'May'? The Case for Modal Polysemy." *Philosophers' Imprint* 16:1–26.

Watkins, E. 2001. "Kant on Rational Cosmology." In E. Watkins (ed.), *Kant and the Sciences*. Oxford: Oxford University Press.

Watkins, E. 2010. "The System of Principles." In Paul Guyer (ed.), *The Cambridge Companion to Kant's Critique of Pure Reason*. Cambridge: Cambridge University Press.

Wiggins, D. 1995. "Objective and Subjective in Ethics, with Two Postscripts about Truth." *Ratio* 8:243–58.

Wiggins, D. 2001. *Sameness and Substance Renewed*. New York: Cambridge University Press.

Williamson, T. 1997. "Sense, Validity and Context." *Philosophy and Phenomenological Research* 57:649–54.

Williamson, T. 2007. *The Philosophy of Philosophy*. Oxford: Blackwell.

Williamson, T. 2013. *Modal Logic as Metaphysics*. Oxford: Oxford University Press.

Wilson, A. 2013. "Schaffer on Laws of Nature." *Philosophical Studies* 164:654–67.

Wittgenstein, L. 1921. *Tractatus Logico-Philosophicus*. London and New York: Routledge. Translated by D. F. Pears and B. F. McGuinness. Introduction by Bertrand Russell. This translation first published 1961, Routledge & Kegan Paul. Routledge Classics 2001.

Yablo, S. 1993. "Is Conceivability a Guide to Possibility?" *Philosophy and Phenomenological Research* 53:1–42.

Index

a posteriori 15, 87, 135, 140n, 141–4, 151, 171, 191, 199, 214–18

a priori 3, 21, 23, 27, 29, 31–3, 40, 44–6, 48, 52, 87, 103, 141, 180, 187n, 192, 214–21

absolute necessity 10, 14–15, 34–5, 157–62, 165, 225–7

abstract 59, 63–4n, 83–4, 86–90, 122, 191–2

actuality 18, 20, 29, 32, 39n, 41, 44, 47, 114–15, 137

alethic 14, 39, 140n, 141, 147, 156–7, 160, 163, 165, 170, 226, 228

Analogies of Experience 32

analytic 37, 118, 134, 137, 141, 144, 153–5, 176, 187n

Analytic of Principles see *Principles, (Analytic of)*

anti-realist 1, 3, 143n, 144

apodictic 19–22, 25

appearances 17, 27, 39, 45–6

Aristotle 51, 200

Aristotelian 3, 14, 85, 177, 184, 186–7, 189–90, 199

assertoric 4, 19–22, 25, 113

Ballarin, Roberta 175n, 182, 187n

Barcan Formula 193–195, 197–8

Barcan Formulas 15, 196–7, 223

Barcan Marcus, Ruth 194, 209

Brewer, Bill 102n, 103, 126n

broadest necessity 226–7

Cameron, Ross 3n, 154–5

Campbell, John 66–7, 203n

categories 4, 17, 19, 25–8, 30–1, 41–3, 45–6

category mistake 110, 183–4

causal 8, 26–7, 32, 39, 65–6, 87, 101–2, 105, 121–4, 134, 138, 142, 145, 172

causality 27–8

causation 27–8, 42–3, 65

classical logic 15, 50, 81n, 82, 161, 178–9, 194, 198

cognition 13, 16–19, 23, 24n, 26–8, 33n, 39–42, 45–6, 48–9, 84, 103, 180, 215, 221
   conditions of/on 19, 40
   laws of 13, 49

compositionality 60–1, 63n

conceivability 15, 151, 191, 219–22, 235

conditional logical necessity 211–12

conditional metaphysical necessity 14–15, 179–180, 201, 203–4, 206, 211, 217–18

conditional necessity 33, 44, 206, 211–14, 217–18

conditions of cognition see cognition

conditions of/on experience 26, 28, 30–3, 35–44, 46, 49, 143

conditions of/on objective thought 13–14, 96–9, 106, 117, 124, 129, 131, 149–51, 170, 172–3, 198, 205, 222, 230, 235

conditions of objectivity see objectivity

conditions of/on possible experience 13, 19, 43n, 49

condition of thought 19, 59, 73, 83, 97

conjunction property, the 15, 223–5

constitutive laws 77, 82, 89

constitutive norms (for/of thought) 13, 15, 72, 76–8, 83, 85, 95, 160–1, 220

contingency 1, 26, 92–4, 134, 189, 214

contingent 14, 23n, 48, 90, 92, 132, 134, 136–7, 139, 151–2, 154, 159, 168, 171, 186, 188–9, 191, 193–5, 198, 200, 214, 224, 231
   existence 14, 90, 151, 171, 191, 193–4, 198

contradiction 18–19, 50–1, 75, 77–8, 82, 96, 118–19, 157n, 159, 162, 227
   law of non- 77, 162
   principle of 19

Converse Barcan Formula 193–4, 197

convention 3, 91–5, 154

conventionalism/t 91–2, 94–5, 154–5

correctness conditions 101, 110–13, 115, 118, 120–31

Correia, Fabrice 86n, 199n, 206n, 207–9, 212

counterfactual 9, 94, 146, 215–16n

course of reasoning 19, 21–2, 25, 53, 58, 69, 70n, 83, 95
   see also logical reasoning

Critique of Pure Reason 1, 16, 17n, 19, 25, 27, 35, 38–9, 46, 99, 104, 121, 142n

Critique of the Power of Judgement 41, 47

de dicto 14, 169, 173–4, 177, 179, 190

de re 14, 30, 143n, 151, 169, 171, 173–9, 181, 183–4, 186, 189–92, 200–1, 205, 214, 217, 223

246 INDEX

deduction model (of modal knowledge) 15, 216–19
deductive validity 50–1, 72, 75
  see also logical validity
Divers, John 2n, 4n, 6–7, 11, 140n, 175n, 176–7, 232n, 233–4
dual 15, 223, 225, 227–8, 242n
duality 151, 184, 223, 225, 227, 229, 231

Eilan, Naomi 99–100, 108
epistemic necessity 12, 34, 141–3
epistemology 5, 15, 87–8, 151, 214–15, 217–19, 222, 235
  of essence 218–19
ersatz 234
essence 1, 3, 85–8, 145, 149–50, 174, 199, 200–1, 205–6, 208–9, 212–13, 218, 219
  epistemology of 218–19
  factual 199–200
  generic 199, 206, 208–9
  individual 200–1
  objectual 199, 205, 209
essentialism 14, 88–9, 177, 186–7, 189–90, 199–201, 205, 208–9
essentialist 15, 85–7, 91n, 105, 135, 137, 150n, 151, 167n, 171, 174, 191, 198–201, 204–9, 212–14, 216–20
essentiality of constitution 135, 199
essentiality of kind 15, 135, 171, 199–201, 203, 205
essentiality of origin 135, 171, 199
Etchemendy, John 51–3, 56
existence assumption 15, 179, 197–8
existential clause 148, 227–9
expressive resources 159, 161
extensional neutrality 134, 136–7, 139, 141–2, 144–6, 153, 205
externalism 125–6, 130

factive 13, 84, 141, 148–9, 168–9, 204, 229
factivity 86, 96–7, 169
falsity 21, 100–1, 116, 118, 149, 184, 227, Fine, Kit 3n, 85–6, 168–70, 174, 187–8, 200n
first-personal 64, 66–9
formal modality 33, 37, 39, 49
free logic 50n, 82n, 178–9, 194, 198, 214n
Frege, Gottlob 60, 84n, 88–9, 207n
Fregean 61, 63n, 84n, 88, 90, 176
function of modal judgment 4–10, 235
functional constraint, the 6–9, 11
functions of judgment 20, 23n, 25, 43, 46

Gardner, Sebastian 98–9, 101–2
generalized identity 15, 86n, 200n, 207–10, 212–14, 218–19
God 17, 191, 193
Gomes, Anil 18n, 24n, 107
grounding 37–8, 90, 200n

Hale, Bob 1n, 3n, 35n, 55n, 78–80, 84n, 85–6, 90, 94–5, 139n, 142n, 144n, 157n, 158–9, 161, 189, 194, 197–8, 200n, 217n, 219n, 224, 226
Herz, Markus 98–9
Hume, David 63

'I think' 23–4, 63–4, 67–70, 73, 129
impossibility 1–2, 26, 119, 134, 141, 145, 148, 167, 219–20
individuate 30, 201, 204
individuation 30n, 202–3
inferential connections 22, 59, 64, 66, 68–71
iteration 151, 223, 228–9, 231–2

Jackendoff, Ray 100
James, William 100, 103
Jarvis, Benjamin 122–3
judging 9, 21–2, 24–5, 58–9, 71
jungle 14, 177, 184, 186–7, 189–90

Kitcher, Patricia 24–5
Kratzer, Angelika 34n, 163–4
Kripke, Saul 125, 127, 135, 199, 209, 214, 216–18
Kripkean 135, 143n, 153

laws of cognition *see* cognition
laws of logic 12, 15, 72–3, 75–8, 82–3, 89, 95, 97, 111, 121n, 134, 136, 139n, 144, 188–9, 194, 198, 220
laws of nature 29, 33, 44, 46, 139, 143, 156
law of non-contradiction *see* contradiction
laws of thought 13, 15, 21, 49, 76–7, 82–3, 89, 94, 97, 111, 159, 161, 170, 194, 198, 213, 220, 235
Leibniz's Law 208–10
Lewis, David 2, 32n, 34n, 105, 116n, 163, 234
locus 23, 64–7, 69–71, 73, 84
logical concepts 85–6, 88–91, 169
logical consequence 50–3, 56, 66, 154
logical entities 84n, 85–6, 88, 144
logical functions 83, 85–8, 91, 145, 198
logical modality 12–16, 18–19, 26, 37, 39, 49–50, 53, 75–6, 142, 144, 160, 177, 182, 189–90, 197–8, 231–2
logical modality question, the *see* question

logical objects 83–4
logical possibility 4, 18–20, 117, 139, 142n, 159–60, 167, 221
logical reasoning 13, 51–2, 54, 57–8, 71–5, 81–2, 218
  see also course of reasoning
  see also reasoning from suppositions
logical satisfaction 187–8
logical validity 52–3, 143–4, 182–3
  see also deductive validity

m-essentialism/t 200, 213, 219n
Mackie, Penelope 86n, 135, 200n, 202, 205
material modality 33, 39, 49
material necessity 32–3, 41, 44, 46, 180
mathematical 37, 43, 122, 135, 137, 154–5, 162, 191–2, 232
mathematics 37, 122n, 138, 192–3
McFetridge, Ian 4n, 51, 54–6, 58, 71–3, 79, 157–8n
metalinguistic 174, 182–3
mind-dependent 3, 220, 222
mind-independent 1–3, 10, 75, 83–4, 87, 220, 222
mere thought 13, 16, 18, 48–9
metaphysical modality question, the *see* question
modal force 160, 166, 168–70
modal logic 2, 15, 140n, 151, 174, 193–5, 198, 223, 228, 234
Modal Transcendentalism/t 150, 160, 171, 173–4, 179, 181, 189–91, 193, 195–6, 200–5, 207, 209–12, 218–19, 235
modalities/y of judgment 19, 20–2, 25
Montague, Michelle 99–100

natural necessity 12, 34, 134, 136, 138–9, 168–70
nature(s of things) 3, 85, 143, 149, 152–3, 198, 200
necessary connection 22–5, 33, 40, 46, 58, 105, 169
necessary existence 33, 44–5, 191–3, 196
necessitism/t 15, 173, 196
necessity of identity 207, 209–12, 214, 223
Newton, Alexandra 43
non-epistemic 39, 137, 141, 143, 156–7, 165
nonjective 14, 48, 99, 109, 111n, 112–13, 115, 117–21, 129, 131, 193n
nonjectivity 112–13, 115, 117, 119
non-objective 107, 110, 115–19, 121
nonsense 82, 104, 119, 183
non-subjective 107, 110, 114–15

non-subjectivity 112, 114, 119
normative laws 76–7, 83

objective-impossible 116, 119–20, 148
objective-necessary 106, 147–8
objective necessity 106, 132, 147–51
objective possibility 106
objective-possible 105–6, 116–17, 119, 148
objective representation 13, 26, 46, 49, 117, 192
objective validity 18, 40, 43
objectively valid 26
objectivity 13–15, 17–19, 47–9, 98–9, 104–7, 109, 111–21, 124n, 129–31, 147–50, 156, 159–60, 170, 171–3, 177–81, 186, 190–3, 195–7, 201, 203–7, 210n, 211–13, 217–19, 221–2, 224–31, 234
  conception of 14, 47–8, 98–9, 107, 120–21, 230
  conditions of/on 14–15, 17–19, 104–6, 116–20, 122n, 129, 131, 147–50, 156, 159–60, 170, 171–3, 177–81, 186, 190–3, 195–7, 201, 203–7, 210n, 211–13, 217–19, 221–2, 224–31, 234
  minimal 108, 114
oomph 1, 3, 160, 166
operator 14, 63, 137, 151, 157n, 158n, 168–70, 174–5, 177, 181–4, 189–90, 194–5, 208, 210, 223, 225–6, 228, 232

Peacocke, Christopher 48, 90, 108, 114
perspective/al 99, 102–3, 107–10, 112, 114
physical necessity 137, 145–6, 153–4, 164, 167
Plantinga, Alvin 134, 138, 232n
practical question, the *see* question
Priest, Graham 137, 153, 161–2, 178n
Principles, (Analytic of) 27–8, 41, 45–6
Prior, Arthur 185–6
Problem of Reality 14, 98–104, 112, 121, 124, 129, 131, 147–9, 159, 172–3
problematic (judgment) 19–22, 25
possible worlds 2, 6, 51, 105n, 234
possible worlds semantics 2, 15, 151, 223, 232–4
postulate of possibility, the 36, 39–40, 42
Postulates (of Empirical Thinking in General) 25–30, 33, 35, 38–41, 44, 150

quantifying in 175, 181–2, 184, 186, 226n
question
  the logical modality 12–13, 53, 75–6
  the metaphysical modality 12–13
  the practical 11–12, 58
  the transcendental 12, 53–4, 58, 75
Quine, Willard Van Orman 14, 92, 94n, 136n, 171, 174–7, 181–7, 189–90

248 INDEX

rational doubt 13, 77–89, 93, 95
immune/ity to 13, 77–82, 84, 86n, 87–8, 93
real definition 85, 199–200
real modality 13, 18–19, 25–6, 39–40, 49,
141–5, 148, 220
real necessity 14, 37–8, 41, 132, 140–50, 153,
155, 160, 180, 198
the strictest 14, 132, 140–1, 145–50, 153, 155,
160, 198
realist 1–3, 8, 143–4
reasoning from suppositions 13, 54–8, 71–3
see also logical reasoning
reduction 1, 154, 234
relative modality 13, 34–5, 37–8, 49, 106,
162–5, 168, 170, 185, 225, 227n, 231
relative necessity 10, 14, 34–5, 38, 106, 150,
157–8, 160, 162, 166, 168n, 170, 177, 179,
181, 184, 195, 224–7, 229
relative possibility 36, 106, 119, 166–167, 225–7
relativization 38–9, 156, 158, 162, 164, 166–8
relevant logic 161
Roberts, Alexander 224n, 226–7
Rosen, Gideon 133, 140–1, 145, 152
Rumfitt, Ian 50–1, 56–8
Russell, Bertrand 56–7, 176, 182

S4/4 15, 92, 168–9, 228–31
S5/5 15, 168–9, 223, 228–9
Schafer, Karl 221–2
self-knowledge 24, 99n
Sellars, Wilfred 77
sensibility 26, 30–1, 47, 192
Sidelle, Alan 3n, 92–3
Sider, Ted 134n, 154–5
Siegel, Susanna 102–3
Skiles, Alexander 86n, 199n, 207–9, 212
Smullyan, Arthur 176, 182n, 188n
sortal 201–6
source 1, 3, 13, 15, 33, 46, 50, 72, 75–6, 83–6,
88–91, 94–5, 97, 142–50, 153, 159–61, 170,
174, 178–9, 186–8, 192, 194, 198, 200–1,
213, 215n, 220, 235
Stang, Nicholas 18n, 29, 33–4, 37–9, 214n

Strawson, Peter 107, 201n
strictest real necessity, the see real necessity, the
strictest
subjective 3, 13–14, 23, 33, 47–9, 99, 101,
107–115, 119–22, 129, 131, 235
subjectivity 107–9, 111–13, 115, 119
substantive 112, 131, 133, 136, 139–41,
143–5, 184
synthetic 23, 37–8, 41–3, 141–2, 144, 214

Table of Categories 25–26
Table of Judgments 20, 25
Tarskian 51–3, 137n
things in themselves 17
thinkability 82n, 117
thinkable 15, 104n, 219, 222
thinker 11–12, 24, 47, 53, 57–71, 73, 75, 78,
80–1, 83, 92, 108, 113, 115, 121, 124–30,
161, 172
Thomasson, Amie 7n, 10, 143n
transcendental argument 42, 44, 221–2
transcendental condition 3, 42
transcendental philosophy 15, 219, 221–2, 235
transcendental question, the see question
truth-preservation 51–2, 72
truth-preserving 52–5, 58, 71–3, 75, 84, 96

understanding, the 20–1, 23, 26, 28, 45–7, 215
unintelligibility 182–3, 189
unintelligible 176, 183–4, 192
unity of consciousness 13, 19, 23n, 49, 58
unity of experience 45–6, 48
unity of self-consciousness 22–5, 45–6, 63–4
unity of thought 59, 61, 64, 70–1, 73, 84, 129
unthinkable 82, 117

water (H_2O) 86n, 87, 135, 199, 202n, 206–8,
213, 216, 218, 220
well-formed 59–60, 78
Wiggins, David 109–10, 200n, 201
Williamson, Timothy 9n, 80n, 140n, 146n,
159, 215
Wittgenstein, Ludwig 117, 127